COMMUNICATION
&
CULTURE

COMMUNICATIONS

George Gerbner and Marsha Siefert, Editors
The Annenberg School of Communications
University of Pennsylvania, Philadelphia

COMMUNICATION
&
CULTURE
A COMPARATIVE APPROACH

Alex S. Edelstein
University of Washington
Youichi Ito
Keio University, Tokyo
Hans Mathias Kepplinger
Mainz University, Mainz

Foreword by Maxwell McCombs
University of Texas

With the collaboration of Leonard Chu, Chinese University
of Hong Kong; Kazuto Kojima, Tokyo University;
Tomoaki Iwai, Tokiwa University; and Kazufumi Manabe,
Kwansei Gakuin University.

Longman
New York & London

Communication & Culture: A Comparative Approach

Longman Inc., 95 Church Street, White Plains, N.Y. 10601

Associated companies:
Longman Group Ltd., London
Longman Cheshire Pty., Melbourne
Longman Paul Pty., Auckland
Copp Clark Pitman, Toronto
Pitman Publishing Inc., New York

Executive editor: Gordon T. R. Anderson
Production editor: Ann P. Kearns
Production supervisor: Judi Millman

Library of Congress Cataloging-in-Publication Data

Edelstein, Alex S.
    Communication & culture: a comparative approach/Alex S. Edelstein, Youichi Ito, and Hans Mathias Kepplinger; with the cooperation of Leonard Chu...[et al.]

        p. cm. — (Communications)
    Bibliography: p.
    Includes index.
    ISBN 0-8013-0335-4
    1. Communication and culture. I. Itō, Yōichi, 1942–.
II. Kepplinger, Hans Mathias, 1943– . III. Title. IV. Series:
Communications (Annenberg School of Communications (University of Pennsylvania))
P91.E33 1989   88-27599
001.51—dc19   CIP

ISBN 0-8013-0335-4

89 90 91 92 93 94 9 8 7 6 5 4 3 2 1

To our discipline:
Communication
and
Culture

Contents

Foreword
The Promise of Problematic Situations

Maxwell McCombs
University of Texas at Austin

There is nothing so practical as a good theory, Wilbur Schramm was fond of remarking. That axiomatic observation appealed to Schramm and to many who have followed him in mass communication research because it succinctly summarizes the relationship between the theoretical and the practical, two concepts often naively assumed to be polar opposites. In fact, all of us use theories about how the world works in order to get on with our daily lives. On a grander level, Schramm had in mind the utility of theory in planning and carrying out social policy. Of course, theory also serves as a guide to scientific practice. It organizes the observations made in an empirical investigation, both at the stage of planning the study and at the stage of interpreting the gathered data. But good theories also have an aesthetic, creative quality that makes them considerably more than a literal map of some phenomena. This creative quality of a good theory extends along two dimensions. A good theory continues to open new doors and to yield a greater depth of understanding for the variables involved in its initial formulation and application. But a good theory also suggests applications in additional areas outside its original ken. By both of these criteria the theoretical concept of the *problematic situation* detailed in this book is both fruitful and practical. It has guided Professors Edelstein, Ito, and Kepplinger and their colleagues down fascinating avenues of comparative research in international communication. Undoubtedly, it also will lead other scholars into fascinating new vistas not originally demarcated by the concept of problematic situations. Like the mountain that must be climbed simply because it is there, this concept of problematic situations holds a similar fascination.

The intellectual roots of this concept are Gallup's "most important problem" question used in American polls as early as 50 years ago and regularly repeated about 200 times since World War II. While there has been some variation in the wording over time, the usual version is "What do you think is the most important problem facing this country today?" Despite frequent use of the MIP data series—to use the common jargon shorthand for this data—researchers seldom have probed very far beneath the topic labels used to categorize responses to this open-ended question. But beyond the general topic categorizing each respondent's nomination for the most important problem is the larger question of what this problem means to the individual. Why does he or she regard the economy, nuclear disarmament, or civil rights, to cite a few typical responses, as the *most important* problem facing the country?

The concept of problematic situations makes a significant contribution to the pursuit of this question. In the research summarized in Chapter 3, for example, the usual topic code for the MIP data is converted into a hierarchical classification in which the array of topics nominated by survey respondents is only the first stage of analysis. In the second stage of analysis the meaning of the problem, why it is considered to be a problem by a particular individual, is coded in terms of what kind of problematic situation is perceived to exist. The coding scheme used at this second level of analysis considers a situation problematic if it involves one or more of these situations:

- Loss of value;
- Institutional breakdown;
- Conflict;
- Need;
- Step toward a solution/proposed alternative solution;
- Indeterminacy.

Chapter 3 begins the detailed explication of these problematic situations.

In the hierarchical coding of the MIP data it is at this second level of analysis that individual differences in the reasons for nominating problems emerge—and in line with the international communication interests of the authors, cultural differences emerge. For example, both German and American respondents frequently cited the economy as the most important problem. In turn, majorities of both described this problem in terms of loss of value, but the differences in the sizes of these majorities are striking. Well over half of the German respondents, but only about 4 out of 10 of the American respondents, described the economy as a problematic situation in terms of loss of value. Other responses are even more strikingly different. For the Americans the economy is a problematic situation because of needs. For the Germans the economy is a problematic situation because of conflict and the breakdown of institutional values. Each of these three types of problematic situations is mentioned by about 1 respondent in 5. The greater detail and variance resulting from this analysis of why something is a problem also offers communication researchers the opportunity to more closely match news content with the pictures of the world in survey respondents' heads.

A COMPARATIVE STRATEGY

The comparisons just made between the kinds of problematic situations described by Germans and by Americans is far more than a fortuitous replication of this theoretical concept in two settings. This comparative approach in the example is part of a deliberate strategy for the study of communication. Employing an analytical model whose elements are structure, culture, and situation, the international collaborative project reported in this book set out to test the efficacy of the concept of problematic situations across a number of different cultures. This research strategy, of course, could be used to test any number of concepts in the communication literature. Here the primary focus is on the problematic situation.

Briefly consider the strategic advantages for empirical research of these three elements: structure, culture, and situation. In the work reported in this book the position of the survey respondents in the social structure is held constant. They are all college students. While the authors acknowledge that quite commonplace practical considerations led, in part, to the use of college students, they also make the argument that youth culture is worthy of study in its own rights. But beyond either of these pragmatic and substantive arguments is the compelling methodological argument for holding constant social structure in order to better understand what differences can be attributed to culture or to individual situations. The authors' emphasis, of course, is on the identification of cultural differences in communication behaviors. Or, to put it another way, their overarching goal is to sensitize us to what is culturally delimited versus universal in human communication.

In the typical poll where respondents are asked to nominate the most important problem facing the country, the sample is selected from the gen-population. The usual result is considerable variance in the responses, and more so if one is comparing general population samples from two different countries. In such a situation the analyst commonly is left with a number of alternative explanations for the results. Among these are competing explanations based on variations among respondents in their position in the social structure, simple individual differences, and, in the case of samples from two or more countries, cultural differences. The strategy of the comparative approach developed by Professors Edelstein, Ito, and Kepplinger helps eliminate competing alternative explanations. In one fell swoop, it also converts the presumed limitations of research on college students into a strategic asset. Since only college student data is under consideration in the various analyses presented here, variations due to cultural differences are more obvious.

The third element in the analytic model is situation. Here the use of the problematic situation, as defined by each respondent individually, has the effect of also controlling for the situation. Only those social problems which are salient to the student are discussed. None are nominated by the researcher. Furthermore, these social problems are discussed in a restricted context, why each student thinks this particular situation is a problem facing his or her country. The specific categories used to describe why these social issues are problematic situations to the student are, of course, creatures of the observer's mind, not the students. But they are broad enough, while at the same time reducing the data to a handful of categories, to be analytically useful in a number of settings.

Professors Edelstein, Ito, and Kepplinger apply this operational definition of the problematic situation to a wide variety of communication settings. These chapters will stimulate your imagination when you read this material and produce many more examples. Here in the Foreword I will draw my examples of the creative potential for this concept from two areas of mass communication research frequently associated with my name: journalism and agenda setting.

NEWS AND PROBLEMATIC SITUATIONS

In his classic, *Public Opinion*, Walter Lippmann emphasized that the daily news is not a representative sample of the day's events. The vast majority of routine events and ongoing situations in our community, as well as across the nation and world, are ignored by journalists. They must be ignored because there simply aren't enough reporters to witness all the happenings in the world. In the entire United States, a country approaching a population of 250 million, there are only slightly more than a 100,000 reporters and editors for all the news media combined. Consequently, the news media position their reporters at a few key posts where news is likely to occur about the departure of people's lives from the routine. In short, remarked Lippmann, "the news is not a mirror of social conditions, but the report of an aspect that has obtruded itself." While there is well-established journalistic tradition about which of these obtrusive aspects of people's daily lives are the most newsworthy, the underlying theory of news remains essentially implicit. One way of articulating this theory is to consider these obtrusions as problematic situations in the individual and collective lives of the community. The concept of problematic situations offers a systematic approach to the daily behavior of the news media. It offers a road map, a general theory, guiding us beyond the morass of specific events and topics covered in the daily news.

Comparisons of news coverage are at the heart of journalism. Local newspapers compare their coverage with the large regional dailies and the *New York Times*. Television news directors read the newspapers. Journalism students and scholars make similar comparisons, only many days later and usually with more precision and rigor. Sometimes all of these comparisons are based on specific stories and events. Scholarly comparisons, however, more commonly are concerned with broad sweeps of news coverage. They usually employ topical categories as the basis of comparison. While such comparisons are useful, they also are limited. Just as a topical catalog of social issues nominated by respondents to the MIP question yields only limited comparisons, context analyses of news topics also are limited. The concept of problematic situations offers a hierarchical analysis of news coverage in which the topic of the story is only the first macro-level of analysis. At the second level we can examine the specifics of the story in terms of what kind of problematic situation is being presented.

Recently, I published a series of comparisons about the news content of newspapers under competitive and noncompetitive conditions in three North American cities, Cleveland, Montreal, and Winnipeg (McCombs, 1987, 1988). Overall, the distribution of news coverage across topics was similar for competing newspapers and changed very little once there no longer was any competition. The findings support a sociology of news perspective emphasizing the influence of professional norms on how the news of the day is reported. The findings did not support a democratic theory perspective emphasizing the importance of multiple voices in the marketplace. At the macro-level of news topics the data are rather unambiguous. But I wonder what the content analysis data at the more specific level of problematic situations might look like. It is entirely possible for two newspapers to be focused on the same topic in their daily coverage, even the same event or situation, and, yet, to take a very different slant on the story. Just as German and American students nominated the economy as the most important problem for vastly different reasons, it is quite possible for two news media to select different aspects of a news event for emphasis. If so, this would be compelling evidence for the value of multiple voices in the marketplace, multiple voices offering different perspectives. Or, is it the case that the professional norms of journalism are now so pervasive that multiple voices are simply a chorus voicing identical problematic situations?

The in-depth portrait of public issues painted by the concept of problematic situations also can be extremely useful in tracing the evolution of a particular issue over time. Sociologists have outlined a variety of theories about the natural history of social issues, the sequence of stages through which most issues pass as they rise and fall on the public agenda. In the course of this evolution the specifics of the issue, the aspects receiving central attention, change. Also changing over time is the amount and kind of attention paid to an issue by the news media. To what extent are these shifts the result of events and manipulations on the public stage and in the political arena? To what extent are these shifts the result of journalistic practice and tradition? Problematic situations—and the operational definitions elaborated in this book's studies—provide a major conceptual tool for tracing the evolution of an issue over time on a variety of agendas, public, political institutions, and the press.

Three timeframes come to mind for the study of the evolution of issues over time. Even across a few weeks or months the aspects of an issue receiving attention are likely to change. My studies of the State of the Union addresses and the President's potential as an agenda-setter have noted the difficulty of simply tracing topics over time (Gilbert et al., 1980; McCombs, Gilbert, and Eyal, 1982). Even if the topics touched on by the President in his annual State of the Union address were to receive continued emphasis by the news media in subsequent weeks, this would be an incomplete portrait of agenda setting because the exact meaning of an issue changes over time, sometimes radically.

With a somewhat longer time frame, the concept of problematic situations is useful for tracing the complete social history of an issue. It would be interesting to see how much—and which aspects—of this social history actually appears in the daily news. Turning completely to the historian's timeframe, the evolution of journalistic practice across decades and centuries, we might ask how press coverage of major social issues has changed. Do newspapers still cover issues the way that they did a century ago? Professors Edelstein, Ito, and Kepplinger speculate that there has been change, but they do not pursue the question in empirical detail. Of course, to pursue such a question in a comparative framework across cultures would be a major intellectual adventure and contribution. And that is the challenge of this book!

AGENDA SETTING AND PROBLEMATIC SITUATIONS

The most exciting contribution of this book to agenda-setting research is its creative elaboration of the dependent variable, the agenda-setting effect. While there has been some theoretical work in agenda setting on explicating the kinds of public agendas involved in agenda-setting effects, most research has concentrated on the exploration of independent and intervening variables. But Chapter 9 presents an exciting array of agenda-setting effects growing out of the concept of the problematic situations. Bernard Cohen's frequently cited definition of agenda setting can be used to outline these effects. As Cohen remarked in *The Press and Foreign Policy*, the press may not be successful much of the time in telling people what to think, but it is stunningly successful in telling people what to think *about*. Taking that final phrase, "what to think about," Chapter 9 suggests three distinct agenda-setting effects:

- Thinking
- What to think *about*
- *What* to think.

Thinking corresponds to awareness and salience, the terms commonly used to describe and define the agenda-setting effect. Operational definitions of thinking are stated in terms of topics, the first stage in the hierarchical definition of problematic situations. Some of the basic research reported here begins with the MIP question, a data source frequently used in agenda-setting studies as well. Testing agenda setting in terms of the correspondence of topics nominated for the most important problem with press coverage of those topics, Chapter 9 reports a traditional agenda-setting study, albeit one conducted internationally.

But that research continues on to the second stage and examines the meanings of these issues in terms of the problematic situations cited by respondents when they explain why the issue was the most important one facing their country. In these analyses the agenda-setting effect is in terms of what to think *about*. The press may do more than suggest general topics for consideration. It also may direct our attention, suggesting particular aspects, particular problematic situations, for consideration. I think of this level of analysis as the attributes of an issue. Just as there can be an agenda of issues, there also can be an agenda of the attributes or aspects of that issue. The operational definitions of problematic situations offer a useful way for measuring and comparing these attributes across a variety of issues instead of relying upon an ad hoc descriptive list of attributes unique to each issue.

The third agenda-setting effect centers on exactly what people *do* think. Can the press so direct our thinking that it frames a perspective for us? Some experimental research reported by Shanto Iyengar and Donald Kinder in *News That Matters* suggests that this may be so under at least some conditions. The news stories included in the TV newscasts viewed by their experimental subjects did establish specific perspectives or criteria which the subjects later used to evaluate presidential performance. Although the experimental data were not analyzed in the terms employed here, they do present evidence of at least two of the three agenda-setting effects presented here. There was agenda setting in terms of topics ("thinking") and in terms of judgmental criteria ("what to think").

Since the original testing of the agenda-setting hypothesis twenty years ago during the 1968 U.S. presidential campaign, several hundred studies have been conducted. The history of these studies can be grouped into four phases. Beyond the initial phase of testing the basic hypothesis, the next three phases represent an expansion of the basic model into new domains. These later phases added intervening variables between the press and public agendas, expanded the model beyond public issues to candidates and the attributes of issues and candidates, and explored the question of who sets the press agenda. We are now moving into a fifth phase, which is quite different in nature. Rather than expanding the model horizontally to new objects of study, this new, fifth phase aims at vertical, in-depth growth. Agenda-setting researchers are shifting from the role of explorer, the most common role in communication research, to the role of surveyor. Rather than seeking new vistas, they place emphasis on the careful mapping of vistas already noted in the literature. The explication of agenda-setting effects presented here is a significant contribution to this new phase.

SUMMING UP

There is nothing so practical as a good theory because it offers a route through the vast arrays of data that can be gathered on any communication phenomenon. For my interests in journalism and agenda setting, the concept of the problematic situation suggests new routes toward the answers for questions that I have pondered about news and about agenda-setting effects. Other readers of this book will find that it suggests routes through quite different data for them. All of this underscores the point made by the rich variety of chapters in this book. The problematic situation is a fruitful conceptual tool, and the strategy of comparative analysis across cultures leads us toward a new era of research and knowledge about human communication.

Preface

This is in the fullest possible sense a collaborative as well as a comparative study of communication and culture.

The project had its earliest beginnings in 1978 at an "information societies" conference of American and Japanese scholars at the Battelle Institute in Seattle. Two years later the University of Washington hosted a second conference at Battelle, this a research workshop designed to address comparative aspects of information societies. One conclusion that emerged was that we should undertake this comparative study of university students.

A Japanese university research team was formed from universities that included Professors Youichi Ito (Keio University), Hiroshi Akuto and Kazuto Kojima (Tokyo University), Kazufumi Manabe (Kwansei Gakuin University), Tomoaka Iwai (Tokiwa University), and Yutaka Oishi (The Research Institute of Telecommunications and Economics). Members met in Seattle and Tokyo to discuss concepts, questionnaire construction, translation, sampling, administration of questionnaires, coding, and data analysis. This led to a third conference in 1982 at Keio University organized by Professor Ito and sponsored by the Japan Society for Promotion of Science (Nihon Gakujutsu Shinkokai), the Hoso Bunka Foundation, the Japan Foundation (Kokusai Koryu Kikin), and the Asia Foundation through the counsel of Mr. James L. Stewart, then director of the Tokyo Office. A special seminar at Keio University was made possible by funds granted by the Toyota Foundation.

Professor Manabe spent the 1984–85 academic year in the School of Communication at the University of Washington as a visiting scholar.

He collaborated in transforming the major concepts in this study, which were tested originally by means of an open-ended questionnaire, into closedended items that yielded unidimensional scales. Professor Masaru Kawamoto, also a visiting scholar at the University of Washington, worked with Dr. Linda Lawson of the faculty at Indiana University (then a doctoral student at the University of Washington) on the content analysis of Japanese newspapers.

Professor Iwai helped to direct Japanese questionnaire coding and Japanese computer operations. Yutaka Oishi (then a graduate student) assisted Professors Ito and Iwai. Professor Masaki Ikuta, now dean, Human Sciences, Tokiwa University, and former director of the Institute for Communications Research at Keio University, helped to finance the Japanese side of the project and gave it his whole-hearted support. Professor Shuntaro Ohta, former director of the Institute, also was helpful at all times. Professor Makoto Tsuruki of the Faculty of Law and Political Science at Keio helped in data collection and provided graduate students for coding operations. They included Atsushi Iwata, Etsuko Shinozaki, and Ken Matsuda. In 1987 Professor Edelstein taught in the Institute for Communication Research at Keio University as Hoso Bunka Foundation professor and consulted with Dr. Manabe at Kwansei Gakuin University. We appreciate also the cooperation of Professor Sumiko Iwao of the institute in Keio.

The project was expanded to other countries by stages: In 1980–81 Professor Edelstein, Aw Boon Haw chair professor at Chinese University of Hong Kong (CUHK), collected data from three universities; Dr. Leonard Chu, now department chairman at CUHK, was the major faculty participant. Graduate research assistants included Victoria Cheung, Clement So, Georgina Pang, and Fanny Wong. In 1982–83 Professor Edelstein taught as Gaste Professor in the Institut fur Publizistik, Mainz University, West Germany, where Prof. Dr. Hans Mathias Kepplinger headed the West German research team.

The German Science Foundation (Deutsche Forschungs-Gemeinschaft –DFG) supported the costs of data collection and coding. Professor Dr. Elizabeth Noelle-Neumann helped to fund the project at several stages. She and Dr. Wolfgang Donsbach contributed intellectually in addressing several aspects of public opinion. Dr. Rainer Mathes of the Institute visited the School of Communications in 1987 and permitted access to several of his studies. He also supplied material on German youth. Uwe Hartung and Thomas Hartmann of the Institut fur Publizistik studies helped with bibliographic research.

The senior author visited Scandinavia in 1987 and collected data for an independent study of Norway. He thanks Professor Niels Thomsen of Copenhagen University in Denmark for facilitating this work, and expresses appreciation to his collaborator in Oslo, Professor Svennik Hoyer. The results of that study parallel this book but are being published independently. An appraisal of Norwegian culture was begun during a visit as exchange professor at Bergen University in the spring of 1986. Professors Per Torsvik and Olav Vaugland enriched that experience.

THE "ORGANIC" PROCESS OF DEVELOPMENT

The book was "organic" in its development, in the words of Marsha Siefert, insightful co-editor of Longman communication books. The first draft took a comparative perspective, incorporating elements of culture.

The name of the book also evolved as the "best fit to the data." Culture, more than situation, was the generic concept that explained the most interesting differences in communications behaviors. As Professor Mc-Combs suggests in the Foreword, although structures often guide us, cultures make the difference.

I had a special interest in this title, harkening back to Alfred G. Smith's book by the same name; however, the thrust of that book as reflected in its subtitle was "Readings in the Codes of Human Interaction." This is not a reader, and intercultural communication is only one of several foci of our cultural perspective. It became evident that student behavior would be more meaningful if viewed in the larger context of general audience behaviors, so these studies were introduced as structural backdrops to the student data. To make relevant the other data we had to establish bases for comparability. These bases were suggested by our comparative perspective:

- Begin with the concepts that are most comparable—these representing a half dozen mainstreams of American communications research that had been taken up by scholars in our participating countries.
- Then demonstrate the conceptual bases for comparison of the cognitive variables, on the one hand, and identify the cultural and situationally determined differences on the other.
- Reach common ground with respect to such concepts as news, credibility, uses, agenda setting, interpersonal communication, and public opinion.

If priorities were established, we would conclude that our first priority was to test the relevance and usefulness of our cognitive variables. We recognize that we have tended to flirt with the mass communication concepts more than to have validated them directly.

Having stated a priority, we find ourselves in the finest of company, that of Maxwell E. McCombs (1981), who in speaking of agenda setting characterized it as a "fortuitously timed metaphor." He recognized that the concept represented a beginning of an inquiry, not a conclusion. Because our work has that some character we find McCombs' statement reassuring:

> Part of the richness of metaphor...is that it allows each individual to make his or her own translation of the comparison....Metaphoric description encourages creative thinking. In the case of [our investigation of comparative communication and culture]...the fact that the central concept (s) guiding this research is (are) expressed as metaphor (s) has encouraged a broad variety of operational definitions and data. (p. 121)

THE SUPPORTIVE STRUCTURE

The senior author acknowledges the useful meetings in Tokyo with Professors Y. Kobayashi, T. Takeshita, and H. Tokinoya, as well as with Y. Sone, and with particular appreciation, recalls helpful discussions with Dr. Hiroko Nishida of Nihon University and Dr. Ofer Feldman of Keio and Tokyo Universities. The senior author must also express his great personal regard for the help given by Professor Ikuo Takeuchi, head of the Institute for Journalism, Tokyo University, and Koichi Ogawa, Tokai University.

A number of other acknowledgements ought to be made. In the early writing stages the graduate secretary at the University of Washington, Pat Dinning, kept an antique version of a word processor in operation. Andy Armour of the faculty of Keio University helped us to bridge some puzzling technological gaps between Japanese and American word processing, and most of the computer runs in Seattle were made by Johan Giffard. Mr. Hyeon-Kyu Lee prepared the graphics. Karen Hedelund, political science librarian, chased down errant footnotes.

Contributions—by the Battelle Foundation, the help of the director, Jamese McDonald, and his assistant, Dr. Clem Chaffee; Charles Kincaid of the Saul and Dayee Haas Foundation, and Provost Emeritus Solomon Katz of the University of Washington—helped to fund the information society meetings and the resulting project.

THE STUDENT CONTRIBUTION

The authors thank the many students who participated in the study. They came from more than a dozen universities in the four countries. A number of young scholars at the University of Washington helped to develop some of the major concepts: Jiande Chen, MA; Dr. Michael Deis; Dr. Linda Lawson; Suan K. Lim, MA; Kenneth Miller, MA; Dr. Barbie Milpacher Mueller; Dr. Hamima Dona Mustapha; Robert Post, MA; Dr. Thomas Spencer-Walters; and Dr. Fred N. Zandpour each utilized concepts in their work that grew out of the development of this book. Mike Hindmarsh, at the time a Ph.D. student, contributed his thinking about the comparative approach.

The writing proceeded by stages. Papers first were drafted by the senior author and submitted to colleagues for review. The senior author thanks Professors Anantha S. Babbili of Texas Christian University; C. C. Lee and Philip Tichenor of the University of Minnesota; Dr. Keith Stamm and Dr. Merrill Samuelson of the University of Washington; Dr. Max McCombs of the University of Texas; Professor William Hachten of the University of Wisconsin; Kurt Kent of the University of Florida; and Dr. David Weaver of Indiana University for their helpful comments. Professor Reynaldo Guioguio of the University of The Philippines visited the University of Washington in 1988 and made valuable suggestions for applications of concepts to mass media development. The senior author collaborated closely with Professors Ito and Kepplinger throughout the process.

THE COMPARATIVE CHALLENGE

Although there were limited resources, as characterizes most comparative studies, there was a compensating advantage in time for a study that was so conceptually oriented. We hope that the conceptual contributions of this book will encourage further funding of more theoretically oriented and basic research in international and comparative communication.

As we will develop in Chapter 1, we will pursue a number of approaches to communication and culture:

- One is a cultural analysis of the context in which each of our student groups is located.
- Another is the analysis of intercultural communication, which will describe interpersonal interactions between American and Japanese college students.
- The third, an analysis of the potential for cross-cultural communication, grew out of our conceptual analysis of news in the newspapers of each of the four societies.
- Finally, the multicultural context permits comparative analysis of the perceived credibility of the media in our four societies, their uses by the individual, their contributions to the holding and per-

ceptions of public opinion, and their agenda-setting functions. Our treatment of these mainstream studies in mass communication will permit us to test the proposition that the multicultural context contributes to an unique understanding of mass communication as a social phenomenon.

In summary, we will try through these cultural approaches to contribute to the fuller emergence of communication and culture as a field of study. In that sense this book is intended as much for American scholars in mass communication as for those who already consider themselves to be internationalists.

It is only fitting that we have devoted our final chapter to a multicultural symposium in which my distinguished colleagues, Professors Ito and Kepplinger, join with me in evaluating the direction of our efforts. It must be understood that without the collaboration and friendship of these and other colleagues this work would not have been possible. Nonetheless, they cannot be held responsible for all the reviews of the literature and the interpretations of the data. I am certain that the final product will surprise them in some respects, for the vagaries of long-distance collaboration are bound to take their toll. Not travel, telephone, cable, tapes, and telexes could deter the insidious introduction of errors. Hoping to be forgiven all errors, not merely by my colleagues but by our readers, we may conclude that the dedication of this book speaks to my coauthors, first among others.

ALEX S. EDELSTEIN

CHAPTER 1

Communication and Culture: A Comparative Approach

Scholars and students have worked with hope and dedication in the fields of communication and culture for more than half a century—on ideas, goals, and a persisting array of global problems. The comparative approach, representative of those ideas, has been directed toward the discovery of generalizations about the roles of information and communication in a variety of cultures.

Communication and culture as an idea is encompassing in its dimensions. More recently, as a self-conceived "information society" (*Johoka shakai*) in which *joho kodo* (information behavior) is the focus of attention, Japan has pointed to the rapid growth of information as an expression of an expanding culture.

Several factors have indicated the importance of information, communication, and culture as the foci of comparative studies. The emergence of Japan, Germany, and the United States as information societies and, at the other end of the technological spectrum, the efforts to bring about "communication development" in Third World countries, have expressed a similar view of the importance of information and mass media institutions.

Decades ago Mowlana (1973) pointed to developments in information technologies relating to computerization and communication that would drive us into global interdependence. As he forecasted, instances of intercultural communication that once were rare events now are witnessed every moment on a global scale. Communications technologies have created windows through which we may view other societies and cultures. Thus Mowlana (1986) recently observed, the world society in general and international relations in particular can only be understood through a study of the messages and communication facilities that belong to it . . . . Culture and communication are the fundamental aspects of the process and must be included in the foci of analysis. (p. vii)

A sensitive observer of international communication (Hachten, 1987) has sought to bring together the world of news and the technologies on which it now depends. He sees dramatic changes occurring in communications technologies that will change the faces of nations as perceived by one another, pointing in this way to the need for constant comparisons to facilitate communication and to audit progress toward their goals:

Few of us can appreciate, much less fully understand, the meaning of the global information revolution . . . a revolution that has enveloped us virtually unnoticed. The major artifacts of this quiet revolution are the computer and the communications satellite—sophisticated electronic devices that have become as much a part of our lives as the electric light. (pp. xii–xiii)

It is not surprising that studies of international communication and culture have mushroomed. To say that one studies "international communication" now requires the identification of one of the fields of inquiry and the cultures that are occupying one's attention. Each field has emerged in distinctive form because of its special purposes, approaches, and matters of concern. Each culture, as well, commands the attention of an identifiable group of scholars. In Japan, as we have suggested, attention has centered on information behaviors as a cultural manifestation.

THE CULTURAL CONTEXTS

Just a few years ago one of our most insightful critics of empirical communication research, James W. Carey (1985), pleaded for a culture-centered reevaluation of the framework within which most communication studies had proceeded: "I have been making an argument for a particular and distinctive point of view toward the mass media, for something I call, without originality, cultural studies" (p. 27).

Although speaking of cultural studies only as imbedded in its own history and not from the perspective of other cultures, Carey nonetheless alluded to the position of observer, a vantage point for the comparativist. Thus the comparativist, by necessity, placed himself or herself in the position of observing the functioning of not merely one but several cultures. Carey urged that observations be keen enough so that we could report not only our observations of the most common bases of those societies but also the more varied manifestations of culture: the *"varieties* of human experience. . . providing the deepest pleasure. . . and the most complex explanatory problems. . . " (p. 35).

It was elements of culture that distinguished societies and revealed their special character, Carey (1982) explained: "we embrace our inheritance from our conversation with our fellow human beings, for. . . you cannot grasp a conversation elsewhere until you can understand one at home" (p. 22).

In the context of the comparative approach Carey might have agreed with us that one may not grasp the nuances of a conversation at home unless one has observed one abroad.

THE EMERGENCE OF A FIELD

The emerging information-oriented field of communication and culture has begun to attract its own critics and advocates. They have acknowledged the relevance of communication and culture to any activity and feel it is vital to validate this relationship by multicultural analysis. One critic (Hur, 1982) has lamented that too many studies have been done on a country-by-country basis in single cultural contexts. He holds that it is necessary to adopt more systematic approaches—as in the case of our multicultural, comparative perspective—if we are to cope with the increasing demands posed by international agendas.

More recently another young critic, Babbili (1987), pointed to other missing elements that have retarded the development of communication and culture as a disciplined field of study. One is the absence of theory, to which our volume is addressed. But another has been the lack of influence of European and Third World cultural perspectives. As a consequence, Babbili observed,

> surveying. . . international communication studies, one finds the landscape at once fertile and barren. Fertile in the sense of. . . scholarship of press systems and issues. . . . The barrenness. . . is. . . an apparent lack of theoretical framework to explain the complexities. (p. 1)

We agree with the call for more systematic studies of communication and culture as a way of gaining recognition for this area as a field of study. We envision several subfields, each of which makes its contribution as a collection of knowledge but each of which also asserts its distinctiveness as a function of its purposes and methods.

In an earlier volume, *Comparative Communication Research*, Edelstein

(1982) suggested ways in which fields of study might be more clearly identified. The argument was made again that each subfield was defined by the works of a scholarly community and within that community expressed a distinctive point of view. The comparative approach is distinctive in its commitment to the discovery of the common bases of societies and the appreciation of the uniqueness of cultural expression as societies pursue their goals.

ADDRESSING SEMANTIC PROBLEMS

One inevitably encounters semantic problems in efforts to articulate an emerging field of study. As a field proliferates it "borrows" words and definitions from kindred disciplines and asks them to do double duty. Later, as foci become sharpened, the utility of borrowed terms becomes questioned. That is no less the case for communication and culture. Up to now, at least, such terms as *comparative, cross-national, cross-cultural*, and *intercultural* often have been used interchangeably. But very pragmatic approaches in methodologies as well as differences in point of view have begun to emerge, each directed to the needs of a substantive and theoretical field of inquiry. Particular research strategies are implicit in each approach. As stated in *Comparative Communication Research* (Edelstein, 1982),

> We have taken a straightforward view of "comparative." It is a study that compares two or more nations (or other entities) with respect to some common activity. In international studies Country A is compared to Country B with respect to leisure time, or Region A is compared to Region B with respect to the flow of news into and out of those and other regions. (p. 14)

In these terms the scholar is an observer looking at nations and regions and comparing their behavior directly with respect to some phenomenon of meaning that is common to both at the same (or equivalent) moment in time and space.

We would contrast the comparative approach with the use of the term *cross-cultural*, which has been used in very precise terms by some scholars to describe messages being sent across borders, but which also has been used metaphorically to mean that a particular phenomenon occurs in many cultures. This meaning does not imply, at all, that a meaningful message is being transmitted from Country A to Country B across national and cultural boundaries. In the first usage no communication act occurs or even is implied.

We would not seek to impose terminology but only clarification where it seems to be required. Acknowledging the value of each of many terms to a variety of scholars, we still think it appropriate to suggest a distinctive term for comparative analysis to be considered along with such terms in use as *cross-cultural* or even *intercultural*. What we suggest is *multicultural*. It would be used to substitute for *cross-cultural* in those references that describe only a comparative setting. Thus *multicultural* would be used to mean "in many cultures, without interaction."

This distinction was made in a comparative study of U.S. and Japanese college students that was reported in 1983 to the Hoso-Bunka Foundation of Japan. The foundation had underwritten the comparative study precisely to determine, *by the comparisons*, the potentialities for *cross-cultural* communication. The question was whether U.S. and Japanese students were sufficiently alike because of their status as students (or so dramatically different by virtue of the variability of their cultures) as to encourage (or discourage) efforts at cross-cultural communication.

The question relating to cross-cultural communication was whether messages through mass media and institutional channels from Japan to the United States and from the United States to Japan could be conveyed in such a manner as to appeal to each culture's values and predispositions. Thus it was framed in the "uses and gratifications" tradition. Did American and Japanese students use mass media similarly or differently? We will answer those questions in Chapter 5.

Also, the question was implicitly related to *intercultural* communication; that is, if values were similar as expressed through media then there were potentialities, as well, for successful interpersonal or *intercultural* communication. Thus *cross-cultural* or *one-way mass communication* was differentiated from *intercultural* or *two-way interaction and interpersonal communication*.

The 1983 Japan study contributes to our efforts in a number of ways. First, as we will describe in greater detail in Chapter 5, it supports our own comparative findings of U.S. and Japanese students and indeed, the findings relating to German and Chinese students as well. That is, all behaved similarly in a number of important ways because of their similar status as students, and all behaved a little differently, as well, because of the differences in their cultures.

Just as importantly, the Japanese study points to the unity as well as the differentiation that we might make between comparative, cross-cultural, and intercultural communication. These approaches contribute to the unity of a field that we have defined as *communication and culture*, substituting for the more common encompassing term of "international communication." Each of three research perspectives into communication contains, as is evident, cultural elements. When we have spoken about *international communication* we have tended, perhaps subconsciously, to minimize aspects of culture.

Differentiation among the three cultural approaches seems less useful when two or more of them are being treated in the same study. Many studies embrace two or more parameters; that is, they may *compare* movements of information across *cultural* boundaries, either by virtue of mass communication or through interpersonal communication. Nonetheless, the differentiation may be observed, as pictured in Figure 1.1.

AN UNABASHEDLY SELF-CONSCIOUS APPROACH

There are obvious advantages to be gained from distinguishing fields of study from one another. We may speak of studies of national and regional communication systems; international broadcasting systems; intercultural, cross-national, and cross-cultural, and of course, comparative. At the least, such differentiation makes easier the search for knowledge in each field.

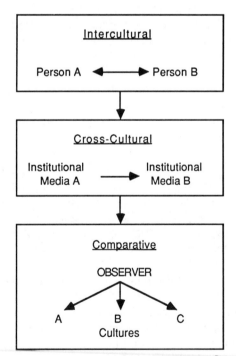

Figure 1.1. Differences in Perspectives in Intercultural, Cross-Cultural, and Comparative Studies.

Scholars in intercultural communication have unabashedly, and self-consciously, asserted their status as workers in a distinctive field of study. Asante and colleagues (1979), for example, have traced intercultural communication studies from rhetoric to speech science, pointing to an outpouring of textbooks, journals, and theoretical and methodological innovations. From anthropology, psychology, and rhetoric and a concern with interpersonal communication in a single culture to interpersonal communication in a variety of cultures, distinctive purposes and approaches were to emerge thàt gave character to the field:

> we are attempting to develop a theoretical and methodological orientation toward intercultural communication as a unified field of study. Scholars from other fields have contributed useful concepts but they have not applied them to interactional situations. (p. 13)

Porter and Samovar (1973) explicitly differentiated intercultural from cross-national and cross-cultural communication: Intercultural stressed interpersonal relations and interaction, whereas cross-national and cross-cultural used institutionalized means of diffusing culture "without interaction."

In fact, intercultural communication scholars were cautioned they must understand the implications of culture before they identified problems for research. Ellingsworth (1977) suggested putting the field on hold until there was a better articulation of cultural variables. Asante saw Triandis's (1972) cultural assimilators and Gerbner's (1976) cultural indicators as providing this necessary "codification" of data: "...much like naming the organic and inorganic materials of the universe....It must be done before other scholars can do their work; the creation of concepts must precede their manipulation" (p. 13). Stewart (1972), as well, made creative efforts to relate aspects of culture to instances of interpersonal communication.

Asante has, however, proposed what seems to represent an unnecessary step toward definition of the field. He suggests that intercultural communication should focus only on culturally determined *differences* rather than identifying similarities: "Cultural differences, not cultural similarities, is the premise of the field of intercultural communication. If this were not the case then all our discussion would be pointless" (p. 14).

Although he stressed the pursuit of differences, Ellingsworth (1976) did not state that similarities should not be observed. He insisted only that the study be designed to make possible a conclusive statement that variances were due to cultural differences and to no other factor. An articulate spokesperson for the differences—similarities position, H. Nishida (1987), has expressed the view that intercultural communications research does not reject traditions implicit in comparative analysis and that, indeed, both intercultural and comparative analyses often are synchronous.

DECIDEDLY MORE BASHFUL, BUT WHY?

In contrast to the zeal demonstrated by intercultural scholars, comparativists in communications research have been much more bashful about proclaiming themselves to be members of a relatively exclusive field of study. Communication scholars generally perceive themselves to be part-time comparativists rather than speakers for a cause. Even such admired leaders in the field as the late Harold Lasswell, Daniel Lerner, Ithiel de Sola Pool, and Wilbur Schramm, although they advanced the comparative approach in a number of important works, did not speak of themselves as comparativists in a communication field of study. Lasswell (1968) wrote of the comparative method as a political scientist and as a part of his personal vision of a global system:

> political scientists have been belatedly responding to the accelerating interdependence of the world arena. . . . The inference would appear to be that an effective demand for more comparative knowledge depends upon the shared expectation of political elites that they will be better off if they broaden the territorial scope and depth of their political information. (p. 3)

Most social scientists, those in mass communications largely excluded, have committed themselves to comparative analysis not merely in terms of global consciousness as a social priority but also as an ordered intellectual and disciplinary imperative.

Sociologists largely have accepted Émile Durkheim's world view (1938) that

> One cannot explain a social fact of any complexity except by following its complete development through all social species. Comparative sociology is not a particular branch of sociology; it is sociology, itself, insofar as it ceases to be purely descriptive and aspires to account for facts. (p. 139)

Although few sociologists would accept Durkheim's view that comparative sociology was sociology itself, they nonetheless accept the centrality in their discipline of an intellectual commitment to explore the extent to which human behavior is universal. Thus the task of comparative sociology, according to Tomasson (1978), was

> to compare values, structures, processes, and behaviors across social systems to distinguish between those regularities. . . that are system-speci-

fic and those that are universal. [It] is a means whereby we can trace cultural borrowings between social systems together with the study of their comparative development. (p. 1)

The search for universality was stressed also by Bendix (1963): "Comparative sociological studies represent an attempt to develop concepts and generalizations at a level between what is true of all societies and what is true of one society at one point in time and space" (p. 532).

Illustrating the semantic problems we have mentioned, Higson (1968) alluded to "inter-cultural" comparisons, but his theme goes directly to the purposes of comparative analysis, noting that variables that had conceptual generality (as our cognitive variables) are more readily validated in the comparative setting. He pointed to the appeal to comparativisits of institutional structures that seem to reflect the common bases of societies.

Anthropologists have been most explicit about the need to identify generalizable and important concepts. Goodenough (1970) described it also as a need for an equivalent set of terms. But he added that "we need some set of universally applicable concepts that will enable us to compare cultures and arrive at generalizations about them" (p. 2). In our case we turned to cognitive concepts as having the most generality.

Kluckhohn early (1953) identified this need, stating that the most common bases for comparison were the "givens" of human life—including, as we have pursued it, cognitive behavior. Reflective of our strategy in this research Kluckhohn wrote, "These [givens]...provide the foci around which and within which the patterns of every culture crystallize. Hence comparison can escape from the bias of any distinct culture..." (p. 521).

Historians, as well, have used the comparative approach to search for universalities by extending them. Thus Bonnell (1980) has described two strategies employed by historians: Utilizing the first technique, the historian juxtaposes equivalent units of analysis to identify variables that explain common or contrasting patterns. Much as we have pursued our strategy, equivalencies are pursued as a way of identifying further equivalencies until, exhausted, they encounter differences. These are explained by cultures or situations.

A RESEARCH STRATEGY

To illustrate: A comparative "point of view" demands a research strategy to advance it. Simply put, as we have advanced it previously (Edelstein, 1974), we begin with our knowledge of the commonalities among student groups that exist across societies, assuming that these commonalities will hold on a global scale. This view expresses the comparativist's assumption that "there are more commonalities across than within." In terms of students, they will express more commonalities with their counterparts in other countries than they will profess with nonstudent members of their own cultures.

The research strategy that is dictated by this intellectual approach is to begin with the assumed commonalities—for example, the equivalence of students—and test empirically the extent to which this assumed homogeneity actually may be observed.

We will expect that the similarities in communications and other behaviors that we will observe are attributable to common roles and identities as students. We do not exclude the possibility that differences also will be observed; certainly, this will be the case. These differences will be explained by cultures and the demands of a variety of situations, as we will further explain and develop.

In his 1974 study Edelstein demonstrated that there were more similarities than differences in media uses and evaluation *across cultures* among groups of similar educational, occupational, age, and sex definition. This was observed despite the fact that extraordinarily different cultures and very different stages of economic development were represented in the comparison countries.

Different political ideologies, religious and philosophical differences, and labor intensive versus technology intensive economies did not affect the results. Now with students as our subjects of study, rather than general populations, we expect to see more dramatic similarities.

A SECOND STRATEGY

A second research strategy adopted by comparativists is to test the assumed relevance of one criterion or one theory to two or more cultures. There are dangers, however, in this approach. The most critical problem is that the criteria that are adopted or the theories that are tested may not be equally relevant to the two or more societies that are being compared. Referring to comparisons of journalists in Third World countries with their compatriots in First or Second World nations, Passin (1963) pointed out that this might only be done with an understanding of traditions and specific historical experiences. But in identifying the close relation ships between literature, politics, and journalism, Passin pointed out an area where multinational and multicultural comparisons might be made.

Two American researchers, McLeod and Rush (1969a, 1969b), attempted to apply the criterion of professionalism in a comparison of Latin American and U.S. journalists. They relied substantially on the concept of equivalence of role to rationalize the comparisons. But the two groups of journalists were more unlike than alike, particularly against the criterion of professionalism. McLeod and Rush concluded that Latin American newsmen scarcely were comparable with U.S. journalists on the attributes of professionalism that they had invoked.

A West German scholar (Donsbach, 1981) attempted to cut through this problem of lack of comparability by suggesting criteria on which all journalists might be compared: competency and legitimacy. The competence would be directed toward increasing the potentialities for public communication, and legitimacy would be defined in terms of the institutional sources of support that contributed to that role. On this basis Donsbach was able to generalize about Latin American journalists as compared to German and Canadian journalists with some degree of success. The appropriateness of the criteria and the relevance of the social theory were all-important to the comparisons.

Where Donsbach sought a basis for comparison that would test his assumptions about similarities of journalistic roles and practices, another German researcher, Kocher (1987), *contrasted* perceptions of role by German and British journalists.

Thus while the Kocher study "compared," it did not take a comparativist point of view or adopt related research strategies. A comparativist would have reasoned that nothing generalizable could be learned from the comparison of roles that were entirely different. Thus Kocher's work would have been viewed as "two studies," one describing German journalists, the other picturing British journalists in their own social and cultural contexts. As she concluded:

> [There were] extensive differences in their perception of their role, their professional motivations and their evaluation of the norm of objectivity. (p. 362)

Kocher saw limits to efforts to compare journalistic roles and practices, asserting that even in countries that enjoyed similar concepts of freedom of the press, journalism practices could develop in completely different directions, these to be determined by political, legal, and historical settings. Our own data on how German students perceived mass media reflected the same political and intellectual values as those identified by Kocher in German journalists; that is, students did not perceive German journalists as neutral or objective but as expressing opinions that mirrored political and intellectual values. British journalists, by contrast, saw themselves in relatively neutral roles as transmitters of information.

Although we may point to conceptual and methodological self-consciousness about the comparative approach in other social science disciplines, mass communications, as a field, has proceeded without self-awareness. This might be a reflection of the state of the field. It is possible that the

comparative approach, searching for its own identity, will encourage movement in mass communication toward a discipline.

INSTITUTIONALIZING A FIELD

In this brief description of points of view in intercultural and comparative
communication we have observed contrasting approaches to the institutionalizing of a field. A pioneer in intercultural communication, Dance
(1978) saw institutionalizing as a process. As seen in Figure 1.2, studies
first proliferate and new boundaries are defined. Then new foci are identi-

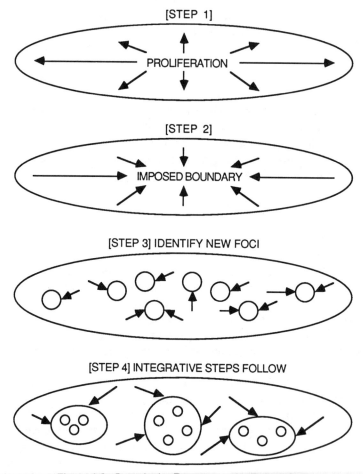

Figure 1.2. Steps in the Emergence of a Field of Study

fied, and new paths for study are discovered. Integrative, theoretical steps follow, often accompanied by innovations in methodologies.

Let us apply those steps to a number of the subfields of communication and culture to determine if they fit the pattern.

National and Regional Systems

Studies of national and regional communication systems proliferated in the 1960s as they took as their foci an array of economic, political, social, and cultural indicators. The increasing availability of masses of data, generated in large part by the initiatives of the United Nations and Unesco, and the ability of new computer technologies to handle those data bases contributed immensely to the development of that field.

What began among scholars as an effort to look at the idea of "system" as a way of observing the relationships of institutions **within** societies (Edelstein, 1982) soon became perceived as a way of comparing functionings **across** societies. Large data sets could be used to describe the shared nature of societies and might even be used to predict their emergence. New technologies of research were leading social scientists to come to conclusions about the emergence of societies. The nature of "data sets" and the capacities of computers and statistical methods to treat them were assigning meaning to those data.

We may go back to some of the earliest and best known studies of communication systems and social systems to observe how "social science technologies" affected the emergence of the field of study of communication systems and social systems, one that we may now place within the broader rubric of communication and culture.

The best known and perhaps least understood of these efforts was that of Lerner (1958). Essentially, Lerner advanced a correlational or "statistical" theory of societal modernization in the Middle East that rested upon the interaction of increasing rates of urbanization, literacy, and mass communication. Other scholars were later to say that his reasoning was faulty and even that his statistics did not bear up. One of Lerner's "steps" did not follow the other, and even the rates of change he projected did not stand up under analysis (Schramm and Ruggels, 1967). Nonetheless, Lerner's work inspired a generation of research on the relationships between economic and social systems and communication systems.

One of the most pressing ideological questions in the United States at that time, as we will note in relation to our discussion of demands for a new international information order, was "freedom of information." Under what social, economic, and political conditions was freedom of information most likely to prosper? The production of various data sets made it possible to submit these questions to the new communications research technologies for statistical manipulation. As expected, the inferences that were made from these data also were to be questioned. Nonetheless, these studies contributed to the emergence of the field of study.

Most central to the concept that freedom of information was related to system variables were two studies by the then editor of *Journalism Quarterly*, a distinguished professor of mass communications at the University of Minnesota, Dr. Raymond B. Nixon. He found that freedom of information was highly correlated with amount of income, degree of literacy, and daily newspaper circulation. A new data set produced by UNESCO five years later contributed more strongly to Nixon's assumptions (Nixon, 1960, 1965). Numerous other studies were to introduce new foci, incorporate more dynamic variables, extend statistical treatments, and suggest alternative interpretations to the data. These were more integrative studies and more conceptually based than the pioneering efforts of Nixon. But like that of Lerner's work, whatever the validity of his findings and their persistence as knowledge, Nixon contributed by his efforts to the emergence of a field of study in communication systems and social systems.

System studies have grown apace. One of the most promising comparative environments is the analysis of emerging broadcasting deregulation policies, notably in Japan, Europe, the United States, and Australia. These studies are taking into account not only the broader social and institutional environments that define broadcasting policies, but as we have suggested, they are taking these internal system characteristics into account in carrying out multinational comparisons.

Cross-National and Cross-Cultural Studies

Studies of cross-national and cross-regional systems, as well, went through stages of proliferation and integration. Early cross-national studies were not thought of as evocative of culture but only as value-free traffic that merely happened to travel across national boundaries. The first studies of mail flow, which were viewed as relatively value free, typically were regarded as exercises in exchange statistics rather than analyses of the cultural relations that explained those flows.

A renaissance of data-based variables emerged in the 1970s and continued into the 1980s. On the one hand the cross-national flow remains relatively value free—commercial data such as bank transfers, stock reports, airline passages, trade statistics, and mail and telephone services. On the other hand, the Unesco-inspired debate over the balanced flow of news has been argued, in part, at the level of the cultural impacts of technological dominance and transfer. In raising perplexing questions about the political, economic, social, and cultural aspects of transmitting and receiving systems, these scholars expanded the boundaries of the debate and defined new foci for research.

Studies of international diplomacy and propaganda have always been clearly cross-cultural. Events such as war and other crises led to the proliferation of the field, embracing studies of the characteristics of communicators, messages, audiences, and processes and effects. The boundaries of the field were extended from the study of politics to that of social-psychology and communication. Communication and attitude change and the social context of persuasion became new foci for research.

Fields also ebb and flow. Propaganda lost status as a field of study after World War II to a larger preoccupation with theoretical inquiries in communication sciences. Studies of public opinion took precedence over propaganda as domestic problems supplanted international conflict. Now a second proliferation of studies has ensued with the renewed interest of scholars in peace research and conflict resolution. Hot spots in the world and the aggressiveness of international diplomacy have produced surges of interest in international political communication, and in 1980 a newly established journal, *Political Communication and Persuasion: An International Quarterly*, began to identify new foci for the study of international communication and persuasion.

Comparative Communication

Comparative studies also have proliferated greatly. Edelstein (1982) described in detail nine substantive areas that had been the foci of comparative analysis, and he referred to a number of other areas as well. Two of the most proliferating areas have been the Unesco-sponsored debate over the New International Information Order (NIIO) and the emergence of information societies.

As is well known, the debate over the NIIO was provoked by demands of the Second (Socialist states) and Third World states. If we follow Figure 1.2 we will look for stages, or steps, in the emergence of research, characterized by proliferation, boundary setting, establishing new foci for study, and integration of substantive areas and concepts leading to theory building.

NIIO: THE FIRST STAGE

Comparative studies of news flow proliferated during two eras, the first in the 1950s and early 1960s, and the second in the early 1970s and 1980s.

The outlooks on the problems were as divergent as the decades in which they occurred. At the conclusion of World War II the Western concern about imbalances in news flow was mitigated by the hope that an easy and palatable remedy might be found. By the end of the stalemated United Nations Conference of 1948 in Latin America, however, guarded optimism had turned to outright pessimism. A number of comparative studies in the 1950s and early 1960s documented the imbalances in news flow and the conflicting outlooks concerning the nature of the problem.

In the most broad-ranging comparative analysis of news flow of this era, Schramm (1959) compared 14 equivalent "elite" newspapers in crises —Hungary and Suez—to observe how good newspapers would describe bad news. The selection of newspapers was based on the assumption that each played a pivotal societal role. Since each newspaper reflected the needs of those societies for elite communication, all of them would be comparable.

Schramm demonstrated, as might be expected, that he was far ahead of most of his contemporaries in exploiting the comparative approach. He went to considerable pains to ensure that the newspapers in his sample were comparable. He postulated that elite newspapers were similar enough to be compared and thus produce useful multicultural generalizations; yet they were different enough to express distinctive elements of (political) culture. Elite newspapers are widely read by leaders and influential people in their own countries and elsewhere. Each is widely quoted, and their viewpoints enter into important decisions. That each newspaper had gained its status by its own or other efforts was less material than their functional equivalence. What mattered was that each expressed a high degree of political and social influence. There was more to be gained by addressing the equivalence of their roles than the sources of their power.

As can be seen in Figure 1.3 Schramm's work touched many bases. He examined patterns and possible distortions in news flow, addressed news

---

* Distinctiveness as well as generalizable patterns of flow and content;

* Distortions in flow and content that might contribute to ignorance and misunderstandings;

* News as well as culture and entertainment;

* Events as well as selected time periods;

* Basic conceptual and methodological issues;

* Concerns with elite or prestige newspapers;

* The need to contribute to a global outlook, and;

* A belief that research contributed to the definition and solution of problems.

Figure 1.3. First Proliferation of News Flow Research

and events, treated conceptual and methodological questions, demonstrated a global outlook in his selection of countries and newspapers, and was guided by a belief that research could contribute to the solution of problems of cross-cultural communication. The study was cross-cultural in asking what countries selected what news, but it was comparative in examining their performance.

Markham's (1961) comparison of news flow, although it followed Schramm's, was first generation rather than second generation in its outlook and sophistication. Markham tied his research to the patterns developed by UNESCO and the International Press Institute in Zurich. They sought merely to identify the extent and quality of foreign news available to readers worldwide. In comparative terms Kayser (1953) found that the 16 foreign newspapers that he examined carried a greater proportion of foreign news than did the one U.S. newspaper, the *New York Times*. But percentages rather than volume of space were reported, producing a distorted outcome for the *Times*.

Comparing Images

Some of the most intriguing studies that emerged during the first wave of comparative analysis of news flow focused on the construction of foreign "images." These studies first proliferated in the 1950s and 1960s and became more sophisticated as they defined new research foci.

Image, of course, was not an easy term to define. Most scholars used Scott's formulation (1965) of images as the totality and interrelationships of attributes—recognized or imagined. To Boulding (1959) images were real, however imagined, and these were the bases on which nations communicated. Mutual perceptions, including perceptions of other perceptions, were the realities that produced friendly or hostile actions. Moreover, images were constantly changing in their elements and therefore in their meanings.

Thus Isaacs (1958, 1962) compared American images of China and India and their peoples; 20 years later Edelstein and Hall (1979) compared American images of traditional and modern China and Japan; earlier, as part of the first wave, Conrad (1955) compared paired newspapers in West and East Germany on their construction of images that represented the ideological perspectives of each social system; and Wolfe (1964) compared images of the United States in 20 Latin American newspapers; in 1981 Pisarek produced findings similar to those of Conrad in his comparison of the United States and the Soviet Union.

All this was indicative of the event-centered and idealistic thrust of comparative analysis, as might be true of any other field. It was captured in this citation from Markham (1961):

Those who believe that peace and security depend upon world public opinion based on international understanding recognize the growing importance of an adequate and meaningful flow of information among peoples as one possible means of achieving such goals. . . . The question of how our press compares with that of other countries in its coverage of the world scene, therefore, is one that merits examination. . . . (p. 50)

The Second Stage

The second stage of proliferation in the late 1970s and early 1980s caused the United States to withdraw its support from Unesco because of what it believed was the adverse and ideological character of the debate. Nevertheless, during this second period the boundaries of the research were greatly expanded and new foci for research were identified.

Attention centered first on the Arab states as a consequence of two Middle East wars and the emergence of OPEC oil diplomacy. As the Arab countries became more powerful actors on the world stage, researchers were motivated to assess and compare their media content to those of other countries. Studies were conceptualized in similar terms to first-stage efforts but were different in point of view.

We may look at Dajani and Donohue (1973) as a useful example. They compared six "prestige" Arab newspapers with respect to amount of foreign news, attention to various countries, and patterns of favorability toward other countries. The hypotheses stressed the influence of political and economic ties, ideological postures, cultural relationships, the national and regional interest (Arabs vs. Israel), and internal political structures. As expected, much of the content was explained by attitudes toward Israel.

Rachty (1978) tested assumptions about tendencies of the Arab press to use wire association news, refuting some prevailing thoughts about those supposed tendencies. As yet another example, Pinch (1978) addressed assumptions about the use of news by Third World countries. His findings also caused some rethinking to occur.

The NIIO issues were reflected in "image" studies, as well. Gerbner and Marvanyi (1977) graphically pictured the world of news as a pattern of reciprocal responses, and Daugherty and Warden (1979) compared editorials in leading newspapers in the United States on their treatment of Israeli-Arab issues.

Schramm and Atwood's second major comparative work (1984) illustrated the foci stage of development and efforts to achieve integration of research findings. In comparing the effects of four press associations on the newspapers of Asia, Schramm and Atwood directed attention to the fact that few cross-cultural effects actually had occurred and that, comparatively speaking, there were few differences in patterns of press association output and media use that were worthy of note. The lesson to be drawn was that social purpose was constrained by media reality.

Another UNESCO study, designed to assess the legitimacy of competing claims about the NIIO, also was unable to settle the issues. Sreberny-Mohammadi and colleagues (1980), in collaboration with an international group of scholars, studied dozens of countries, and a supplementary sample of nations was studied by a U.S. team headed by Stevenson and Cole (1979, 1980). It was difficult to agree on foci, although strenuous efforts were made.

Although surprising to the researchers, the results were generalizable across nation-states with disparate cultures and from different regions of the world. The commonalities observed in the study are in Figure 1.4. Stevenson and Shaw (1984) amplified these data.

Stevenson (1988) observed about the report, "Mostly it contained numbers, which were surprisingly similar to those in dozens of other studies carried out at different times with different samples, definitions, and techniques" (p. 129).

Thus more intensive comparative analysis was used to carry out an auditing function, but comparative studies yielded other benefits as well. Having moved beyond the most direct—although sometimes the least comparable—observations, researchers learned enough to redefine problems in ways that might permit solutions, given the appropriate remedies. As Giffard (1987) put it, it was a myth that new technologies could provide a "quick fix" for information imbalances. However, new communication infrastructures could be planned and new information services could be instituted that might provide the news that was needed. Probably the most successful of these "globally induced" information services was Interpress (Giffard, 1984, 1985), which offered services in seven languages in several world regions.

---

* Certain types of news will appear in all media systems, whatever their characteristics as societies;

* News, itself, demonstrates a homogeneity;

* Regionalism is a strong predictor of news flow and content;

* Developing countries are more likely to qualify as "hot spots" in the news than industrial countries;

* Some geographical areas are more invisible than others, explained largely by political attributes.

Figure 1.4. Structurally Based Generalizations about News Flow

INTEGRATION AND THEORY EMERGE

Integration and theory began to be introduced into comparative analysis of the NIIO as scholars switched from looking only for discrepancies in news flow to identifying some of the equivalent conditions that promoted balance. These were found in such common bases for exchange as regionalism, former colonial dependencies, trade, security, language, and cultures.

In 1971 a well-known Norwegian scholar, Galtung, theorized that a great deal of the pattern of news flows depended on colonial and former colonial relations. This meant that the patterns would be as similar between Britain and her Pacific colonies as between France and her African colonies. In other words, the dependency relationships were functionally equivalent although the actors and the locations were different. Thus if one did a comparative analysis of news flow involving dependency relations one could expect to observe similar outcomes. The idea, roughly, is that there would be more flow from the center nation (the colonial power) to the peripheral (colonies) than vice versa and that there would be more communication between center nations than peripheral nations.

This theory was amenable to testing, which was carried out in the Pacific islands by two researchers at the East West Center in Hawaii, Nnaemeka and Richstad (1980). The study supported the broad outlines of the Galtung theory but encountered the suggestion of emerging differences, that is, that regional cooperation among the colonial dependencies in that area—French as well as British—and the introduction of satellite communication technologies now made it useful and feasible for the former colonies to communicate among themselves. Formerly this communication had not been possible. The authors concluded that this new point-to-point communication was not a "quick fix" for those societies but that satellite communication would further erode the former structured relations between center and peripheral nations.

Summarizing the place of studies of news flow in the context of comparative studies, Edelstein concluded, "...the debate stimulated new ways of looking at old problems...encouraged the use of theory...and narrowed and provided foci on the most promising parameters for study..." (1982, p. 60).

INFORMATION SOCIETIES

Although the NIIO and related issues spurred comparative studies and ultimately produced integrational and theoretical works, "flow" research nevertheless settled into a well-defined set of boundaries. As the boundaries of flow studies became more pronounced, the first studies of the new technologies of communication began to be introduced. An even more profound proliferation of studies about information societies began as the flow studies waned.

The Information Society Defined

At the third in a series of information societies conferences between 1978 and 1983, the first two held in Seattle, Washington, and the third at Keio University in Tokyo, our colleague Professor Youichi Ito (1981) defined an information society in Japanese terms as *johoko shakai*: "a society characterized by abundant information in terms of both stock and flow, quick and efficient distribution and transportation of information, and easy and inexpensive access [to] information for all members of society" (p. 672).

In 1984 Ito and a colleague, Koichi Ogawa, described more recent trends in information societies research and referred to first and second *johoko shakai* "booms." The two authors concluded that Japan was unique as a culture in its fascination with the concept of an information society because of

> Socio-economic conditions in the 1960's, strong Japanese curiosity about novelties and...progressive attitudes toward social change....These achievements have occurred in advanced technology, business, governmental policies, and social scientific research. (p. 16)

Studies of information societies began in Japan as early as 1966, but the term was not coined until 1969.

Masuda (1979) saw the social nexus of the information society as a collision between desires for privacy and demands for homogeniety brought about by the promise of technologies that would sustain and even extend cultural homogeneity. Even the larger concept of "informationalization" in Japan has been viewed as having possibly negative effects on the value of privacy. Masuda (1980) forecast an environment in which some rights to privacy might become subordinated to an ethic that required the sharing of information. This took on universal as well as comparative dimensions:

> in the information society...the satisfaction of achieved goals will become the universal standard of values....The spirit of the Information Society will be the spirit of globalism, a symbiosis in which man and nature can live together in harmony, consisting ethically of strict self-discipline and social contribution. (p. 33)

At this point, however, the human rights debate has not occupied a great deal of the research stage. The focus of attention of scholars has been fastened on a variety of research on information behavior, in both its larger cultural forms as well as individual behavior. Ito (1988) characterizes these studies as representing the "macro" and "micro" interests of an information society, as macro studies try to grasp the social phenomenon "whole" and micro studies examine the behavior of individuals in the aggregate. Thus macro studies have described national, regional, and even global systems, and micro studies have particularized the behavior and needs of "acting units," that is, individuals.

Many of these investigations have been directed to the analysis of "informationalization," that is, the relationship between consumption and stock of information in the society at a particular time. Tomita (1978) characterized this development as a need for Japan to develop information and communication policies in an age "oversupplied with information," a situation in which the production of information was far greater than the consumption. This unique observation, stated as a policy perspective, has its echo globally in concerns about the extent and nature of investments that must be made in communication infrastructures to optimize production and consumption while at the same time assuring diversity and an enhanced quality of life (Takasaki, 1978). We summarize the thrust of this research in Chapter 8.

Expressive of universalism of communication, and inviting comparison, the more complex communication infrastructures are now increasingly subject to policies directed at deregulation of all telecommunication systems, most notably in the United States and Japan. The comparative approach would take technological innovation and diffusion as its causal agent and then look to see how it affected comparable (in industrial and similar terms) societies, in each case looking at cultural factors for more sensitive indicators of the likely course of those policies.

The Japanese view of the information society is holistic, and its views beg comparison where they may be found. To Japanese scholars, information behavior does not simply represent audience exposure to media; it also requires responses to the environment. It requires an active audience that abstracts meanings from information and uses those meanings to maximize the pleasures of its participation. Thus individuals interact with information, which does not possess any properties until the individual gives meaning to it. This occurs in a deeply embedded cultural context. Thus Ito (1988) proposes that the research question is "what kinds of individuals have what kinds of needs for what kinds of information?"

Ito (1988) sees the potential for comparative analysis along these dimensions of information behavior. As new technologies are introduced, such as the highly interactive systems in Japan, Hi-OVIS and CAPTAIN, the comparative question would be "what kinds of technologies, in what kinds of societies, most satisfy the culturally determined needs of individuals for information and communication?"

It would be instructive, as one instance, to compare the cultural commitment of Japan in introducing CAPTAIN with the case of Britain and its offering of PRESTEL. Viewing innovations in technologies as the independent variable, and adoption and utilization of systems as the dependent variable, one becomes fascinated by the explanatory power of the intervening elements of social organization and culture in predicting outcomes. In those terms one must hypothesize that it is far more likely that Japan will move more quickly than Britain to set down definitive, progressive, wide-reaching regulations and policies regarding interactive communication technologies.

Ito believes that this advanced state of informationalization already has placed Japan beyond the stage of proliferation of research to the establishment of boundaries and foci that will guide more sophisticated analysis. Integrative concepts are at hand, which encourages the interest in globalism. For one thing, the observation of similar audience-media interactions in multicultural settings would validate generality of the Japanese approach. There are a number of indications that Japanese scholars share Ito's sense of the future. Utilizing concepts that described information environments, Maejima (1973) concluded that individuals engage in "transmission" and "collection" processes of information behavior that promise a universality of findings in cultures. In each case,

- The content of information that individuals collect from mass media is basically the same as what they transmit to other people.
- There is a high correlation between an individual's need for information and expected social role.
- The satisfaction an individual derives from transmitting information decreases as its focus shifts from self to family to the local community and the nation.

Fujiwara (1969) complemented those findings by pointing out that exposure to media or usage of media constituted only a small part of a Japanese individual's information behavior as a whole. This was discerned from studies of "information types" and "consciousness types" among audiences.

The thrust of these and other studies is to define information behavior in the larger context of culture, setting, and lifestyle. These are merely some of the foci that might be tested in the multicultural setting. All innovations, including technologies, make demands on the cultural fabric. The essential question centers on the ability of a culture to adapt to those demands. Our intellectual goal, as we discuss in Chapter II, the symposium of authors, is to observe the nature of cultural responses to similar and different stimuli in multicultural contexts.

DEFINITION OF A FIELD: AN INVITING VISTA

We have been moving toward the conclusion that the field of communication and culture offers an inviting vista for comparative analysis. The comparative approach has acquired a boundless array of knowledge, defined parameters, and foci for research, as well as evidence of integration and theories. This book is intended to advance that process. In doing so, we try to make more evident

- The distinguishing characteristics of *fields of research*, such as the comparative approach
- The links between studies of communication and culture and major streams of mass communication research
- The future of the field, as it addresses technological and social changes that will affect our information and communication environment.

USING THE BOOK

We hope that teachers and students find this book useful and a source of gratification. As we have suggested, it is intended to be as useful for a class in mass communication that has had no experience in international issues as for those who are steeped in internationalism but who have had no empirical background. Students who have neither considered the major traditions of mass communication research nor gained any experience in the international and comparative context will enjoy their first opportunity to do so.

Much more common to faculty and students in international communication has been the study of comparative *institutions* rather than the behavioral concepts that we consider.

A recent exemplar of the institutional approach has been the work of Martin and Chaudhary (1983). But it is interesting to observe that they have, from their perspective, made observations similar to our own, that is, that although media systems are functionally equivalent as institutional structures they vary as a consequence of the uniqueness of cultures. Different political cultures assign different roles and tasks to their media to govern their performance. We think of Martin and Chaudhary as representing an advanced stage of comparative analysis of press institutions, complementary to our largely behavioral approach.

Let us now briefly, chapter by chapter, introduce the book itself. The purposes of each chapter are to introduce in each case a major tradition of mass communication research in its original setting—in some cases American, German, Japanese, or Chinese.

As a next step we examine the multicultural relevance of each concept. The always implicit question is how we would study that concept if we approached it comparatively, that is, multiculturally. How well does the concept travel? For example, is credibility a multicultural concept or is it only an American cultural illusion? If we find that other cultures entertain the same concept, although embedded in their own cultural context, what conceptual steps do we take to engage in the comparisons? And in each case, how do we observe the cultural and situational determinants?

In Chapter 2, we take the view that comparative analysis is not so much a method as an approach to a problem. In describing student values, we realize that culture and/or situations may explain more behavior in one national setting than in another. Political cultures have limited the sense of personal efficacy of German and Japanese students, whereas situational factors have constrained Hong Kong Chinese. In contrast, a greater sense of access to the political culture is reflected in the communication behavior of American students.

Chapter 3 introduces the "idea of the problem" and describes how a variety of individual problems are transformed into institutionally defined (macro) social problems.

At the micro level this leads us to the "problematic situation," which is framed as a cognitive challenge to the individual; in collective terms, the aggregate of problematics becomes defined in social terms that are resolved by institutional actions.

The problematic situation is defined as a "condition of discrepancy," which demands attention and behavior. These conditions of discrepancy are observed at both individual and societal levels as *conflict, deprivation, need, blocking, uncertainty,* and *steps toward solutions.* The "problemization" by the individual of any of these conditions of discrepancy induces a motivating force that produces information and communication behaviors.

One of the tests of a theory is its productivity; may it be applied to a consideration of other problems and in other cultures? In Chapter 4 we examine the relevance of the theory of problematic situations to a discrepancy theory of news. The theory proposes that media in their socially defined roles "scan" the environment for evidence of discrepancies that are accessible to observational and reporting methods. Within the scanning capabilities of the media, the discrepancies that they are able to observe take on the character of news.

Let us take as an example the clean water bill recently passed by the U.S. Congress. That was a social problem that had emerged and created public opinion and public action. Because of its problemization by individuals and the society, the clean water problem was observed by the media to represent discrepancies of several kinds.

1. *Deprivation*, in that something of value had been lost (clean water)
2. *Societal needs*—to clean up the water
3. *Uncertainties* about the extent of the needs and the efficacy of the *proposed solution*
4. *Social conflict* perceived (between the president and the Congress)
5. *Steps that were taken* to solve the problem
6. *Breakdowns* in those steps (if the clean-up program were not working as planned)

We will expect each of these problematic situations to be recognized by media and exploited as news.

One of the major criticisms of the uses approach is that it has not demonstrated convincingly the causal connection between needs experienced by an individual and uses of communication; that is, a motivational state. In Chapter 5 we put forward the concept of problemization by the individual to address that suggestion by the critics of the uses approach; that is, problemization by the individual induces motivation. We propose (although we cannot at this point demonstrate conclusively) that the perception of a discrepancy and its problemization are antecedent to the uses of communication.

In Chapter 6 we reevaluate another tradition of mass media research—the credibility of the medium. But our multicultural perspectives suggest that we adopt new and more meaningful (from an audience point of view) criteria to assess how various publics evaluate media.

Our data support observations made in Japan, as well as in the United States, that the social outlook of media (such as "respect for the individual," "sentiment," and similar values) is more relevant and important to audiences than the more limited criterion of credibility.

In Chapter 7 we shift the focus of coorientational studies in public opinion and communication from evalutive to cognitive dimensions. The question to be addressed is whether actors perceive that they are communicating about the same opinion objects or different opinion objects.

The use of cognitive foci also will permit us to conceptualize a "communication step theory" of public opinion. As a first step individuals and/or publics might focus on the consequences of a problem; at a second stage, they might communicate opinions about its causes, and ultimately they might discuss solutions.

The logic of the process, which gains support from our data, is that consequences are easier to observe than are causes or solutions, and they are the first to be observed, as well. We describe the extent to which students perceive that they and their peers, or they and public opinion, are cooriented to the same or to different cognitive aspects of public opinion.

Chapter 8 shifts attention, as Ito has suggested, from primary attention on media and social institutions to the important roles played by personal observation and interpersonal communication.

With respect to personal observation, the different nature of problems and their physical environments produce different degrees of opportunity for students in each country to observe events at first hand. In contrast, we look to cultural factors to account for differences in interpersonal communication. We have accessible to us extensive comparisons of the cultural context of interpersonal communication of Japanese and American students.

Chapter 9 places the major assumptions of agenda setting in a multicultural context. We hypothesize that different media have somewhat different agenda-setting effects and that cultural homogeniety-heterogeniety contributes also to effects.

We suggest that cognitive objects that are "thought about" as foci of agenda setting should be specified in meaning terms, such as problematic situations. Three degrees of "thinking" are proposed as agenda-setting effects—"thinking only," "thinking about," and "what to think." They are proposed as elements of a multieffect, multistep model, in which a variety of actors—politicians, social critics, bureaucrats and managers—join with journalists in setting agendas.

We propose that although agenda setting may be a limited behavioral hypothesis, it actually implies maximal conditions of communication. If individuals are successfully told what to think rather than only to think or what to think about, they are more bounded and there is less impetus for communication.

Our impetus for taking a cognitive approach to agenda setting, as with problematic situations, was based upon two related matters:

One rested upon the advantages of the use of cognitive variables in comparative analysis. As we have said, people in all cultures have problems, think about problems, and try to solve problems. Hence, cognitive variables are directly comparable and lend themselves to comparative analysis.

Our second perspective was guided by the importance of placing thinking and communication at the heart of our analysis. Most communications research has taken the direction of the study of attitudes rather than of thought, itself.

In a plea to fellow communication researchers that expresses our interests, Carter (1981) asked his colleagues to devote far greater attention to studies of cognitive behavior. He suggested that the study of cognitions and communication could help to prevent the curtailment of civic freedoms —not only in America but in all democratic societies:

I have seen reports that our freedoms may have to be curtailed because democracy is too difficult, too slow to operate under contemporary stresses. If we do not seriously, and carefully, begin to look into the problems of mass cognition and mass communication, to develop new solutions to them, we would certainly deserve what happens to us.

Without informed citizens there is no socially responsible mass medium . . . And there are no informed citizens if people cannot contribute cognitively and communicate their cognitions adequately. . . Indeed, "informed citizen" is a contradiction in terms if the(se) [communications are not] cognitive efforts. (p. 8)

We see, therefore, our cognitive approach as a step toward achieving a better comparative understanding of cognitions and communications.

Our approach in Chapter 10 is (1) intended to be as value free as possible because of the comparative context and is (2) designed to enhance opportunities for interaction and communication between researchers and subjects. As a second step we develop and test scales that measure each of our major concepts. The results are compared to those obtained with our basic instrument.

The form of a multicultural symposium in Chapter 11 enables us to restate in the "first person" the challenges of comparative analysis of communication and culture.

As a part of this process we suggest additional parameters for study. We propose that the comparative approach be applied to other problems and audiences for mass communication, and we conclude that the study of the values, perceptions, opinions, and communication behaviors of university students be the focus of continued attention. The recent and continuing student disorders in China and Korea are only symptomatic of deeper currents of unrest in those and other societies.

Robinson (1987) recently reported remarkable similarities in the outlooks of American and Soviet youths. Although conscious of cultural and situational imperatives, we may not conclude that trends are universal across nations; we need to observe and compare to discover common bases for behavior. Ultimately, this is the challenge to scholarship of comparative communication. Its degree of success will establish the significance of our field.

CHAPTER 2

Sources of Student Values: A Cultural Analysis

The comparative approach represents not only a point of view but an analytical approach as well. It enlists three concepts to explain the sources of student values: *structure*, *culture*, and *situation*.

These concepts are both exclusive and inclusive. They are exclusive in that they mark some discernible boundaries, but they are inclusive in that interdependencies exist among them. In explaining our data, therefore, we attribute similarities of communications and other behavior to the likelihood that these are characteristic of students in all the cultures. But there are bound to be differences among these groups as well. We attribute those differences to one of two basic sources: (1) distinctive elements of culture in the societies, or (2) the uniqueness of situations—so-called "conditions of contingency," a term borrowed from B. F. Skinner (1972). Under these conditions it is difficult to account for behavior exclusively in terms of social structures or cultures.

Anthropologists see structure as a valuable analytical instrument. They assert that what might be called "laws of society" define the boundaries of any culture, leading us to observe similarities across cultures as well as differences. They argue that any comparison of the social life of different peoples will prove that the foundations of their cultural development are remarkably uniform. It would then follow that there are laws to which this development is subject. The discovery of those similarities—and the laws that govern them—should be an important goal of any field, including that of communication and culture.

Durkheim (1938) and Parsons (1951) placed comparative studies at the core of sociology as a discipline. But in looking for laws of societies, Durkheim only implicitly recognized the need to rationalize similarities that occurred across different societies. Payne (1973) pointed to Durkheim's work as illustrating the fact that the comparative method was not simply an exercise in the collection of differences from a number of societies. Rather, it required a recognition of similarities and their bases as well. Tyler (1978) was able to observe that social relations (including, presumably, communication) were often more complex within cultures than across social groups in different cultures.

We also gain support for our analytical approach from Parson's general theory of action. It suggested three major societal impulses or forces.

- We treat the first of these, which he described as social systems, as social structures.
- Parson's second, cultural systems, incorporates our uses of culture and values.
- The third, which he characterized as personalities, represents the responses of the students to situations. In these situations they perceive conditions of contingency that they had not experienced previously in their social and cultural milieux.

We have found it convenient to think in terms of social institutions that carry out the functioning of social systems or structures. These institutions are relatively permanent and formal in their outline and draw support from the society. They are embodied in such forms as government, law, education, health services, and the family. As social institutions, they are given protections and allocated resources to perform tasks in behalf of the society.

Figure 2.1 illustrates the manner in which the comparative approach

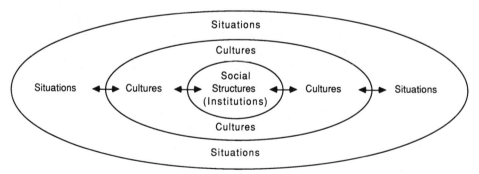

Figure 2.1. Structure, Culture, and Situation

incorporates the concepts of structure (expressed through functioning social institutions), culture and situation.

The model in Figure 2.1 establishes social structures and institutions as the instruments of societies. Cultures supply the core of values and beliefs which guide their functioning. Situations, in contrast, may be indefinable and almost boundless. Although many demands on the individual in society are predictable, others occur unexpectedly and thus require adaptation and response. Situations make demands on the capacities of institutions and cultures and contribute to culture as a dynamic and changing force.

We have taken the view that the four societies have been equally subject to social forces. Tensions between adaptation in terms of existing values and the challenges of innovation and social change have created situations with which our students were required to cope. Our colleague (Manabe, 1982) pointed to the rapid and extensive changes that have occurred in postwar Japan and characterized Japanese society as functioning somewhere between "value maintenance and value change." Kepplinger (1975), among others, described similar forces in Germany, and we will observe parallel conditions in both the United States and Hong Kong.

As comparativists, we expect to observe these tendencies in each of the societies. The comparative perspective will encourage us to determine the extent to which the students behaved in ways that permit generalizations and theories of society to emerge.

STRATEGIES FOR RESEARCH

Holt and Turner (1970) emphasized that the comparative approach implies not only a point of view but also a strategy of research and analysis. The strategy that we have adopted is first to identify similarities in the functioning of societal institutions. Once these have been established, we may look for cultural and situational differences.

Weber's classic studies (1922) of the relationship of the Protestant ethic to the rise of capitalism rested largely on his adoption of that research strategy. He first identified what was equivalent across cultures, such as population base, climate, geography, social organization, and other factors. Eventually, he isolated a factor (now questioned) that appeared to explain differences. This research strategy literally pursued equivalencies until they led to differences. The similarities were explained by structure, the differences by culture.

In our case, we assumed that those individuals who were located in similar places in the social structure—as in student subcultures where there was contact with humanists, social scientists, and intellectuals—would face similar kinds of problems and communicate similarly about them. We took up Tyler's (1978) observation that students might find it easier to communicate within their subculture and, globally, with similar subcultures than to relate to members of different social classes within their own cultures.

Martin (1976) has made precisely this case:

> To say that a person belonging to the Western culture and another to the Oriental culture is to suggest mutual exclusivity certainly does not exist. Two individuals belonging to the so-called Western culture may be more different in many of their cultural traits than [if] one of the individuals is someone belonging to the so-called Oriental culture. (p. 431)

The research strategy of first identifying similarities in social and individual values before pursuing differences is illustrated by the work of Edelstein (1974). He held a number of factors constant—the importance of problems, the similarity of social groups, and access to media content. He then looked for the influence of cultures and situations on communication that was employed by individuals. He observed that the similarities in social groups, the importance of the problems they described, and the similarity of access to media content produced similarities in communication. Beyond that, however, he found differences that were attributable to the three cultures that were under study.

It is important to note, however, that *structures* are loosely defined terms. Some structures might actually be different rather than similar; if so, this would produce differences in media uses and evaluation.

To illustrate: although the Japanese students were similar to students from other countries in class role, were dealing with problems of comparable importance, and had equal access to the media, Japanese media structures are different from those of Germany, Hong Kong, and the United States. Japan has a much stronger national newspaper structure and a strong national and regional television system as well. The United States, in contrast, has a weaker national newspaper structure with a stronger local television structure. Germany has strong local as well as national newspapers, and Hong Kong lacks influential indigenous media structures.

As we compare and counterpose our student groups, our task of interpretation becomes challenging. Within the contexts of structure and function, culture and values, and situations of varying importance, we encounter students' opinions and communication behaviors that are responsive to each of those forces. How students, as a subculture, behave is our structural question; how students behave in America, Germany, Japan, and Hong Kong is the cultural question; and what special conditions or contingencies affect behaviors is the situational question.

THE CULTURAL APPROACH

We need now distinguish structure from culture. As pointed out, we are using structures to describe the workings of institutions created by societies to permit them to function as a community. That is why societies lend their resources to institutions such as the family, education, government, business, and welfare. Cultures, in contrast, are defined as the understandings that have been generated among individuals and groups about the nature of human relationships, how those relationships were established, and the social outcomes that are predicted for its members. Culture describes a history of experience that has been shared by a people in the context of a nation. Each national culture expresses itself in a way that asserts normativeness, gives vent to expression, encourages thought, and permits action. Culture is cognized and communicated. It adopts means to pursue its ends.

Defining culture in everybody's sense is difficult, if not impossible. Kroeber and Kluckholm (1952) counted almost 200 definitions of culture. This number was explained by the fact that scholars in each case defined culture in terms of those aspects and dynamics of behavior that they sought to observe. Kluckholm (1951) later defined culture as what we learn from others (through communication) plus what we may add to it. Thus culture (and the values that are abstracted from it) is learned through actions, including communication. We are describing a "subculture," what our colleague Kojima (1986) described as a "generation of youth." This subculture developed its character and its values as a result of common and basic experiences generated by age and place. Values were abstracted by individuals as a consequence of their history of experiences.

We are fortunate in that Atwood (1984) has brought together cultural perspectives that are related directly to communication. Similarly, Dodd (1977) proposed that we consider both social systems and cultural variables as antecedent factors to communication. Kim (1979) noted that culture was imprinted on the individual as a perception that was accepted and expected by parties to communication. And Harms (1973) said that communication between communicators of similar cultural backgrounds was usually easier, more reliable, faster, and safer than communication between those of different cultures. These intellectual contributions facilitate our treatment of communication as a culturally inspired behavior.

Rosengren (1986) made an even stronger statement. In his view youth subcultures provided guidelines for each of the students against which they judged situations and determined how and what they would communicate. Rosengren placed culture at the hub of his "wheel of culture." This view contrasts with our use of structure as the core. The difference lies in point of view: In adopting a cultural rather than a comparative approach, Rosengren found himself first searching for differences in behavior that were inspired by cultures. Later he discovered commonalities. But in adopting structure as our first step we are seeking first to extend our knowledge of similarities.

As we have noted in the case of media structures, social institutions are not always cohesive within or precisely similar across societies. In different societies different institutions compete with each other. Swingewood (1977) proposed that cultures and even youth subcultures are not entirely cohesive nor marked always by consensus. Struggles occurr over lifestyles and values. Rosengren said that because culture is dynamic, it encourages conflict as well as consensus. Although each society actively socializes its youth, students nonetheless question values and construct their own guidelines for action.

FROM CONCEPTS TO OBSERVATIONS

How does one actually make the broad conceptual leap from the more abstract concept of culture to the actual behavior of individuals, in our case college students? This is a difficult task. As one useful precedent, Nishida and Gudykunst (1981) noted Skinner's observation that individuals conform to and express the values of their culture because they are positively reinforced for doing so: "This is all part of the social environment called a culture, and the main effect. . . is to bring the individual under the control of the remoter consequences of his behavior" (p. 173).

Skinner (1972) went on to distinguish, as do we, between culture and values: Culture represents social contingencies, whereas values are derived from positive or negative reinforcements experienced by the individual.

Rosengren (1986) paid particular attention to youth culture. He conceptualized "ideal types" of youths who were products of family socialization, paralleling to a remarkable extent the observations of Chaffee, McLeod, and Atkins (1971). They asserted that the family is the most pervasive means for transmitting culture because it teaches children the behaviors that would be expected of them. Families socialize children in two basic value orientations—intellectual divergence and social consensus. From their juxtaposition, four basic types of youth emerge, two of them reactive and the others consensual.

One type of consensual student, possessing both intellectual and social skills, was encouraged to address a variety of societal concerns, that is, social problems. The other consensual student, possessing fewer social and cognitive skills, was permitted to become passive and withdrawn from social life. The more socially and intellectually skilled students not only adopted the values of the society but also articulated them in unique ways; but students who had not been taught these intellectualizing abilities were able simply to seek cues—from family, peers, or the mass media—concerning how to perform.

Rosengren described the student types in analagous ways but saw the intellectual dimension expressed also in conflictual terms. The conflictually oriented students were either humanistic (consensual) or radical in their outlooks and temperaments and were reinforced for each of these behaviors.

We must observe, however, that Rosengren's types appear to be more typical of Western than Asian cultures, for it will become plain that Japanese students, particularly, did not encounter positive reinforcement for conflictual behavior. Nonetheless, the paradigms may be helpful to us at some point in suggesting why students in some of the more consensual cultures perceived that they were in a better position to observe the behaviors of members of the broader culture—that which extended beyond their peer contacts.

THE SITUATIONAL APPROACH

The symbiosis among structure, culture, and situation becomes evident when we seek to differentiate between the concepts of culture and situation. We distinguished between structure and culture by defining structure as made up of formal institutions whereas culture reflects the accomplishments of the society. We also incorporated elements of Rosengren's "wheel of culture," which saw cultural accomplishments as the content and form of art, literature, and philosophy.

But culture at certain points becomes almost indistinguishable from situations. For example, we spoke of youth culture as generational and thus bounded by 10- to 20-year time periods. But it is true that some situations persevere over generations, as we point out in the case of Hong Kong.

Culture is more often thought of as extending over more "space" as well as "time," encompassing an almost infinite array of values. Yet situations may create their own values, transforming the meaning of culture. Situations may also be prolonged, in that way approaching culture in its hallmark of continuity. Perhaps the best way to distinguish culture from situation is to see the former as representing defined, related, and predictable circumstances. Situations, in contrast, interrupt the flow of culture to call attention to problems.

Nishida and Nishida (1981) used situation in much the same sense as Skinner (1972). An individual in a situation deals with elements that are newly encountered and for which no traditional approaches are available. Situations thus imply the acknowledgment of new contingencies.

METHODOLOGICAL IMPLICATIONS

As we discuss in our chapter on methodology, we have taken a situational (rather than a cross-situational) approach. Situational analysis implies that the individual must deal with contingencies that might, in fact, be bounded more narrowly in both time and space. In this sense situations might represent smaller pictures than cultures, and the narrower boundaries might serve to spotlight events and make behaviors more observeable.

Atwood (1986) and others see the situational approach as a philosophical position in which the researcher adopts a methodology that takes the point of view of the individual rather than that of the observor. If this stratagem is accomplished, an otherwise subjective condition is made objective from the point of view of the individual in the situation.

Although situations may be more narrowly bounded and thus more amenable to observation, to the extent that a kind of objectivity is served, a problem nonetheless emerges; that is, the infinite number of situations to be observed. Atwood replied that a carefully chosen and limited number of situational observations should permit generalization.

There has been a growing commitment to the situational context of research. A number of investigators has advanced conceptual bases for the situational approach. Stewart (1978) said that although culture transcends the individual, the individual nonetheless carries the burden of picturing those values and elements of culture in his or her own mind. Hall (1977) agreed and observed that situational frames are the building blocks of both individual lives and institutions.

Saral (1977) actually compared culturally derived differences in data sets with those that were associated with situations. He concluded that cultural differences are more apparent in some contexts than in others, and what seem to be cultural differences in communication are sometimes better accounted for by situational differences. Howell (1978) concurred that every communication act is of necessity localized in time and space, and Nicassio and Saral (1978) called for methodological approaches that would allow us to observe the variability of behavior across situations.

Prosser (1978) and Casmir (1978) reflect some of the central concerns of this book. Prosser observed that the consideration of situational differences and similarities placed the idea of culture closer to a consideration of cognitive processing and communication, whereas Casmir suggested we should move toward a focus on situational communication processes within and between individuals from a variety of cultures. These, of course, are our purposes.

FROM BOUNDARIES TO PARAMETERS

Our discussion of structure, culture, and situations defined the parameters and boundaries of each of those concepts. But to address these concepts to the analysis of our data, we need also describe the parameters of culture that characterized each of the student groups. It will be apparent that each youth culture was explained better in generational than in traditional terms. Within these limits, however, some nuances were seen.

In brief, American youth culture has been portrayed as influencing the wider culture as well as being affected by it. This view carries implications for student perceptions of the utility of mass media, not merely as consumers but also as conscious manipulators of the media. German youths, in contrast, have felt a symbiosis with journalists but have recognized, at the same time, the inability of the media always to bring about social action.

The Asian context is markedly different. Japanese students were more characterized by the privatization of their beliefs and values than by active societal participation. This, too, has been a postwar phenomenon. But Japanese media in many respects have maintained a culturally mandated aceess that has intersected with the public and government, and in that sense the media have become arbiters of public opinion.

Hong Kong students have coped with a perception of powerlessness. As members of a British crown colony, whose hegemony will soon become the province of the People's Republic of China, they have adjusted their cultural tendencies to cope with a great deal of political indeterminacy.

We may now consider each youth culture in more detail.

The American Experience

Uniquely among our cultures American student values have extended beyond the university boundaries to bring about social change (Hoge, Luna, & Miller, 1981). In music, dress, human relationships, and issues of war and peace, there has been innovation by youth. Yankelovich (1974a & 1974b) characterized the basic pattern of cultural change as diffusion from college students to other young people and then to the total population.

American youth values were the most transient of the four cultures, being marked by dramatic change from one decade to the other in response to significant events. Hoge, Luna, and Miller (1981) pointed to changing youth values from the 1950s to the 1960s and 1970s. The most marked changes came as a consequence of Vietnam although unexpressed emotions by students whose criticisms about Korea were repressed in the 1950s also were tapped.

Hoge, Luna, and Miller (1981) asserted that the alienation of youths from military and nationalistic ideologies increased markedly from Korea to the 1970s. Privatism replaced political commitment; educational goals turned from liberal and philosophical to vocational and privatized values. Attitudes about economics and government became more conservative. But there was continuity in religious beliefs, self-other relationships, basic faith in human nature, and the tendency to criticize the college experience.

Edelstein (1962) charted changes in student political behavior over three and one-half decades. He concluded that students had become less ideological over time, a trend that reflected decreasing conservatism as well as liberalism. This swing was seen in less emotional and doctrinnaire commitments to positions on political, social, and economic issues and an independence of thought from prescribed liberal and conservative doctrine. Yet it was marked also by political awareness, knowledge, and party identification. He noted that this loss of ideology created a vulnerability to the impact of events, as was to be witnessed later in the students' response to the Vietnam War.

The Jacob report (1957) saw students' behavior as working "with the grain" of external influences. In that sense the college culture became a medium of communication for newly prescribed social values. A similar case has been documented for outside intervention as the major force in mobilizing college students to protest against the Vietnam War.

Guardo (1982) asserted that changes in youth values were not so much generational as situational and reflected a realistic appraisal of the world around them.

> Social, national and world events almost defy individual control...complex political policies attempt to harness an almost out-of-control economy...Middle East (and now Central American as well as nuclear) tensions, continuing energy problems, and whatever else...on the newscape...to confront, challenge, and virtually overwhelm any sense of individual influence, impact, or control...the only seeming locus of control is oneself and those close to self. (p. 502)

Guardo concluded that it made sense that personal relationships would become more salient and that preferences would develop for work and other commitments that demanded less rather than more. At points of possible control the student would be pragmatic and problem oriented rather than ideological and philosophical.

Studies reported in 1971 by Yankelovich and the Columbia Broadcasting System News supported the inference that students' values were responses to situations. During a time of newfound affluence for parents, it was ironic that most changes in values were among students who enjoyed this affluence. The new values centered on self-expression, creativity, and freedom from constraints. Although money, success, and traditional morality were deemphasized, a majority still clung to traditional values of career-mindedness.

Yankelovich (1971) added to Guardo's assessment of situational influences the finding that value gaps were greater within generations than between generations; that is, students were closer in their values to those of their parents than to those of other students. Hence generational influences were subordinated to situations. The study described what was characterized as the "cooling of American [youth]." Although cultural values relating to marriage, authority, religion, work, money, and sexual morality continued to change, political deviation became less marked. The radical, Marxist left made up only 11 percent of the college student population. What gave the political movement strength was its symbiosis with emerging social values and styles of life.

American students were pessimistic about the welfare of the society and distanced themselves from it. Institutions were perceived as having broken down, the uncertainties and dangers of war as having increased dangerously, and the economic system as being threatened by its built-in inadequacies. Students did not wish to support either internal or external policies based on this structure.

Yankelovich (1971) pointed to a political alienation that was comparable to that felt by Japanese students 15 years later. He observed that

> students [were] pessimistic, discouraged, skeptical and even cynical [and did] not believe that our system of American democracy function[ed] in practice as it is supposed to in theory. Rather, they believe[d] that government [was] manipulated by special interests and that the mass of the public has been brainwashed into believing that what it thinks really counts. . . . They believe[d] that major institutions [stood] in need of drastic reform, including but not confined to the major political parties . . . . Only 1 in 10 believe[d] that the real power in the country [was] in the hands of the people. (p. 29)

A number of studies carried out at Harvard University in the 1960s and 1970s directed their attention to causes of unrest on American college campuses. These were historical as well as contemporary in scope and addressed both the character of students, including their values and those of their parents, and the nature of the causes which they adopted and which gave vent to their frustrations. These feelings were displaced against the oppressive demands of college but they were triggered by such traumatic and historical events as World Wars I and II, the war in Korea, and protests over American actions in Vietnam and Cambodia.

By and large, student political behavior in the United States over that expanse of time proved to be more continuous and predictable than discontinuous and random—in its logic if not in its actions. This was to be expected, for over time students have continued to be representative of similar social classes. Many of their idealisms have grown out of their roles

in the university. Most variations in behavior can be attributed to differences in demands posed by situations and events. By and large, generations
of students have been much more alike than different in their selection of
social milieux in which to express their values.

Lipset (1967) sees this as a global phenomenon, pointing to the crucial
role of Russian students in the nineteenth and early twentieth centuries in
paving the way for, and in creating, many of the revolutionary movements
which led to the revolution of 1917. As we will point out, Chinese students
were key to revolutionary upsurges in the early twentieth century and
caused much of the intellectual ferment, as well as supplying the cadres,
which contributed to the overthrow of the Manchu dynasty and to later
political developments in China—including the Communist grasp of power
in 1945–49. Similarly, student groups in nineteenth-century Western
Europe often provided the ground swell for revolutionary movements.

Lipset's *Student Politics* offers comparative perspectives on student
movements worldwide, including those in Third World countries such as
Burma, India, Nigeria, and several countries in Latin America. These perspectives are merely illustrative of the nature and the impact of student
unrest and uprisings throughout the world—in Africa, Asia, Eastern and
Western Europe, Latin America, and North America. These movements
not only addressed internal dissension about matters affecting the personal
welfare of students but expressed equally passionate feelings about societal
and world conflicts. These have taken on generational as well as broader
social character.

Lipset and Schaflander (1971) used structural, cultural, and situational
determinants to assess student movements in the United States. They have
made the structural case of equivalence by pointing to the similar ages of
students as well as the similarities of their social and class environments.
The American college generation of the 1960s, as an example, shared the
experience of being the children of parents whose social and political values
were shaped by the economic depression of the 1930s and participation in
World War II.

As children of this generation, the college students of the 1960s had as
their legacy the moralistic and liberalizing spirit of the 1940s and 1950s, the
wartime and postwar periods, as efforts were made to reconstruct societies
in Europe, Asia, Africa, and Latin America. The United States, although
victorious in the war, found itself groping for peace and seeking its proper
role in a turbulent new world.

Students also found themselves born into a changing university institutional framework, one which became larger, more bureaucratic, more
research oriented, and more impersonal. Whereas there were about 1
million students and only 80,000 faculty in 1930, by 1970 there were 7
million students and more than a half million faculty.

These phenomena were mirrored externally by the advent of new industrial practices and empires and their accompanying technologies and bureaucracies. These made enormous demands upon the universities and reshaped their character. Burgeoning institutions such as government, business, and social agencies required a greater fund of more precise information to guide their activities. Foundations anticipated these needs and soon funneled large amounts of money into research that would shape the social policies of a changing nation.

The university campus, itself, as a microcosm of society, became attacked by students who found themselves to be as much victims as partners in this process. Problems have always abounded on college campuses, but students have perceived many of them as amenable to solution, bringing to bear upon them a spirit of idealism. But as a group that is bounded in both space and time college youth also have proved to be susceptible to mobilization by radical thought and action. External events often have provided the catalysts for these values.

Lipset and Schaflander (1971) suggest that the civil rights movement and the war in Vietnam were the most powerful forces to mobilize American college youth in the 1960s and 1970s. The 1968 assassinations of the Rev. Martin Luther King and Senator Robert Kennedy, charismatic spokesmen for nonviolent, antiwar, egalitarian, and progressive social change, evoked the passions of American youth. But while the radical student movement renounced traditional values and pointed to the corruption of the "system," other students were less intense and more pragmatic in their idealism. They would in the 1980s, as they had in the 1970s and the 1960s, support moral causes relating to nuclear arms, racism and apartheid, worldwide pollution, and other problems that appealed, universally, to college students, but they would not make demands for radical change in the system. Illustrative was this statement by the V and V student organization at Boston University in the 1960s, who were reacting to revolutionary leaflets that had been distributed by student "extremists, disrupters and anarchists":

> We are unalterably opposed to "takeover"...This is totalitarianism, not democracy;
>   We are unalterably opposed to the guerilla Left policy of taking the law into "our own hands"; opposed to vulgar and vile name-calling and all nondemocratic forms of protest...
>   We may be naive and idealistic and branded phoney liberals—but we still have faith and hope in the democratic dream that our parents and schools have drummed into us. (Lipset and Schaflander, 1971, p. 338)

This expression of sentiment of a divided college student body at Boston University was expressive of the national mood of students, described as more marginally active than radical A massive national nonviolent demonstration was triggered in October and November of 1969 that enlisted most students but was attacked bitterly by the radical student Left. A report by the President's Commission on Campus Unrest (1970) concluded that there were two crises on campuses; one a spasm of violence and the other a gap in understanding of the attitudes of students toward racial injustice, war, and the university itself.

The foreword to a 1980 Carnegie Foundation report on the college generation of the 1970s concluded that there were apparent discontinuities between those students and the generation of the 1960s, but a number of similarities nonetheless existed. Students in the 1970s were optimistic about their own futures yet pessimistic about the future of the country. They were idealistic about the world they would like to live in, but they were pragmatic about the world they actually lived in; while they were liberal about social trends and life styles, they were more conservative than earlier generations had been about political issues. The illusions about American society had been lost and the society had been weakened by the misdeeds of its leaders. The task force commissioned by the government to assess student attitudes concluded that students' viewpoint could be described as "me-ism," an absorption with the self and a loss of identification with society:

> One senses the development of a lifeboat mentality...Each student is alone in a boat in a terrible storm, far from the nearest harbor. Each boat is beginning to take on water. There is but one alternative; each student must singlemindedly bail. Conditions are so bad that no one has time to care for others who may also be foundering. (Levine, 1980, p. 22)

The evidence, however, is that the American college student in the 1970's and early 1980's, at the time that we conducted our survey, was concerned not only about himself but about social problems, as well. It was not the self at the expense of the society, but an expression of self in the society.

In summary, American college students were aware and concerned about social problems. They responded not as a generation but individually to events that eroded their confidence in government and led them to conclude that drastic changes were required. Although at an early point they had no natural allies, the unfolding horrors of the Vietnam War gave them a target at which they could direct their hostility to enlist parents, the public, and the media in that cause.

The success enjoyed by students over the Vietnam War was opportunistic and situational. Some argued that students were more followers than leaders. But their success may have fueled a sense of political efficacy. The contemporary battles against apartheid in South Africa and against nuclear arms might argue for this conclusion. However, the activities of minorities and other groups outside the universities have suggested that American youths have expressed elements of a culture more than a youth subculture, giving support to a situational rather than cultural interpretation of their behavior.

The German Youth Experience

Describing the emergence of the German youth movement in the 1960s, Karl (1970) noted the "ever new and spectacular events" that unfolded during that period. These events were worldwide in scope, were relatively independent of political systems and social structures, and shared a common ethos. Yet as we have seen in the case of American youths, the youths of each country were motivated by particular causes and events.

Karl (1970) made a case for both structural and situational perspectives. In comparing the student protestors of the 1960s to a variety of youth movements in Germany spanning half a century, he noted that similar social structures over time produced astonishingly similar values among youths, whereas special conditions, such as life under national socialism, produced complete contrasts in values and behaviors.

An internal "structural-cultural rationale" showed up in the disposition over time for German youths, as a social class, to protest against the materialism reflected in bourgeois-capitalist values. Leaders of youth groups were similar in background—emerging from upper and middle classes and families able to give them a university education—and engaged in similar protests. Several generations of youths criticized the rigidity that sprang from traditional values and institutions that inhibited their judgments and creativity.

Karl (1970) thus argued for continuity of youth culture rather than for generational change. Although a sense of solidarity was created among German youths by the recognition of common values and the attraction of social action, reinforced by intensive and satisfying communication, it led to problems of communication with outsiders. The development of an "internal language," which was inaccessible to outsiders, caused misunderstandings. Only "other outsiders" could relate to this language.

But Karl (1970) saw these internal structures as generalizable across youth cultures. Ideas that bridged nations and cultures were based on common experiences, and generalization was possible because of comparable conditions. Contrary to what a national cultural hypothesis proposed, students behaved similarly across cultures when conditions were parallel and motivating.

Karl (1970) emphasized that the youths (*Jugendbewegung*) of Germany in both the pre- and post-1960s were consistent in their perceptions of the nature of mass society (and its problems) and of those who held power. Across five generations of German students the unifying ideology was a protest against social and intellectual control by the social and political order.

The protest movements in Germany in the 1970s and early 1980s may be seen as an extension of the student revolts of the 1960s in that those who led them were university educated and were part of a "humanistic intelligentsia" who were graduated from human and social science faculties. The techno-economic and juridical-administrative intelligentsia remained relatively passive in the face of emerging social movements.

Situationally, the critical environment for protest in the 1980s centered on seemingly antihumanistic issues, primarily the placement of intermediate nuclear forces in Europe, aroused after the decision of the North Atlantic Treaty Organizations (NATO) to place medium-range missiles in Europe in December 1979. The most dramatic peace demonstrations took place at a convention of the Lutheran church in Hamburg in 1981 and at a disarmament and détente agenda in Bonn for which 300,000 persons were mobilized.

A parallel antinuclear energy movement combined protests against nuclear energy plants and uses of nuclear energy. The focus of this movement was a protest in Wackersdorf, Bavaria, which continued in one form or another from 1981 to 1985. A larger interest in ecological questions began in the 1970s, which also took up the thesis of limits of economic growth. This impulse found expression throughout Europe in the preservation "year" of 1970 and the Stockholm conference of 1975. It was linked, as well, to protests against large technological or industrial developments. The women's liberation movement also gathered support in the 1970s. Women for Peace linked up with the environmental movement and was expressed politically by the emergence of the Greens. Similarly, tendencies emerged toward adoption of alternative forms of life and economic structures, diminishing profit orientations and asserting the equality of employees in the industrial order.

These related outlooks toward the quality of life not only were a reflection of the maturation of university students but also continued to attract them to social issues and movements that invoked social change.

Kepplinger (1975) added to the impact of events a number of factors that relate strongly to our emphasis on media and communication. He saw the most significant intellectual influence on students of the generation of the 1940s, 1950s, and 1960s as emerging from the activities of the Group of 47, a collection of avant garde artists, intellectuals, writers, and journalists who questioned postwar values of materialism, at the same time giving legitimacy to the new left in German politics. However, Kepplinger points out that the values of the Group of 47 would not have been favorably received had those values not already existed, particularly among students.

The Group of 47 (which actually contained 70 members) forged an intellectual link between literature and politics; in this relationship literature was to instruct politics and journalism. Thus a symbiosis was created between journalism and German youth that was to persist for generations. Kepplinger identifies *Der Spiegel*, the provocative weekly newspaper, as the publicist and even exploiter of the Group of 47.

Once having exploited the idealism of the Group of 47, *Der Spiegel* shifted its emphasis from culture to political conflict as it took up new causes. *Der Spiegel* amplified incidents and themes of violence. Disproportionate attention was given to acts of violence by the police against persons rather than to the acts of demonstrators (many of whom were students). In its coverage of culture, general political culture, and political conflict, *Der Spiegel* reflected the youths' values much more than those of the general population.

The Group of 47, according to its mentor, Hans Werner Richter, one of a number of radical socialists who had lived through the Nazi era, was not really a group; it just called itself that. There was no formal membership. Group life took the form of an annual meeting of writers, social critics, and academics, convened by Richter. The first meeting took place in the fall of 1947 when some contributors to the literary magazine *Der Ruf* met in the house of Ilse Schenider-Lengel at th Bannwaldsee near Hohenschwangau in the Bavarian countryside. A similar scenario was followed for the next 20 years, with the exception of 1966, when the group met in Princeton, New Jersey.

The Group of 47 was conceived as a literary society. Its métier was humanistic, avant garde, and reactive to material values and any return to mainstream values. Among young authors who made their literary debut were Heinrich Boll, Gunter Grass, Martin Walser, and Peter Handke. For most young German authors an invitation to present themselves to the Group of 47 opened many doors although it did not ensure artistic or financial success.

Grass, arguably the leading German writer today, made his way with the help of the Group of 47. Prior to his invitation to a group meeting in 1958 he had published an unnoticed book of poems. At that meeting he read from his novel *Die Blechtrommel* (*The Tin Drum*) and was awarded the group prize. When the book was introduced to the public at the Frankfurt Book Fair a year later, Grass had been able to sell the rights to the book to seven foreign publishers. Dieter Lattmann (1980), who had read before the group himself, described Grass's success as "an example...of the mass media mechanism which the group was then capable of setting in motion" (p. 73).

One gains awareness of the lasting effect of the Group of 47 by a consideration of its membership·

- **Heinrich Boll:** Winner of the group prize in the 1950s and a Nobel Prize in 1972, he was an outspoken critic of German society, anti-militaristic, anticleric (although himself rooted in Catholicism), anti-Nazi, novelist, essayist, a moral institution up to his death in 1985, and the most widely read contemporary writer.
- **Hans Magnus Enzensberger:** Poet, essayist, severe social critic, advocate of political engagement of artists, he proclaimed the death of literature in the 1960s but continued his critical writing.
- **Gunter Grass:** A novelist, poet, essayist, sculptor, artist, and the leading German novelist, he gained popularity with critics and public in the 1950s but became a political moderate in the 1960s and lost some of his popularity as a consequence.
- **Peter Handke:** He made his debut in a 1966 meeting where he actually attacked the group; later that year he published his first novel. *Der Spiegel* gave his appearance before the group heavy emphasis and published an advance review of the book. He publishes novels and essays and has been accused of escapism.
- **Uwe Johnson:** He was born in Mecklenburg, later under the control of the German Democratic Republic. He escaped in 1959 to West Berlin and later moved to New York. He died in 1984 but often was compared to major English authors of the twentieth century.
- **Johannes Mario Simmel:** A best-selling author regarded with contempt by serious literary critics, he nevertheless brings attacks by these critics as he combines contemporary problems of sex, espionage, crime, drugs, and so forth with moral imperatives.
- **Martin Walser:** He is a prolific novelist and among the most outspoken authors in politics, engaging in union activities among writers.

The Group of 47 met for the last time in 1967 when the student movement and emergency laws in Germany were the foci of public attention. The group as a whole had become politicized by this time, issuing manifestos about the *Der Spiegel* affair and other controversial issues of the 1960s. Lattmann (1980), however, was ambivalent concerning the extent to which politics put an end to their association. It was significant that the student movement was not entirely welcomed by the group. Some members were appalled at the radicalism of the movement even though it echoed substantially the beliefs they, themselves, had held. Yet they resented the fact that some of their fellow authors joined with the student movement and adopted its radicalism.

It can be argued, under all these circumstances, whether German youth values are continuous or generational. The generational case was made by Noelle-Neumann and Kocher (1987), who pointed to data that show the values of German youths to be more discrepant with those of adults than is the case in other Western countries (Belgium, Denmark, France, Great Britain, Holland, Ireland, Italy, Spain, and Sweden). Answers of German youths to questions addressing values associated with marriage, divorce, religion, perceived closeness and obligations of family ties, and respect for authority and institutions showed much more discrepancy with values asserted by adults than did the answers in any of the other cultures. What was more, this discrepancy had emerged only in recent years—which argues for a generational effect.

One might contend that the magnitude of the discrepancy between youth and adult values, measured in this fashion, is not as important as the fact of a discrepancy, and this fact has not changed during the postwar period. Thus, more than generational, we might argue that the discrepancy is situational and to some extent brought about by cultural responses to events. Cultural precedents existed for accepting the advent of social change. German youths in this respect were consensual as members of a subculture but autonomous with respect to adult values; similarly, they were autonomous in relation to the family but dependent on their peers. Yet our data show that German students were able to perceive orientations of the larger society even if these orientations did not reflect their own values.

The Japanese Experience

Kojima (1986a) saw continuity also in generations of Japanese youths in their commitments to a constitution and a modern democratic system, greater respect for human rights, and the search for peace. More than preceding generations, postwar youths expressed an aversion to social pathologies and the corruption of individuals and institutions.

Paradoxically, Japanese students showed a greatly decreased social participation and a turning inward toward their private lives, including family and friends. Although they resisted public influences on their personal desires and expression of feelings, they also reasserted a respect for traditional norms.

Manabe (1982) pointed to the situational forces that gave Japanese students a "generational" character. He agreed that despite these influences students' values remained relatively constant, testifying to the strength of culture. At the same time, industrialization, democratization, the rise in living standards, extended opportunities for education, and the prevalence of information came about in rapid order.

Japanese also were shaken by the end of rapid economic growth and the almost unbridled period of consumerism (Edelstein et al., 1982), the oil crisis, the implications of American withdrawal from Vietnam, the Lockheed scandal that brought the fall of Prime Minister Tanaka, the increased value of the yen, and the embroiling of Japan in trade disputes. Students found themselves in the vortex of these changes.

A report on *Japanese Youth in a Changing Society* (Naka, 1977) supported the view that changes in Japanese youths were more generational than cumulative. The dividing line generationally was drawn after World War II, as with German students. Young people before the war ascribed more to societal values, whereas postwar youths—while still attached to the family—became less responsive to more broadly defined societal values.

There is some dispute concerning what actually occurred. The report to which we allude took the view that young people before the war had, "in principle, at least, a group-oriented attitude to life, [whereas] their postwar successors have individual-oriented life targets." The evidence cited was that fewer than half the postwar students, as compared to prewar students, responded favorably to statements reflecting a willingness to fight social injustice, lead an upright life, set aside personal needs and dedicate oneself to the common good, work hard and save money to get rich, and so on. Rather, the mood shifted to a desire to live according to one's own tastes and to lead a less involved life. The competing view is that while Japanese youths became more "inner directed," they continued to hold group values, particularly with respect to the family, a "duality of self and other," although identification with the society was weakened.

The argument for duality was supported by a 15-year study (Kojima, 1985) that demonstrated an increased desire by Japanese youths to get along well with "people around me." During that same period there was a decline in favorable responses to values that addressed individual autonomy, and there was no strengthening of values related to individual affluence.

The studies reflected a broad range of changes in the values of youths (Akiyama & Muramatsu, 1985; Kazama & Akiyama, 1980; Kojima & Kazama, 1975). Values placed by youths on social relationships actually increased rather than declined in generational terms. But less value was placed on broader societal concerns. There was a continuing emphasis on personal feelings and mood; less value was placed on efficiency and work and more on the balance between work and leisure.

These moderating tendencies were apparent in the larger context of Japanese culture. There was increasing approval for the employment of women and for more egalitarian roles for men and women in marriage. There was more expression of religious faith and a stronger sense of national pride. But political changes were marked even more by a continuing decline in attention to political processes accompanied by a substantial loss of a sense of political efficacy. There had been a loss of confidence, as well, in the effectiveness of public opinion. Akiyama and Muramatsu (1985) concluded,

> Nearly 80 per cent now believe that the opinions and wishes of ordinary citizens are not much reflected in the governing process. Furthermore, two thirds believe that demonstrations and petitions can have little effect, and over 40 per cent believe that even voting can have little influence. In all respects, the sense of political effectiveness has declined during the decade:
>
> Since the ruling Liberal Democratic Party has been in power for so many years, despite its internal struggles and financial scandals, the public may believe that constructive change is unlikely. Feeling that it no longer responds to them, the people apparently are turning away from Japan's political process. (p. 26)

Kojima earlier (1977) took a less pessimistic view. He agreed there was a strengthening of "private life first" and liberalizing and democratizing tendencies, but he concluded that nationalism and traditional social norms had persisted, although undergoing changes, a "co-existence of Japanese change and tradition in daily life, culture, society, and politics." Kojima concluded also that changes in public opinion corresponded with fluctuations in the economy. The discrepancy between ideal and actual functioning of political institutions came about because of increased political understanding, not because of a lack of commitment to free political institutions. The question was *how well* institutions were functioning, not *whether or not* the institutions were viable.

Kojima asserted that although the four major postwar trends in opinion—increased national pride, strengthening of democratic tendencies, precedence of private life, and transformation of some social norms—differed in character, they were nonetheles complementary. Giving priority to personal needs rather than to societal goals affected social norms, but increased national pride strengthened democratic processes.

Akuto (1978) concurred with Kojima's interpretation and pointed out that value orientation, operationalized as lifestyle, better explained voting than did party identification, issues, or imagemaking by candidates. Akuto also agreed with Rosengren (1986) on the cultural primacy of what one learns as a child rather than from a political party. Thus Akuto characterized the Japanese voter as "diligent" rather than "involved," noting that almost two-thirds gave reasons of duty or responsibility for voting compared to only 20 to 25 percent who cited party identification. Therefore the "apolitical but diligent" citizen represented the political majority. We need to determine, as well, if college students were also merely "diligent" or actively involved in the social problems that they defined.

In summary, Japanese youths retained some traditional values and commitments while at the same time they demanded a greater personal autonomy. They were pragmatic in their acknowledgement of their lack of political efficacy. They recognized political culture as based on system elements of political power and the media. This belief foreclosed radicalism and demanded consensus as a means to an end much more than as an end in itself. Thus the capacity of Japanese youths to initiate actions based on their perception of situations was constrained by political culture. Situational determinants were minimized and structural elements dominated. Cultural norms assured the continuing dominance of structures.

The Hong Kong Experience

The values of Hong Kong youths were shaped by similar experiences: the place of the youths in relation to others, to families, and to society in terms of access to political power. These values had their source in Chinese culture and a special limiting set of conditions created by British political culture.

We found, nonetheless, a powerful case for a youth culture. Students were the first to pick up on modern beliefs and to internalize them as values. The rapid and unpredictable pace of events in Hong Kong accented the appeal of modernism to youths and at the same time imposed strains on traditions and culture.

A recent study by Chen (1987) found that Chinese youths had a propensity toward political participation. A variety of motivations, including a strong sense of history and national pride, a pervasive idealism, a belief in modernism, and an ability to speak for the society around them, contributed to the spontaniety of youths in mounting demonstrations against the central government and foreign enemies, particularly the Japanese. At the same time, Chinese youths showed themselves to be essentially opportunistic, exploiting the political vacuum that developed as a consequence of civil war, and demonstrating against Japan both for its earlier political aggression and military imperialism in China as well as for its more recent economic penetration of Chinese markets.

Chen (1987) pointed out, however, that over a period of seven decades the student movement in China declined perceptibly in autonomy and effectiveness. From the mounting of spontaneous demonstrations in which the students could advance their personal as well as idealized goals, the demonstrations became influenced by the civil war and by student Communist leaders who had positioned themselves among them.

Although Chinese university students may continue to demonstrate spontaneously, they have little real power. High school and middle school students were exploited dramatically in the Cultural Revolution. Now only small and relatively short-term demonstrations by students are permitted to occur, and these demonstrations have been snuffed out quickly. Because the people depend on the government for jobs and personal security, what we might view as cultural tendencies have been suppressed by the political culture.

The Hong Kong Parallel. The lack of access to the political structure in Hong Kong has been a traumatic phenomenon also for Chinese adults and youths. To some extent it parallels the limited and unpredictable franchise that existed in China. Only the first steps toward political participation in Hong Kong were taken after World War II, when Chinese formed political organizations to cope with a British oligarchy that had suppressed economic and political participation. But the Reform Club and later the Civic Association were only nascent political organizations. Their resentment expressed itself in the Kowloon riots of 1956 and 1966 and the strikes, police confrontations, and bombings of 1967. There were extensive letter writing, petitioning, debates, resolutions, and recommendations about such problems as rental increases, utility costs, and demands for off-course horse-race betting centers and to establish Chinese dialects as official languages of Hong Kong.

The Chinese University of Hong Kong (CUHK), whose students made up one-third of our sample in this study, was established in Shatin in the New Territories in response to these demands. The Heung Yee Kuk, or Rural Council, representing New Territories residents, led this drive. Students at CUHK published in their newspaper a demand for more Chinese language usage, and public opinion polls there and at the University of Hong Kong (whose students also are in our sample) strongly supported the goals.

One of the problems that greatly troubled students, and which recurred in our study, was their feeling that examinations for all universities favored those who spoke English. By this time, the Hong Kong media had also begun to devote belated attention to the social problems that had brought about the deep sense of political alienation. In the constricted setting of Hong Kong, societal problems are student problems, as well, and the media began to demonstrate an awareness of that linkage. Hoadley (1973) observed that barriers to participation were formidable, being rooted in an admixture of cultural and situational factors that reinforced one another.

Cultural Legacies. It has been argued, however, that little has changed in the basic assumptions and core of beliefs of the Chinese. Whether they came to Hong Kong when it was first settled by the British in the 1850s or fled from the People's Republic of China, they brought their culture with them. It included existential propositions and sets of abstractions that helped them to form ideas about themselves, their families, and their place in society. A knowledge of the strength of these values helps us to comprehend a culture-bound environment where students are faced with burdensome decisions brought about by the collision of culture with politics and social change.

The core of beliefs, in the form of traditional Chinese culture, is founded on two basic philosophies: Taoism and Confucianism. Taoism holds that human nature and the universe are a mixture of good and evil—made up of two opposing forces—the Yin and the Yang. These forces interact and intertwine, like Heaven and Earth, male and female, strong and weak, and good and evil. There is a little of each in the other, but together they form a harmonious unity. Confucianism, as a complementary philosophy, stresses the social environment and the ordering of interpersonal relationships. Here the emphasis is placed on humankind's relationship to humanity rather than on humankind's relationship to God, as in Christianity Emphasis is on this life, and now (Kluckholm & Strodtbeck, 1961).

Hsu (1955) pointed out that Confucianism requires each individual to occupy his or her proper place. When the individual is right, the family will be right; when the family is right, the nation will be right. One must fulfill the duties and obligations inherent in the five human relationships (the so-called Five Cardinal Relations): between emperor and subject, between father and son, between husband and wife, between brothers, and between friends.

Yang (1959) noted that Confucian values also demand a high degree of achievement—thus the pragmatic willingness of the Hong Kong Chinese to make pacts with the colonial ministry to enable themselves to do that which might be done. Not to make the best possible compact with the Devil would be out of keeping with values derived from the culture. The individual must recognize problems and cope with them despite personal costs and barriers:

> the...moral standards demanded not merely self-sacrifice from the individual but also that he take responsibility for self-cultivation according to Confucian ethics, and try to find the solution...in his own efforts at self-perfection. (p. 27)

A study carried out in 1972 by Shively and Shively at Kwun Tong Estate, an essentially middle-class housing development, identified two kinds of individuals—the *traditionalists*, who were more pessimistic and felt less of a sense of personal efficacy, and the *modernists*, who were more optimistic and demonstrated more personal confidence. The traditionalists were older and less educated and their social relationships were tied much more to the family. They maintained a required piety, were less likely to speak English, occupied fewer professional-management roles, and were less mobile in social and occupational terms.

The modernists, in contrast, were younger and college educated and had added to traditional values those values that permitted them to function in the broader, societal setting. The modernists identified roles for government, institutions, and citizens and saw them as complementary and integrative. The traditionalists depended on one or another of these agencies without regard to their interaction. The modernists also expressed a greater sense of efficacy with respect to their ability to play a role in solving social problems. Thus two major forces were at work: a living culture that was sustained under enormous pressures, and an emerging modernism, which youths, as a social class, adopted as their credo.

One cultural view that explains the lack of active political participation by Chinese is an "idealized relationship" between the government and the people, a symbiosis analogous to that which should exist between parents and children. This illusion was strengthened and even exploited by the traditional conservatism of elitist Chinese, to whom the British delegated power and who most opposed liberalization.

Novelist Han Suyin wrote that the population of Hong Kong, rooted in a freer society than the one they had escaped in China, nonetheless was more characterized by transience than permanence. Despite an "air of belonging," each Chinese in Hong Kong thought in terms of his or her origin—usually a village in South China. China was the sea, and Hong Kong was a lifeboat on the sea. No one wanted to rock the boat.

The situational conditions contributed to the air of apathy. It was evident that despite its evils, the colonial government functioned efficiently, it was more responsive to press criticism, and social services received more attention and money. There was also a general recognition, despite the liberalization and participation gestures of the late 1970s and early 1980s, that colonial rule was not relinquished easily. Many Chinese believed their votes did not count and channeled their energies into their careers. Their position was that reforms must precede participation, not the reverse. Finally, concerning the politics of Taiwan in relation to China, students wondered if two Chinas could continue to exist.

Situational Relevance. The politics of Hong Kong require us to reconcile cultural interpretations and situational relevance. Wong (1970—1971) tended toward situational relevance, arguing that cultural values such as paternalism (accepting government as a "brother's keeper"), "boat on the sea" (Hong Kong as the boat, and China as the sea), lack of identification with Hong Kong and its problems, or even the conflict between the Kuomintang (Taiwan) and the Communists were not the most relevant determinants of student behavior.

Wong suggested that cultural traits may, however, explain responses in situations. Confucious, she said, did not propose that people be politically indifferent; rather, Confucious said that while government should be paternalistic it must be benevolent and meet the needs of the people, or else the people have a right to revolt. This view underlines the conclusion that the lack of political involvement in Hong Kong has been a product of a long-drawn-out process of alienation from the political system—including also a sense of student powerlessness, meaninglessness, and isolation. There has been a pragmatic sense that power resided in London. Deutsch (1968) concluded that the real Hong Kong mood was one of masterly expedience and crisis-to-crisis adjustment and recovery—in cultural terms, a gambler's mentality, partly fatalism.

A public opinion poll in 1966 by *Kung Sheung Yat Po*, a popular Chinese-language daily, found that a majority considered voting to be a meaningless act. The gap was caused not by any denial of civil liberties but by a lack of popular control over government; public opinion was of little use if that opinion had no impact on official policies.

The Kwun Tong study showed that whereas 20 percent said political affairs were important, 38 percent said they were not important, and 19 percent did not know or care. Although 49 percent said they followed public affairs, only 7 percent claimed to do so regularly. As for political efficacy, only 1 percent thought they could do something about an unfair regulation; 82 percent said they could do nothing. But the greatest sense of political efficacy was held by the educated and the young. Wong (1970–71) cited an Urban Council report (1966b) that college youth increasingly would reject the status quo:

> it is debatable whether any traditional view is accepted [among these college youths]. The great majority...are of Hong Kong birth...as distinct from any traditional way of life and thought. It would be natural for this rising generation, equipped with education and impelled by new hopes and ideals, to tend to dissociate itself from any traditional viewpoint and to assimilate more modern ideas on the proper relationship between government and people. (pp. 11–12)

An earlier report by the Urban Council (1966a) suggested that education would equip and motivate youths to increase rather than to reduce political participation.

Townsend (1967) noted that in Hong Kong and in other Third World societies there was a highly centralized political structure and a great degree of political control. Thus one could not equate interest with participation because power was not distributed or shared. But McClosky (1968) described Hong Kong colleges and universities as incubators for civic duty, political competence, interest, and responsibility, as well as for the personality characteristics of self-confidence, dominance, and articulateness.

In summary, Hong Kong students are required to lend traditional values to the consideration of immediate situations, which in many cases, are beyond their personal control. But a modern Chinese youth has learned to adapt situationally in an intricate political culture.

SOME COMPARATIVE STUDIES

We do not have direct comparative data for all four student groups. But some comparative studies have included one or more of the groups and occasionally compared them to each other as part of a larger study. Some of the findings are suggestive of our own findings despite the differences in the research settings and some of the questions that were asked.

Gillespie and Allport (1955) conducted one of the earliest comparative studies of youth values. American students were characterized more than other groups by the inclination to seek a rich, full life for one self and one's family; to think in concrete and practical terms about jobs home, and recreation; and to be relatively unconcerned about social problems. However, the comparisons did not include students from other industrial countries, notably either Germany or Japan.

The Youth Bureau (1978) of the Office of the Prime Minister of Japan conducted two comparisons of youths in 11 countries, one in 1972 and the second in 1977. Three of the countries surveyed were Japan, the United States, and West Germany.

Of the three groups, German students were most likely to be characterized as diligent (followed closely by the Japanese) and intellectual, practical, and peace loving (closely followed in each case by the Americans); the American students were perceived as most broad-minded (followed by the Germans). Japanese youth were rated very low on intellectualism, practicality, and broad-mindedness. Interestingly, Japanese youths themselves agreed with these appraisals except that they perceived themselves as being more peace loving.

Japanese youths, surprisingly, perceived themselves as less fearful of bringing disgrace either to themselves or to their families. They were more concerned about creating problems for people around them. American students were far more concerned than either the Japanese or German students with bringing down the wrath of God. A comparison of American, German, and Japanese students on beliefs about personal control found that the U.S. students perceived greater internal control than did the Japanese students, were less likely to perceive "powerful others," and saw events less as due to chance. A later comparison with German students showed U.S. and German students to be similar in perceptions of internal control; the German students were highest on the "powerful others" scale, and the U.S. and German students were lower on the chance scale (Krampen & Wieberg, 1981). But the same basis of comparison used by Lao (1977) showed no differences across the three cultures.

Our own data suggest the extent to which the four groups of students actually demonstrated similarities and differences in values and behavior. Students continue to be dissatisfied with society and society with them. It has been suggested that the dominant student mood in the 1970s and 1980s throughout the Western and democratic world may represent a shift on a broader basis from societal consciousness to self- and group interests. We offer evidence only from four cultural settings, but these data may be indicative. What becomes real is the need to undertake an even more comprehensive and perhaps worldwide study of the values of youths.

ANALYSIS

Our cultural analyses give us some sense of the differences in communications behavior that we expect to observe in the data that we will present. We do not propose a variable by variable set of predictions, for the comparative model proposes as much an inductive as a hypothetico-deductive approach. We expect to observe similarities based upon the constancy of student roles in all societies. The differences will emerge as a consequence of variations in the larger cultures and the special demands posed by specific situations.

American Students: Media Manipulators

The American pattern has been essentially one of the persistence of a core set of college values that are critical of existing institutions, make demands upon them, and experience varying degrees of success in achieving their purposes. The protests against Korea met with only limited success; these stifled demands were restated on the occasion of Vietnam by those college students who had been rebuffed in the 1950s. The 1970s and 1980s saw a series of demands that were related to civil rights, equal rights for women, and more freedom of personal choice. As those demands were met by an expanding economy and a political structure that sought to co-opt college youth, twin currents developed—continued claims upon the society and increased co-opting by it.

This pattern of social legitimacy of claims and the assimilation of "claims-makers" argues for the usefulness of mass communication and interpersonal discussion to the individual. Thus we should expect American students to use mass media as they advance their purposes. To this point, it might be reasoned, American students have learned to manipulate mass media to achieve their purposes.

German Students: Constant Claims-Makers

German students also have been claims-makers, but they have not defined their purposes in the same terms as American students. While seeking to legitimize their activities, they have viewed social institutions as not deserving of legitimacy. They do not wish to manipulate or to join the system but to change the system. The mass media have helped them to achieve the legitimacy they seek; thus we would expect them to utilize those media and appreciate them in more intimate terms. As members of a group that is making demands upon the society which are more difficult to achieve, German students find themselves communicating more as a discreet entity. Thus interpersonal communication takes on more significance and mass media contribute more directly to that internal dialogue among students.

Japanese Students: Observers and Participants

Japanese students are preparing themselves to become a part of the social order. Yet as a group they recognize that social change constantly is occurring and their values are evolving. Thus they have intellectual and emotional needs that must be articulated. We would expect Japanese students to look to the mass media for articulation of the forces and the pace of social change and a recognition of their needs. Given these intellectual demands, students would identify with mass media more in cognitive than in affective terms. They would act out their emotional needs within the family and in intimate friendships. This would confine the role of interpersonal communication to the private rather than to the public domain.

Hong Kong: The Communication Dilemma

Chinese students in Hong Kong are subject to a great number of situational demands. They are buffeted by a political environment to which students as well as ordinary Hong Kong residents have little access. These Chinese students see many problems about them. They are intimately portrayed: housing, transportation, employment, crime, and the breakdown of the family. Chinese students are seeking their place in an environment that is subject classically to Yin and Yang—expressed primarily in the constant tugs of war that are being fought surreptitiously among political and economic forces within and beyond Hong Kong itself. Over these forces the Chinese student may exercise little control. Mass communication in this context is itself highly situational. Students may not rely completely upon the institutional sources of information. They must rely also upon interpersonal and family networks, no matter how fragile these might become.

PURPOSE

The purpose of this chapter has been to create a cultural framework for the analysis of student communications behavior.

We began by outlining the research strategy:

1. an assumption of the functional equivalence of student groups;
2. an awareness of cultural differences that might produce variations in communications behavior;
3. a sensitivity to the importance of situations which might transcend both structural and cultural influences.

We provided a cultural analysis of each student group—Americans, Germans, Japanese, and Chinese. We also described situations which affected students own values or determined their perceptions of the needs of the society.

These analyses permit us to state broadly relevant hypotheses which exploit the appeal of a metaphor. The metaphorical approach was suggested by two almost identical references to the notion of a "sinking boat," one metaphor describing the Chinese in Hong Kong and the other American students in the 1970s and 1980s.

In the first figure of speech, Chinese were wary of "rocking the boat" in Hong Kong because of the imposing presence of the British Crown Colony administration and the great fears of Red China. Rocking the boat could disturb the delicate political balance of the colony and bring on China. In the second instance, American students were paddling their own canoes, so to speak, and would not rock them to help one another, expressing a "me-firstism." Yet, as we pointed out, we did not buy the thesis that American students in the 1980s, at least, were insensitive to the needs of others.

Thus a slightly different metaphor is suggested, as follows:

- American students are willing to rock the political boat, but it depends upon the cause or the issue. They do not wish, however, to sink the boat.
- German students are quite willing to turn over the boat, their cause being superordinate; in any case, the boat is not worth keeping afloat because it is not going anywhere.

- Japanese students are not in the boat, but they expect to go along later for a ride. They are keeping their eyes on the boat to see where it will pick them up to take them to their destination.
- Chinese students are not in the boat, either, even though they think they should be. They wonder if the Chinese, who will replace the British in Hong Kong, will permit them aboard, much less give them permission to rock it.

Given the extended metaphor, it is possible to express some expectations for the ways in which students in each group might use and evaluate mass media in relation to what they consider to be important problems. A few inferences might be made at this point:

First, all students would use media more or less similarly as a function of their structurally defined and generally equivalent roles in the society;

Second, students would evaluate the efficacy of media based upon their problem-oriented expectations for performance. By groups:

- American students, orienting to specific problems, would assess media in terms of problem-specific performance. Because American students expect problems to be solved, they would be pragmatic in their assessment of the utility of media as a part of this process.
- German students, governed by reformist ideals expressed in the Group of 47—embraced, as well, by many working journalists, would ally themselves intellectually with those ideals and trust the mass media to support their political activism.
- Japanese students, aware of the cultural demands of a highly integrated society, would monitor media actively with a view to assessing the functioning of the system which they are prepared to enter.
- Chinese students, aware of the political uncertainties associated with the changing sovereignty of the Hong Kong colony, and observant of the potentialities for social conflict, would address problems that were most immediate and susceptible to solutions. They would interpret mass media performance cautiously, measuring their own participation and constraining their evaluation.

THE STUDY SETTINGS

Our settings were university campuses in the United States, West Germany, Japan, and Hong Kong. The samples of students were drawn from the social sciences and the humanities. They represented similar values and orientations. They are more easily compared than students from professional schools simply because across a number of cultures and universities each university may be host to a different array of professional schools, ranging from medicine, engineering, computer science, and law to other colleges, many of which vary greatly in nature and scope. The social sciences and humanities are most equivalent in their outlooks and teachings.

We selected several universities in each country, seeking to represent degrees of quality, programs, outlooks, and values. To illustrate, religious values are prominent in a number of universities in the United States, Japan, and Hong Kong. We selected Seattle Pacific University in Washington State, Kwansei Gakuin University in Japan, and Chinese Baptist College in Hong Kong because of their denominational status.

Washington State

The University of Washington (UW) lies along Lake Washington in a heavily urbanized setting in the Puget Sound region in the northwest corner of the state; nearby is Seattle Pacific University. Washington State University (WSU) is located in a vast agricultural region in the southeast portion of the state. The two major universities are quite different; UW is substantially larger (36,000 students as compared to 16,000) and is a major research institution. It is the center of a megalopolis of approximately 2.5 million people. However, about 75 percent of the students at both universities come from Seattle and its coastal environs, the population base of the state.

Seattle is a media center that has spawned a computer culture, film companies, theater, ballet, opera, symphony, and Northwest arts. There are three network television outlets, national cable networks, public television, and independent television stations. Seattle has more than 40 radio stations and several commercial and cultural weekly newspapers. There are numerous specialty book shops and two daily newspapers, one with a circulation of more than 250,000 and the other approaching that figure. National newspapers are at hand daily.

Nevertheless, in Pullman, Washington, the WSU students have access by cable to a similar menu of national television and film. The university itself is a cultural oasis, offering many of the arts, although on a limited scale.

West Germany

Our two major sources of interviews in Germany were the University of Mainz and the University of Munich.

Mainz is the smallest of four cities that form the Rhine-Main area, one of the major industrial zones of West Germany. The nearby cities are

Frankfurt, Wiesbaden, and Darmstadt. Mainz has a population of 180,000 but the area includes about 2 million people, similar in number to the greater Seattle metropolitan area.

Mainz was founded more than 2,000 years ago by the Romans and in the Middle Ages was the residence of the most powerful archbishops of Germany. Johannes Gutenberg, the inventor of modern printing techniques, was born in Mainz in the fourteenth century, and the Gutenberg Museum is a showpiece. The Johannes Gutenberg-Universitat Mainz was founded by the French military government after World War II. It replaced an older university that was closed because of revolutionary activities.

The university is situated outside Mainz, but many students live in the city. It has about 24,000 students and offers courses in all disciplines. Mainz is the capital of the Rhineland-Palatine region and is the center of regional government, parliament, and several ministries.

The Rhine-Main area is Germany's largest media center. The largest TV organization in Europe, ZDF, is headquartered in Mainz. There are three TV outlets in all, including SWF and HR; two radio stations; and seven subscription daily newspapers, among them the prominent *Frankfurter Allgemeine Zeitung*, a regional newspaper with a circulation of approximately 165,000.

An old city, Mainz offers a rich cultural life of opera and theater, churches, and historic sites. Book shops and kiosks are everywhere, and international magazines and newspapers are available. As a kind of contrast, a computer culture is developing, in which IBM is a major factor.

Our other German university center, Munich, is one of the largest, wealthiest, and most beautiful cities of West Germany. It is located near the Alps and several attractive lakes. Despite its 1.3 million population, it still retains the character of a traditional Bavarian town. The capital of Bavaria, it hosts a regional government, parliament, and ministries.

Munich has attained the status of a European-wide center of film (Geiselgasteig), auto (BMW) and electronic industries (Siemens) and satellite technology (MBB), and it is an international trade fair center. It has a rich cultural life in its opera house (Muncher Nationaloper), its museums (Deutschese Museum, Alte Pinakothek), and playhouses (Residenztheater, Kammerspiele).

The university is the second largest in Germany, with 47,000 liberal arts students. Its departments are scattered throughout the city, so the university has a prominent place in the social and cultural life of the community. Munich is also a media center. It has a large film industry and a local TV and radio station, it also has access to several other TV and radio stations, among them Austrian stations. All major national and international newspapers and magazines are available at a multitude of book shops and kiosks.

Japan

We obtained our interviews in six universities in Japan: Keio, Tokyo, Kwansei Gakuin, Saitama, Tokai, and Nihon. Tokyo and Saitama are national universities, and the other four are private universities. Keio, Tokyo, and Nihon are in Tokyo, and the other three are in other cities; they are either (1) national, (2) prefectural or municipal, or (3) private in their character.

Students of Keio, Tokyo, and Kwansei Gakuin Universities represent the elite class of Japan because graduates are likely to become elite or their parents already belong to the elite classes. The images of Keio and Kwansei are similar; in fact, Kwansei is often called "Keio University in the West." It is located near Kobe City, about 400 kilometers west of Tokyo. These students have been described as "sons and daughters from established, wealthy families, sophisticated, playful, and often easy-going although intelligent by birth." The students are oriented toward the business community. The Tokyo University students are stereotyped as "straight A students from high schools all over Japan, serious, square, and hard-working." They have drives for power and success and are oriented toward government, academics, and journalism. A joke about Keio and Tokyo students says that an ideal life is to date a Keio student, marry a Tokyo graduate, and send the children to Keio.

Tokyo University is the highest-rated institution, and its student and graduate complexion indicate this status: Almost one-fourth of its students are in graduate programs. The total number of students in this very select university is not high. It was founded as *Tokyo Daigaku* in 1877 and was made up of departments of law, science, literature, and medicine. The agricultural unit in the sciences dates back to 1789. Its name was changed to *Tokyo Teikoku Daigaku* (Tokyo Imperial University) in 1897. In the post-World War II expansion it added and expanded programs in law and engineering; they now are the most prominent degree-granting colleges, along with medicine, agriculture, and other sciences.

The founder of Keio University, Yukichi Fukuzawa (1835—1901), is often called the intellectual father of modern Japan. In 1858 he opened a school of Western studies in his own residence, which grew into Keio University. In his prolific writings, his basic theme was to sustain ideals of self-respect and democratic ways of thinking. He also founded a newspaper, *Jijsshimpo*, which propounded his philosophy. Keio has a somewhat larger enrollment than Tokyo University and a smaller proportion of graduate students. It has a higher proportion of social science and humanistic programs and students.

Tokai University is somewhat larger than Keio and has a number of special institutes and centers. About one-third of its students are in letters, humanities and culture, and political science. Nihon University is a comprehensive educational system that incorporates junior and senior high schools, junior colleges, and technical and professional programs at the university and graduate levels, the system has an enrollment of almost 106,000 students, about 69,000 of whom are university undergraduates. Parallel in some respects, Saitama University began as a high school and then evolved into a prefectural college, teachers' college, and junior college. It now is a university with graduate programs in the sciences, social sciences, policy sciences, and engineering. It is the smallest university of the group.

Kwansei Gakuin University began as a seminary and middle school but now is strongly oriented to the social sciences and humanities, with schools of economics, literature, law, sociology, theology, and sciences. Seven undergraduate schools emphasize culture, language, social and natural sciences, and professional studies. It is located in the Kwansei (Osaka-Kobe-Kyoto) area.

The media environment is unique in that all students read the same national newspapers in addition to local media; journalism is not local in the same sense as in other countries. The national newspapers include the largest, *Yomiuri*, *Asahi*, *Mainichi*, *Sankel*, and *Nikkei*. *Yomiuri* has editorial staffs in three major cities and printing facilities in five locations. Japanese newspapers originated in the early seventeenth century. Later, in the nineteenth century, daily newspapers emerged as organs of political opinion, especially critical of government as *bokutaku*, or wooden warning bells. As we learn from our student sample, they are no longer perceived in this way. As for television, the Nippon Hoso Kyokai (NHK) is the national subscription channel; in addition, there are a half dozen commercial entertainment channels and a variety of special channels. Japan ranks fifth, behind the Soviet Union, America, West Germany, and Italy in number of books. A large number of weekly magazines, some of them popular and sensational, are directed toward the ordinary Japanese reader.

Hong Kong

We gained interviews in three major institutions in Hong Kong. One was the University of Hong Kong (UHK), a traditional university in the British pattern. The second was Chinese Baptist College, primarily an undergraduate teaching institution, at one time much more sectarian in its curriculum and students' interests than at present. The third, the Chinese University of Hong Kong (CUHK) near Shatin in the New Territories, was formed from an amalgam of several small colleges, including religious schools. It is connected by electric train, subway, and bus to Hong Kong.

Baptist College is in Kowloon itself, the old Hong Kong, and is primarily an undergraduate teaching institution. It offers very few graduate

programs and is professional and job oriented in its undergraduate programs. It concentrates heavily on the social sciences and the humanities. Its
students are drawn more broadly from among the social classes than are
those at either CUHK or UHK.

UHK is the major graduate-degree-granting institution in Hong Kong.
It, too, is strongly grounded in the social sciences and humanities. Whereas
both Baptist College and CUHK operate on the American system of classes
and examinations, UHK operates almost entirely on the British model. Its
students tend to be older and drawn from wealthier families and British
Commonwealth emigrants. The faculty is primarily Western, and a far
larger proportion of Western students attend the university.

Hong Kong is not noted for its cultural environment, yet it has many
ethnic film houses and cultural centers, and an active Western arts center
runs months-long Western art and music festivals. It is a tourist paradise
for shopping and eating and is noted for the great number of stalls that
mass-produce kitsch art. It has two television channels in English and two
in Cantonese and Mandarin; radio is limited to three channels. There are
countless Chinese-language newspapers and a number of English-language
dailies as well, notably the *South China Morning Post*, which ranks as a
prestige newspaper.

Although we may assume a certain structural equivalence in our samples because we are dealing with university students of similar ages and
orientations to the social sciences and humanities, we face subtle questions
of comparability of media structures. Nonetheless, the United States, West
Germany, and Japan are among the top four information societies in the
world in the quality and extent of their media structures. Hong Kong has
the advantage of being a communication and transportation center for
Southeast Asia.

The student samples were compared by sex and class standing and
were found to be representative of the populations that we had defined.
The Japanese sample, by sex, contained three-fourths men, but the 26
percent women slightly overrepresented the actual female population.
Overall, the proportion of women ranged from 10 to 22 percent in the six
institutions we sampled. However, a larger proportion of women was
enrolled in the humanities and social sciences. To check the possible
impact of any variation in sex ratios, we correlated the variable with other
behaviors; we found very few differences tied to sex roles in any of the
countries.

We discovered also that U.S. students were predominantly in the third
and fourth years of their programs, whereas most students from the other
countries were in their first and second years. But an examination of age
distributions showed a rough equivalence, suggesting that U.S. students
entered universities at an earlier age; in any case, the differences between

the samples were not significantly different. Somewhat more of the Japanese students came from the higher grade levels.

We also correlated the year in school with major variables and found no large or consistent relationships. The implication of our analysis is that the total experience and role of a student in a university explained behavior more than did differences in sex or the year in school.

SUMMARY

We sampled students from the humanities and social sciences in several universities in each of four cultural settings. We described the media environments of each of the universities. To maximize comparability, we combined the university samples into a country sample. We compared the samples across institutions for sex and year in university. We discovered two sources of substantial variation: sex with respect to Japan and the year in school with respect to the United States Based on correlations with other major variables, however, neither of these sampling factors appeared to bias our data or their comparability.

CHAPTER 3

The Problematic Situation as a Multicultural Concept

The communication processes by which society comes to recognize its problems, and cope with them, are neglected aspects of two important research traditions: the idea of the problem itself and the functions of communication in coping with problems. The idea of the problem has with us for a long time, but the suggestion that we study *communication about problems* is relatively new.

Almost two decades ago, the grand theorist Pecci (1968), overwhelmed by what he perceived to be the enormous growth of world problems, said it was imperative that we begin to comprehend more fully the nature, the seriousness, the interrelatedness, and the deeper meaning of those problems.

Writing in *Futures*, Judge (1975) spoke of a range of world problems and of agencies that were the sources of problems or were trying to deal with them. A team of futurists from the Center for Study of Social Policy (1977) sought to anticipate societal problems so they might benefit from science and technology. The problems they saw were occurring primarily in industrial nations, and they thought that they could be approached best in a comparative framework.

Harms (1980) saw the need for the gathering and cross-referencing of information pertinent to worldwide problems that were occurring within and among societies, and he saw linkages between those problems and problems of communication. A world communication problem, as Harms defined it, invited comparative analysis as a means of arriving at policy-oriented generalizations that could be global and regional in scope.

A RESEARCH HISTORY

A number of distinguished social scientists and pollsters, Buchanan and Cantril (1953), Cantril (1965), and Gallup (1976–1977), have long been concerned about the problems and aspirations of people. UNESCO decided in 1948 that information on the perceptions of individuals about their prospects for personal happiness and world peace was essential. Buchanan and Cantril discovered gaps in knowledge and understanding and reported that stereotyping was endemic within what they characterized as "tight cognitive frameworks."

Cantril initiated a second study in 1965 in which he observed that there were new problems requiring new solutions. Although carried out 20 years ago, and with noncollege as well as college students, the problems mentioned by the respondents from nine countries were in important respects quite similar. Personal economics were mentioned twice as often as any other problem; family and health problems were next, and values and employment also were univerally mentioned. Other findings were equally relevant to our present study:

- The individual worked within narrow limits of job, security, and location in a social structure.
- The norms for social classes varied from one society to another, but individuals defined themselves in relative terms within those structures and became comparable cross-culturally on that basis.
- Individuals projected their own views on the nature of the individual in society, and these views varied as a function of the capacities of the individual—educational attainment in our own case.

Gallup (1976–1977) extended the work of Cantril on the nature of problems and efforts to solve them. He sought, also, to determine how satisfied people were with their lives and which qualities of life were most important to them. He identified problems of employment, family life, and the urban community and nation, and he perceived global interdependence in solving them. These considerations also emerged in our study.

THE MOST IMPORTANT PROBLEM

American pollsters have for many years used lead-in questions about the importance of social problems. Smith (1980) pointed out that Gallup asked "the most important problem" question in his American studies as early as 1935 and has asked it nearly 200 times since World War II. Smith utilized 125 Gallup surveys from 1946 to 1976 to chart most important national and world problems. Other pollsters have asked variants of the Gallup question.

Page and Shapiro (1982) plotted the flow of policy preferences from 1935 to 1979, among which were expressions of opinion about national and world problems and issues. Funkhouser (1973a, 1973b) related media coverage of social problems and social issues to polls about those problems in efforts to identify agenda-setting effects.

In West Germany Noelle-Neumann and Kepplinger (1981) studied the most important community, regional, and world problems in Mainz. Atwood (1984), as we describe in more detail, analyzed problem perceptions and media use in Hong Kong. Edelstein (1973, 1974) related uses of communication about social problems to public opinion in both Yugoslavia and the United States. Each of these studies was cognitive in approach; that is, each addressed such behaviors as awareness, knowledge, problem definition, problem solving, and decision making.

Japanese researchers also have focused their attention on the problem as an object for research. They have seen the problem in terms similar to that of the event; that is, both problems and events are situational as matters to be dealt with here and now.

The Japanese in the mid 1980s became interested in learning more about the role of broadcasting in regional Japan, emphasizing the region as an element of social consciousness and community. Up to that time the questions posed by researchers that had addressed local or community interests had tended to be abstract—to generalize about problems and events, rather than focus upon particular problems or events, and to generalize these over time, so that little contemporariness was afforded.

The researchers adopted the "problematic" or "events" approach so that they could anchor opinions in a "concrete" situation. The "problems" that they elected as being contemporary and specific related to the concerns of local people about their safety or security. The most important of those problems were selected—those that had produced demands by people that something be done about them.

The citizens cited ten problems. Topically they included the arts, business and economic development, corruption, crime, politics, sports, and the weather. Dynamically, in terms of the concept of the problematic situation, the problems were articulated as losses of value (because of corruptiona and crime, typhoon damage, etc.) and steps toward the solution of problems including business reorganization, construction, and changes in business practices.

People also mentioned events that had commanded their attention. Topically, again, these related to the contemporary effects of natural disasters, crop failures, unusual weather patterns, and factors related to everyday lives, such as the progress of children in school, the adult's perceived ability to pay particular kinds of taxes, and individual rights to receive and live adequately on pensions.

The study (Takashina, 1984) was devoted to our second and equally inmportant consideration—communication about problems. In all three regions—Fukui and Shizuoka prefectures and Kobe City—television was the best source of information about natural disasters (more markedly so in Fukui and Shizuoka), sports, and the weather. Newspapers were the best sources for information about business and the economy, the progress of children in school, public discussion, and shopping. Public information bulletins were most depended upon for information about personal health and hygiene.

Thus the Japanese study illustrated several major considerations that we will now treat in greater detail:

- The focus of attention was the problem or the event in their highly situational settings;
- These problems were characterized topically, but they revealed dynamics that we have described as "problematic situations";
- Different communication media were more useful for different problems—and for their implied character as problematic situations.

THE PROBLEMIZATION OF TOPICS

Beyond the topical nature of any problem is a larger question of its meaning. We have described our efforts to determine the kinds of meanings that are attached to problems. This same search was pursued by our colleagues Elisabeth Noelle-Neumann and Hans Mathias Kepplinger (1981). In conducting a study of a local community they documented the fact that individual and social problems were not objective realities but the outcomes of the problemization of a topic by an individual or by the society.

They noticed that problems were perceived by individuals in both personal and social terms—in personal terms as "a threat to the individual" and in social terms as "threats to the society." They described the process of problemization as the "problem of the problem." This required respondents "to construct reality:"

> Problem dimensions are the characteristics or the effects of individual problems thought to be particularly serious and forming the "problem of the problem." We then speak, say in the case of unemployment, of its problematic nature for the workers concerned, their dependents, and the general economic situation of the country. (p. 24)

Noelle-Neumann and Kepplinger (1981) observed that individual problems became social problems by threatening an ever larger number of persons, as in the case of an epidemic, or by becoming a symbol of a social fact that is seen as so dangerous or undesirable as to require change.

A SOCIOLOGICAL VIEW

Sociologists have theorized that social problems must go through well-ordered "steps," or stages, before society collectively is able to cope with them. Different social actors and institutions become key participants at each of these stages. It is easy to see by looking at a newspaper or carefully watching a television news program that some actors are more central than others at different stages of the emergence of problems.

The actor most often cited as a news source in stories about social problems tends to be a public official. For reasons that are not fully understood, experts, social critics, social scientists, and most certainly students are far less likely to be portrayed by the media as critical actors or participants in the emergence of social problems.

Blumer (1971) characterized emergence as the first stage of society's recognition of a social problem. Various actors play a variety of roles at this stage. Most typically, the mass media perform a publicizing role, pointing to the problem and describing it in terms of its consequences for the society.

This leads to the next collective step; that of mobilization, in which student and other "claimant" groups typically engage in actions that are designed to call public attention to steps that might be taken to solve a problem. When the German government announced its proposed action on employment of missiles, the antinuclear, antiwar, and environmental forces joined in a protest and demanded that alternative actions be taken. There is a latent structure of concern about problems of this kind that permits mobilization of groups whose interests coincide at some point.

But before social problems can be addressed collectively, Blumer explained, the problem must be legitimized. This cannot be done by the mobilization tactics of protestors alone, although it is said that opposition to the Vietnam War became legitimized at a later stage of the war by the involvement of white-collar citizens in protest marches. The media may be enlisted most effectively in the legitimation process by confering legitimacy. German students sought the active support of the media in trying to win the support of authorities, experts, and others in the political mainstream.

Once an action is taken it may not be permitted to rest, Blumer suggested. It must be implemented. Here the major role of the media is to maintain surveillance over those actions. This is not the easiest role for the media to fulfill; to carry it out, they require events (often staged) that dramatize or provide evidence of the success and/or failure of implementation.

Sociological thought has continued to be occupied with the study of how social problems emerge as a collective process. We might cite many such authors, as Manis (1974), Spector and Kitsuse (1974), and Zygmunt (1986). Although each proposal differed in substance and focus of attention, the studies were similar in an important respect: Each attempted to examine the collective, step-by-step process of the definition and resolution of social problems. It is the steps that these models address that provide the context for individual definition of a problem and what became for the students an exercise in transforming them into problematic situations.

In the context of problemization, John Dewey (1910) once asked, rhetorically, "What is a problem?" He observed that every problem was accompanied by indeterminacy; there was always a point at which one experienced a condition of discrepancy for which there was no appropriate response. Thus the individual was faced with the need to engage in definitions of situations in ways that would permit problem solving to occur.

THE INFLUENCE OF JOHN DEWEY

The distinguished educator and pragmatist John Dewey greatly influenced the thought of America, and he may be considered to be one of the parents of the study of communication in the situation. Dewey recognized also that situations were problematic in their character, and that communication was most useful in a defined situation rather than in the abstract. He remarkably, in his discussion of *Democracy and Education* in 1916, observed:

> Society not only continues to exist . . . *by* communication, but it may fairly be said to exist *in* communication. (p. 5)

Dewey defined the problematic situation in a number of ways. He spoke constantly of the presence of individual and social needs, the many expectations that were generated in the society, the inevitability of social conflict, the need to creatively address problem-solving alternatives, and the importance of each step that might be taken toward solutions to individual and social problems. He saw the relationships between communication and community, and he warned against the potential loss of value to the society if it proved unable to preserve a sense of community.

As early as 1910 in *How We Think* Dewey spoke of the many ambiguities that faced individuals and the uncertainties that existed in group life—the kinds of uncertainties that demanded that steps be taken to solve problems. To Dewey, ambiguity was an attractive concept—it described the beginning of the creative process that would resolve a dilemma—the need to construct alternatives to resolve the ambiguity. Thus he saw ambiguity as part of the process of thinking, not as a vague or complex condition that could not be resolved.

Dewey was fascinated by cognitive processes as they expressed the relationships of thinking to doing. Both of these behavioral steps, he suggested in *How We Think*, were universals in any society. In that volume he demonstrated an absorbing interest in problem solving, particularly in the conditions of ambiguity in a situation:

> A question to be answered, an ambiguity to be resolved, sets up an end....Every suggested conclusion is tested...by its pertinence to the problem at hand. (p. 11)

During the mid-1920s, Dewey turned more of his thoughts on thinking to the problems of a society although never deserting his concerns for the responses of individuals to situations of their own definition.

Dewey now (1927) saw political democracy as the sum of individual adjustments to a number of problematic situations, no two of which were alike but which, taken together, tended to converge as a common outcome. Dewey believed, as a part of this larger picture of society, that social change had a life of its own, brought about by a collective dynamic in which changes were related and cumulative in character. Perhaps Dewey's greatest regret, which he expressed repeatedly, was that a cumulative critical sense in society lagged behind the problems that emerged and cumulated. The Problem of the public was to improve communication so that people could address their problems adequately.

But in larger terms Dewey remained an optimist. In *Problems of Men* (1946) he saw society as replete with problems. But he was not discouraged. Actually, he said, these conditions gave democracy its vitality— a problem was not a problem but a challenge to the intellect and to communication:

> The...idea of democracy...must be continually explored...constantly discovered and rediscovered...The institutions in which it (democracy) is embodied have to be remade...to meet the changes that are going on in the development of new needs...and new resources for satisfying those needs. (p. 47)

It is not surprising that Dewey's search for the relationship of communication to problematic situations stimulated generations of educational psychologists to study problem solving in education. These scholars contributed to the final matrix that we developed for the study of communication in the situation. They helped us to define a taxonomy of problematic situations. From there we could take the next step—that of identifying the implications for communication in *each* situation. As examples,

1. Nordbeck (1971) observed that children identify the existence of a problem by experiencing a discrepancy between two situations. They observe, or imagine, that this discrepancy requires action on their part; in the psychologist's terms, to solve the puzzle the children are required to move from one behavioral state to another. This recognition that they had to move from their present position to another position led us to our identification of a problematic that we called *need for value* as a present-future situation. Needs could be defined in individual or in societal terms.

2. Jensen (1978) agreed that problems were defined not so much by "what is" but by "what is wrong"; that is, again, a condition of discrepancy. What most often "went wrong" among the students described a sense of deprivation in a temporal present-past condition. That is, they had enjoyed some privilege or action that now was denied to them. We conceptualized those now-then conditions as *losses of value*. Again, loss could affect individuals or societies.

3. Berlyne (1965) saw a problem as a failure to reach a goal on one's first attempt. There was nothing problematic about a situation just because someone had a goal; it was the acknowledged failure to attain the goal that produced the problem.

    We later encountered instances among the students when they felt they had been thwarted in their efforts to achieve their goals, often because of confusion or ambiguity. Being thwarted represented a form of *blocking*, and the confusion and ambiguity associated with it represented a condition of *indeterminacy*.

4. Getzels (1979) observed that children felt it necessary to define problems; the first step in problemization. Problem definition is, in fact, a significant step toward problem solving. We conceptualized that idea in more programmatic terms as *steps toward solutions* because the examples represented movement toward a goal.

5. A major communication implication for our problemization approach was suggested by Bunge's (1967) definition of a problem as a difficulty that could not be resolved immediately *and which required a search*. That search also represented a *need for value*, in this case formulated in communication terms.

    This formulation made us mindful again of Festinger's (1957) motivational aspect of cognitive dissonance; the cognitive discrepancy that produced the dissonance might impel some individuals to engage in a search of some kind.

* Loss of values: A condition of discrepancy where the individual once possessed something of value and had not yet moved to replace it, a present-past temporal condition.

* Need for value: A condition of discrepancy where the individual sought to gain or to achieve some value that had not been attained, a present-future temporal dimension.

* Institutional Breakdown: A loss of value on institutional rather than on an individual basis, a situation where a social institution such as government, education, or the family no longer was functioning adequately or failing to meet societal needs, a present-past temporal dimension.

* Social conflict: The individual observed conditions of conflict between or among other actors or institutions, including issues of war, trade and other competition between individuals or between or among governments; this could occur along any temporal dimensions, past, present and/or future.

* Indeterminate situation: Conditions of uncertainty, ambiguity, chaos, confusion, questioning, prioritizing, etc.. This, too, could take place within any time frame.

* Steps toward solutions: Demands for, proposals for, or observation of any steps that might lead to solutions. This, too, could take place in any time dimension.

* Blocking: An individual or a collectivity that was proceeding on a path is interupted by an actor. This could take place in any time frame.

Figure 3.1. Seven Conditions of Discrepancy

On the bases of these and other studies of problem defining and problem solving we generated (see Figure 3.1) a formal scheme of problematic situations that included seven conditions of discrepancy.

INDIVIDUAL STUDENTS' PERSPECTIVES

In the present study we asked students to name three important problems *and* to tell us which of those was the most important to them personally; we then questioned them about that problem. Thus the question should be interpreted as "which of the important problems that affected the society was the most important to you personally?"

We first classified the problems topically, using conventional categories of media content. These were added to, as necessary, to accommodate the particular concerns of one or more of the countries. For example, trade is particularly important to Japan, and housing and population are highly relevant to Hong Kong students. We then looked at the topically defined problems for their behavioral dynamics, that is, the problematic situation(s) they proposed.

The topics perceived as most important in each student culture varied substantially, and each group selectively attended to just a few topics. Note that we are still talking about "topics" at this point, and not about problematic situations.

With respect to topical categories, American students were preoccupied primarily by only two problems: economic issues, 40 percent, and nuclear arms and war, 26 percent.

In Germany the economy, nuclear war, and the environment accounted for 88 percent of all problems.

Japanese students focused on questions of trade, domestic politics, and international conflict, and these problems accounted for 72 percent of the topics they named.

Hong Kong students were more broadly concerned with five topical areas: social problems, the politics of 1997, housing, education, and population. These accounted for 88 percent of all problems.

Thus the groups were more or less equivalent in focusing their attention on a few major topics, although these were very different.

Students' comments illustrate and give personal definition to the concepts.

An American student cited economic problems: High interest rates and the lack of a balanced budget were limiting the vitality of the market system. Interest rates affected him personally, and this item was coded *loss of value*; the federal budget and the market system were more broadly conceived of as evidence of *institutional breakdowns*.

As a second problem he saw nuclear arms as necessary to maintain a balance of power, but he wondered how many nuclear weapons actually were required. In raising both the literal and metaphorical question, he described an *indeterminate situation*.

The third problem he mentioned was the plight of Third World countries, facing hunger, unproductive economies, and political instability. His statement that "a plan of action" was required was coded as a *need* for *steps toward a solution*.

He said the most important problem was the economy. Once the market system was allowed to operate freely and interest rates came down, the system would work, but this could occur only with a balanced budget. In this response the student went beyond the specification of the problem itself to propose *steps toward a solution*.

A German student, expressing anxiety about the prospects for world peace, perceived great uncertainties in this area. He felt an understanding was lacking that the armament spiral could and must be stopped by one side. Only that would reduce the danger of atomic warfare. Thus he described a condition of *indeterminacy* and *proposed alternative solutions*, in that way defining two problematic situations.

He cited as a second problem the stagnation of economic growth—an *institutional breakdown* that produced problems for individuals throughout the entire economic system. His reference to the impact on the individual was coded as *loss of value*.

He mentioned unemployment as the third problem. He saw this in systemic terms as a "period of economic growth that had been overtaken by economic events; the good times had not lasted." This perception of loss of value on a systemwide basis was coded as an *institutional breakdown*.

He said the most important problem was world armament and the securing of peace. The fear of war affected everyone, and social benefits that once came from the state were limited by the costs of the arms race. Here, too, he linked individual *loss of value* to systemic problems, or *institutional breakdowns*.

A Japanese student expressed concern about trade and perceived *conflict* between Japan and the European Economic Community. She acknowledged that Japanese exports hurt the European community, a loss of value on a systemic basis—hence, *institutional breakdown*—contrasting this aspect with the observation that the Japanese market itself was protected.

She cited as a second problem the military buildup in Japan. It was making a "dead letter" of Article 9 of Japan's Constitution; guarantees built into social institutions were not functioning as they were intended, thus revealing an *institutional breakdown*.

The national debt coupled with a tax increase to deal with it was the third problem. From her perspective, there must be a limit to the size of the debt that the economy could sustain, and now she was being asked to pay taxes to remedy errors in policy. This, to her, was a personal *loss of value*.

The "pocketbook" problem was most important. She saw herself paying more in taxes and more for public utilities, and she feared inflation, another potential *loss of value* to her as an individual.

A Chinese student said that housing, youth, and the economy were the three most important problems. Juvenile delinquency was the one most important problem.

Housing was a problem because of the substandard squatter villages in which people lived. This situation represented a deprivation, or *loss of value*, at the level of the individual.

As a second, related problem, youths were increasingly attracted to materialism and the good life at the cost of spiritual values. These represented personal *losses of value*.

As a third problem, industry nationwide had suffered a cutback, resulting in a widespread loss of employment, or a *breakdown* of the economic system.

FROM TOPICS TO PROBLEMATICS

The transformation of topical concerns into the cognitive dynamics of problematic situations created several important opportunities:

1. As we had intended, it created a behavioral context for analyzing topics in behavioral, meaning terms.
2. It contributed to the creation of a theory of problematic situations, which we would apply to a number of other situations.
3. It contributed to our ability to generalize about a large number of topics—which produced an "economy of scale."
4. It represented realities conceived by individuals and articulated as problems rather than as ambiguous topical categories of content.
5. It linked us with a broad field of cognitive theory that incorporated information behavior and communication. In pointing to the importance of cognitive theory in communication, Pavitt (1982) said that since communication was largely intentional and designed to achieve specific purposes, cognitive models such as problem solving and decision making were highly relevant. He urged that there be more work on the cognitive aspects of information and communication.

A FRESH EXAMPLE: XINHUA AND THE ASSOCIATED PRESS

An ongoing comparison of the wire services of Xinhua, the official Chinese news agency, and the Associated Press (AP), the premier Western agency, has tested the usefulness of topical categories of news as contrasted to problematic situations in determining the similarities and differences in the two news services.

On the face of it one would expect Xinhua and AP to differ dramatically in the kinds of situations they portray in the news. Atwood (1987) of Southern Illinois University decided to test two approaches. One was to do a topical comparison, as is the usual practice. The other was to compare them on their construction of problematic situations, adopting our approach.

Atwood was surprised by the results of the topical comparison. It showed that the two services were much alike—a .66 correlation of categories such as economics, international relations, education, and so on.

Atwood then examined the results produced by the comparison of problematic situations. He found that Xinuha, dramatically more than AP, focused on the consequences of problems, acknowledging the existence of many problems faced by individuals and by society. But the related "problematics" stressed the kinds of steps that were being taken to bring about solutions—instances of cooperation and negotiation and suggestions for alternative approaches.

In contrast, AP, much more than Xinhua, reported conditions in which the context of problems included instances of confusion, uncertainty, questioning, and doubts. The Associated Press also reported many more situations involving individual and social conflict, individual deprivation, and needs expressed by individuals (as compared to needs of the society). It reported three times as many instances of conditions of indeterminacy—situations of doubt, uncertainty, questioning, confusion, and anxieties—and twice as many incidents involving individual and social conflict, deprivations, and needs. In contrast, Xinhua reported twice as many instances of negotiation and a third more instances of cooperation, and it devoted three times as much space to Third World news.

It should be acknowledged, of course, that both the AP and Xinhua reports represented their own constructions of reality for their own patrons and readers. Most illustrative of the differences was the surprising finding, pointed out by the Chinese coders, that even Xinhua sports reports contained few elements of competition or conflict.

The more important finding, to us, was that whereas topical comparisons showed no differences between the two agencies—flying in the teeth of expectations to the contrary—the analysis of problematic situations showed that there were sharp differences in approaches to news. This finding is highly relevant to the issues that we raise in Chapter 1 about the quality of news flow, and it is germaine to the issues we develop about news in Chapter 4.

Figures 3.2a through 3.2d introduce us to the distribution of problematic situations as they were perceived by students' and percentages are reported in Table 3.1. Despite cultural differences and some situational influences, the students' answers proved to be comparable along a number of dimensions.

First, as we indicated, each student culture focused its concerns on three or four major kinds of problematic situations—needs, losses, institutional breakdowns, and perceptions of social conflict. Only Hong Kong students did not address social conflict. As we have pointed out, Hong Kong is not a sovereign nation but a crown colony and is externally administered. Hong Kong students joined in the perception that they were experiencing deprivations and that their needs were not being met. Like

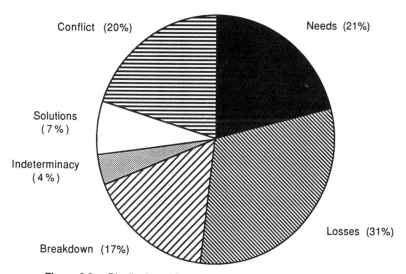

Figure 3.2a. Distribution of Problematic Situations: United States

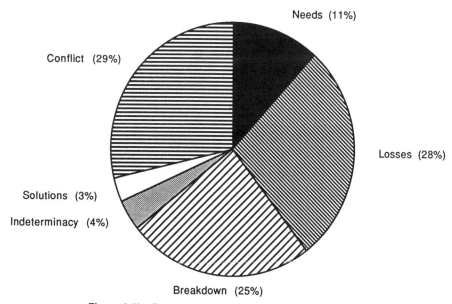

Figure 3.2b. Distribution of Problematic Situations: Germany

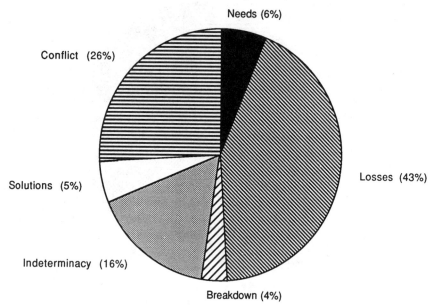

Figure 3.2c. Distribution of Problematic Situations: Japan

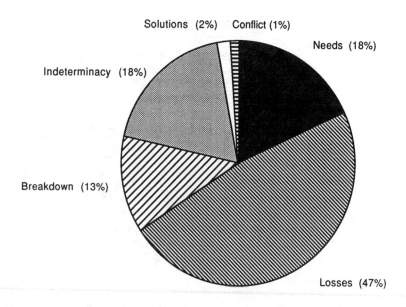

Figure 3.2d. Distribution of Problematic Situations: Hong Kong

TABLE 3.1. PERCENTAGE DISTRIBUTION OF PROBLEMATIC SITUATIONS

Problematic Situation	United States (n = 678)	Germany (n = 470)	Japan (n = 667)	Hong Kong (n = 636)
Needs	21	12	6	18
Losses	31	28	43	47
Institutional breakdowns	17	25	4	13
Indeterminacy	4	4	16	18
Solutions	7	3	5	2
Conflict	20	29	26	1
Totals	100	100	100	99

the other students, they blamed social institutions for not being able or willing to respond to their needs. Perhaps the most interesting common behaviors among the student groups were that they avoided conditions of indeterminacy and ambiguity, and in each case very few of them were oriented to solutions. This finding runs counter to emphases in the mass media on steps toward solutions to problems.

ASSESSING DIFFERENCES

Inevitably, there were differences in emphases, attributable either to elements of culture or to the uniqueness of situations.

Americans were most anxious about various kinds of deprivation; that is, about *losses of value* to the individual. These losses of value were perceived as the consequences of inflation, unemployment, interest rates, crime, and drugs.

Coupled with perceptions of individual loss was the perception of needs, in many cases to address problems of unemployment. For example, it was necessary to create jobs, expand opportunities, and bring about social equity.

About one of five students pointed to a variety of social conflicts, including national and international issues relating to nuclear power and nuclear armaments and, as a related consideration, East–West relations. A fourth element was the breakdown of social institutions that had failed to be responsive to those needs.

More than one in four of the German students also stressed deprivation at the individual level and, as well, perceptions of the breakdown of social institutions. They felt personally deprived by the lack of assistance given to students, and they were distressed about the lack of responsiveness of politically conservative institutions to important social problems.

In contrast to Americans, German students expressed fewer individual needs, implying they did not consider it likely the government would address those needs. Why, then, should they mention them? However, to the same extent as American students, German students perceived the danger of conflict through the threat of nuclear war, the state of Third World countries, and the East-West conflict.

Almost one-half of the Japanese students expressed concerns about personal losses of value. These were rooted in fear of the loss of spiritual values in youths and a breakdown of the family as a consequence of social and economic mobility. At the institutional level there were deeply rooted concerns about environmental pollution and the lack of forcefulness of steps taken by the government.

The Japanese students least expressed personal needs, which might be attributed to a clearer perception and even acceptance of what was possible to bring about in personal terms in that society. This general sense of acceptance also would explain a lesser tendency to perceive failures in the functioning of social institutions.

One surprising finding was the extent to which Japanese students perceived the existence of social conflict. More than one in four students pointed to business competition, the debate over the Constitution, issues regarding the environment and nuclear power, and policies that governed Japan's trading position.

Even more than Japanese youths, Hong Kong students were concerned by a sense of personal loss growing out of perceptions of delinquency, crime, and the increasing adoption of materialistic values. More than one out of eight expressed need for the reform of social institutions, and they voiced anxieties about the transfer of political sovereignty to China in 1997.

Hong Kong students dealt little in policy terms with social problems, nor did they express concerns about international conflict. As we have pointed out, this result is understandable in the context of centrally administered social agencies and the lack of involvement in international problems because of the status of Hong Kong as a crown colony rather than as a sovereign state.

TOPICS AS PROBLEMATICS

As we have discussed, the transformation of topics into problematic situations had the function of assigning *meaning* to topical categories. By viewing topics as problematics we were able to observe that the *same meanings* occurred with *different topics*, whereas *different meanings* often were associated with the *same topics*. To illustrate, what one person sees as

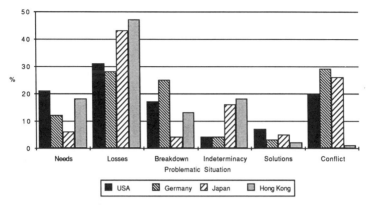

Figure 3.3. Comparative Array of Problematic Situations: By Country

deprivation caused by economic policy will be perceived by another person as economic opportunity. To still others this same event may be seen as evidence of ideological conflict or a breakdown in the economic order.

Figure 3.3 compares problematic situations by countries, and Figure 3.4 pictures countries by problematic situations; data are in Table 3.2.

We note in Figure 3.3 that the U.S. and Hong Kong students most expressed needs, Japanese and Hong Kong students losses or deprivations; West German students were most concerned about the breakdown of social institutions, Hong Kong students the most indeterminacy, and German and Japanese students the most perception of conflict. Figure 3.4 allows us to visualize the importance across each culture of losses of value, conflict, and concerns about the viability of social institutions.

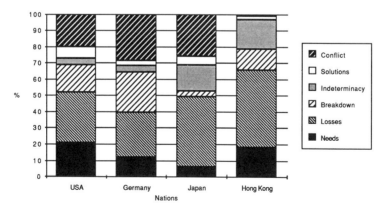

Figure 3.4. Comparative Array of Countries: By Problematic Situations

TABLE 3.2. TOPICAL PROBLEMS AS PROBLEMATIC SITUATIONS

Transformed into Problematic Situations	Topical Problems Mentioned by Students								
	Economic	Education	Housing	Politics	Population	Social Problems	Trade	War	International Relations
The United States									
Need	22	27	—	20	—	30	21	14	29
Loss	42	28	—	20	—	36	29	20	13
Breakdown	13	40	—	43	—	19	8	12	30
Indeterminacy	4	3	—	2	—	5	8	6	7
Conflict	7	6	—	2	—	5	12	11	9
Solutions	11	5	—	12	—	7	21	38	13
Germany									
Need	16	—	—	15	—	20	—	10	—
Loss	56	—	—	18	—	28	—	24	—
Breakdown	21	—	—	38	—	17	—	15	—
Indeterminacy	—	—	—	1	—	2	—	8	—
Conflict	20	—	—	23	—	14	—	41	—
Solutions	—	—	—	—	—	2	—	3	—
Japan									
Need	22	29	—	24	4	22	8	19	31
Loss	26	24	—	27	30	39	17	22	32
Breakdown	24	33	—	28	11	21	34	18	13
Indeterminacy	4	4	—	18	52	7	29	—	14
Conflict	17	7	—	—	—	8	8	31	14
Solutions	6	4	—	2	4	3	3	9	10
Hong Kong									
Need	25	32	30	13	14	18	—	—	—
Loss	49	34	50	23	57	61	—	—	—
Breakdown	13	28	11	13	21	10	—	—	—
Indeterminacy	13	6	6	46	7	8	—	—	—
Conflict	—	1	1	4	—	2	—	—	—
Solutions	1	—	1	1	—	1	—	—	—

NOTE: Each of the scores represents a proportion of 100. Blanks indicate no data.

THE NATURE OF TRANSFORMATION

One of the most critical questions we have raised is the way in which topics are translated into problematic situations. Are economic problems always instances of deprivation or loss? Do they strongly suggest needs? Do they point to breakdowns in social institutions? Answers to these questions go to the heart of our theory; that is, that problematic situations are varied and meaningful. For example, we should not expect all economic problems to be translated into deprivations; also, we should not expect all educational problems to be translated into questions of needs. There might be tendencies in one of these directions, but there should be variation as well.

Figures 3.5a–3.5d picture the results of the transformation of topics into problematic situations, also represented in Table 3.2.

First, we should point out that for ease in handling, topics such as inflation, employment, and so on were combined under economics, and crime, delinquency, welfare, and so on were grouped as social problems.

Second, problems that applied substantially only to one country, such as trade (in the case of the Japanese), population (with respect to the Japanese and Chinese), and housing, (only to Hong Kong), were retained although inapplicable to other students.

The findings are interesting and confirm our suspicions. In each country the transformation from topics into problematic situations usually resulted in emphasis on more than one problematic situation. As many as three problematic situations usually accounted for most of the dynamics implicit in a category. Any purely topical categorization, therefore, would necessarily be ambiguous. This aspect varied also by country, although similarities can also be seen. Topic by topic there were a variety of transformations into problematic situations; within topics we observed great similarities as well as differences across the four graphs.

Economics

Students in each country viewed economic topics largely in terms of loss of value. This is not surprising because it is not often that we view gains in value in the economy as a "problem." Yet there were differences among the groups. For one, more German students felt a sense of loss than did other students. Japanese students felt least deprived by economic problems.

The most emphasis on needs was expressed by Hong Kong students and the least by German students, but those differences were not great.

Hong Kong students experienced the most economic uncertainty, as well as a greater need to resolve it.

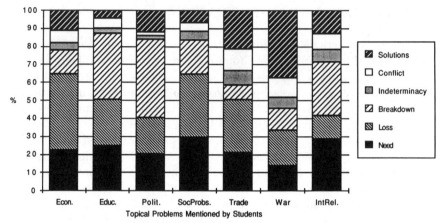

Figure 3.5a. Topical Problems as Problematic Situations: United States

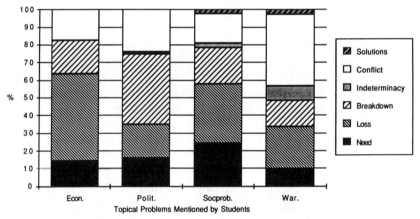

Figure 3.5b. Topical Problems as Problematic Situations: Germany

Japanese students were somewhat more concerned about breakdowns in the economic system; German students expressed similar fears.

Finally, German and Japanese students saw economic problems more in conflictual terms, the German students because of internal frictions and the Japanese students in terms of external trade.

Education

Again, there were similarities and differences in education.

Germany did not perceive education to be a problem, in contrast to the other three groups.

In each of the other three countries education was seen as demonstrating needs, deprivation, and breakdowns in institutional functioning.

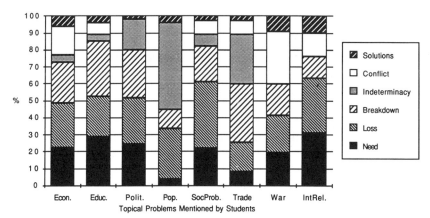

Figure 3.5c. Topical Problems as Problematic Situations: Japan

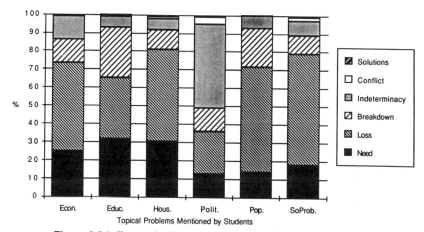

Figure 3.5d. Topical Problems as Problematic Situations: Hong Kong

The three groups saw few ambiguities concerning the problems of education; they were all too clear, and there was little evidence of steps toward solutions.

In substantive terms Japanese students expressed concern about the nature and quality of the system, Hong Kong and Japanese students disliked administration of the system, and American students decried the lack of support for them and the system.

Housing

The topic of housing was mentioned only by students in Hong Kong. Transformed into problematic situations it expressed primarily feelings of need and deprivation in being unable to obtain housing.

Politics

Again there were similarities across the groups for politics. American, German, and Japanese students did not see the political process as responsive to them.

Approximately half the Chinese students saw the politics of Hong Kong primarily in terms of the uncertainties relating to the future sovereignty of the crown colony, as can be seen in Table 3.1. The quality of administrative functioning, therefore, was a moot question.

Japanese students also perceived uncertainties about the political picture, but this area was much less pervasive and could be attributed to national elections occurring at that time. In any case, political power was not expected to shift greatly.

A similar phenomenon occurred in Germany, where elections also were occurring. German students expressed little uncertainty because the outcome, again, was in little doubt. Rather, they saw the election in conflictual terms.

Population

The two Asian countries were both concerned about problems of population but viewed the situation in different terms.

Whereas a great many Japanese students expressed anxiety about the declining birthrate, Chinese students saw the influx of "boat people" from China as causing crowding, housing shortages, transportation breakdowns, and crime. Thus population, although a "same-named topic," represented dramatically different problematics for the two Asian groups—an uncertainty felt by Japanese students and a sense of fear and deprivation on the part of the Chinese.

Social Problems

There was a great deal of consensus among the student groups that social problems such as crime, welfare, and the deterioration of the family unit added up to deprivation or loss of value. The most widespread perceptions of problems of this kind were seen in Hong Kong, where students feared a breakdown of cultural stability and values.

American students more than others defined social problems in terms of needs; this outcome expressed the sense of American students that all social problems could be solved if skills and resources were brought to bear on them. American students also recognized that social problems represented conflicts of values and beliefs about steps that should be taken to solve these problems.

Trade

As might have been expected, only American and Japanese students thought that trade was the most important problem; no consideration was given to problems of trade by the other two groups.

Again, however, the reasons were different: American students saw the problem of trade more as representing deprivation and a need for action. Japanese students, in contrast, saw trade problems in system terms and as a product of ambiguities about the true nature of trading relations.

As might be expected, the American students demanded solutions to the problem whereas the Japanese students, seeing the problem in more complex terms, were less able to address solutions.

War and International Conflict

We may note quickly that Chinese students excluded themselves from considerations of war and international relations. As subjects of a crown colony, they perceived that Hong Kong had no foreign policies other than trade policies.

If there were any one topic that we thought would be perceived similarly—in terms of problematics—by the other three groups it would be war. That is, it would be perceived in terms of its elements of conflict. But that did not turn out to be the agenda.

American students, for example, focused most of their attention on solutions to war and conflict rather than simply restating the nature of the conflict. In that respect they were unique. Actually, only one out of nine American students stated the problematic of conflict as a conflictual state. That is a remarkable figure, and it demonstrates how topical categorization can obscure the underlying dynamics relating to a subject.

German students, in contrast, saw conflict much more in its basic terms, and very few were oriented to solutions. This reaction reflected an underlying pessimism about the potential for conflict resolution.

Japanese students also transformed instances of social conflict into problematics that expressed elements related to the conflict itself. Like the American students, they saw conflict in the pragmatic terms of need for action and the breakdown of political, economic, and social institutions.

International Relations

The category of international relations was addressed *exclusive* of war and conflict. Only U.S. and Japanese students addressed international relations in terms of diplomacy, compromise, and negotiation. The two profiles were similar in several respects, but there were differences as well.

Surprisingly, fewer American students than Japanese saw deprivations arising from efforts to relate to the problems of the United Nations and UNESCO and the conduct of diplomacy with the Soviet Union and client states. Rather, American students saw these problems primarily in terms of the breakdown of traditional diplomacy and the consequent need for action. Only a modest number of students demanded or perceived the possibility of immediate solutions.

In contrast, Japanese students saw international diplomacy and negotiation (centering on international trade) as a lost cause although a sizable group also saw a need for action. Like the American students, only a few Japanese saw the prospect of immediate solutions.

In summary, topical categories contained within them a number and variety of problematic situations; these were implicit in the many-faceted nature of the problems themselves and in students' perceptions of them. The nature of the problematics varied to some extent by topics and to some extent, as well, by cultural concerns.

We are drawn to the conclusion that by engaging only in topical categorization one is likely to obscure differences in the meaning of things. The meanings grow out of the social experiences of individuals, the broader culture and institutional framework, and the uniqueness of situations.

MEDIA USE AND PROBLEMATIC SITUATIONS

As we have noted, Chapter 4 reports on a content analysis of the presentation of problematic situations by the newspapers in the four cultures. There we compare the emphasis on problematic situations by newspapers with the constructions of problematic situations by the students. The often-stated question is whether or not the students are influenced by the construction of meanings that are given emphasis in the news.

In this chapter, however, we will engage in a different comparison—the extent to which expressed preferences for newspapers or television as sources of information are linked with the constructions that students have placed on problematic situations. As stated, the question we will ask is whether or not preferences for newspapers and/or television are associated with tendencies to construct particular kinds of problematic situations. For example, is the perception of conflict associated more with newspapers or with television?

Figure 3.6 and Tables 3.3 and 3.4 address two kinds of data:

1. A comparison *across* the four groups of the extent to which the two media were associated with the construction of particular problematic situations
2. *Within* each group, a comparison of the two media with respect to the presence of each type of problematic situation

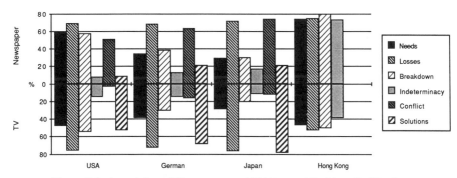

Figure 3.6. Association of Newspaper and TV Use and Problematic Situations

TABLE 3.3. ASSOCIATION OF NEWSPAPER AND TELEVISION USE AND PROBLEMATIC SITUATIONS

Problematic Situations	United States		Germany		Japan		Hong Kong	
	Newspapers	*TV*	*Newspapers*	*TV*	*Newspapers*	*TV*	*Newspapers*	*TV*
Needs	$y59$	47	34	39	29	29	$y74$	47
Losses	$x69$	76	68	73	$x71$	77	$y75$	53
Breakdowns	57	55	$x38$	31	$x30$	21	$y80$	51
Indeterminacy	$x8$	15	13	15	17	12	$y73$	39
Solutions	9	4	21	17	$x21$	13	—	—
Conflict	51	53	63	69	74	79	—	—

NOTES: $x = .05$; $y = .01$. Blank indicate no data.

TABLE 3.4. USES OF NEWSPAPERS AND TELEVISION FOR INTERPERSONAL COMMUNICATION ABOUT ASPECTS OF SOCIAL PROBLEMS

	Germany		United States		Japan		Hong Kong	
	Newspapers	*TV*	*Newspapers*	*TV*	*Newspapers*	*TV*	*Newspapers*	*TV*
Causes	$x38$	50	34	37	46	42	22	17
Consequences	$x81$	96	74	79	33	34	67	66
Solutions	70	65	78	76	$x89$	80	—	—

NOTES: $x = .05$. Blanks indicate no data.

Our first observation is that the patterns of preference for media were generally similar for the American, German, and Japanese students but quite different for the Chinese students. In the first three groups, newspapers were associated with some problematic situations, but television was associated with others. In Hong Kong, in contrast, newspapers were preferred over television for all problematic situations.

That near symmetry in Hong Kong also existed to some extent for American, German, and Japanese students. They demonstrated few differences with respect to media associations with those problematics that involved needs, losses, and breakdowns of social institutions. Apparently, media were perceived as performing similarly along those dimensions. Newspapers and television similarly treated the goals of individuals and whatever deprivations were experienced by them. They also assessed the functioning of social institutions in a comparable way.

Differences did occur, however, in preferences for newspapers and television with respect to conditions of uncertainty, social conflict, and efforts to address problems. These were similar for each of the three student groups.

Television was perceived as the most used source of information about conditions of uncertainty and efforts to solve problems, that is, "good news." In contrast, all student groups associated newspapers more with the portrayal of social conflict. These differences were dramatic.

In addition, most use of both media was associated with reports of losses of value. Some of the conditions of loss of value were expressed by unemployment, inflation, crime, and divorce that were observable by the media; newspapers were perceived, apparently, as more associated with such news.

A mid-range of media use was associated with needs for value and breakdowns in system functioning, that is, the lack of functioning of economic, social, and political institutions, again actively reported by the media.

With the exception of Hong Kong, neither newspapers nor television was seen as a primary source of information about conditions of indeterminacy—explained in part in Chapter 4 in describing the tendency of headline writers to minimize elements of ambiguity in the news stories. Other than questions raised during political campaigns, natural catastrophes such as earthquakes, and similar "unexpected" events, little media coverage is directed to indeterminacy because it is recognized that audiences find it difficult to cope with uncertainties.

Although we cannot document cause and effect, whatever the direction, it seems apparent that newspapers and television in some instances functioned similarly and in other cases differently; interestingly, this pattern held across cultures.

It is less easy to justify the low association between the audiences' conceptions of steps toward solutions and their use of media—or particular media. Our content analysis of the media in Chapter 4 actually shows that newspapers gave a great deal more attention to solution-related news than was reflected in the students' concerns. Students associated their thinking much more with problems than solutions, particularly German students, as noted earlier.

SUMMARY

We introduced a behavioral dimension of "problematization," which proposed the transformation of more commonly used topical categories into the dynamics of problematic situations.

To rationalize our approach, we noted Dewey's comment that "a problem was a problem." We traced the research history of the problem and found that it had a number of intellectual roots. One of them was in educational psychology, the other in sociology.

Behaviorists were interested in individual problems, whereas sociologists were concerned about social problems. Our linkage of these two traditions lay in our articulation of the kinds of problemization engaged in by the individual as he or she observed the nature of problematic situations that were faced by the society.

We compared perceptions of the distribution of problematic situations and attributed these perceptions to several factors.

- One was the common basis for the behavior of students, suggesting shared perceptions of the nature of problems and situations.
- Another was a probability of differences in their construction of problematic situations because of the different values that characterized their larger cultures.
- Finally, we identified situational factors such as the transfer of sovereignty in Hong Kong, trade, and international relations.

We then asked about possible relationships between uses of media and how students "problematized" various topical problems. Comparing newspapers and television, we found similarities, which we attributed to the common bases of media, and we found differences as well, which reflected the nature of each of the media.

The concept of the problematic situation generated a great deal of explanatory power, both in itself and in relation to media uses. Given the data, an encouraging basis exists for further studies.

CHAPTER 4

Walter Lippmann Revisited: The Problematic Situation as a Multicultural Theory of News

It was Walter Lippmann (1922) who suggested that news represented "obtrusions" on the environment. News was not a mirror of social conditions but the report of an aspect of behavior that had obtruded itself. The media scanned the environment (as would radar or sonar impulses) for these obtrusions, which revealed themselves as "news blips" on a journalistic screen. Lamenting that so many of society's manifestations were hidden or concealed, Lippmann urged that a basic challenge to the press was to gain greater access to evidence of these obtrusions.

If one thinks for a moment about Lippmann's characterization of news, it seems almost to impel us toward a theory of news as a recognition of those obtrusions—which we have defined as problematic situations. A theory of problematic situations might help to give a systematic cast to the endless varieties of obtrusions that are monitored by the media. At present we lack such a theory.

In acknowledging the need to construct theories to explain what was observed and reported and defined as news, McQuail (1983) suggested that a starting point might be to consider and perhaps to reconcile at least three points of view on the nature of news: one was that of the *journalist*, another was from the perspective of the *reader*, and the third was the view of an *outside observer*. He characterized these approaches as

1. *Commonsense definitions:* These played an important part in the audience's ability to appreciate the nature of news.
2. *Working theories:* These guided the daily routines and observations

of the journalist and news organizations, but although journalists have been taught to "recognize" stories, criteria are stated only loosely and are anecdotal rather than systematic.

3. *Social science theories:* These have been inspired by studies of news as a product of the media in its environment.

Two Norwegian social scientists (Galtung & Ruge, 1965) attempted to bridge these three perspectives by melding commonsense audience perceptions and journalistic characterizations of news. As a first step, they first described news in terms of its most evident properties and common coinage, for example, elements such as novelty, conflict, importance, prominence, and proximity, which give news its commonsense character and reader appeal.

They began this process by wondering why some events rather than others were selected as news. Something was always happening to someone in the world, they reasoned, and since everything could not become news, the media obviously were selecting from among a myriad of events. What rationale could be drawn that would explain those selections?

The simplest explanation, they thought, could be drawn from perception (and cognitive) theories in psychology. Some events, as Lippmann proposed, stuck out more than others because of their character; the more they obtruded in a situation, the more likely they would show up as news blips on the journalistic screen. Lasswell (1948) called this the "surveillance" function of the media.

Galtung and Ruge (1965) identified a number of obtrusions that were most likely to capture the attention of journalists. For one thing, an event was more likely to be recognized as having news value if its life span fit, in terms of time, into the production cycle of the newspaper. Events that were the most violent, least ambiguous, most interpretable culturally (and thus more meaningful); most consistent with what was expected (but nonetheless novel); most consonant with existing values; and most often previously treated as news became current news. Editors kept watch over the news menu and tried to present a balanced fare. Elite persons and nations could be personified more easily for consumption than could nonelites, and negative news was easier for the reader to comprehend than was positive news.

The Norwegians were not content simply to rest their case for a theory of news on their deductions. They tested hypotheses derived from the theory by comparing the news selection processes of four newspapers during international conflicts. They won support for most of their assumptions, but because some reservations were attached to those findings, they suggested that their ideas had to be formulated more explicitly to be tested adequately.

THE TOPICAL APPROACH

One of the most prevalent "commonsense" means of categorizing news has been to label it topically with such terms as *economics*, *energy*, *housing*, *national*, *international*, and so forth. These labels or topics typically have reflected as much the "location" or the "environment" of a story as its meaning, a "classification by convenience" that created its own limitations. It should have been no surprise to editors that stories classified under different topical headings often contained similar dynamics, and stories that were topically the same reflected different dynamics.

The American Society of Newspaper Editors (1982) discovered the implications of these underlying dynamics when they reviewed a study they had commissioned that looked into the ways in which editors, reporters, and readers categorized news topically. Each was asked to assign news stories to topical categories, and their judgments were then compared. Substantial areas of disagreement existed among editors, reporters, and readers concerning how news stories should be categorized. Whereas editors might classify a story as "economics," reporters thought it smacked of "politics." However, readers were not classifying content on those lofty planes; rather, the stories were subjecting them to a number of anxieties, including a sense of uncertainty about their ability to make intelligent budgeting decisions based on the outcomes of economic policies. It became quite clear that similarly designated topics incorporated a broad variety of meanings and behavioral consequences. Few stories reflected a single, unambiguous stimulus.

TOPICALITY AND IDEOLOGY

The problem of topicality has surfaced in a variety of ways, most recently in ideological confrontations among developed and Third World countries about issues of fairness and balance in the international flow of news. The debate began with condemnations of the lack of balance and reciprocity of news flow worldwide and invoked, as well, questions of fairness of content and "objectivity."

The disputants were brought together by UNESCO to produce a conclusive report but foundered on topical and ideological shoals. Whereas Stevenson (1985), a key American participant, pointed to the world flow of news as a generally stable exchange (in topical terms), with the exception of the socialist states, and thus relegated the dispute to a "pseudo debate," Nordenstreng (1985) asserted that the topical approach reflected an ideological position, for topicalization concealed more meaning than it described. The question was not one of quantity but of quality—what stimuli, in terms of meaning and point of view, were implicit in each topical category? The approach taken by Stevenson, he insisted, represented a blind positivism.

> An understanding of foreign countries as reflected in news coverage requires a much more delicate methodology than the simple counting of how much attention is devoted to such categories (in topical terms) as politics, natural catastrophes, etc. . . . the fact that certain aspects of reality lend themselves to convenient measurement does not mean that those aspects are necessarily most essential to our understanding of reality. (p. 634)

The topical approach to news raised other problems as well. For example, the reporting of radical changes in government and natural disasters was widely described as an absorption with "coups and earthquakes" and "bad" rather than "good" news. But contrary to this conventional wisdom, Stevenson found that few stories in any country were explicitly negative or positive. Stevenson referred to an earlier study (Stevenson & Greene, 1980), which concluded that most of what people saw as bias in the news was a function of the expectations that they brought to it. Sreberny-Mohammadi et al. (1985) observed that tone, moral judgments, and political orientations formed the wider ideological frame of reference of each media system and were as important, if not more important, in the construction of social consciousness than the total amount of news coverage described by topical categories.

Proposals for a "meaning" rather than a merely topical approach to news has come from a number of other directions. Schudson (1978) and Schoenbach (1983) endorsed a "cultural hypothesis," which saw news as a reflection of patterns of development and national character. Thus Schudson suggested that Americans in a bountiful environment expected problems to be solved and viewed any failure to solve them as discrepancies worth noting in the form of news. In other words, members of productive societies expected achievement, and failure was news, but in societies that experienced failure, achievement was news.

Schoenbach (1983) concluded that news was an ideological product and thus a construction of meaning. Referring to Galtung and Ruge's (1965) contrast of socialist and capitalist orientations, Schoenbach pointed out that these orientations would lead socialist news to emphasize structures whereas capitalist news would stress personalities. Echoing Schudson (1978), Schoenbach suggested that negative news was worth reporting in societies that took for granted inevitable positive change; however, in cultures in which progress was more elusive, success was news, failure was "olds."

The debate about news has clearly been approached by Third World countries in political and ideological terms. Ogan, Fair, and Shah (1984) characterized this orientation as "a little good news." Ogan and Swift (1982) earlier discovered that about half the stories in all countries—developed and Third World—were positive in tone and only one-fourth actually were critical, a finding that our own data will parallel. Ogan and Swift further noted that private newspapers were more balanced in tone than government-owned or socialist newspapers. But in political and ideological terms there was a substantial need for evidence of success, if not success itself.

Two insightful Third World researchers have also seen behavioral implications in the selection of news. One of them, Vilanilam (1980), pointed out that behavioral dynamics were implicit in topical categorization of development news. He noted that these categories concealed the underlying dynamics of needs, deprivations, and programmatic approaches. Similarly, Aggarwala (1979), a Third World critic, called for news that addressed needs and actual implementation rather than government-inspired development news.

TOWARD A FUNCTIONAL APPROACH

The criticisms of the form and content of news have raised a related question of its usefulness to members of a society. Schulz (1976) advocated a functional approach in which producer values and the individually centered "usefulness" orientations would be brought together. Based on an extensive analysis of West German media, Schulz found general support for the functional approach. He argued that news selectivity (or objectivity) actually represented efforts by journalists to provide audiences with cues for judging the reliability of claims that were made by news sources. Thus events that threatened the system would be dealt with extensively. Gans (1979) constructed his definition of news on those premises:

> news is information which is transmitted from sources to audiences, with journalists...summarizing, refining, and altering what becomes available to them...to make the information suitable for their audiences (p. 80; cited in Schoenbach, 1983, p. 39)

A number of critics do not agree, however, that there is a great degree of emphasis in news on audiences' values. Rather, they offer evidence that journalistic approaches to news actually are more producer than reader or audience oriented. For example, cognitive psychologists Findahl and Hoijer (1981) have noted that the journalistic rules covering the "who, what, when, where, and why" have been used more to guide news gathering and writing than to ensure understanding by audiences. If comprehension were the primary goal of the five-w approach, more emphasis would be placed on the "why." It is the "why," in the shape of causal factors, that gives readers the most understanding of an event. And the "why" is less often stressed than the "who," "what," "when," and "where."

Based on an analysis of comprehension of television news, Robinson and Levy (1986) concluded that the "why," or causal elements, in a story had the most influence on viewers' comprehension because it allowed other elements to be cognitively integrated into an overall story theme. However, the criteria varied with the nature of the story. Some stories required more emphasis on the "who," "what," and "where," whereas other stories, such as reports of foreign policies, required more emphasis on "why" and "what" elements.

Robinson and Levy (1986) raised very practical questions about the impact of the clustering of news that evoked the same cognitive dynamics. For example, the clustering in a single newscast or newspaper page of accidents, crime, and disasters might, because of their cumulative impact, produce a "deadening" effect on audiences. Called "proactive interference," this cognitive effect might cause audiences to tune out more instances of the same dynamic and, as well, reduce news comprehension. Thus news producers must provide more varied menus of meaning for audiences.

FORMALIZING A DYNAMIC OF NEWS

Many of the dynamics of news are intuitively recognized by journalists, but they have not been formulated in terms that permit easy application. We may reconstruct, in more formal terms, the implications for cognitive dynamics that characterize certain "locations" or reporting "beats." Each tends to produce a particular kind of problematic situation that describes the cognitive dynamics that affect audiences in their efforts to assign meaning to news.

For example, the police beat produces reports of crime and social deviance that cause (or promise to bring about) a sense of loss, or deprivation, both to individuals and institutions. A report on a single day may incorporate threats to the person, the loss of objects of material value, or the breakdown of social institutions. Crime news also projects a picture of an unremitting battle between criminals and the law that reflects underlying tensions in the society and contributes to a disturbing perception of social conflict.

The steps that are taken to cope with these deprivations and conflicts have their genesis in the criminal justice system. Robinson and Levy (1986) would argue that the police beat, because of the cumulative nature of its behavioral dynamics, should not be isolated as a source of news. Rather, it should be reported as an aspect of the larger and more behaviorally diverse environment of criminal justice. System reporting would invoke a variety of other behavioral dynamics, such as the ways in which the system takes steps to cope with deprivation and other dysfunctioning. Investigatory and court procedures may be reported as steps toward solutions and seen as part of a more understandable system of criminal justice.

A reporter operating in this larger milieu would be stimulated to explore the environment for variations on otherwise more narrowly defined and constant behavioral dynamics. Robinson and Levy (1986) warned against the deadening of the cognitive processes of reporters as well as readers. Reporters sense this possibility and often are stimulated to find variations on otherwise constant themes.

CONSTRUCTING MEDIA LOGIC

Jensen's (1986) "reception" theory moves us from cognitive dynamics to the institutional dynamics that affect the meaning of news. Jensen concluded that because the newsroom organization had been created to deal with "ritualized" topics, it had, in this way, neglected dimensions of audience "meaning":

> the communication of meaning through the media should be conceived as a sequence which moves from the media institutions through the content to the audience.... At each stage of the communication process, meaning is subject to negotiation and reformulation, and the process does not stop as soon as the message has moved through the channel from sender to recipient. (p. 25)

Jensen (1986) argued that this chain of news production to news consumption produced cumulative distortions in meanings, as selective processes of news gathering and processing became exaggerated by selectivity on the part of media audiences. These selective processes, he argued, reduced greatly the opportunities for building consensus in society.

Altheide (1976), among others, pointed to a complex of economic, organizational, and personal factors that determine the biases built into news reporting. He observed that interactions among business people, political activists, and reporters influence the selection and treatment of news. Indeed, Altheide and Snow (1979) suggested that the processes of news gathering and forms of presentation add up to a "media logic." Only by taking audiences into account, however, could an interplay be created between media logic and what might be observed as "audience logic."

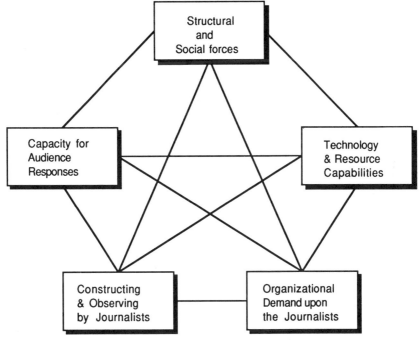

Figure 4.1. Contexts for the Definition of News

A generation of scholars has contributed to a definition of *media logic*. Shoemaker and Mayfield (1987) described the sources of influence on media content as (1) the routines of news gathering, (2) journalists' orientations and attitudes, (3) institutional and social influences, and (4) ideological influences.

We are not too distant from this formulation, as Figure 4.1 indicates. We look first at the structural nature of media, the broad social and technological forces that have influenced the emergence of the media as a social institution, and the organizational and social forces that have defined the capacity of the journalist to observe and report on events. But the conditions that contribute to the construction of news, and the ability of audiences to address meaning in the news, represent the ultimate equation.

We might discuss, briefly, each of these forces:

1. *Structural:* The structuralist view postulates that economic ideologies and ownership have created the social forces that define the nature of news and how it is presented. Structuralists see media as produced by elites for the maintenance of elite values. Gerbner and Gross (1976) proposed a "cultivation hypothesis," in which media,

driven by structural and technological forces, propound and rein-
force normative values.

2. *Technological:* This view proposes that the emergence of new
communication technologies affect (often enhancing) the abilities
of media (notably, print and broadcasting) to construct reality.
Williams (1982) described an emerging electronic environment and
even new modes of living in new societies. Snow (1983) proposed
that the influence of the information environment extends beyond
the more obvious characteristics and constraints of media technologies to ways of thinking. Electronic games, video, and radio
produce a media culture in which reality is constructed and altered
continuously through linguistic strategies that media employ in
interpreting phenomena.

3. *Organizational:* Tunstall (1971) described the impact of the interplay among journalists, news organizations, news sources, and
competitor-colleagues.

   A journalist-sociologist, Warren Breed (1955a, 1955b, 1956,
1958) earlier spurred a generation of resarch on the interplay between the character of the journalist, the social forces that molded
the nature and presentation of news, and external cultural and
social forces that molded the media opinion-leaders. White's
pioneering study (1950) of the "gatekeeper" described problems of
news selection, and Brown (1979) and many others have reconsidered that concept.

   A host of researchers has described the interplay between the
size and nature of news organizations and the values of journalists.
Johnstone, Slawski, and Bowman (1974) described the values of
American journalists; Becker (1979) reassessed those values;
Weaver and Wilhoit (1986) carried out an extensive comparison of
American print and broadcast journalists; and Ettema and Whitney
(1982) collected and presented a range of data describing the pro-
ducer-artist-writer as governed by the media environment—in
music, book publishing, screen acting, commercial and public television, and the press. These pieces are of a genre inspired by Elliott
(1972).

4. *Observational:* Lang and Lang (1960) and Halloran, Murdock, and
Elliott (1970) analyzed how media construct reality by the nature of
their observing techniques. They cited as examples the coverage of
public events such as parades and demonstrations. Kepplinger (our
German colleague) and Roth (1979) described the oil crisis as a
creation of media reality.

Nimmo and Combs (1983), among others, pointed to the construction
of "politically mediated realities." Bennett (1983) described news as the

"politics of illusion": personalized, dramatized, fragmented, and normalized—knowable but meaningless. The journalist is not a conscious observor but is caught up in the process of "objectifying" life and society.

In contrast, an early tradition of research (summarized by Edelstein, 1966) described the many roles of the journalist. Such classic works as White (1950) identified the gatekeeping function; Gieber (1960a, 1960b, 1964) described the many conflicting social and psychological environments of the journalist, weighing desires for personal autonomy against numerous role demands; Swanson (1956) described the journalist as one of a class of publicists; Pool and Shulman (1959) offered insight into how journalists played out their fantasies in the process of news gathering and writing; and Bauer (1964a, 1964b), who described interactions between journalists and their perceived audiences.

More recently Molotch and Lester (1981) looked at news as "purposive behavior" and noted that journalists and media exploit events to fit them into a journalistic rubric. This is a view shared by Tuchman (1973, 1977) who described the "routinization of news" and the function of the journalist as the "objective" form and processes of news gathering.

Capacities of Audiences

Lang and Lang (1971), acknowledging the symbolic environment, have nonetheless advocated examining the responses of individuals to the media. Even with the new and powerful means of visual and audio transmission, communication systems are still human systems and events are still the precipitants of communication processes, although best observed as collective definitions. Thus a cognitive approach to news would occur in a social-psychological environment.

FROM WORKING THEORIES
TO A TESTABLE THEORY

Our purpose is to move conceptually from what McQuail (1983) called "working theories" of news to a "testable theory." Despite the dozens of newswriting texts which have described working theories, it must be said that the question "What is news?" has not been answered in any meaningful way. The fourth edition of a widely used and highly regarded textbook, *News Reporting and Writing*, as does many other assessments, answers the question "What is news?" simply by restating the values that journalists assign to news. These familiar values include the impact or the importance of the event, its timeliness, the prominence of the people involved, the closeness of the event to audiences for news, and elements of conflict, novelty, and contemporariness.

These characterizations reflect McQuail's notion that "working theories" guide the daily routines and observations of journalists and news organizations. But these characterizations actually fall far short of a working *theory*. They actually represent a set of rules, embodied in a loosely held inventory of news values. As a working *theory* such elements should be linked conceptually and describe a system and a hierarchy of values. Most critically, if news values were expressive of a theory, the audiences for news would express their values in similar terms to those of journalists and be guided by the same rules and cognitive values. By contrast, there are numerous criticisms that the world of the journalist does not describe the world of the audiences. Jensen's (1988) reception theory of news, to which we referred earlier, argues that audiences utilize their own strategies for understanding the news, contributing to great differences in understandings of the same news events.

Schramm (1949) very early recognized the need to describe the nature of news in terms of cognitive dynamics. Thus he proposed a construction of audience needs and satisfactions that incorporated "immediate" and "delayed" reward news. The immediate-reward news was the more simple and dramatic and required little exercise of thought either by the journalist who constructed the event or the audience that addressed it. The delayed-reward news implied complexity of content and the need for reflectivity on the part of both journalists and audiences. As Atwood (1970) and others were to point out, while Schramm's idea offered some utility, and seemed to be very promising as a cognitive construct, there were too many instances where immediate rewards for some persons produced no rewards for others and where delayed reward content often brought immediate satisfactions to more sophisticated audiences. Schramm's notion of cognitive process was inviting but his content categories were unreliable.

Following upon a dozen or more efforts to assess the utility of Schramm's theory, two young researchers (Badii and Ward, 1980) concluded that there was a clear "reward" dimension in the nature of news, but they did not validate the "immediate" and "delayed" constructs as Schramm had intended them. Rather, they suggested that whatever the temporal or substantive nature of the reward, it could be rationalized by the journalistic commonsense elements of news of significance, prominence, and normality.

Other than Atwood's (1970) comparison of journalist—audience responses, few other cognitive specifics have been gathered to address the implications of a symbiosis between journalists and their audiences. Bauer (1964a, 1964b) very early spoke of an "anticipation of audience" effect by which the journalist "imagined an interaction" between them. More recently McLeod, Kosicki, and Allen (1987) have suggested a cognitive model of news that incorporates both journalists and audience. Toward this purpose, McLeod and colleagues suggest that the simplistic stimulus-response (SR) model of news should be seen as a more complex process in which audiences bring something to a message and the message brings something to the audience.

McLeod and colleagues suggest, therefore, that any theory of news must incorporate the efforts of media and audiences to process information. They explain that the examination and unravelling of the nature of news and the active processing of news by audiences brings us inevitably into the field of cognitive psychology:

> the analysis of the process and effects of mass communication should study the processing of media messages and how they are structured by various segments of the audience. The free verbal responses of the audience member seems to be data indispensable to such analysis. (p. 4)

A cognitive perspective. McLeod and colleagues asserted, implied a much broader definition of what people get from news other than mere knowledge or data. The representation or meaning of the news content must be assessed, and this must be done from the point of view of the audiences. The emphasis must be placed not only upon actual information processing but on the meaning of news to the communicator and to the audiences. We have offered as a construction of the "meaning" of news of both journalist and audiences the concept of the "problematic situation."

Schramm and Atwood (1984) testified to the need for behaviorally defined rather than topically identified theories of news. In their study of news flow in the Pacific, the two researchers attempted to infer the meaning of news—so-called qualitative dimensions—from a topical analysis of newspapers. But they concluded that the use of topical content categories might not describe how the reader understands or reads the news:

> Economics, for instance, is a "scholar's" word. What we classified as economics the readers were likely to see as money, or finance, or investments, and even to divide these items into foreign and domestic topical subcategories [so they could deal with them in meaning terms].
> A story of an insurance company being cleared of fraud charges was classified by our [the study] coders as a legal and judicial story, whereas the readers apparently thought of it as a financial story.
> Foreign relations also is a scholar's distinction. Readers seemed to think of foreign news items less in terms of international relations and [more] in terms of the dynamics [or meaning] of news, which in most instances has been couched in violence and conflict. (p. 79)

Schramm and Atwood said that they had not given up entirely upon their system of topical categories, but that they had discovered the dangers of equating categorical analysis and readership studies and making inferences as to motivations. What was needed, they concluded, was a system of analysis that would reflect audience interests with the dynamics of news.

As we have suggested, the motivations of audiences and the content of news are best described by problematic situations, and topical categories would fall within those conceptual boundaries. Thus news stories categorized simply as "economics" might imply a number of problematics. One of them would incorporate losses of value that were associated with inflation; another would describe needs for value related to investments. In the same sense, news stories categorized topically as foreign relations could incorporate a number of problematics; one might be dimensions of conflict, while another might address global steps that were being taken toward the solution of world problems.

A cognitive approach to news, as we have suggested, contrasts an "internal" appraisal of news with social analyses of "external" forces. Shoemaker and Mayfield (1987) have incorporated a number of external concepts suggested by Gans (1979) and Gitlin (1980) to build a social theory of news. Incorporating the structural, cultural, and socio-political perspectives we earlier described, a social theory requires news to reflect social reality without distortion, be responsive to social routines, express the influence of journalists' socialization and attitudes, be responsive to structural and technological forces, and reflect ideological positions.

This need to construct a social theory of news does not obviate the need to treat cognitive processes which are utilized by both journalists and audiences. The problematic situation offers a *lingua franca* of news that can be seen within the cognitive framework proposed by McLeod and colleagues. In pragmatic terms, the problematic situation defines the dynamics of news construction and news consumption by addressing directly the internal content and meaning of news. Even as an emerging theory, the problematic situation must meet several conditions, which are listed in Figure 4.2.

---

    *   It must be exclusive as well as inclusive in its meaning;

    *   It must be integrative of concepts;

    *   It must be systematic in its structure, and;

    *   It must be parsimonious as to its description of content.

Figure 4.2. Necessary Conditions for Emerging Theory

We take the view that our theory meets these conditions:

- It is *exclusive* in that it excludes or minimizes other elements such as ritualization.
- It is *inclusive* in that it incorporates elements of news such as importance and prominence, as illustrated in Figure 4.2.
- It is *integrative* in that producer and consumer may be seen in relation to one another as each "problematizes" the news.
- It is *systematic* concerning the relations that are established among problematic situations along meaning and temporal dimensions.
- It is *parsimonious* in its reduction of an infinite number of topical categories to a finite and limited number of meaning categories.
- And, we might add, it is *explanatory* in that it directs itself to meaning elements rather than to categorization (in atheoretical frameworks).

UTILITY OF A THEORY

We believe that theories should also be useful to those whose behavior they explain. The problematic situation offers several possibilities for applications of a pragmatic kind.

- It might provide editors with a limited number of reference points against which judgments of news might be compared.
- It could sensitize journalists to the variety of obtrusions in the environment, aiding in their identification and construction of meaning.
- It might address equivalence in meanings of news to the journalist, to audiences, and to the society.

We offer Figure 4.3 to illustrate the taxonomy of efforts that have been made to map the meaning of news. It runs the range from common-sense elements, to Lippmann's idea of obtrusiveness, to the categorization of news as topics, and thence to our formulation of "news is discrepancy, operationalized by problematic situations."

THE ANALYSIS OF NEWSPAPERS

Our content analyses of newspapers addressed both topics in the news and the meaning of news as defined by problematic situations. We discovered, as had been suggested by Galtung and Ruge (1965), that a single news

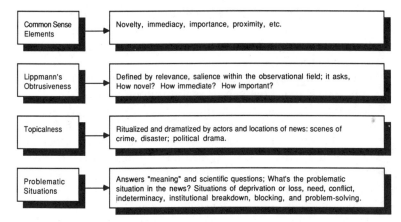

Common Sense Elements	Novelty, immediacy, importance, proximity, etc.
Lippmann's Obtrusiveness	Defined by relevance, salience within the observational field; it asks, How novel? How immediate? How important?
Topicalness	Ritualized and dramatized by actors and locations of news: scenes of crime, disaster; political drama.
Problematic Situations	Answers "meaning" and scientific questions; What's the problematic situation in the news? Situations of deprivation or loss, need, conflict, indeterminacy, institutional breakdown, blocking, and problem-solving.

Figure 4.3. A Taxonomy of Efforts to Map the Meaning of News

story usually incorporated a number of dynamics—in our analyses, a number of problematic situations. Consistent with the Galtung and Ruge theory of the "cumulativeness" of these dynamics contributing to the context and appeal of news, we reasoned that the greater the number of problematic situations present in a story, the more likely it would meet the definition of news and the more likely it would be read.

Our data provided us with assessments of

1. The overall array of problematic situations in the news
2. Their distribution by topics
3. The relationship of headlines to story content, that is, any tendency by headline writers (whether journalists themselves or editors) to emphasize one problematic situation over another
4. The extent of similarities across cultures of definitions of news as problematic situations
5. The presence of culturally defined differences

Our expectations for similarities in the definition of news grew out of our earlier assumptions about the similar structures and functions of newspapers. Habermas (1962), among others, observed that structural determinants such as similar needs for social institutions (including media structures) produce similarities in news content. In our case, this outcome was likely because we were comparing urban daily newspapers from similarly industrialized societies. Habermas observed that media played out this structural role in what he termed the "public sphere." That sphere provides the environment for the society to utilize democratic processes to define goals and means for cooperation between state and public. Media provides the basic ingredient utilized in this process—news.

Our characterization of news will permit us to address implicitly the contention by Habermas (1962) that the media (as one of a number of institutions) compete for autonomy rather than strive for cooperation and integration. It will be interesting to note the extent to which media take a normative perspective in dealing with events that Habermas would see as inviting centripetal social forces to assert themselves.

Operational Steps

In operationalizing our content analysis we noted immediately that news stories were far more detailed in their treatment of social problems than were the descriptions provided by students in survey questionnaires. Without altering our basic conceptualization we were able to capture these nuances by expanding categories rather than reconceptualizing existing ones. In student questionnaires we had combined references to "personal" deprivation, needs, and so on with references to "societal" deprivations and needs. The detailed treatment of news allowed us to categorize items as "individual" and "societal," recombining them as necessary.

For example, we expanded the concept of problem solving to categories that differentiated steps toward solutions from actual problem solving. We added a category of "consequences of problem solving"—incorporating both positive and negative consequences. To illustrate, the Hong Kong *South China Morning Post* reported a solution to housing problems of the elderly that placed them in shelters previously used by "street sleepers"; the negative consequence was that the street sleepers were being forced out into the open again.

One conceptual consideration was that many news reports about such seemingly routine events as meetings, announcements, reports, and so on did not state explicitly that the events were held in response to observable problematic situations, present or future. But it could be reasonably assumed that meetings carried implications of that kind, that is, problematics that created the need for meetings, announcements, and so on or that might, as a consequence, create problems. We coded stories of this kind as "implications for problematic situations."

Finally, in encountering national elections in both Japan and West Germany, we observed a common technique of political campaigning in political cultures where positions were contested—criticisms, on the one hand, and refutation, on the other. Normative Western journalistic practice requires the reporting of accusations of wrongdoing or neglect; it similarly requires the reporting of responses to accusations. Because responses often take the position of denying that problematic situations exist, we adopted a category that we defined as "denial of problematic situations." Denial also was illustrated in a political example, although outside the context of an election. The *South China Morning Post* reported that former President Ferdinand Marcos of the Philippines had "denied" that he or his family was involved in the disappearance of a man who, against the wishes of the family, nonetheless had married his daughter (in secret).

We analyzed newspapers for the six-month period before and during our student interviews. In most cases, we began with the issues of November of the previous year and continued through April, the month of data collection. We were guided by the suggestions of agenda-setting scholars that it may take up to six months for newspapers to establish an agenda for their readers. We did not analyze television, radio, books, or magazines.

In Germany, we selected the *Frankfurter Rundschau*, a national daily of liberal political direction, and the *Allgemeine Zeitung* of Mainz, a newspaper that is also read by students but is more conservative.

In Washington State we selected the *Seattle Times* and *Post-Intelligencer*. Although both newspapers are published in Seattle, each has a statewide circulation; the *Post-Intelligencer*, a morning, daily newspaper, is the most widely circulated statewide.

We chose the *Yomiuri News* and Mainichi Times in Japan; both are national newspapers and are read by university students. Most Japanese daily newspaper circulation is accounted for by five national newspapers.

In Hong Kong we selected the *South China Morning Post*, the English-language newspaper with the largest circulation, and the *Oriental News*, the Chinese-language newspaper with the largest circulation.

We sampled in each newspaper the six most prominent stories beginning on page 1. If there were too few news stories displayed prominently on page 1, we turned to inside pages. We constructed a sample incorporating each day of the week, for example, a Monday paper for the first week, a Tuesday paper the second week, and so forth throughout a week-long publishing cycle. We made 24 coding decisions for each issue of each newspaper—six headlines and three paragraphs in each of the stories, a total of 18 paragraphs.

We classified separately the headlines of each story and the first three paragraphs. Our purpose was to compare the thrust of the headlines with the content of the stories. Did the headline portray the same problematic situation that was represented by the lead of the story? The second or third paragraph? What inferences might be drawn from these decisions by editors?

Some problems of comparability occurred because of different typographical styles of newspapers in some countries. We resolved this problem by coding at least three headlines per story. In some cases newspapers used only one headline; in others, they used several. Some Japanese newspapers "bled" headlines into the text, but they were still coded as headlines because of the typographical emphasis. In a complementary study in Norway (Edelstein & Hoyer, forthcoming) it was noted that *Aftenposten* (*Evening News*) both illustrated and summarized top news stories on page 1, all of which were treated in detail inside the newspaper. In this case we coded the first three problematic situations in each summary, by phrase, rather than the first three paragraphs of each inside story. We had determined previously that the summaries and stories were consistent in their content.

The Findings

Relevance. The analysis of newspaper headlines (of the six dominant stories on page 1) affirmatively answered our question of relevance: Could *all* news stories be coded?

Except for announcements of meetings and similar events as carrying implications for problematic situations, 75 percent (Hong Kong) to 86 percent (U.S.) of the stories on page 1 contained references to the kinds of problematic situations reflected in interviews with students. Other than conflict in the individual and individual needs, all categories were represented.

In adopting our category "implications for problematic situations," we were able to code *all* news stories in *all* newspapers.

Emphasis. We also were able to assess the degree of emphasis accorded to problematic situations and compare tendencies across the four cultures.

As we would expect from a structural hypothesis, there were similarities in the portrayal of problematic situations. For examples, there was far less portrayal of conflict than would be supposed from a perspective of media criticism. Only 10 to 12 percent of headlines across all newspapers stressed social or international conflict. There were, however, instances of blocking of actions involving individuals and bureaucracies. However, even if those actions were defined as forms of conflict, only 15 to 17 percent of all content would be conflictual.

All media devoted a great deal of attention to problem solving. One-fourth of the page 1 headlines in U.S. newspapers described steps toward solutions to problems, and another 7 percent detailed successful outcomes. In all, one-third of the headlines were oriented to solutions. Japanese newspapers devoted 25 percent of their page 1 headlines to steps toward solutions. Hong Kong newspapers devoted 21 percent of their headlines to stories of this kind, although they did not favor all the solutions.

Differences were also observed. These could be attributed largely to events and political cultures. West Germany represented a special case

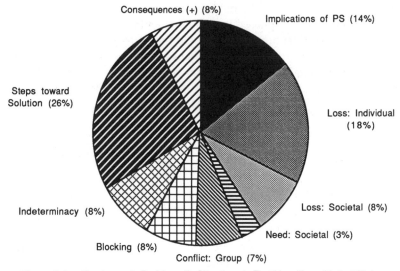

Figure 4.4a. Emphases in Problematic Situations in First Headlines: United States

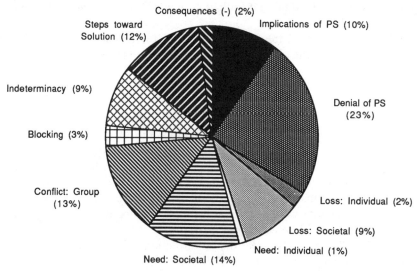

Figure 4.4b. Emphases in Problematic Situations in First Headlines: Germany

because the country was embroiled in a national election in which the more conservative newspaper, the *Mainz Allgemeine Zeitung*, gave prominence to campaign denials of wrongdoing by conservative Chancellor Helmut Kohl. Thus the newspapers reported few steps toward the solution of problems.

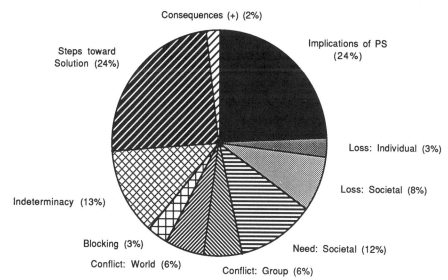

Figure 4.4c. Emphases in Problematic Situations in First Headlines: Japan

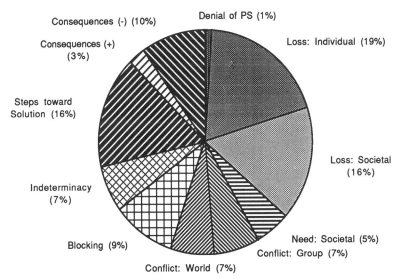

Figure 4.4d. Emphases in Problematic Situations in First Headlines: Hong Kong

As a second variation, both the U.S. and Hong Kong newspapers, more than those in Germany and Japan, stressed individual and societal deprivation. These reports were related to the persistence of such social problems as crime and delinquency and the loss of efficacy of social insti-tutions such as education, health and welfare, and the economy. West German and Japanese students reported many fewer incidences of deprivation, having expressed their personal and societal concerns as needs rather than as deprivations.

Interpretation of Findings

Figures 4.4a to 4.4d (and Table 4.1) lend some support to Habermas' (1962) expectations for evidence of structural homogeniety, which was shown, as we have suggested, by similarities in the distribution of problematic situations. But Habermas' view that institutions competed excessively did not gain an equal measure of support. There were, of course, portrayals of societal conflict, some of which were resolved "unequally." But there were as many instances of losses suffered by individuals as societies, and there were more instances of steps toward solutions than references to social conflict.

Correspondence between Headlines and News Stories

There has always been a sense that the news is sensationalized by headline writers, who are seeking to gain the attention of readers. Thus they emplasize the most sensational elements of the story. To what extent does this commonsense knowledge stand up under scrutiny?

The way in which we addressed this question was to look for variations between portrayal in headlines and in stories. We assumed that reporters are told to introduce the most important element into the lead—that is, the first paragraph—and the headline writer bases the headline on the lead. However, headline writers enjoy some degree of freedom; they must encapsulate in a few words the major elements of the story. On some occasions the headline writer must reach deeper into the story to find a suitable element. It must be recognized, as well, that some reporters write their own headlines. But even if this were the case, the headline writer "puts on another hat" when shifting from writer to editor. The differences that we found would simply make more evident the perceived differences in perception of the functions of headlines versus stories.

Figures 4.5a to 4.5d and Table 4.2 reflect the degree to which the contents of headlines were faithful to the themes developed in lead paragraphs.

The U.S. Pattern: Minimal Variation. A high degree of fidelity in emphasis was found between headlines and leads. There was only a small tendency in headlines to minimize references to indeterminate situations, either because of the difficulty in writing a headline of this kind or because of a belief by editors that indeterminacy does not attract readers.

TABLE 4.1. EMPHASES IN PROBLEMATIC SITUATIONS IN FIRST HEADLINES

	United States	Germany	Japan	Hong Kong
Implications	14	19	25	—
Denial	—	21	—	1
Combined	(14)	(40)	(21)	(26)
Loss (individual)	17	2	3	14
Loss (societal)	8	8	8	12
Combined	(25)	(10)	(11)	(26)
Need (individual)	—	1	—	—
Need (societal)	3	13	12	4
Combined	(3)	(14)	(12)	(4)
Conflict (individual)	—	—	—	—
Conflict (group)	7	12	6	5
Conflict (world)	—	—	6	5
Combined	(10)	(12)	(12)	(10)
Blocking	(7)	(3)	(3)	(7)
Indeterminacy	(8)	(8)	(13)	(5)
Steps toward solutions	25	11	25	12
Consequences of solutions (+)	7	—	2	2
Consequences of solutions (−)	—	2	—	7
Combined	(32)	(13)	(27)	(21)
Totals	99	100	99	99

NOTE: Blanks indicate no data.

TABLE 4.2 DISTRIBUTION OF PROBLEMATIC SITUATIONS BY FIRST HEADLINE AND LEAD PARAGRAPHS

Problematic Situations	United States		Germany		Japan		Hong Kong	
	Headline	Lead	Headline	Lead	Headline	Lead	Headline	Lead
Denial or implications	—	—	—	—	—	—	1	1
	14	13	26	17	21	6	25	13
Loss (individual)	17	19	4	2	2	—	14	17
Loss (society)	8	9	11	10	8	8	12	5
Needs (individual)	—	1	—	—	—	—	—	—
Needs (society)	3	4	17	—	12	15	4	3
Conflict (individual)	—	1	—	21	—	—	—	—
Conflict (domestic)	8	6	10	13	6	14	5	3
Conflict (world)	3	2	—	1	7	8	5	0
Indeterminate situation	8	13	13	8	14	23	5	17
Blocking	7	5	4	4	3	2	7	9
Solutions (steps)	25	22	12	22	25	23	12	22
Positive or negative	—	—	—	—	—	—	7	5
consequences	—	—	(2)	(2)	—	—	2	4
Total consequences	5	5	2	2	2	1	21	31
Totals	99	100	100	100	101	100	100	99

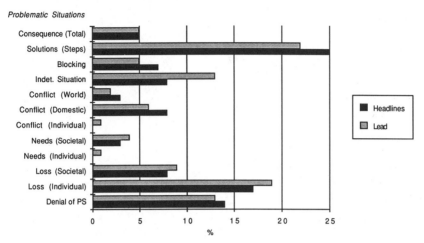

Figure 4.5a. Distribution of Problematic Situations by First Headlines and Lead Paragraphs: United States.

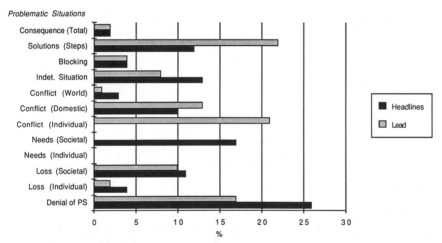

Figure 4.5b. Distribution of Problematic Situations by First Headlines and Lead Paragraphs: Germany.

The German Pattern: Great Variation. In contrast to the U.S. findings, there was great variation between headlines and first paragraphs in Germany, for two reasons: One was the election campaign; the other was artifactual because of the use of several headlines per story, each treating a different element of content. But several of the discrepancies were dramatic in scope. For example, 17 percent of the headlines were keyed to individual needs and orientations, most of them tied to the election. Yet fewer than 1 percent of the first paragraphs emphasized these problematics. The key to

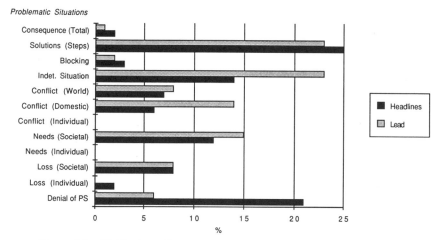

Figure 4.5c. Distribution of Problematic Situations by First Headlines and Lead Paragraphs: Japan.

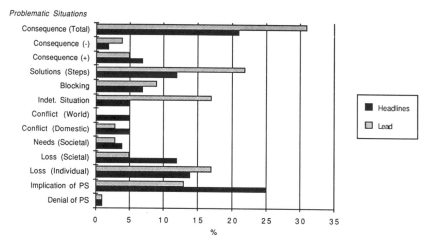

Figure 4.5d. Distribution of Problematic Situations by First Headlines and Lead Paragraphs: Hong Kong.

editorial treatment was found in the category of "conflict within the individual." Some 21 of the first paragraphs were devoted to this condition of internal conflict—in most cases voters trying to make a decision about the election.

The contrast in headlines and stories is particularly interesting in the German case because many of the writers also produced their own headlines. Thus although they began their stories by describing how voters were trying to make decisions, their headlines pointed to the importance of the decisions being made. In this sense the story was subject oriented, whereas the headlines were more audience oriented.

Another discrepancy between headline writing and newswriting was illustrated by our earlier suggestion that it was difficult for an incumbent politician to assert progress during an election campaign. Although 22 percent of the first paragraphs described actual steps that had been taken toward the solution of social problems, only 12 percent of the headlines picked up on this dimension. We inferred that headline writers minimized the significance of steps toward solutions. By the same token, although only 8 percent of the leads described conditions in which individuals or groups were being thwarted, or "blocked," by contending candidates, parties, and governments, 13 percent of the headlines followed this theme.

German headlines also featured more indeterminacy than was reflected in lead paragraphs, an inversion of findings in other countries. The headlines seemed to insist that their subjects cope with uncertainties—which again seemed to indicate that headline writers were consumer as well as subject oriented. Finally, German headlines tended to "neutralize" leads by stressing procedural aspects of events that were not emphasized in the stories; they were more likely to say in a headline that a meeting was held (26 percent) than what actually was reported in the story (17 percent). Once again, the headlines took account of the interests of readers in what was occurring.

The Japanese Pattern: Reducing Conflict and Indeterminacy. The Japanese pattern differed in its emphasis on neutralization and on reducing conflict and indeterminacy. For example, some 21 percent of headlines compared to 6 percent of lead paragraphs mentioned only the "implication" of a problematic situation, in that way minimizing references to actual problematic situations. Headlines also reduced the amount of domestic conflict (6 percent compared with 14 percent in lead paragraphs) and indeterminacy (14 percent compared to 23 percent in leads). In terms of our previous discussion, we might see in both these findings implications of producer-mindedness.

Headlines maintained a high degree of fidelity, however, in relation to other social processes, notably societal losses, societal needs, and steps toward solutions to social problems. These data are particularly noteworthy because they came at a time of regional elections. Perhaps without themselves recognizing it, the media softened the conflict that was inherent in the political process.

The Hong Kong Pattern: Caution in All Things. The Hong Kong headlines demonstrated more caution than did the first paragraphs of leads, again indicating producer-mindedness. For example, 25 percent of the headlines implied that there were only implications of problematic situations, as contrasted to 13 percent of the leads. Similarly, only 5 percent of the headlines pointed to conditions of uncertainty compared to 17 percent of the leads. What was remarkable is that only 12 percent of the headlines described steps toward solutions as compared to 22 percent of the leads. Headline writers were more skeptical about solutions than were reporters. But headlines were more assertive than leads in highlighting social problems such as crime and delinquency when there were deprivations to the individual and the society.

Point of View

Returning to Habermas' (1962) thesis of competing institutions, we look at our data in terms of the points of view represented in the news story. Media logic, as we have suggested, yields control of most of the activity in a news story to the source of the story. Thus it has been said that one should not look to the journalist or even the newspaper for bias in the news but rather to the source of the story. Since government actors and institutions carry out the major tasks of the society, and they are more accessible to media than economic institutions, it was not surprising that government officials and bureaucrats were the major sources of news. Habermas implied that this common condition produced multicultural similarity of news.

A story in the *Seattle Times* illustrated that the source determined not only the focus of the story but also the point of view that explained its treatment as news. A government statement about how the tax base was to be reformed was represented as a step toward a solution to taxation policy. Here the government source controlled the activity. Similar stories that quoted members of Congress on the tax policies and actions that might be taken continued to report from the point of view of the administration. Reports that the proposed tax legislation would not be passed by those chambers were treated as instances of blocking the government action rather than an initiative or a step toward a solution.

Our conceptual approach was to code the story from the point of view of the source that was portrayed as controlling the activity. But if both sets of actors were quoted in the same story, we coded both problematic situations, one of which was steps toward a solution, the other blocking.

A story in the *Hong Kong Standard* described the arrest of two men who had attempted to rob the passengers in a minibus. From the point of view of the initiators of that action, the police, the story reported a normative perception of steps toward the solution of a crime. The police, as representatives of a social institution, were the source of the news report. But from the standpoint of the robbers, who were caught in the act, the arrest represented a blocking of their efforts.

A story in the *Seattle Times* reported that a man convicted of a crime had won a judicial appeal; from his standpoint that was a step toward a solution to a problem. But from the perspective of the police and the prosecution, which earlier had controlled the situation, it was a solution that had failed to be implemented. Habermas (1962) might see this story as an instance of institutions competing with one another for autonomy whereas the media presented the picture of contending forces.

The Good–Bad Argument

We called attention earlier to assertions by Third World nations that Western media presented too much "bad news." Our use of the theory of problematic situations will not resolve that argument, but it may illuminate the observation that judgments about news are not only ideologically bound but also, as Stevenson (1985) suggested, in the eyes of the beholders.

Recognizing the dangers as well as the potential benefits of addressing the "good-bad" argument, we characterized cognitive elements of problematic situations by the most obvious "value" perspectives. We then classified stories as "good news," "bad news," "balanced," and "neutral," concluding as follows.

Implications for Problematic Situations. The absence of any explicitly stated problematic situation suggested neither good nor bad news. Until problematic situations actually were addressed, stories that carried only implications for problematic situations would be characterized as neutral news.

Denial That Problematic Situations Exist. On the face of it, a refutation reports that no problems exist, and in that sense it is good news. Yet the story is linked to an earlier report of bad news. As a process, therefore, a refutation story might be construed as balanced news: The media balanced earlier reports of bad news with the report that there actually was no bad news.

Loss of Value to Individuals and to the Society. Reports of this kind represented deprivations to the individual and to the society and were characterized as bad news.

Needs for Value of Individuals and the Society. On the one hand, such events implied needs, wants, or desires that were not satisfied, and hence might be characterized as bad news; on the other hand, the story reported recognition of a need that might be satisfied at some future time. Since the story carried the implication of both bad news and good news, it was coded as balanced news.

Conflict in the Individual, Group, or Society. The political process of making choice—which is the context in which stories of this kind usually are found—is good news in the sense that it describes a functioning individual; on the other hand, one might view any reports of personal difficulties as bad news.

One may make a similar case for domestic conflict: Strikes, attempted business takeovers, and so on demonstrate that democratic processes are at work. On the other hand, the conflicts are unresolved and various outcomes might pose threats to the individual and to the society.

Similarly with world conflict: Competition in trade, even when there is disagreement and imbalances, may be perceived in favorable terms as the consequences of free and compensating market forces. But there is a negative view, as well. Competition and imbalances may be seen by Third World and socialist nations as inevitable outcomes of a predatory economic order.

Because of the ideological flavor of these categories, we present two different sets of data. One set coded conflict as bad and the other coded it as balanced; that is, there were different outcomes and implications of conflict.

Indeterminacy. Stories that incorporate uncertainties, confusion, ambiguity, and crisis make excessive demands on the individual and may be perceived as bad news. Although in the Western political environment indeterminacy is inevitable and even expected, particularly during election campaigns, we nevertheless coded instances of it as bad news.

Blocking. Some individuals might judge that the veto of a trade bill is good news, whereas others might think it to be bad. Western political cultures would see positive benefits in the exercise of a constitutional right. But socialist and Third World countries view blocking by actors other than the government itself as unwarranted and illegal—hence, bad news.

In the United States the veto by President Reagan of the bill that would limit textile imports from Southeast Asia was viewed by Congress as blocking, and hence bad news; but from the standpoint of Southeast Asian countries, and for the Pacific Northwest in the United States, the veto was good news.

Since it might be argued from a behavioral perspective that any action that is interrupted or held up signals a problem, we coded blocking as both good and bad, and hence balanced, news.

Solutions. Our solution categories describe different steps and stages or problem solving. Taking steps toward solutions was considered to be good news, although we did not address the value of any specific step. Generally speaking, people like to see problems solved. In value-free terms, we coded steps toward solutions as good news.

Consequences of Solutions. There may be negative as well as positive consequences of solutions, hence good or bad news.

Based on these judgments we reconstructed Figures 4.6 and 4.7, and Tables 4.3 and 4.4 to portray problematic situations in headlines as neutral/balanced, bad, and good news.

Figure 4.6 now portrays a virtual balance between the combined categories of balanced neutral and good news as opposed to bad news. The United States and Japan, interestingly, reported the most good news.

Taking an entirely Western perspective, however, Figure 4.7 and Table 4.4 produce a substantially different picture of reality. In this table we have recoded perceptions of social conflict, indeterminacy, and blocking as balanced rather than bad news. And rather than bad news being the dominant category, the emphasis shifts from bad news to balanced news as the dominant category. So-called bad and good news are more or less equivalent in degree. This holds true for all four countries, although the United States may be seen as offering a more balanced agenda.

It becomes tempting at this point to speculate on the implications of our approach for a number of ideological issues related to the dispute over the quality of news. For example, we might speculate about what might be perceived in these tables as "intellectual imperialism" in the export of news?

Let us speculate that news stories that convey underlying assumptions about such values as problem definition and problem solving are exporting

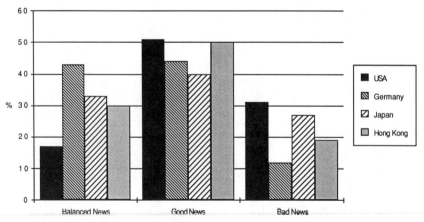

Figure 4.6. Problematic Situations as Good, Balanced, and Bad News: Third World and Socialist Perspectives.

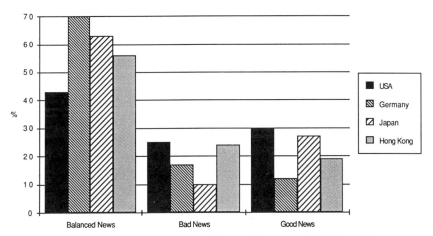

Figure 4.7. Problematic Situations as Good, Balanced, and Bad News: Western Perspective.

TABLE 4.3. PROBLEMATIC SITUATIONS AS GOOD, BALANCED, AND BAD NEWS: THIRD WORLD AND SOCIALIST PERSPECTIVES

Situations	United States	Germany	Japan	Hong Kong
Balanced or neutral news (denial, needs, Implications)	17	43	33	30
Bad news (loss, conflict, indeterminacy, blocking, negative solutions)	51	44	40	50
Good news (solutions)	31	12	27	19
Totals	99	100	99	99

TABLE 4.4. PROBLEMATIC SITUATIONS AS GOOD, BALANCED, AND BAD NEWS: WESTERN PERSPECTIVES

Situations	United States	Germany	Japan	Hong Kong
Balanced or neutral news (denial, indeterminacy, needs, conflict, blocking)	43	70	63	56
Bad news (losses, negative outcomes of solutions)	25	17	10	24
Good news (steps toward solutions; positive outcomes of solutions)	30	12	27	19
Totals	98	99	100	99

these values as elements of culture. Whereas one culture might assume that steps toward the solution of problems are good news, a number of political cultures might take the view that it is important to emphasize first the causes of problems before any steps are taken toward solutions.

The nature of the steps and the openness of the process also are subject to cultural interpretation. Some of the steps that we conceptualized in relation to solutions—negotiation, compromise, due process for the individual (in criminal proceedings), and the exercise of civil rights with protections under the law—quite clearly are threatening and even alien concepts to some Third World and socialist countries. These nations, in part because of their perceived economic and political vulnerabilities, are much more oriented to the rights of the society than to the individual.

SUMMARY

We observed that so-called "working theories" of news, which addressed "inventories of news values" (i.e., elements of importance, prominence, novelty, etc.), described essentially journalistic rules of the road and that audiences did not always construct meaning along those same dimensions. Therefore, a lingua franca of news was required that was utilized similarly by both journalists and audiences. We utilized the cognitive construct of the problematic situation to provide equivalence in the meaning of news to both producers and consumers of news.

Our application of a cognitive framework has pointed to the subjective bases for judgment that have contributed to the debate over the quality of news. As we continue to make clear, the debate cannot easily be resolved, for each point of view is based on radically different conceptions of the role of media in society. No matter how extensive the debate or the remedies proposed, the quality of news will continue to be in the eye of the beholder.

Our cognitive theory of news is consistent with the pioneering ideas of Lippmann, and it extends through the theorizing of Galtung and Ruge and other colleagues. We have transformed topical approaches to news into problematic situations, and we have suggested that journalists and audiences "co-orient" to those problematics that reflect the meaning in the news.

We have explained that the production of news is part of a process of information gathering and processing that is carried out in a broad social context. Structural, technological, and social forces impinge on the work of the journalist.

We conducted a content analysis of issues in newspapers to determine the extent to which we could observe and record problematic situations. We compared our findings across the four cultures. Similarities were explained by the common structures of institutions, including the daily newspaper; we also found differences that we could attribute to cultures and situations.

We reviewed our data to see if they could address such concepts as good and bad news and intellectual imperialism. These characterizations of news have come up repeatedly in media criticism in the international environment. We concluded that good and bad news could be defined from several cognitive perspectives but that evaluations of this kind were subjective. Cognitive aspects of news also fitted into the debate over intellectual imperialism. Western democratic cognitive processes, particularly those that are openly portrayed, run counter to cognitive strategies of both style and substance that are pursued in Third World and socialist countries.

CHAPTER 5

The Problematic Situation as Motivation: Addressing Gaps and Missing Links in Uses and Gratifications

Established in the 1970s as a reaction to the concept of "powerful media," the uses and gratifications approach has sought to establish that American audiences are active, if not powerful, partners in the communication process. From the "uses" perspective the audiences are not merely passive consumers but individuals who select consciously from an array of media and content. From those channels of information and entertainment they satisfy their personal and social needs.

An imposing number of studies over the past two decades seemed to testify to the vitality of this approach. But predictably, as more and more evidence accumulated, critics placed the approach under more careful scrutiny. Some challenged its underlying assumptions; others sought merely to add context and elements of process. Almost all these scholars were American, Israeli, or British, and in some cases they collaborated with one another. The approach was not embraced immediately either in Germany or Japan.

The critics of the approach brought a variety of points of view to the debate. These included functionalism, advanced by American sociologists Charles Wright (1959) and Elihu Katz (Katz, Gurevitch, & Haas 1973), who also is an Israeli; formalism as a means of addressing steps in the process, proposed by Katz, Blumler (British), and Gurevitch (Israeli) (1974); cultural and humanistic perspectives, introduced by McQuail (British) (1985); and a cognitive framework, also proposed by McQuail in the context of cultural and humanistic values.

Earlier McQuail and Gurevitch (1974) and Johnstone (1974), followed by Blumler (1979), had introduced a structural model. This model suggested that the use of mass communication was linked to such factors as the place of the media and their audiences in the economic, political, and social structure, and it linked media uses to critical theories in mass communication.

We try in this chapter to reconcile various points of view and to supply what we consider to be one of the "missing links" in the uses approach—the element of motivation. We suggest that the motivations produced by the problemization of needs may serve to bridge the gaps that critics have said exist between the assessment of needs and the uses of communication to satisfy those needs.

THE FUNCTIONAL APPROACH

As a functionalist, Wright (1959) attempted to accommodate the contending views to one issue—whether, in fact, individuals who were selecting among channels and content truly were autonomous beings as they engaged in those selection processes or if, as seemed also to be the case, they were operating within limited degrees of freedom that were permitted to them by the values of their social group:

> If individuals select certain media, or certain types of content, in their roles as...[students], we gain insight into the relationship between the attributes of the media (real or perceived) and the...functions (individual and social) which they serve. (cited in Katz, Gurevitch, & Haas, 1973, p. 33)

Katz and colleagues offered evidence to show that needs were first generated by individuals, who then looked to the media to help them to satisfy those needs. This step permitted individuals in some cases "to strengthen, to weaken, to acquire, and to contact others" for purposes of gaining information, knowledge, and understanding. In addition, the individual could through the media establish personal credibility, demonstrate self-confidence, and maintain social stability. This conception of "uses" is illustrated in Figure 5.1.

Katz saw each of the media as having different capabilities for making "connections." For example, books were the best means for understanding oneself and film the best medium for enjoyment, followed by television and books. Newspapers most encouraged self-confidence and stability and described "what was going on."

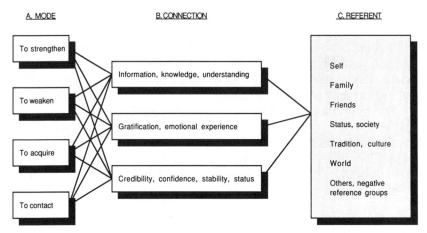

Figure 5.1. Katz's Classification of Media-Related Needs

FORMALISTS AND STEP TAKING

Although accepting, in part, the Katz schema, critics nonetheless raised a number of questions about it. Those whom we might call the "formalists" wondered how Katz's connections could actually be drawn. To establish a connection between the individual's needs and use of media, it must be demonstrated that motivations actually existed and were directed toward that use.

Several of the criticisms of the uses approach came too late to affect many of the studies that had suffered from these limitations. Thus Katz, Blumler, and Gurevitch (1974) concluded that a formal statement was needed to make the uses assumptions more plain and susceptible to testing. Toward this end they specified "necessary and sufficient" conditions under which uses and gratifications might be demonstrated.

The researcher would be required to specify

1. The social and psychological origins of needs
2. The expectations that were held for media that led to their use
3. The conscious selection of media sources that were thought to carry the greatest potential for meeting those needs
4. The actual satisfaction, subsequent to use, that occurred

As Blumler and Katz (1974) restated this approach, connections needed to be established among the audience's motives, expectations of media, and actual uses and gratifications. Each was a necessary although not sufficient condition to establish that uses actually occurred. Sequences of steps as well as the steps themselves also needed to be established so that they might be more easily tracked.

Finally, Blumler (1979) pointed to confusing aspects of the uses and gratifications approach. He wondered if the concept of the "active" audience, used to rationalize the approach, might not actually work to confuse it. The activity element, he suggested, implied more intentionality, prior motivation, selectivity, tastes, and interests than actually might be the case.

HUMANISTIC AND CULTURAL PERSPECTIVES

At the same time, suggestions were made for more humanistic and cultural perspectives. A number of British critics who saw society more in collective than in individual terms objected to the implications that "atomized" individuals made media choices to satisfy privatized needs, that is, needs that did not take into account the concerns of the individual that grew out of the social and cultural environment.

It was McQuail (1985) who suggested that a failure to account for the humanistic and cultural millieu in which motivations occurred represented another gap in the definition of the uses process. Individuals were consumers of culture as well as of information, McQuail pointed out. Thus he did not object to the uses approach itself but only to its failure to specify elements of culture that would place it within the humanistic tradition.

McQuail (1985) defined *culture* in terms that are quite analogous to those we used in Chapter 2, that is, a collective sense on the part of members of a society of values and meanings that are accessible to them *as members of that culture*. McQuail saw individual choice, as an expression of "taste," evident in all cultures. Media content, as well as all other cultural production, was constructed according to a knowledge of an audience's values and tastes and had built-in appeals to individuals as members of audiences. The term *audience* did not represent a simple aggregation of individuals but carried societal implications, which assumed a common core of culture.

McQuail (1985) thus accepted a uses approach that assumed an active, choice-making individual—provided that the choices were culturally framed. The creative acts of artists, designers, musicians, filmmakers, stylists, advertising agencies, editors, commentators, journalists, and so on dipped into that core of culture. Mass communication responded to the anticipated tastes and values of its audiences; it produced culture for consumption, and thus for uses.

McQuail (1985) actually offered two uses models, represented in Figures 5.2 and 5.3. One stresses elements of culture; the other is cognitive

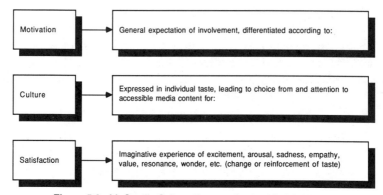

Figure 5.2. McQuail's Culture-Communication Model of Uses

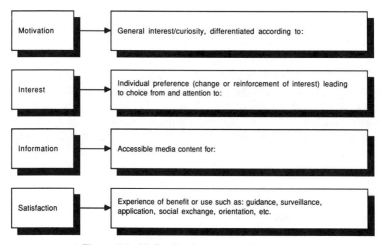

Figure 5.3. McQuail's Cognitive Model of Uses

in that it describes the steps by which the individual processes information of value.

THE STRUCTURAL/CULTURAL PERSPECTIVE

The structural/cultural perspective offered by McQuail and Gurevitch (1974) saw a connection between the social structure and cultural values. Individuals do not operate in a self-contained system. They are connected to various locations in the social structure. Many of the audience's expectations and satisfactions are explained by structural aspects of media, notably their role in the market system and the messages they construct to meet the demands of that system. These exploit the customs, norms, and conventions of societies.

Johnstone (1974) also insisted that members of mass audiences do not experience the media as anonymous and isolated individuals but as members of organized social groups and as participants in a social environment. And Blumler (1979), in turn, proposed that the needs of individuals that are satisfied by media grow out of the social class and place of individuals, and interactions are permitted only in their social environment. Thus structures as well as cultures define appropriate means of using media content.

The German Experience

The German "uses" studies relating to information have not been caught up in the same considerations of motivations and satisfactions as in the United States, Britain, or Israel. Rather, it might be said that German research has approached uses of public affairs information as roughly equivalent in their functioning to media exposure, the uses being more implied than stated.

Illustrative are two studies by Schulz (1976, 1982), which reported that young people consumed more television and radio and local (and tabloid) newspapers than national or qualitative newspapers. This finding was associated as well with greater interpersonal communication, indicating the intimate context in which mass media functioned for students.

Similarly, our colleague Kepplinger (1984) related the uses of mass communication to the disposition of leisure time. Thus he observed that as working hours fell sharply over a period of almost two decades, more leisure time was created. Germans put much of the "new" time into new mass media, notably television. Time spent on all media increased from about 3.1 hours to almost 4.5 hours, most of it going to television and some to radio. In addition, more nonleisure time was also invested in media, in this case radio, newspapers, and television. The enormous increases in time spent with media paralleled changes in the number of acquisitions of television sets and additional purchases of radios. In the two decades the percentage of those who owned TV sets increased from 18 to 83 percent. By 1982 some 98 percent of the population owned TV sets.

Kepplinger abstracted a number of his findings from the work of Keifer (1984), who went on to observe that beginning in 1980 Germans spent less of their newly found leisure time at home and much more of it outside the home. The attrition was greatest among the college educated and the young, and the loss of time was felt primarily by television and newspapers. For the first time in Germany, there was less interest in television than in radio and newspapers.

The implication that gratifications exist for news, but merely have not been greatly studied in *the* Germany, may be drawn from findings generated by Weiss (1978a, 1978b). He related needs to satisfactions associated with books, magazines, newspapers, television, radio, and personal conversations. As we observe of the German students in Chapter 8, interpersonal communication was seen as superior to mass media for satisfaction of most needs. Television most filled needs for entertainment and newspapers for information. Several of the findings satisfied the motivation dimension of the formal uses model.

- Mass media use was most associated with low personal involvement but an interest in topical information.
- In contrast, interpersonal communication was most related to high personal involvement and interests in topical information.
- Finally, all mass media were considered as functionally equivalent information alternatives to one another, but interpersonal communication and books were seen as unique channels of information and communication. The findings by Dehm (1984a, 1984b) that 30 percent of her sample of television viewers could be characterized as "information seekers" led to the conclusion that there was no dichotomy between entertainment and information.

The Japanese Experience

The Japanese context for the study of uses and gratifications is different from that in Germany. Whereas German scholars have not pursued the concept vigorously, Japanese scholars have been both aloof and critical. Writing from the perspective of Japanese culture, the director of the Tokyo University Institute for Press Research, Ikuo Takeuchi (1986), joined the British critics in their evaluation of the uses and gratifications approach.

Takeuchi questioned the purely empirical model and the rational approach that it implied. Uses and gratifications, he observed, operated more clearly in Japan at the structural or social level. He pointed out that although a few Japanese researchers had explored uses and gratifications approaches, a much more substantial and longtime interest had been expressed in the *kokuminsei* approach to studies of national character. These studies took individual behavior into account, but behavior was seen as expressive of personality and social status. This approach assumed more homogeniety than heterogeniety on the part of the audiences.

Takeuchi pointed out that the Institute of Statistical Mathematics (1983) had been conducting basic *kokuminsei* studies through surveys that defined and tracked changes in values and opinions (Hayashi et al. 1982). Only the later surveys extended the scope of the *kokuminsei* studies to answer questions raised by uses and gratifications studies.

It was not surprising that the Hayashi groups should find the formalist criticisms of the uses approach so relevant to their own pursuit of the concept. The Japanese, themselves, had felt it necessary to adopt a formal model, one that would state explicitly the steps that would occur in uses and gratifications as a process. This model would guide their systematic inquiries.

As a first step, the Japanese approach assumed that individuals came to social situations as a consequence of the interaction of their personalities and their place in the social structure; an awareness of those situations then gave rise to needs; the media in some instances became the means for satisfying some needs; and where needs were satisfied by media, the use of media for these purposes might become a habituated behavior.

Testing these assumptions, the Japanese compared American and Japanese students on their needs, satisfactions, and reasons for using media. Similar to our own observations, the Japanese research team concluded that Japanese and American students had similar needs for information, but Japanese students rated more highly the need to acquire information that would help them to know how to act in social situations. Japanese students were more satisfied with television and magazines, but they were less satisfied with radio. In contrast, American students expressed more dissatisfaction with television. One of the findings that forecast our own observations was that the Japanese media satisfied Japanese youths more than American media satisfied their youths, suggesting that in Japan there is a more integrated culture that prescribed more functional roles for the media.

Tokinoya (1986), who has worked with American colleagues, undertook an indirect comparison of findings from his own data obtained in Japan. He compared those with data reported previously for American audiences by Rubin and Rubin (1981, 1982). Tokinoya applied American uses and gratifications questions to a national election, giving special attention to uses of media by the elderly.

As for the uses themselves, Tokinoya found that elderly Japanese used TV content more than Americans as something to talk about, as simply a routine, and because it helped them to forget the tensions of daily life. The elderly American viewers more exploited the inexpensive nature of the entertainment provided by Television and reported that it generated a great deal of excitement in their otherwise constrained lives.

The Hong Kong Tradition

The Hong Kong studies of uses have been uniquely utilitarian. A study of TV homemaking programs (Ha, 1986) tested the concept of involvement as a need and as a generalized motivational state. The study rejected the idea of a *generalized motivational* state that explained attention to the information content of public affairs programs. In contrast, the author provided evidence that demonostrated the satisfaction of needs relating to the utilitarian character of "how-to" programs.

The closest approximation to the American approach was a study by Tang (1986), which addressed need satisfaction and decisional utility in an assessment of the uses and gratifications of TV news. She found that high exposure to TV news meant greater need satisfaction and a greater sense of decisional utility, and the more that people watched the news, the more they discussed it with others.

These findings fit into the formal models of uses and gratifications that have attempted to account for motivations and satisfactions and for uses as a process, rather than restricting uses to the fact of media exposure.

ADDRESSING MISSING LINKS AND GAPS

Although we are not proposing our own formal model, we do utilize our concept of the problematic situation to address one of the criticisms made by the uses critics, that is, that the uses scholars should demonstrate a link among needs, motivations, and other steps in the uses process. Katz, Blumler, and Gurevitch(1974) have been most specific about defining steps that the uses and gratifications approach should demonstrate. These are illustrated in Figure 5.4.

As can be seen, one should first specify the social and psychological origins of needs. Second, one should identify motivations that are linked to those needs, and these motivations should be linked to expectations of rewards. The individual then makes selections among sources of information. That done, satisfactions are experienced through the use of those sources. Let us take these steps one at a time to note now the problematic situation contributes to that process.

MOTIVATION AS A MISSING LINK

One of the most evident missing links in the uses model is the element of motivation. If one thinks in terms of the processes implied by Figure 5.4 one may observe that motivations appear to be a product of both "push"

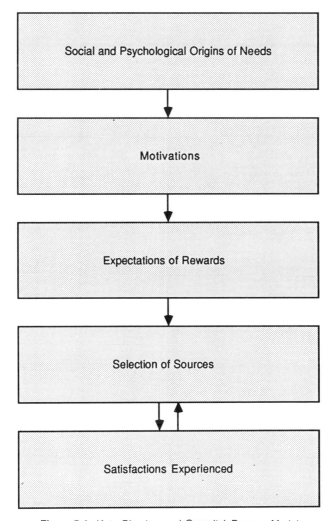

Figure 5.4. Katz, Blumler, and Gurevitch Process Model

and "pull." Push, in our schema, represents the problematic nature of
needs; the problemization of a situation as a need produces a motivation to
address that need. Motivations also are predicated on the expectation of
rewards, which represents the pull. Problemization of need evokes these
processes.

The precedent for treating a need as a motivation state may be found
in Festinger (1957). He postulated need as a product of a perceived discrepancy between expectations and observation. The discrepancy produced
a motivation to resolve the discrepancy. Nonetheless, Festinger's theory

presented difficulties: One is that it defined only a single condition of discrepancy—that of cognitive dissonance. The other was suggested by Carter, Pyszka, and Guerrero (1969). As they put it, it is not enough to be motivated; one must demonstrate the ability to learn and to function on the cognitive level, that is, to construct problematic situations.

As discussed in Chapter 4, our conception of the cognitive process pictured the media as presenting problematic situations in the form of news. Audiences identify and interpret these problematics in a selective manner, in some cases in agreement with the media formulation and in other cases themselves formulating the problematics in different terms. The problematic situations that are in the minds of the audiences, and the problematic situations that are pictured by the media, represent possible bases for making connections between the individual and the media.

The expectations for media use and selectivity of sources were described by Palmgreen (1984) as a scenario in which the individual has decided what he or she expects from the media and evaluates the extent to which those expectations are met. Interestingly, evidence has shown that television most closely approximates in its results what has been expected of it. You get what you see, so to speak, which may be why some audiences select television rather than print. The printed word is less predictable; the process of reading and thinking may generate new questions, which themselves take the form of needs.

Finally, when needs are satisfied, a reinforcing effect occurs and the individual is encouraged to repeat the experience. If a failure occurs, the individual is less likely to use those media again. This result produces discriminations in media use and content choices. In comparing the preferences that the students expressed for media we assume that they were based on expectations that were formed on the basis of experience. Finally, satisfaction with uses is implied by the discriminations made in selection of media and the reasons given for those choices. In many cases the characteristics of media channels were equated with media content; thus the evaluation of content also implied the evaluation of media.

We were encouraged in our cognitive approach by the early work of Weaver (1980). He linked two concepts that are integral to our information-processing approach to the uses of mass communication.

One step that Weaver proposed was that we differentiate between the cognitive activities associated with information processing and the diversionary rewards associated with the gratifications approach.

As a second step. Weaver stressed the motivational element of cognition as it expressed needs for information.

These two elements represented what Weaver termed "need for orientation." It spoke to the need for information that was relevant to a situation and presumed an active audience that assessed its own needs and the relevance of information to the satisfaction of those needs.

Weaver rationalizes the "active" audience in commonsense terms. He points out that while it might be argued that initial exposure to information in mass media often is haphazard, it is difficult to argue that regular exposure, especially to the more demanding print media, would be entirely random. Some degree of selection based upon specific needs should be anticipated.

Weaver introduces a problematic situation—a condition of uncertainty—into his assessment of "need for orientation." A high degree of uncertainty (which we have described as conditions of indeterminacy), coupled with a strong sense of relevance, would produce a high need for orientation in the situation; hence, a motivation would ensue "to use" relevant information.

Weaver reported an important finding for the uses approach. That was that cognitive needs for orientation were more related to newspaper use than were psychological satisfactions associated with participation in politics. The same finding held for the discussion of politics. Thus it could be said that the information processing aspects of politics were more related to media use—particularly newspapers—than were psychological gratifications associated with knowing about politics.

The paradigm that Weaver suggests offers great comparative potential. One might ask to what extent his findings would hold true across political cultures. Are some cultures more attuned to information processing than to the psychological gratifications associated with participation in politics; do these two "uses" covary in some cultures? From our data in Chapter 5, there is the suggestion that uses and gratifications covary in Germany but not in the U.S., Japan, or Hong Kong. A more direct measurement of these effects and the inclusion of a greater diversity of political cultures would lead us to more broadly comparative insights and generalizations.

HUMANISTIC METHODOLOGY

We took steps to permit students to describe events in their own terms—a "humanistic" approach to methodology. We permitted the greatest possible degrees of freedom in both the identification and evaluation of sources of information. We did not suggest sources to students; we required them to suggest their own bases for evaluating the usefulness of their sources. They proposed such attributes of media performance as informational quantity and quality, channel dimensions such as sight and sound, and credibility (reliability, trustworthiness, and accuracy). These attributes described expectations for how the media would perform and judgments about their usefulness in coping with problematic situations. Students not only provided their own criteria for judging media but also described the problematics in their own terms.

This methodological approach also addressed problems of comparison. Because each student in each culture proposed a different problem, we were required to utilize a means of comparison that would rest on conceptual equivalence rather than literal sameness. The conceptual basis of equivalence that was adopted to compare problems was the *importance of each problem to each individual*. Thus comparisons were based on the similarity of the degree of "personal salience" to each student, no matter what the content of the problem.

Finally, we took account of cultural variations by expanding the topical categories to accommodate the concerns of students in each culture. Trade conflicts were most salient to Japanese students, whereas housing was most important to Hong Kong students. In addition to the equivalence of salience, we achieved another kind of comparability by viewing problems as problematic situations. Thus we could compare economic problems to political problems, and social to world problems, if each of these problems invoked a similar problematic situation.

STUDENT PERSPECTIVES

Statements made by students illustrate our approach and permit insight by the reader into the great variety of problems and the problematics that were proposed by students.

An American student said that high interest rates and the lack of a balanced budget were affecting the vitality of the market system; in topical terms, both were economics stories. In terms of problematics, however, he saw high interest rates as a loss of value, whereas his doubts about the vitality of the economy carried implications of a system breakdown.

A German philosophy student said unemployment had created difficulties for students entering the job market. How could there be jobs for them when jobholders were being dismissed? In topical terms this was economics; in problematic terms she saw it as a condition of indeterminacy, or uncertainties.

A Japanese student called attention to trade disputes between Japan and the European Economic Community. The topic was trade, of course, but the problematic was international conflict. She was also concerned that the militalry buildup in Japan—topically domestic politics—was making a dead letter of Article 9 of the Constitution; thus her focus was on a possible breakdown in the social order.

A Chinese student said housing, youth, and the economy were the three most important problems. These have different topical character, but she viewed each problem as representing a form of deprivation; thus the problematic situations were characterized as losses of value.

THE CULTURAL CONTEXT

We also conformed to McQuail's (1985) suggestion that the individual be evaluated in the cultural context. We first examined, however, the equivalence of the social structures, which extended across cultures. The reason was that the equivalence of social groupings, such as college youths, was a major source of similarities in behavior across cultures. Given social structure as a source of equivalence, we looked to cultures and situations for variability.

The structural context allowed us also to extend the relevance of the concept offered by Gerbner and Gross (1976) that the media, responsive to elements of structure, actively cultivated values. In that same sense we could conceive that media also cultivated problematics. Zillman (1980) suggested that coping with media-produced problematics permitted satisfaction to the individual who dealt with them. Rosengren (1986) also incorporated problematics into his concept of uses, addressing problems that were embedded in needs, one of the problematic situations we have conceptualized.

REVIEW AND ANALYSIS

To review briefly, we conceptualized the problematic situation as a cognition that provides the missing link between needs and motivations. The cognition of the problematic situation is necessary to bring about an action state; that is the individual is motivated by the problematic situation to act in some way. We present data that describes how student groups perceived the existence of problematic situations and how they coped with them.

As we have proposed previously, we hypothesized that because of their similar place in the social structure, students would be more alike than different in their perceptions of problematic situations, and differences would be explained by elements of culture and the uniqueness of situations.

The results are presented for each country in two forms. Figures 5.5a through 5.5d describe the distribution of problematic situations for each student group. Figure 5.6 permits easier comparison across each group. As can be seen, we were able to observe many similarities in behavior among the groups.

American, German, and Hong Kong students expressed a similar degree of need as a problematic situation; they also were similar in the extent to which they perceived the existence of institutional breakdowns, that is, failures to deal with broadly based social, economic, and political problems. All four groups paid the same amount of attention to steps that had been taken to bring about solutions to problems.

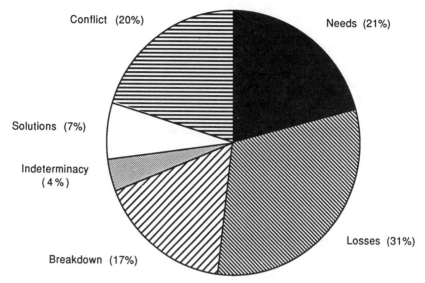

Figure 5.5a. Distribution of Problematic Situations: United States

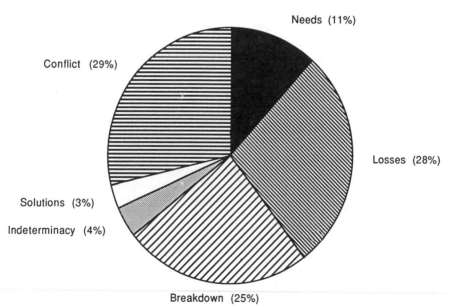

Figure 5.5b. Distribution of Problematic Situations: Germany

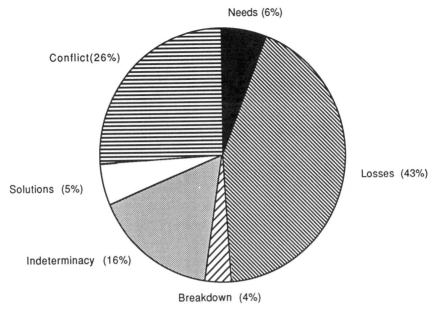

Figure 5.5c. Distribution of Problematic Situations: Japan

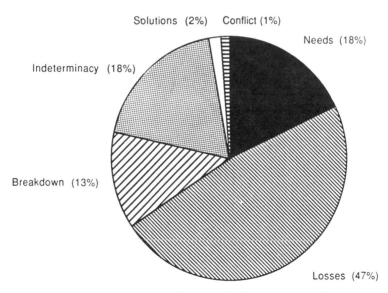

Figure 5.5d. Distribution of Problematic Situations: Hong Kong

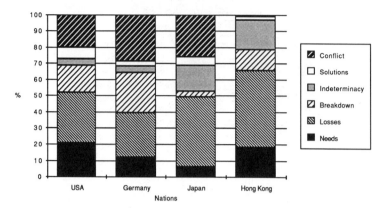

Figure 5.6. Distribution of Problematic Situations

Japanese and Hong Kong students were alike in their recognition of conditions in which losses of value had occurred, and American, German, and Japanese students were similar in identifying indeterminate situations and instances of social conflict.

These and other similarities supported our assumption that the similar places of students in the social structure produced similar outlooks about the functioning of their societies. Acknowledging these similarities, we may also point to cultural variations.

Many fewer Japanese students, as contrasted to the other groups, asserted either personal and societal needs or pointed to breakdowns in institutional functioning. Japanese culture suggests that this confidence in institutions and a sense of well-being produces expectations that needs will be satisfied.

Cultural indicators do not explain the behavior of Hong Kong students, however. They appeared to be governed almost entirely by situational rather than cultural factors. For one thing, they faced the prospect of political indeterminacy caused by the transfer of sovereignty to China to 1997. Conditions of indeterminacy often stifle motivation rather than generate it, as individuals retreat from ambiguity, confusion, and doubt. Thus different problematics carried different implications for motivation and action.

Similarly, Hong Kong students were less motivated to address international conflict, acknowledging their colonial status as a crown colony. Thus whereas many Japanese students were cognizant of conflict about international trade, Hong Kong students found international conflicts to be nearly irrelevant.

Figure 5.6 makes it easier to see that American students expressed the most concern about four problematic situations—a sense of deprivation, an emergence of needs, a breakdown of social institutions, and perceptions of social conflict that emerged from the failure of social policies. We may speculate on the steps by which this process occurred for each of the groups, thus creating an "ideal type."

American students felt deprivations that generated needs. When those needs were not satisfied, they attributed the failure to political, social, and other institutions. They perceived that rather than attending to their needs, these institutions were competing with each other for resources and dominance. This view mirrored perceptions of social conflict as well as the breakdown and failure of valued institutions.

German students were similar to the Americans in that they, too, addressed the same four problematic situations—deprivations, needs, perceptions of social conflict, and breakdowns in social and political institutions—but these cognitions painted a more textually rich cultural scenario than a situational one. The German students felt a sense of economic deprivation that produced unsatisfied needs. This lack was explained by the conviction that the system did not wish to respond to student needs. Social conflict was perceived in group terms, the outs versus the ins.

The hypothetical processes we might infer for Japanese and Hong Kong students are simpler because both groups focused most of their attention on a single problematic situation—a perception of the loss of values that were rooted in the family and group life. These feelings were generated by similar concerns—the tenuousness of relations of self, family, and society as a consequence of social and economic change.

We should add that Japanese students also were concerned with the problematic nature of international social conflict, primarily with regard to trade and nuclear arms. But their ability and motivation to deal with these problems were bounded by the inability or unwillingness of their government and institutions to address them.

In summary, problematic situations permitted motivations to be aroused. But it is important to the uses approach to restate that the motivation to use mass communication depended on students' expectations for content and actual media choices. Selectivity of media to respond to problematic situations was governed by the expectations that students held for those media.

EXPECTATIONS AND MEDIA CHOICES

The discriminations that were made among sources support the suggestion that students held different expectations for each source.

As has been true at each stage of our analysis, students in all cultures tended to be more similar than different in their choice of sources. As

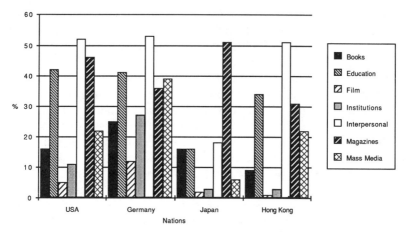

Figure 5.7a. Sources of Information about Problems

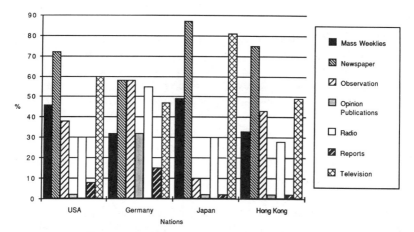

Figure 5.7b. Sources of Information about Problems

shown in Figures 5.7a and 5.7b, all four groups used newspapers and television greatly, and all mentioned films and formal reports about events or policies least. All used mass weeklies to about the same extent, although the character of those weeklies was different.

Three of the four groups relied to the same extent on formal education (Japan excluded), social institutions (Germany excluded), personal observation and interpersonal communication (Japan excluded), radio (Germany excluded), opinion publications (Germany excluded), and books (Hong Kong excluded). The U.S. and Japanese students tended more toward magazines.

Differences that reflected culture and values were seen in the tendency of German students to differ from the other three groups in several ways. For one thing, they cited opinion publications dramatically more than did other students; as we have suggested in our summaries of other studies, they used radio substantially more, and they mentioned institutional sources, official reports, books, and personal observations much more often.

Japanese students also revealed some striking differences. Japanese mass weeklies, known as *shukanshi*, have a unique character, roughly equivalent to a blend of the American *People* magazine and an illustrated tabloid weekly. *Shukanshi* report rumors rather than always telling the truth. But Japanese students were remarkably less likely to report the use of interpersonal communication and personal observation. (We touch on cultural aspects of this situation in Chapter 8.) Japanese students participated in the public process primarily through the mass media.

Hong Kong students ranked lowest in the use of books, perhaps because the fewer Chinese-language books that addressed Hong Kong problems.

COMPARING MEDIA SELECTIVITY: MASS AND QUALITATIVE

Generally speaking, the designation of "qualititative" characterizes media that complement mass media. Whereas mass media work in a limited time frame, qualitiative media exploit a larger context. They employ larger and more professionalized structures, space, talent, and technologies. By comparing qualitiative and mass media we may test Katz's (Katz, Gurevitch & Haas 1973) hypothesis that different needs—problematic situations—are served by different media.

We defined mass media as newspapers, radio, and television and, for the Japanese students, the *Manga* cartoon mass weekly and the *shukanshi* magazines. For qualitative media we combined books, magazines, opinion publications, reports, and educational experiences. Each student got one point for each source named. The greatest number of points possible was five; the fewest was zero. We defined three categories of use, either 0 or 1 mention, 2 mentions, or 3 to 5 mentions. These made up an index for comparison of both mass and qualitative media.

We could then determine the extent to which students used

- Mass and/or qualitative media to connect with what they said was their most important problem (MIP)
- *Mass* media more in relation to one problematic situation than another
- *Qualitative* media more for one kind of problematic situation than another

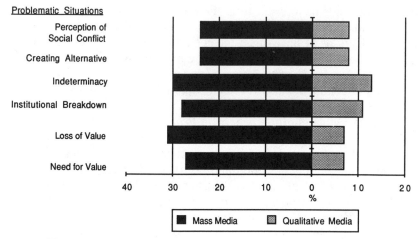

Figure 5.8a. Problematic Situations and High Media Use: United States

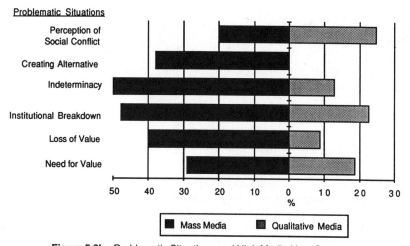

Figure 5.8b. Problematic Situations and High Media Use: Germany

Because mass and qualitative media, qua media, serve similar functions in all societies, we expected to observe similarities in their use across our groups. But media also reflect differences in cultural values and situations.

The uses of media for problematic situations are portrayed in Figures 5.8a to 5.8d. We divided the users into three categories: high, moderate, and low. For purposes of presentation the high-user group was most illustrative.

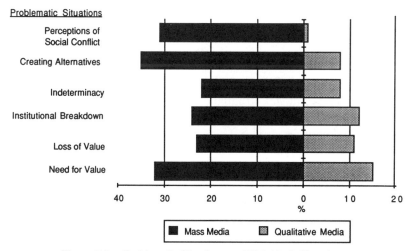

Figure 5.8c. Problematic Situations and High Media Use: Japan

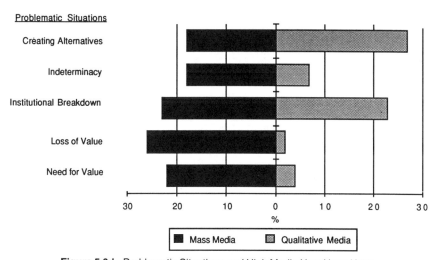

Figure 5.8d. Problematic Situations and High Media Use: Hong Kong

EXPECTATIONS FOR FINDINGS

We entertained our customary hypotheses. Status and role should produce similarities across the groups. These influences were apparent. All groups perceived that mass media and qualitative media gave different degrees of attention to different problematic situations, and all groups said they used mass media much more than qualitative media to connect to problematic situations. But differences that were attributable to cultures and to situations also asserted themselves. These findings may be represented, again, by drawing media use profiles.

U.S. Students: "Bad News Mass Media"

American students perceived that mass media differentiated among problematic situations, but not strikingly. Four problematics—needs, losses, indeterminacy, and social conflict—were most visible. Given the deprivation associated with these, U.S. students might conclude that mass media are "bad news" media.

The picture of qualitative media was somewhat different. Overall, there was less use but a similar degree of differentiation. Less attention was given to personal functioning related to losses and needs for value than to institutional breakdowns, indeterminacy, social conflict, and creating alternatives. Thus qualitative media emphasized societal more than individual values. For mass and qualitative media, we see much more dependence on mass media in all four groups.

German Students: Mass Media as Mirror

German students reflected more variability in uses of both mass and qualitative media. As regards mass media, students saw more attention to conditions of indeterminacy (part of the election process), institutional failures, and loss of values as individuals. These foci expressed contrasting student outlooks. Mass media acknowledged social problems and student deprivation, sought to advance new solutions, and acknowledged needs, but they appeared to minimize social conflict.

Qualitative media there pointed more to social and class conflict. They acknowledged institutional failures and individual needs, but offered no new solutions, nor did they acknowledge sufficiently conditions of indeterminacy and the extent of individual deprivation.

Japanese Students: All Systems Go

Japanese students saw different emphases in mass media on problematic situations. Mass media identified more individual needs, conditions of social conflict, and new alternatives. They dealt less with indeterminacy (despite predictable national elections) and individual deprivation.

Qualitative media minimized social conflict but also expressed relatively great concern for individual needs. There was little differentiation in their attention to problematic situations.

Hong Kong Students: The System Isn't Working

Hong Kong students perceived that mass media did not differentiate greatly among problematic situations, giving most attention to individual deprivation, the needs associated with that condition, and the breakdown of social institutions. They saw much greater differentiation in qualitative media, contrasting their relative concerns with solutions to problems and institutional failures to much less concern with indeterminacy (associated with 1997) and individual concerns.

Figures 5.9a and 5.9b show additional support for the uses perspective that audiences discriminate among sources. Figure 5.9a shows high, medium, and low use for both quantitative and qualitative media and supports our structural hypotheses that patterns will be similar among the four groups. Figure 5.9b shows disproportionate overall use of mass and qualitative media, as representing differentiation in choice. The patterns are similar across groups with the exception of Japan, where there is less discrepancy between use of the two kinds of media.

MEETING EXPECTATIONS

We operationalized "meeting expectations" as a third necessary condition of the formal uses and gratifications model by examining the attributes that students gave to the media. At a means of deriving attributes for the media, students were asked to respond to three sequential questions:

- What sources of information have you used to be informed about this problem?
- Which of the sources that you have named was the most useful?
- Why was this source of information more useful to you than the other sources you have mentioned?

Since the questions were asked subsequent to the media behavior, the attributes given to the media reflected the condition of "having used" rather than "expectations for use" and, in this way, obtained a measure of actual rather than intended use.

Students gave five reasons why sources were useful. Some of the reasons given were similar to those suggested by Katz, Gurevitch & Haas (1973).

1. *Channel dimension, that is, the unique characteristics of each channel of communication:* Television, for example, was characterized by visual factors such as sight, sound, color, and movement. Print media permitted the reader to control the amount and the pace of the stimuli. Radio provided a condensed aural stimulus.
2. *Cognitive processes:* The audience used media to gain understand-

ing, as Katz had suggested, and to engage in comparison and analysis. The implication was an active audience.

3. *Cognitive effects:* The media provided the audience with facts or information. The members of the audience indicated that they used these facts and information as given. The implication was a more passive audience.

4. *Accessibility:* The media were at hand, requiring no great effort on the part of the audience; the TV or radio sets were playing, the newspaper or magazine was subscribed to, and so on.

5. *Reliability:* The media were accurate, trustworthy, credible, and thus reliable.

Some personal accounts illustrated these appraisals:

An American student said his sources of information were TV news, newspapers, magazines and books. Books were his most useful sources because they, rather than newspapers, gave him a sense of participation and of what really was occurring.

A German student said his sources of information were television, newspapers, radio, and leaflets. He was an activist in problems of the environment and NATO. He found daily newspapers to be more useful because they provided more information and clearer background material.

A Japanese student mentioned books, newspapers, and special programs on television as her sources of information. She said the TV special programs were most useful to her because very clear images or impressions were conveyed by the TV screen. Thus she was as involved in the medium as in the message.

A Hong Kong student said that Television Pearl, one of the two English-language stations, was most useful because she could relax and watch the news with her family after a hard day and long trip home by bus to the New Territories. These were channel and access effects.

Channel Dimensions

Three of the four student groups saw significant channel effects, German students for qualitative media and American and Japanese students for mass media—television in each case. Thus German television was perceived as more common than unique as an informational source, while American and Japanese students saw television as a distinctive informational medium. It is interesting that German students saw themselves as more passive cognitive users of mass media, perhaps because of the informational role of television. Overall, German students demonstrated more expectations for each of their media. Six of ten discriminations assigned

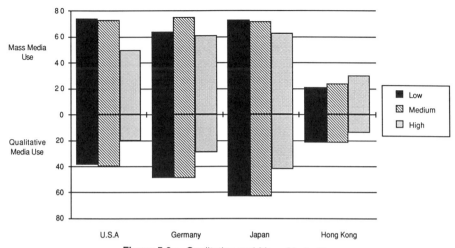

Figure 5.9a. Qualitative and Mass Media Use

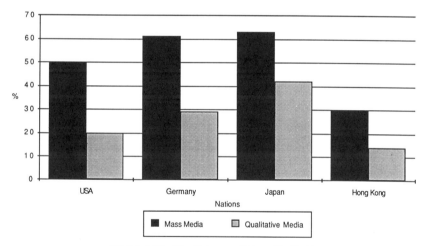

Figure 5.9b. Qualitative and Mass Media Use

media a specific quality, with mass media stimulating their cognitive processes and being distinctively accessible and reliable.

Cognitive Processes

We had conceptualized qualitative media as more reflective and directed at achieving understanding of problems rather than simply informing. American and Japanese students conformed with these expectations. But Ger man students again afforded a contrast. They perceived that mass media were more useful for thinking and understanding, possibly because the students thought alike on many subjects. American and Japanese students, in contrast, did not see their mass media as harbingers of thought. Rather, they acknowledged that qualitative media aided understanding and enlarged perspectives.

Cognitive Effects

Cognitive effects, as contrasted with processes, implied a less active audience and less demanding media. Students would have a sense of being informed rather than learning in a deeper sense. There was less active processing of information.

American and German evaluations contrasted greatly. The U.S. students saw mass media as meeting somewhat less demanding requirements than qualitative media, whereas German students saw mass media as contributing to greater understanding. Qualitative media for German students thus was more passive. But Japanese students saw mass media as more passive than qualitative media and less reflective.

Hong Kong students significantly evaluated their media primarily in terms of providing information, with newspapers more informative than television; but they did not say that the media stimulated them to understand problems to any greater extent.

Accessibility

The value of accessibility was cited by both the American and German students, but Japanese students said media could not be useful simply because they were close at hand.

Different shades of meaning entered into these responses. German students viewed accessibility as availability. Was it more or less difficult to procure in the campus kiosk or in Mainz itself? For the American students it was a matter of convenience. How close at hand was it? In those terms qualitative media were less useful becasue they were not as close at hand. It required effort to gain access to them, whether at a news stand or because of their cost.

Reliability

As we discuss in greater detail in Chapter 6, we did not expect reliability (e.g., source credibility) to explain a great deal of media use. This expectation generally was confirmed across the groups. Only German students found mass media useful because of their reliability. We noted earlier the symbiotic relationship that existed between German students and mass media.

German students just as emphatically rejected reliability as an attribute of qualitative media. The more they used qualitative media, the less likely they were to suggest that those media were reliable. From other data we have inferred that German youths see qualitative media as representative of a political status quo with which they are at odds.

The American students found qualitative media more credible, but again, this belief did not translate into a sympathy with the content; it seems rather, to be a recognition of the status of qualitative media as national media. The Japanese students again did not invoke reliability, suggesting it was not a relevant attribute.

If we look at Figure 5.10 we gain insight into the nature and extent of the uses to which qualitative and mass media were put by our student groups.

The German students, perceiving a sympathetic mass media, utilized four of the five categories of evaluation (cognitive processes, cognitive effects, accessibility, and reliability); they evaluated qualitative media along only two dimensions. The other three groups did not reach the German level of varieties of mass media use, notably Hong Kong students. They used the fewest bases for evaluation of qualitative and mass media among the four student groups. This suggests a less active audience that is relying on the media only for raw information rather than depending upon the media to guide their thinking and decision making.

In our operationalization of "expectations" as "evaluations" we must acknowledge that we are borrowing some meaning; that is to say, evaluations do not address all of the expectations that audiences may have for media. We know that media, as is the case with other institutions, do not

	Germany (N=470)		USA (N=678)		Japan (N=667)		Hong Kong (N=639)	
	Mass	Qual.	Mass	Qual.	Mass	Qual.	Mass	Qual.
Channel Effects	NO	YES	YES	NO*	YES	NO*	NO	NO
Cognitive Processes	YES	NO	NO	YES	NO	YES	NO	NO
Cognitive Effects	YES	YES	NO	NO	YES	NO	YES*	YES*
Accessibility	YES	NO	YES	NO*	NO	NO	NO	NO
Reliability	YES	NO*	NO	YES	NO	NO	NO	NO

*=<.05   Note: All other references to "yes" and "no" indicate tendencies. As examples, German students tended to evaluate mass media on the basis of cognitive effects, accessibility and reliability.

Figure 5.10. Evaluation of Sources of Information

always come up to our expectations. Nonetheless, there is a case to be made that value received must be related to value expected, else little activity, as Weaver (1980) suggested, would occur.

We may also make the case that our cultural and situational analyses have led us to anticipate the nature of the expectations that each student group—as representative of a culture, or responding to critical event—might hold for each of the media. The extent to which this "expectation"—a kind of hypothesis—actually is being met is indicated remarkably by the data for Germany and Hong Kong. The German data reflect cultural attachments by students to mass media, while the seeming neutrality of Hong Kong evaluations points to a persisting political alienation of students from the media and, of course, the system itself.

In considering elements of structure, culture, and situations, we encountered our greatest variability. There was not as much evidence to support the structural hypothesis that because students are similar across cultures they evaluate media similarly. Rather, the variability suggested otherwise. Students may have access to media without having access to the political culture, as appeared to be the case in Germany and Hong Kong. In Hong Kong students apparently felt that they had access to neither the press nor the political structure. Only American students did not make distinctions between access to the political and media systems, as distinctive entities.

SUMMARY

We reviewed several approaches to uses and gratifications research, focusing on missing links and gaps pointed to by critics of the approach. We addressed those criticisms by proposing the problematic situation as producing a motivational state, thus providing a missing link in a formal analysis. Gaps were represented by the lack of critical, humanistic, and cultural perspectives. We proposed our methodological approach as humanistic in its procedures.

We summarized approaches to uses and gratifications research in Japan (an emerging formalist model), Germany (largely treated as simple exposure to media, with gratifications inferred), and Hong Kong (a synthesis of the American and German models).

We compared the four student groups to derive generalizations concerning their uses of and gratifications from information. We found that their media behavior could be characterized as produced by needs, energized by motivations, and guided by expectations and evaluations of sources of information. This result met, to a considerable extent, the demands of a formal model.

CHAPTER 6

Multicultural Perspectives on the Credibility Factor

The study of how people evaluate the credibility of their sources of information has a considerable history in the United States, and similar studies have been conducted in Germany and Japan. More recent studies in Japan and the United States have caused a significant reversal in thinking about credibility. Where once credibility was a narrowly defined concept that centered solely on considerations of accuracy and reliability, it is now being approached in both Japan and the United States in more contextual terms as an expression of cultural forms as well as professional media considerations.

Credibility has been linked as well to the concept of uses, an instrumental or functional approach, as discussed in Chapter 5. The individual has purposes and motivations that guide the use of communication. In this process communication may represent the active processing of information or, in some cases, its relatively passive acceptance. The source of information is more or less credible and accessible to the user. And as a very important consideration, each source of information—print, picture, and sound—has its own unique capabilities as a medium of communication.

In Germany, mass media, particularly, have been viewed by students as their intellectual allies in a variety of situations in which there have been demands for the solution of social problems and the establishment of social justice. In Japan, the culture has brought to the concept of credibility questions about the intimacy of the relations that should exist between the media and the public. Thus credibility no longer is limited to elements of factual accuracy but includes an evaluation of the conduct and performance of media as these might affect the pursuit of dignity and harmony in life by the individual. A similar extension of the concept has occurred in the United States to the extent that credibility refers to ethical as well as to performance aspects of media.

These developments pose a challenge to the comparative process, which proposes that we should discover common concerns about media performance and compare them to the expectations held for the media. To what extent do individuals in different cultures develop common expectations for media performance? On what bases are judgments made? How insistent is the public in all societies that media respect the rights of individuals and take into account social norms?

The comparative context becomes a means of gaining insight into the common bases in cultures for the evaluation of media. We may observe whether all cultures have seen the emergence of a broader relevance for a once narrowly defined concept of credibility, once defined primarily in terms of the attributes of the source of the communication—its status, power, and prestige—evolving later into criteria of reliability, trustworthiness, accuracy, and factual presentation. Charting that path comparatively gives us deeper insight into the growth of a concept.

THE LONGEST HISTORY

Of our four media systems, the concept of credibility has the longest research history in the United States. Credibility emerged as a powerful question as a consequence of World War II studies on communication and persuasion, typified by the experimental work of Hovland, Janis, and Kelly (1953). Hovland believed that when sources were credible they also influenced the audiences' attitudes toward the channels through which messages were transmitted. At that time the Hovland group focused attention on the speaker who was conveying the message, either in person or by film or print. Some credibility effects were attributed to the character of the speakers and some were attributed to the channels themselves.

Hovland and his colleagues had generated their research in response to political forces and conditions. Societies in mortal conflict looked to the credibility of their leaders for definitions of reality. After the war, it was logical that the concept of credibility would be transported from the political to the economic marketplace. Now credibility of the source was to refer more to mass media channels such as television and newspapers than to leaflets or films. A new question was framed: Which of the major media in the increasingly competitive media market—newspapers, television, radio, and magazines—could most be believed?

Television's emergence as the newest market force led it to compete with newspapers and magazines for audiences and prestige. One way in which it proceeded was to seek knowledge about itself in relation to its rapidly expanding audiences. Conscious of its visual appeal and its freshness as a medium, television found to its delight that the criterion of credibility was an advantageous way to assess its impact on audiences. The Television Information Office, the association that speaks for the television industry, hired Roper (1985) to conduct comparative studies of media.

The Roper polls were soon to supplant in the public consciousness the studies of newspaper effectiveness that were reported in 1958 and 1961 in behalf of publishers by the distinguished pollster George Gallup. The Gallup studies had shown newspapers to be the best source of both local and world news. But even Gallup acknowledged in 1961 that television was emerging as an important source of world news. In Gallup's own effort to address the credibility factor, newspapers could take comfort from the fact that about 70 percent of the respondents in each survey said that newspapers were accurate with respect to facts. This was the narrowest basis possible for defining credibility.

THE EMERGENCE OF THE USES APPROACH

It was the Roper (1985) organization that saw the advantage of extending the meaning of accuracy to that of credibility. It also linked credibility to the concept of how much audiences used each of the media. Thus Roper asked audiences to tell his interviewers where they got most of their news. Audiences were asked to rate the credibility of each source—newspapers, television, magazines, radio, and people—in relation to how much they depended on it. The report that Roper gave to the Television Information Office and distributed to the public was to surprise everyone who had expected newspapers to continue to be portrayed as the dominant medium. As more people bought TV sets and used them, they also adopted new evaluative criteria for news.

The first Roper results were strongly suggestive of later outcomes. Only 57 percent of respondents said newspapers were the sources of most of their news, whereas television was named by 51 percent—a much smaller gap than was anticipated. Radio was named by 34 percent, magazines by 8 percent, and people by 4 percent. By 1967 the rankings were reversed. Some 64 percent named television and only 55 percent newspapers (some people named both sources). On the next sampling television retained 64 percent, whereas newspapers dropped to 40 percent.

The assessment by audiences of the credibility of each source paralleled responses to the uses question. Again, at the outset, newspapers were narrowly favored. Some 32 percent said that in a situation in which there were conflicting reports of the same event they would most believe news-papers, and 29 percent said they would most believe television. But as more TV sets were placed in use and people spent more time with their TV sets, the picture had changed. By 1964 some 36 percent said that they would believe television, and only 24 percent said newspapers. Ten years later 51 percent said they would believe television, and only 22 percent said newspapers. By 1984 the figures stabilized at 53 percent and 24 percent. Because these trends had been plotted over a 25-year period, they themselves achieved credibility. Yet a stream of studies by social scientists questioned the conceptual bases of the credibility and uses questions and the methodological procedures that produced such surprising data.

EXPANDING THE CONCEPT

Despite the great differences that Roper began to demonstrate between television and newspapers, his findings flew in the face of conventional wisdom. Granted that logic dictated that if news was news, differences in perceptions of it must be attributed to the differing nature of the channels. But was the criterion of credibility the only concept relevant to comparisons of media performance? Since television more easily invoked visual images, might not this feature give the medium an unfair advantage? And more important, might not credibility incorporate more complex responses than the phrasing of the question implied?

Lee (1978), who had set out to assess credibility in keeping with the Roper approach, therefore was not surprised to discover that his respondents perceived television as more trustworthy than newspapers. But Lee did become surprised as he carried out his analysis to discover that a meaning dimension also emerged that only could be described as "intimacy," that is, a special relationship of news to the individual. Lee concluded that news was not simply news "but a product that had become an intimate part of our lives."

SOME METHODOLOGICAL QUESTIONS

Other scholars wondered about the constraints placed on the individual by the framing of the Roper questions. In a comparative study that enquired into the uses of information by the individual, Edelstein (1974) made a distinction between reports about trivial events and important problems. When this criterion of importance was utilized, the Roper results were reversed. Newspapers became more useful. What made these data persuasive was that they were consistent across three cultural groupings—in Belgrade and Ljubljana in Yugoslavia and in Seattle, Washington. Newspapers in all three settings were used as much or more than television for addressing important problems.

Edelstein (1974) was surprised, in turn, to discover that when respondents were given the opportunity to link credibility to uses they failed to dc so. Very few respondents volunteered credibility as a reason for finding television or newspapers useful. Rather, all respondents in the three cultures characterized the media in other terms. They differentiated among the media on the basis of their effectiveness as conveyors of information and images. Each medium delivered the messages in a different form.

THE APPEALS OF TELEVISION

Television, however, in its easily accessible and dramatic form, provoked unique emotional and humanistic responses. Andreoli and Worchel (1978) demonstrated that television alone, among other media, had a greater impact when audiences perceived it as trustworthy and had inversely less effect when it was perceived as untrustworthy. In that these findings applied exclusively to television, not to other media, the medium appeared to be the message.

Keating (1972) provided a partial explanation of this phenomenon. He observed that television magnified the characteristics of the communicator. Indentification with a live actor personalized the communication process and contributed to higher ratings for trustworthiness, expertise, attractiveness, and other attributes of the communicator. Keating at the same time observed different learning patterns: Television produced more immediate learning effects but was less effective when messages were complex.

Several investigators saw related dimensions of credibility, one of which was the extent of "criticalness" that individuals were able to bring to a medium. For example, Greenberg (1966) and Mulder (1980) found that their respondents had different perceptions of the functions of two media. They viewed television primarily as an entertainment medium and newspapers as an information medium. Since television was viewed primarily as a medium of entertainment, viewers were not as likely to look for errors.

Other investigators (Chaiken & Eagley, 1976) also found that the stimuli of television were distracting and impaired the critical capacities of audiences. In contrast, when audiences actively sought out information in newspapers, they were less critical of the content. Thus sensory or entertainment involvement with television, and active seeking of information in newspapers, each worked in its own fashion to reduce the criticism of audiences.

MULTIDIMENSIONAL PERSPECTIVES

Another step toward demonstrating the multidimensional nature of credibility was taken by Gaziano and McGrath (1986). They observed that perceptions of credibility extended to the ability of the media to be responsive to public views and to "morality" in the selection and treatment of actors in the news. In their ability to take the view of the public, the ratings given to daily newspapers and television were more similar than different.

Among the differences, however, newspapers were rated higher with respect to responding to their readers' interests, telling the whole story, and being concerned for the broader public interest. Understandably, heavy television users thought television to be more credible, and high newspaper users thought newspapers were more credible. Gaziano and McGrath (1986) also were able to link attitudes toward credibility to the relationships of journalists to their communities. Journalists, as a group, differed in their characteristics and values from the norms of the local community, which had an effect on their credibility.

A study by Richardson, Detweiler, and Bush (1988) has confirmed that one source of the perceived credibility of the newspapers is the "social distance" that people feel between themselves and those media. This promoted the idea that, where publics feel that the media are expressing community values and advancing community goals, the publics will not only be more appreciative of the media but more trustful as well.

Alarm therefore has been expressed that journalists are fighting a hopeless cause, because the character of any profession tends to isolate members of that profession from other groups in society. Thus as Breed (1955) first put it, "ingroupness" developed in the newsroom, and "social controls" defined the values and the performance of the journalist.

A study by Burgoon, Burgoon, and Atkin (1982) noted that, while most journalists maintained "public" contacts, there were groups among them who engaged in substantially more communication with their peers than with members of the local community. To the degree that this existed, there would be less of a sense among members of the community that the newspaper reflected their values and upheld their standards. Thus credibility would be reduced.

The researchers concluded:

> a substantial subset of journalists are insulated from their publics. This is particularly true of editors and young staffers. (cited in Richardson, Detweiler, and Bush, 1988, p. 7)

A substantial number of American researchers have pursued this question of the impact of professionalism on contacts with publics and the implications for media credibility. The extent of the expression of this interest might suggest that this consideration of credibility is endemic only in America.

A comparative perspective might argue otherwise, however. It would suggest that where journalism is pursued in any society according to a code of professionally determined values, it would fall prey to the creation of social distance between the media and their publics. By the same token, where journalists could find acceptance by corresponding elites, the loss of credibility might be minimized. Journalists and other elites would exchange the benefits of their associations, although they could not escape, at the same time, being constrained by them.

A distinguished journalist–scholar returned to the observations made by Gaziano and McGrath (1987) to emphasize the significance of the bonding of the newspaper to the community as an element of credibility. Meyer (1988) told an international meeting of public opinion scholars in Barcelona, Spain, that the two essential elements of credibility in the American context were the commonly recognized and interrelated factors of accuracy and objectivity, on the one hand, and community consciousness, on the other. What was more, community was bound up intimately with the elements of accuracy and objectivity. Viewed in relation to the expressions of regard for personal and community consciousness by media in our Japanese data, the findings by Meyer suggest multicultural analyses that would compare the relationships between perceived accuracy and objectivity of the media and perceptions that they reflect a sense of community.

CREDIBILITY OR CREDULITY?

A contrasting view of credibility has suggested that, coupled with attention to the functioning of media, it might also be well to give attention to the capacities of audiences. Thus Edelstein and Tefft (1973) asked if "credulity," as contrasted to "credibility," might not explain some of the results of credibility studies.

This view dictated that research attention be shifted from the media as a source to the needs and capabilities of individuals who were using media content. A sample of readers of a small daily newspaper in Washington State was asked if there were anything about Watergate (the Nixon administration's coverup political scandal) *that they found hard to believe.* Almost every person found at least one thing hard to believe, and many persons listed two or more things. Very few (no more than 13 percent) attributed their problems to a lack of credibility of the media. Yet the media were the major sources of information.

The failure of respondents to refer to credibility established for

Edelstein and Tefft that what had passed in many studies as a problem of *source credibility* might well have been a problem of *respondent credulity*. They suggested that rather than ask if the individual trusted the media, researchers should ask if the individual trusted oneself. When a person said, "That's incredible!" it described oneself and not the source.

There are other ways in which the message resides in the audience rather than in the message but which ultimately may affect media credibility. An instance of this was revealed in a study of the relationships of media criticism of government to people's trust in government.

A group of political scientists (Miller, Goldenberg, and Erbring, 1979) found that readership of a newspaper that was critical of government resulted in public distrust of government. This, in turn, was intensified by the degree of partisanship felt by audiences; if the other political party was criticized, audiences mistrusted the government even more.

The political scientists were surprised by some of the results. For one thing, although it appeared that the media in most instances had been very restrained in their criticism of highly corrupt government practices, as in the case of Watergate, the effect of the media criticism was to produce marked distrust of government. Further, even though the media held individuals, rather than government itself, responsible for the corrupt practices, the public still distrusted the government as a political institution. Apparently the people feared the government's capacity to do harm more than that of any individual.

In effect, publics distrust institutions more than individuals, no matter the situation. Publics sought to impute generalized wrongdoing to the institutions more than to the individuals. In this context, the media, as institutions, would not themselves escape distrust. As we have suggested, the message—"blame the institutions"—was in the public, not in the media, which had been restrained in their criticisms.

LEARNING, NOT CREDIBILITY

Robinson and Levy (1986) took a parallel course to the Edelstein and Tefft (1973) study in that they did not impose the concept of credibility on their audiences. Rather than asking about uses or credibility, the two researchers asked about "learning." How much did audiences learn about the world from television news? A number of qualitative differences emerged between those who read newspapers and those who were more dependent on television.

The newspaper readers demonstrated a broader use of vocabulary, possessed more information at similar educational levels, were more likely to recall information in the news, and were more aware of issues in an election campaign. Newspaper readers were also more familiar with the identities of major news figures and were more likely to discuss news. Finally, they did more political reasoning and expressed a longer time perspective on news and personalities.

However, a comparative study of magazines in three countries, one of them in Germany, suggested that audiences appraised their media in over-all terms. Johnson (1984) identified evaluative clusters that included edi-torial tone, communication potential, and perceived utility. Only editorial tone incorporated the element of credibility of the medium, which itself was judged on the basis of its perceived intentions with regard to the giving of information. But Burgoon and Burgoon (1980) said that a critical factor in determining the overall appraisal of the source was its perceived fair-mindedness, and that perceived accuracy, also a credibility factor, was important whatever the perception of the informational motives of the source.

Johnson's findings in Germany help us in two ways. First, they de-monstrate that credibility is a multicultural concept which must be taken into account in doing comparative analysis. The implicit lesson from this is that nations have something to learn from one another about publics' per-ceptions of media. Social factors that affect media credibility, particularly those that contribute to changes in the social meaning of the concept, will emerge similarly in equivalent societies. In comparing post-industrial or information societies we may expect credibility to take on a similar charac-ter, given the cultural and situational differences that might assert them-selves in each case.

We should see evidence that West Germans see their media "whole" as indicative, as well, of what we might observe in the United States, Japan, and Hong Kong. In Johnson's study he observed that the Germans assigned credibility to the media in terms of what they perceived as the media's broader intentions and performance, including motives that might go beyond the mere provision of information.

Considerations of this kind should be taken into account in assessing our own data. We will not suggest that media credibility is not an important variable; rather, the evidence suggests that credibility cannot be viewed in isolation from other aspects of press performance. A path, so to speak, usually may be drawn between the content and performance of the media and the ways in which they are used, and trusted.

A 1982 report by the American Society of Newspaper Editors noted that readers were capable of drawing a line between viewpoints of the editors of newspapers, news as editorial content, and views held by the readers themselves. About seven of ten readers were able to assess the opinion orientations of their newspapers. They evaluated their newspaper's political orientation, its degree of objectivity and fairness, its breadth of perspective, and its consistency with their own views.

Again, two lessons may be drawn. One is that publics feel that they are able to assess their newspapers and are likely to do this along many dimensions. The other observation that can be made is that these dimensions often interact with one another in ways that make credibility a complex rather than a simplistic concept, one that is likely to be more similar than different across cultures. However, this is not to deny cultural factors nor the impact of unique circumstances that influence the performance of media in societies at particular times.

Addressing the question of the relevance of the credibility factor, Gaziano (1988) concluded from a review of four major surveys of public attitudes conducted during 1985 that there was no crisis of confidence in the media. The researcher summarized the results of four industry-sponsored surveys and concluded that publics held a generally favorable impression of the media. Within media, as we have ourselves concluded and as Edelstein (1974) previously has reported, television is better regarded than newspapers on less important problems, but newspapers were rated more highly than other media when topics were complex.

The question of credibility went far beyond the more limited perspective of accuracy to larger conceptions of fairness in the treatment of political figures and institutions, invasion of privacy, and sometimes abuse of the average citizen. In these emerging situations the public believes that the media could report more accurately and impartially. At the same time, the public strongly supported the media as the watchdog of government.

These somewhat conflicting views contribute to the sense of a society in transition that is experiencing tensions between social institutions. The media seemingly have moved into unanticipated social environments where social institutions have broken down, in part because public figures have failed to come up to the standards of the society. Yet the institutions that have suffered these losses have failed to cope with the problems. In these cases, where the media have in the course of events intervened in the process, objections have been raised as to their actions. It is a dilemma that may face all societies where institutions—such as government and media—confront one another, and it represents a social environment which may be multicultural and which thus invites comparative analysis.

An extensive study by Izard (1985) asked the extent to which media were perceived as covering up stories, violating the privacy of individuals in the gathering and publishing of news, and placing the selling of newspapers ahead of other values. Were journalists too argumentative in their tactics, did they lack real autonomy as journalists, were they accurate, and did they sometimes contrive information? Izard decided that audiences judged the media on their treatment of sensitive issues and their relations with the government.

All these studies—and many others—provided the backdrop against which a concerned American publishing industry decided itself to explore the nature and scope of the credibility factor. A little earlier, the Japanese Association of Newspaper Publishers had decided on the same course of action.

EVOLVING PROFESSIONAL CONCERNS

It was a fear that the public distrusted the news media that led the American Society of Newspaper Editors (ASNE) (1985) to take a broader view of credibility as a concept. The study explored credibility as it related to audiences' conceptions of press performance on social issues such as privacy, personal interests and the public interest, the well-being of the community, and the capabilities of journalists.

The society discovered that the 18-to-24 age group gave lower credibility scores to newspapers and higher scores to television than did older groups. One reason was that the younger group was reading newspapers less than the older groups and watching television more. Credibility scores were tied to the amount of attention given to media—the more time spent watching television or reading newspapers, the more credibility was accorded to each.

Other press agencies conducted similar studies. The *Los Angeles Times Poll* (1985) addressed perceptions of political bias, evaluations of media performance, accuracy, social responsibility, and the press role as a critic of government. The Gannett Center (1985) studied public knowledge, media use, and personal experience with the media as components of credibility and public opinion. The *Washington Post Poll* (1981) earlier had identified sharp public complaints about media invasion of the private as well as the public domain. A majority said that the media invaded the privacy of individual citizens, interjected too much of their own opinions into the news, and didn't care much what people thought. The ASNE study was less severe on media but the same broad concerns emerged.

THE GERMAN CONTEXT:
FOLLOWERS AND CRITICS

Most empirical studies of the credibility of the media have been in the American pattern, but critical and analytical studies have addressed links as well as gaps in understanding among the media, their audiences, and social critics. German youths, and university students in particular, developed an early intellectual and ideological attachment to those mass media that supported their attempts to intervene in the political process. Yet students have played an intellectual role in the evolution of media criticism as well. Acknowledging the persisting intellectual attachment of German youths to newspapers, Kepplinger (1983) described the heightened criticism as "decreasing approval" rather than marked negativeness.

Noelle-Neumann and Piel over the period 1978–83 (1983) asked the German public questions about media credibility, eliciting a remarkable 59 percent who found television more credible, followed by newspapers at only 12 percent.

Kepplinger (1984) asked about the completeness, the truth, the speed, and the ease of understanding of mass media. Again, television got the best ratings, followed by (public) radio and newspapers, but these ratings were less favorable than in previous years—a period from 1964 to 1980. This tendency was most marked among the young, educated students, yet almost half rated television and radio positively and 31 percent rated newspapers favorably.

Kepplinger (1984) provided explanations for these trends. For one, the level of education in Germany has increased markedly, leisure time has expanded considerably, and interest in politics has increased sharply. These factors all breed social criticism, including criticism of the press. At the same time, Germans have devoted an increasing amount of attention to most media. The exception is the newspaper, where circulation has remained at approximately the same level. The penetration of radio and television, in contrast, has increased considerably. This process is virtually complete, however.

By and large television faced the fewest critics, radio was somewhat more criticized, and newspapers drew the most attention. But all audiences (other than a single exception for television in 1970) have rated their information content less favorably in every four-year period since 1964. This finding contrasted with their growing appreciation of the entertainment content of media, where radio has become most favored. Young persons, however, have been less approving of the information content of television (a public corporation), with which they have had less experience than with newspapers.

Kepplinger (1984) described as an unique development for Germany the phenomenon of mass media criticism of itself. Thus television newscasters have increasingly criticized radio and newspapers, radio has condemned television and newspapers, and newspapers have pointed to the deficiencies of radio and television.

Kepplinger (1984), however, rejected the idea that the growing criticism of media was instructed by media self-criticism. Rather, he held to the thesis that becoming more informed and engaging in more political participation, particularly among youths, contributed to a spirit of criticism of all social institutions, including mass communication. As the public became more literate and informed it could be anticipated that greater criticism and less appreciation of media would ensue.

In summary, we may observe that the German perspective has been one of social criticism of the media, among other social institutions, while Roper-style questions about credibility continue to be asked.

JAPANESE PERSPECTIVES: THE PUBLIC AS PERSONAE

Although Japanese media also have addressed narrow questions of credibility as journalistic concerns, they recently have given a great deal of attention to the public as personae. As early as 1979 the Research Institute of the Nihon Shimbun Kyokai (NSK) (Japanese Newspaper Publishers and Editors Association, 1984) conducted studies of credibility and the attention of media to human and social values. As we have noted, NSK asked questions about accuracy, impartiality, and trustworthiness as journalistic problems; but they added a number of more intimate concepts of media performance such as permitting the "dignity of the individual," seeking to be relevant to daily life and to the society, permitting personal reflectivity, and demonstrating a concern for human rights.

These studies did not deny a "credibility factor." Actually, the term became popularized and adopted as a Japanese "jargot" as its meaning was broadened. By 1986 an NSK study reported increases in credibility scores for newspapers. This finding was based, in part, on an open-ended question that asked; "Do you think newspapers are reporting accurately the developments in the world around us?" The questions stressed the importance of interactions of readers with their newspapers. Audiences were characterized as in "active and passive affirmation, negation, or neutral evaluation" (see Figure 6.1 and Table 6.1).

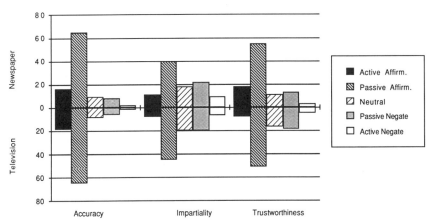

Figure 6.1. Comparison of Japanese Newspapers and Television on Three Credibility Measures.

TABLE 6.1. COMPARISON OF JAPANESE NEWSPAPERS AND TELEVISION ON THREE CREDIBILITY MEASURES

	Active Affirmative	Passive Affirmative	Neutral	Passive Negative	Active Negative
Accuracy					
Newspapers	16	65	9	8	2
Television	18	65	9	6	2
Impartiality					
Newspapers	11	40	18	22	9
Television	8	45	20	20	7
Trustworthiness					
Newspapers	18	55	11	13	3
Television	8	51	17	19	5

Contrary to the Roper results in the United States, newspapers and television differed very little. Japanese readers said both media were more accurate than impartial. Newspapers were more trustworthy, but accuracy was distinguished from trustworthiness. Accuracy reflected the interaction between reporter and source, whereas trustworthiness described interactions between journalists and audiences.

In areas that impinged most intimately on the individual (see Figure 6.2 and Table 6.2), the media gained much less approval. Television was

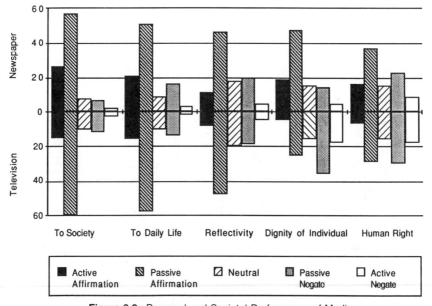

Figure 6.2. Personal and Societal Performance of Media

TABLE 6.2. PERSONAL AND SOCIETAL PERFORMANCE OF MEDIA

Areas of Relevance	Active Affirmative	Passive Affirmative	Neutral	Passive Negative	Active Negative
To society					
Newspapers	26	57	8	7	2
Television	15	60	10	12	3
To daily life					
Newspapers	21	51	9	16	3
Television	16	58	10	14	2
Reflectivity					
Newspapers	11	46	18	20	5
Television	8	48	20	19	5
Dignity of individual					
Newspapers	19	47	15	14	5
Television	5	25	16	36	18
Human rights					
Newspapers	16	37	15	23	9
Television	7	29	16	30	18

less approved than newspapers, which was apparent in concerns about the dignity of the individual and human rights.

USES AND CREDIBILITY

In approaching our analysis of student behavior we relied on a number of criteria for both uses (as outlined in Chapter 5) and credibility. When a student used a source of information, how was it evaluated? What criteria were brought to bear on its utility for the individual?

We allowed our students to respond freely to this question: Why did you find this source [the one described as "most useful"] more useful than the other sources you had utilized?

As outlined previously, responses could be grouped into a number of categories that described the functional aspects of uses. One of these was the characteristics of the channel of communication—whether print, sight, sound, color, or movement. We described these as "channel dimensions."

Two others incorporated informational utilities. We adopted the suggestion by the Japanese research team that we develop a means for distinguishing between replies that suggested active processing as contrasted to passive acceptance of information. The NSK in Japan had applied these distinctions successfully to a sample of Japanese adults. We hypothesized that these informational values would prove to be much more of a factor in explaining preferences for media than the more narrowly defined construct of credibility.

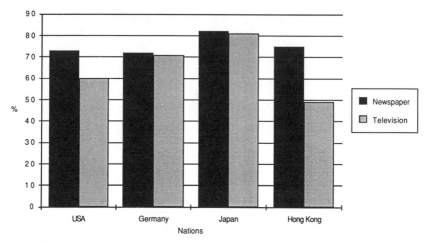

Figure 6.3. Comparative Uses by Students of Newspapers and Television

TABLE 6.3. COMPARATIVE USES BY STUDENTS OF NEWSPAPERS AND TELE-VISION

Sources	United States (n = 678)	Germany (n = 470)	Japan (n = 678)	Hong Kong (n = 639)
Newspapers	73	72	82	75
Television	60	71	81	49

We also expected that because of the universal availability of all media to the students, mere accessibility of sources would contribute only in a minor way to media use. It was not surprising, therefore, that students reported similar or greater use of newspapers than television, as portrayed in Figure 6.3 and Table 6.3. Finally, students could evaluate their sources in terms of such credibility constructs as reliability, accuracy, or credibility itself.

COMMENTS BY STUDENTS

As the reader will observe, statements by students tended to support our conception of the functional nature of uses and the evaluative criteria that grow out of them. Most students evaluated the media on the bases of informational utilities and the characteristics of channels of communication rather than credibility or accessibility. Only the German students proved to be an exception to this generalization.

An American student found foreign newspapers to be her most useful source. She said they gave her insight into how other nations viewed the arms buildup; the views of western European nations were particularly useful. This, too, represented active processing of information, for an "insight" implies active cognitive behavior. Another American student said news magazines were most useful because they were more detailed than television and easier (because of the way they summarized events) to understand and follow than newspapers on a day-to-day basis. Because the reader, herself, did not do the job of interpretation, we classified her behavior as passive acceptance.

A German student said newspapers were most useful because they were more objective than televison, less one-sided, as she put it. These are credibility factors. Another said daily newspapers were more useful because they contained more information and clearer background material. We classified that use as active processing because the term *background* implied perspective.

Another German student said her own personal observation of the political scene was more reliable than any other source of information. As we have noted, the German students felt the strongest sense of participation and personal autonomy, yet they were open about their sense of intellectual identification with certain of the mass media. This relationship contributed to their tendency to cite credibility factors; they experienced a sense of interdependence in these terms.

A Japanese student said television news was most useful because very strong impressions could be obtained by visual and auditory information. This assessment was directed to the characteristics of the channel.

Another Japanese student named television and radio, saying that while doing other things, such as cooking, television and radio were easy to understand because they appealed to the senses of sight and hearing. That answer called attention to the characteristics of television as a channel. Another said weekly magazines were most useful because they gave long-range perspectives and showed diverse opinions, indicating active processing. One Japanese student liked the mass magazine *Manga*, which is noted for its graphic presentations and the simplicity of its content. Because the student reported no thinking on his part and made no specific reference to graphics, we coded his response as passive acceptance.

A number of Hong Kong students stresed that the print media provided much more detail about community problems than did television. We coded this type of response as passive acceptance because no reference was made to integrating these details into a framework of thought. At the same time, a number of students expressed a sense of a lack of analysis and interpretation. We coded this as active processing on their part although it did not imply that the newspapers or television had met that standard.

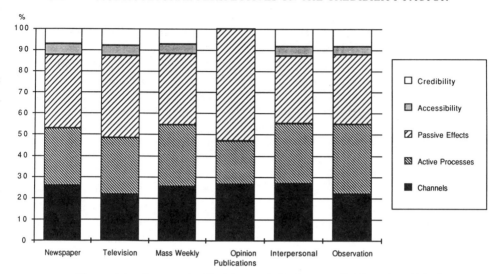

Figure 6.4a. Reasons for Usefulness of Six Sources of Information: United States

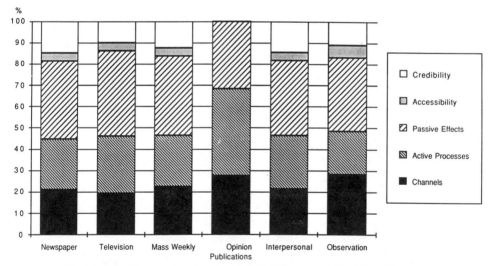

Figure 6.4b. Reasons for Usefulness of Six Sources of Information: Germany

EXTENDING THE ANALYSIS

The individualized statements by students were very illustrative. But aggregating the data across the student groups permitted a broader picture to emerge. We were able to test our assumptions about the ways in which students as a whole—and comparatively across cultures—expressed their

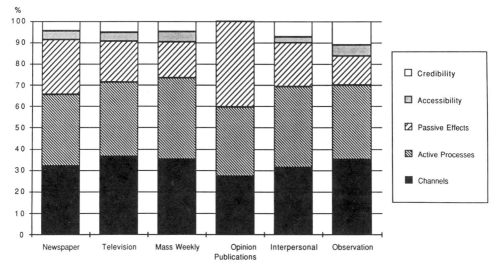

Figure 6.4c. Reasons for Usefulness of Six Sources of Information: Japan

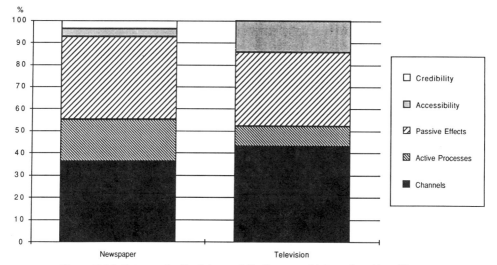

Figure 6.4d. Reasons for Usefulness of Six Sources of Information: Hong Kong

preferences for sources of information and the reasons that they gave for doing so. Figures 6.4a through 6.4d and Table 6.4 confirm many of our expectations.

Informational values and channel characteristics were cited much more often as reasons for the utility of information than was the criterion of credibility.

TABLE 6.4. REASONS WHY MEDIA CHANNELS WERE MOST USEFUL

	United States	Germany	Japan	Hong Kong
Newspapers				
Channels	35	34	41	65
Active processing	37	38	43	34
Passive effects	47	59	33	67
Accessibility	7	6	5	6
Credibility	10	24	6	7
Television				
Channels	27	32	42	82
Active processing	33	45	40	18
Passive effects	48	67	22	64
Accessibility	6	6	5	27
Credibility	10	17	6	—
Mass weekly				
Channels	35	37	44	—
Active processing	40	40	48	—
Passive effects	46	62	21	—
Accessibility	6	6	6	—
Credibility	10	21	6	—
Opinion publications				
Channels	18	46	50	—
Active processing	14	68	60	—
Passive effects	36	53	74	—
Accessibility	—	—	—	—
Credibility	—	—	—	—
Interpersonal				
Channels	36	35	38	—
Active processing	38	41	46	—
Passive effects	43	58	25	—
Accessibility	6	6	3	—
Credibility	11	24	9	—
Observation				
Channels	29	55	41	—
Active processing	44	40	41	—
Passive effects	43	68	16	—
Accessibility	5	11	6	—
Credibility	11	22	13	—

NOTE: Each figure is a proportion of 100 percent. Blanks indicate no data.

The Hong Kong students most applied informational criteria to newspapers, while most German students appreciated the informational content of opinion publications. At the same time, 67 percent of the German students saw informational uses for television, but they described uses more passive than active.

We had created two measures of information use: passive and active processing. The latter was established by evidence that the student used information to gain understanding or comprehension, or think in new terms, as contrasted with situations in which students did not themselves engage in integrative or other active thinking—although they might use a great deal of information or detail.

German students were unique in the extent to which they used the credibility criterion—many more students credited newspapers with being reliable and trustworthy; in fact, about 1 in 5 German students referred to factors of credibility as a way of explaining their preference for other media as well. We anticipated this cultural variation when in Chapter 2 we described the special relationships that existed between German students and mass media.

Lacking this same special relationship, other students did not employ the credibility criterion to this extent. Only about 1 of 10 American students referred to credibility compared with 1 of 8 students in Japan. Generally, credibility was mentioned by fewer than 1 out of 10 students.

As we had also hypothesized, factors of accessibility or availability also were seldom described as a reason for preferring one medium of communication over another. Very few German students (1 out of 9) described accessibility as vital to direct observation, but for all groups and for all media most other scores were far less.

CHANNEL ANALYSIS

Figures 6.4a through 6.4d permit additional insights into the impact of different media. We may with these same figures assess students' evaluations for each of the media.

Newspapers

Japanese students used newspapers more actively than passively, which was unique among groups. We attributed this difference to the importance that was attached to newspapers in areas of government and public opinion. In our discussion of agenda setting, Chapter 8, we describe the active "mediating" role taken by newspapers as journalists communicate freely with politicians and the public to facilitate debate.

The greater passivity that characterized Hong Kong students with respect to the informational content of newspapers was expressed in an unusual way: They tended much more to compare newspapers with television rather than judge each independently. Most comparisons were expressed in terms of the greater detail to be found in newspapers, but no explicit references were made to greater understanding or perspective. The implication could be drawn that Hong Kong students did not see newspapers or television as doing any thinking for them.

Japanese students more than the others pointed to channel dimensions of newspapers as a reason for expressing their preferences. One cultural reason may be the fact that *kanji*, the Japanese print character, is quite distinct from Roman script. But this also is true of the Chinese-language newspapers in Hong Kong. One explanation for this discrepancy is that Japanese media generally are more striking in their appearance than American, German, and even Chinese newspapers. Beniger and Westney (1981), among others, have pointed to the more graphic style of Japanese newspapers to attain visual effects. Newspapers such as *Yomiuri* and *Asahi* employ multiple headlines (although not in their English-language editions). Japanese newspapers also are much more likely than Western newspapers to use graphs and cartoons to illustrate a variety of news events— not merely to plot economic trends as is common in Western newspapers.

The relative passivity in information uses expressed by the German students is actually misleading. It grows out of their identification and agreement with intellectual and ideological positions that are articulated by journalists and shared by the students themselves. The markedly higher degree of credibility accorded by German students to newspapers supports this inference.

Television

Only one major difference in preferences for television was expressed by the students—the more active than passive use of television described by Japanese students. We attribute this finding, again, to the air of excitement generated by Japanese television through its visual qualities. Almost all Hong Kong students (4 out of 5) expressed a preference for television because of its channel characteristics. This might have been their way of characterizing the language accessibility of those stations—English, Mandarin, and Cantonese.

The Mass Weekly

There were few differences concerning the mass weeklies other than the continued tendency for the Japanese students to prefer their visual character and simplicity of presentation. These picture/cartoon/news magazines, as well as the more purely cartoon publication called *Manga*, or informative comic book, have enormous circulations among young people particularly. Ito (1987) observed that the term Manga first meant a cartoon in newspapers, magazines, or on television but later came to describe comic books or magazines that were entirely cartoons.

The Functions of **Manga.** A brief discussion of the *Manga* phenomenon will contribute to an understanding of the Japanese affinity for highly visual mass media.

A survey by the Youth Affairs Administration in the Office of the Prime Minister (Office of the Prime Minister, 1981) reported that *Manga* were read by 89 percent of primary schoolchildren and 72 percent of university students; the figures were 66 percent for working class youths and 26 percent for adults over 35 years of age.

The best-selling comics exceed 4 million copies annually. In 1985 one comic book sold 34 million copies. Although many are of dubious value, some have artistic merit and educational value, and many cartoonists are considered to be contributors to popular culture. The most respected cartoonist, Osamu Tezuka, has published more than 300 comic books and has received awards recognizing his merit, one of them from the Japanese Ministry of Education. Tezuka graduated from the prestigeous Osaka University and practiced medicine. His cartoon books reflect a profound intelligence, a knowledge of science and history, and keen insights into human nature. One cartoon story consists of more than 50 volumes, which university students read as if they were textbooks. It spans battles, rebellions, friendship, love, and most human activities in seventeenth-century Japan. The story line is thought to be patterned after Marx's theories of history and social change. Most of the world's great literary works, including those by Dickens, Twain, Stendahl, and Tolstoi, are presented in *Manga*. At *Manga* coffee shops customers enjoy a choice of comic books and magazines, and social critics speak of a "Manga culture."

Opinion Publications

American students read opinion publications much less frequently and, curiously, were more passive than active in their use. We drew the implication that American students think of opinion publications as authoritative and thus accept their point of view. In contrast, by being more active than passive in their interaction with these publications, the German student asserted more of a dialogue than a client type of interaction. The Japanese students, too, interacted with their opinion media, although many were also more accepting than were the German students. In general terms, we might characterize the German students as interacting with opinion elites, Japanese students as actively surveying them, and American students looking to them for direction. Possibly the intellectual quality of magazines such as *Harpers*, *Atlantic Monthly*, and the *New Yorker* contributed to this.

Interpersonal Communication

Chapter 9 examines cultural dimensions of Japanese interpersonal communication in great detail. We simple note here that interpersonal communication in Japan proved to be less an exercise in information giving and receiving than a means of checking on the appropriateness of one's beliefs and behavior and learning how consensus might be reached. Japanese students actively engaged in interpersonal communication when that opportunity presented itself.

Personal Observation

Japanese students also defined social problems much less by means of personal observation, but again, when they did so, they were actively engaged. In contrast, more American and German students adopted personal observation as a channel but, relatively speaking, saw it less as involving a means of learning or knowing. German students, through their more active participation in political processes, were most able to observe events at first hand. German students again most explained their preference for channels by referring to their credibility.

CULTURAL PROFILES

Figures 6.4a to 6.4d also permit us to develop individual profiles for each of the four cultures.

American Students: Passive When Active

As we already observed, American students reacted in unique fashion to opinion publications. This was their most distinguishing behavior. There were fewer evaluations of opinion publications, based in part on lesser use; but the most remarkable fact was their more passive than active use. American students seemed to suggest by this behavior either that their thoughts were shaped by opinion publications or that they engaged in a higher degree of selectivity of publications, which echoed rather than challenged their views. American students also gave less emphasis to the characteristics of channels of information. They appeared to be less conscious of the impact of the uniqueness of channels on their thinking and observational capabilities.

German Students: Interdependent and Participant

German students expressed their degree of interdependence with mass media and their own sense of participation in events by their references to the credibility of sources. The lowest score they accorded to a medium—17 percent to television—was higher than that given by any of the other cultural groups to any media. The greatest trust was expressed for newspapers and interpersonal communication, 24 percent in each case. If we consider that the roots of credibility as a variable are found in the interdependency felt by individuals—as they engaged in collective behavior and interpersonal communication—their participatory role contributed to their special relationship to the media.

We may see this fact as explaining their seemingly contradictory mode of using information in *mass* media channels—reportedly more passive than active. Our explanation is that the mass media largely expressed their views. In contrast, German students reported more active processing of information from opinion publications, which represented challenges to their views. American behaviors were quite the opposite—the students demonstrated more passivity with regard to opinion publications but more activity with respect to mass media. This finding contributes to alternative explanations, none of which we can establish explicitly.

The explanation toward which we lean is that American students are more reactive to mass media than to elite media because mass media are more pluralistic in their approaches to problems, and American opinion publications are more easily identified with a point of view. Thus students could be more selective with regard to opinion publications, permitting them to find a medium with which they agree. This fact could contribute to a passive acceptance of information.

Japanese Students: Consensus, Passivity, and Activity

Japanese students were, in almost every case (the exception was the mass weekly), more active than passive users of channels of information—particularly with newspapers, television, interpersonal communication, and personal observation, but not with opinion publications.

One explanation parallels that which we have offered for American students. It is made even more appealing by the fact that most Japanese newspapers are national and most television is regional or national in character. These high-circulation, high-exposure media would require cognitive activity to sort out the diversified content and approaches. In contrast, the kinds of special and opinion publications that we have described would permit greater selectivity. If we look at the extent to which Japanese students actively processed information from the mass media, we may see that consensus building in Japanese society is more than a passive process, no matter what the style is that characterizes communication activity.

Hong Kong Students: Situation More than Culture

Our Hong Kong data on these variables are sufficient only to report on newspapers and television. These data, however, are quite revealing. They show the most dramatic contrast between active and passive media use. We would explain this result by the uncertainties that exist in the political environment and the fragmented nature of the mass media in Hong Kong. These data appear to be explained better by situational rather than cultural parameters.

Chan and Lee (1986) have explained in the situational context the political and economic factors that have governed the ways in which audiences have utilized the diversified press of Hong Kong. The political context is explained to some extent by the interparty struggle between a Communist and capitalist press—one of which is aligned with Beijing and the other with Taiwan. The economic context is promoted by the highly indigenous Chinese press, which is attuned in very pragmatic terms to the booming market economy. These newspapers tend to neglect greatly what we would describe as the public sphere.

In both political and economic terms, The *South China Morning Post* and the *Hong Kong Standard*, both English-language newspapers, are committed to maintaining the status quo and supporting the policies and actions of the colonial government. The many Chinese-language newspapers (*Ming Pao Daily News, Ming Pao Evening News, Hong Kong Economic Journal, Sing Pao Daily News, Star, Tin Tin Yat Pao,* and *Oriental Daily News*) emerged in the 1970s as "centrist" media loyal to Hong Kong and critical of both Beijing and Taipei. While devoting attention to political issues, they are also attentive to social problems. The *Daily News* is the largest in circulation of the popular Chinese-language newspapers. (We included it with the *Morning Post* in our analysis of news in Chapter 4.)

There are also a substantial number of what Chan and Lee call "rightist" and "ultra-rightist" as well as "ultra-leftist" newspapers. The rightist papers tilt mildly toward Taiwan out of political ideology and personal histories, yet they are responsive to social problems. The ultra rightist newspapers were once propaganda organs and have shrunk in number because of ideology and unresponsiveness to problems. The numerous leftist papers are owned outright in Beijing. *Wen Wei Pao* appeals to students and to laborers, *Ta Kung Pao* attracts intellectuals and business people, and other newspapers cater to lower classes. The *New Evening Post* was designed to attract a general, cross-sectional circulation. None of these newspapers, nor the rightist papers, has a significant audience of university students.

Television does not reflect the political diversity of newspapers, which appears to explain the evaluations of television as providing information or details rather than treating events in a manner that encourages reflection and discussion. The two English-language channels cover news routinely and give little indication of underlying conflicts. The two Chinese-language channels are, if anything, less concerned about social problems. All channels are entertainment oriented. There is no educational channel per se, as in American, German, and Japanese systems. Educational content is transmitted over the regular channels.

Noting the failure of media to meet expectations in relation to problems of housing (with which we have dealt), Atwood (1984) commented that all media sources may have been perceived as of little use: "Perhaps newspapers were really of little value in this situation, but television was perceived to be useless." Atwood speculated that housing was a problem that could not be solved; hence information was less useful. Yu (1981) concluded that the chief reporters on Hong Kong dailies did not feel it necessary to report a great deal of political information. Atwood found that most Hong Kong subjects were "constrained" and "fatalistic" about politics, and he attributed this finding to cultural as well as situational factors.

These special media conditions—politically conscious but somewhat muted newspapers, political apathy on the part of residents, and a passive television (and radio) system—explain the nature of the perceptions of newspapers and television by the Hong Kong students.

SUMMARY

The credibility factor has been transformed from a narrow measure of the accuracy of reports to more inclusive individual and societal values. These look to the performance of the media and ask that media acknowledge more broadly the importance of social norms. Informational values, channel characteristics, and the importance of problems tend to influence the ways in which news is used and information sources are evaluated.

We do not take the position that credibility is not a relevant criterion for the evaluation of mass media—only that credibility may not be the *most* relevant factor in people's minds. Interestingly, this is particularly the case where important problems are at stake. Here, it would seem, people trust themselves more than they trust the media.

As a second consideration, credibility may vary by culture, as we have shown in the case of the German students and as has been demonstrated in studies of general populations in Germany as well.

Finally, we are encouraged to think of credibility as a calculated intellectual judgment rather than as a blind, emotional, and unvarying response that indicates a generalized hostility toward the media.

A young American scholar, Gunther (1988), recently took this same perspective. He concluded that judgments about the credibility of a source were characterized by thinking, were not lightly made, and served to illuminate the relationships between thinking and mass media evaluation.

Multicultural applications and possible generalizations are suggested by the finding by Gunther and Lasorsa (1986) that partisan or biased persons are likely to impute bias to the media. Other scholars have pointed to similar phenomena, notably the conclusions reached by Anast as early as 1961, and the supportive findings by Roberts and Leifer (1975).

Gunther (1988) has gone on to demonstrate that people who hold extreme attitudes with respect to issues are likely to reflect those attitudes in their evaluations of the media. Interestingly, this holds for those who are the least extreme as well. Gunther explains that paradox in these ways:

- The attitudes of those who are most extreme are reflected by intense cognitive activity;
- The attitudes of those who are least extreme are not explained by cognitive activity but by the lack of activity; they thus become most susceptible to social influence.

The multicultural implications of these suggestions are intriguing. Do media in different cultures vary in their tendencies to produce greater or lesser controversy and thus stimulate those who hold extreme views and are cognitively active? We might easily think of some of the German mass media in these terms, and consequently we would expect them more to invoke in audiences considerations of credibility.

Are individuals in different cultures more or less involved or attracted to controversy? Do media accurately reflect these tendencies or, perhaps, constrain them? How would this impact upon the latitudes of trust for mass media? We can observe tendencies of this kind in the comments about the media by Hong Kong students.

Finally, we might ask if individuals in different cultures are more or less given to cognitive activity and hence might become more apt to view media in terms of their credibility. A partial answer to this question is provided by the behavior of Japanese students, who more than the other students in our study demonstrated active information-processing.

Nonetheless, active cognitive-processing alone, as demonstrated by our Japanese data, does not produce tendencies to weigh heavily the credibility of the media. Cognitive activity must be accompanied by a degree of bias. Rather, our data support the expectation that credibility, as a criterion, is greatly influenced in its application by the cultural and situational contexts in which media perform and in which individuals act out their beliefs.

Audiences were more concerned with channel characteristics and informational content than with credibility or accessibility. Only the German students employed credibility as a relevant variable. None of the four student groups saw accessibility as a vital factor.

The *Manga* cartoon books were discussed in terms of Japanese culture, and situational factors in Hong Kong explained the students' perceptions of the media. The participatory values of German students and attachments to media expressed cultural and situational values.

The dispute over credibility has raged over the competition between newspapers and television; this may be more of a market situation than a matter of social relevance. In contrast, participation, interpersonal communication, and direct observation possess built-in factors of credibility for one who may check or see for oneself. In comparative terms, credibility must be viewed not only within a journalistically narrow framework but also within the broader cultural contexts of social relevance, the perceived relationships of audiences to the medium, and the pragmatics of political situations and market economies.

CHAPTER 7

Perceptions and Cognitions: A Comparative Approach to Public Opinion

Ever-present concerns and challenges in the world community lend themselves to the comparative analysis of public opinion. Many of the problems that our students identified are endemic worldwide: housing, ecology, human rights, social relations, and quality of life. These concerns are equivalent multiculturally because they are basic to individuals and are present in all societies.

Glock (1952) made the case almost four decades ago for the comparative study of public opinion. He viewed it as a complex process whose study brought together all of the social sciences, and he was intrigued by the implications of the concept of "holding an opinion" as it expressed itself in a variety of cultures and through the use of mass communications: "...the way in which 'holding an opinion' is valued in a society is likely to influence whether or not the individual seeks out news, what news he seeks, and the way in which he interprets it..." (pp. 447–448).

Glock today would look at poll data and other indicators of public opinion and sympathize with the many views held about world problems. But he would, at the same time, lament that we have not learned enough about the processes of opinion holding to undertake comparative analysis. Although we are rich in our knowledge about attitudes toward world problems, we lack an adequate understanding of the underlying dynamics of those opinions. To complement our knowledge of points of view it was necessary to examine the structures and foci of opinions. A knowledge of these elements would help us to be comparative.

Our approach in this chapter acknowledges the importance of the concept of opinion holding and adds to it the concept of *cognitive opinion objects*—which are the foci of opinions that are held. This concept argues that each opinion is more than the expression of a larger idea; it is the aspect of that idea that commands attention at that time. Individuals form opinions about aspects of problems as a problem takes on form and character.

Our search in this chapter is to identify for study opinion objects that help us to be comparative. Toward this end we will introduce the concept of cognitive aspects of problems as foci of opinions. We will use these cognitively defined opinion objects also to describe the opinion-forming processes by which individuals focus their attention on different aspects of problems at different times.

This approach is compatible with two major research traditions in public opinion: (1) studies of perceptions and cognitions and (2) communication studies of co-orientation.

Studies of co-orientation focus on the attitudinal or evaluative context of self and other perceptions. According to this construction, individuals perceive that they agree or disagree with the opinions of others—interpersonally or in relation to a more abstract concept of public opinion. More recently, however, communication scholars have stressed the importance of understanding as well as agreement as a focus for the study of communication and opinion processes. The cognitive approach that we suggest follows the steps taken to address understanding.

Kim (1986) identified the search for understanding as productive of more communication behavior than the search for agreement. One needs more information to achieve understanding than to like or dislike or agree or disagree. Kim pointed out that the content of communication is not limited to values. He proposed that co-orientational matrices be constructed to determine nonevaluative cognitions—as objects of orientation—to determine the focus of communication as well as how the opinion objects are evaluated.

It is important to realize that the intellectual bases for co-orientation studies were defined by sociologists and psychologists and that these expressed their own interests, not those of communication scholars. McLeod and Chaffee (1973) pointed out that these perspectives limited the study of human communication because they focused upon *intrapersonal* rather than *interpersonal* aspects of communication. The "personality" of a communicator described values residing only in that individual; communication and co-orientation required that at least two persons be observed.

As a second consideration, the interest of our field in the processes of mass communication, with its emphasis upon the transmission of information, gave increased value to the study of cognitive processes as well as the social conditions affecting those cognitions. What people were thinking about and what they communicated to others should be the foci of study.

The two Wisconsin researchers suggested five conditions that should govern the study of co-orientation. Let us look at how our study addresses those conditions:

- The first condition is that the persons who are interacting in a particular situation express affective and role relationships to one another. This particularly characterized the relationships expressed by our students;
- It is necessary not only to observe cognitions themselves but changes in cognitions as well, to permit communication to be studied at several points in time.

By contrast, we focused upon the movement of problems, rather than the movement of students, through a time sequence. A time dimension was incorporated in the cognitions that students reported about problems as those problems changed in their nature over time.

- The third condition is that sequences of messages and acts related to those messages must be observed. As suggested above, we observe the number and kinds of cognitions that students expressed at each stage of the emergence of problems.
- The fourth condition requires simultaneous communication. Our study incorporates a number of reports of perceptions—of self, of peers, and of general publics. These are in the same time frame.
- Finally, the Wisconsin researchers suggested that there should be mutual assessments by the parties of the cognitions of others and that all related cognitions should be assessed. Our study does precisely this—it incorporates *a number of kinds* of self and other perceptions.

An important aspect of the McLeod–Chaffee (1973) model is that it proposes a model of co-orientation that has accuracy as its objective, for with accuracy, there may be greater understanding. This is where our approach is most consistent with that model. Our cognitive approach permits us to assess *the accuracy of co-orientations to the conceptual location of each social problem*. We define conceptual location as the *causes, the consequences, and the steps toward solutions* of all problems. We permit students to tell us if they are co-oriented to peers and publics at each of these stages of emergence of the particular problems with which they are concerned.

PERCEPTIONS AND COGNITIONS

The approach we take in this chapter advances the view that opinions about problems or issues are the product of perceptions and cognitions by the individual, and public opinion represents an awareness that others are engaged in the same perception and cognitive processes. We take a cognitive approach when we assert that perceptions are important not only when they stress the *content* of opinions but also when they indicate the presence, or absence, of a *common focus of attention*. To learn about foci of attention we must ask what public opinion is as well as what it is about. As we point out in our discussion of agenda-setting effects in Chapter 9, a knowledge of what people actually are thinking about may lead us to new discoveries about preconditions for communicating opinions.

Our data, therefore, address *cognitive* accuracy—the accuracy of the perceptions that people are thinking about and talking about the same aspect of a problem, that is, its causes, consequences, and/or solutions. Up to now the cognitive aspect of the element of accuracy has been directed to the *evaluations* or the attitudes that people have expressed in their opinions about problems.

We believe that a cognitively oriented research agenda represents the minimum prior condition for assessing the meaning of any agreement or disagreement, for before we assess whether or not people agree or disagree as to the evaluation of problems we should first determine that they are dealing mutually with the same aspects of those problems at the same point in time.

The larger consequences of that minimal first research question lead us to important societal questions:

- First, is it possible that media might be focusing upon causes of a problem while publics might still be concerned about the consequences of problems or insisting that the time is at hand for these problems to be solved?
- Second, is it similarly possible that public opinion polls may be asking publics about, let us say, solutions to problems while publics are not yet at that intellectual point, still concerned, as we have suggested above, about the consequences of those problems?
- Finally, we may see that media—qualitative and mass, print or electronic agendas—might or not agree at a particular time as to what aspects of problems should be addressed. Publics would be caught up in these discrepancies in agendas. In short, putting aside agreement or disagreement about certain causes, consequences, or solutions, the society would be at odds as to what aspect of the

problem was, or should be, on the national agenda at a particular point in time.

The questions that we asked students were designed to provide information that would address these questions:

- To what extent did students perceive that they and their friends were holding opinions about the same aspects of a problem or different aspects of the problem?
- To what extent did they perceive that their focus on aspects of public opinion was similar to or different from the focus of the publics?

Perceptions of convergence—focusing, or as we might say more easily, thinking and talking about the *same* things—carry different implications for communication from perceptions of thinking and talking about *different* things. We based our analysis on the extent to which there was *cognitive* co-orientation rather than *evaluative* co-orientation. Where there was evidence of the former we thought of it as convergence: Co-orientation to evaluative components is thought of as congruence.

To obtain the data that would permit us to determine the degree of cognitive co-orientation we identified three foci:

1. The nature or the consequences of a problem
2. The causes of a problem
3. The solutions to a problem

We will match the foci of attention reported by students themselves with their perceptions of the foci of others—their peers and public opinion. We will be able to determine in this way the amount of perceived convergence on the three kinds of opinion objects: nature or consequences, causes, and solutions.

With data of this kind we could answer questions such as the following:

- At a given time, and with respect to specific problems or issues, is the society largely attentive to the same or different aspects of the same problem?
- Or is the society largely attentive to the same or different aspects of another problem?
- Are the perceptions of the society congruent with reality?
- Are perceptions more accurate with respect to some aspects of problems than others, without regard to the problems themselves?

These questions, in turn, raise another, more subtle question: What is more important to consider, those aspects of particular problems or issues to which the public is attentive in a particular instance, or the behavioral logic of a certain public always being more focused on the consequences, causes, or solutions, without regard to the problem itself?

In addressing those questions it becomes clear that we are required to gain a greater understanding of the nature of critical events and how they develop and the nature of the actors—social critics, politicians, media, and so on—who exert influence on them, what we describe in Chapter 9 as agenda-setting processes.

THE COMPARATIVE PERSPECTIVE

Comparativists point to a number of reasons for taking a renewed interest in perceptual and cognitive approaches to public opinion. First, as discussed in Chapter 1, individuals in all cultures entertain perceptions and form cognitions. Second, these perceptions and cognitions are equivalent across societies and, as such, are easily compared. Finally, perceptual and cognitive approaches grow out of important research traditions.

Despite his respect for a definitive state of knowledge as the foundation of democracy, Lippmann (1922) offered a perceptual and cognitive definition of public opinion as "the pictures in our heads." He described how individuals felt themselves forced to deal with a "virtual flood of symbols, stereotypes and images." Allport (1937) said it was important to acknowledge from a psychologist's standpoint that public opinion had no discrete quality; it existed only in the eye of the beholder.

Contemporary American scholars have also called attention to perceptual and cognitive aspects of public opinion. Boorstin (1974) wrote from a historian's perspective that public opinion in modern life had become "whatever people think it is." And Lemert (1981) wrote from the standpoint of mass communication studies that "public opinion is the perception that public opinion exists." Noelle-Neumann (1979) director of the Allensbach, West Germany, Institute for Public Opinion, contributed a world view to the perceptual and cognitive approach. Her empirical studies in West Germany suggested that individuals were able to perceive accurately the ebb and flow of popular and unpopular ideas and their climates of opinion:

> today we can *show* it, we can prove it: Man has an organ to perceive opinion, the gift to perceive with great subtlety, the development of opinion in his environment. We can ask questions [of anonymous sub-

jects] about almost every matter of common interest....Their replies
mirror the actual changes of opinions as measured by public opinion
research; not as uncertain suggestions, but on the contrary...with [the
most minute] decreases and [notably] increases...in the opinion climate.
(p. 147)

Noelle-Neumann (1979) qualified this ability in a number of ways. She
did not expect people to assess the absolute nature of public opinion but
only its tendencies, in one direction or another, and primarily in situations
in which there are conditions of moral or social conflict. Further, she asked
about cultural relevance. As a consequence, studies of the climate of
opinion and the "spiral of silence" have been reproduced in the United
States and, as she hoped, have stimulated additional inquiry.

Noelle-Neumann's work is rooted in perceptual and cognitive theories
and affords linkages to a variety of other perceptual and cognitive approaches. For one, Breed and Kitsanes (1961) much earlier created popular
interest in what they called "pluralistic ignorance," a condition that is
brought about by misguided perceptions by individuals about what con-
stitutes majority opinion. These "ignorant" perceptions (of racial and
religious bias) are projected onto a "plurality" of the social group; hence
the individual is guilty of "pluralistic ignorance."

Studies of pluralistic ignorance in public opinion were pursued by a
number of scholars (O'Gorman, 1975, 1979, 1980; O'Gorman & Garry,
1976). Taylor (1982) established the link between pluralistic ignorance and
Noelle-Neumann's concept of climates of opinion by suggesting that they
both rested on the ability of individuals to judge the nature of public
opinion.

The recent work of Davison (1983) is in this same tradition. Davison
suggested and Glynn (1986a, 1986b) supported the idea that there are
important "third party" effects of public opinion. These are based on
perceptions of probable consequences of public opinion on others that the
observers need to take into account. Although these individuals feel themselves to be unaffected directly, they perceived that others consider themselves to be affected and would act in some way. The question was how
these actions might affect the observer, the third party. If the observers
thought that the actions of the public would affect them, they would act
accordingly. Davison and Glynn said it was curious that almost everyone
exaggerated the effects of public opinion on others while minimizing the
effects on themselves.

Critics of perceptual theories have questioned the accuracy with which
people judge the opinions of others. They point out that actions may not be
taken on the nebulous basis of estimates of what people think other people
think. They doubt the ability of individuals to judge climates of opinion or

even tendencies. Tichenor and Wackman (1973) noted that many of their respondents could not judge the opinions of others nor did they wish or attempt to do so.

Commenting on the difficulties inherent in discerning the opinions of others, Lippmann (1922) wrote,

> In putting together our public opinions, not only do we have to picture more space than we can see with our eyes, and more time that we can feel, but we have to describe and judge more people, more actions, more things than we can ever count, or vividly imagine. We have to summarize and generalize. We have to pick out samples, and treat them as typical. (p. 148)

This statement, of course, does not put the question of the validity of the perceptual approach to rest. Fields and Schuman (1976), among many others, pointed out that some perceptual cues are unmistakable in social communication, although in other situations one's beliefs about what other people think might well be inaccurate because direct communication is absent.

Perceptual approaches and the related cognitions help to explain what otherwise might be considered to be surprising results in our data. Why, for example, should university students in four different cultures perceive more similarity in focus of attention between themselves and generalized public opinion than between themselves and their peers?

PERCEPTIONS OF CO-ORIENTATION

Several American studies bear on our comparisons of perceptions of co-orientation among student groups. The accuracy of perceptions has most attracted the attention of communication scholars. They asked individuals what they think and what they think other people think; those others were then asked directly what they thought, and these data were compared with the perceptions. This process usually operated in two ways: A's perception of B, and B's perception of A. The degree of accuracy varied according to a number of conditions. Glynn (1984) found that people were able to judge the opinions of neighbors more accurately than those of people who were more distant. In this context of public opinion the use of interpersonal communication would be more reliable than mass communication in guiding perceptions.

The accuracy of self-other perceptions has been evaluated in relation to a number of different actors—government officials, press, and various publics. These studies have been characterized generally as evaluations of positions on problems or issues. Researchers have asked each individual how he or she and others defined the nature of a problem and how strongly each felt about problems or actors involved in the process.

Bowes and Stamm (1975) compared the accuracy of mutual perceptions of groups such as journalists, community leaders, and publics to determine who most accurately perceived the opinions of others with regard to local problems. By comparing the perceived and actual favorability of these groups toward local issues, they were able to identify gaps in understanding of public opinion.

A study in Hong Kong (Lai, 1983) compared the accuracy of perceptions of newspaper editors, students at the Chinese University of Hong Kong, and a general sample of the population. Editors and readers were asked to evaluate the sensationalism of the coverage of a murder case and to assess each other's perceptions.

Lai found significant disagreement between the judgments of editors and students, but this finding contrasted with the perceptions of editors that there was little disagreement. Hence a perceived co-orientation on the part of editors was not justified. The students, however, more accurately perceived that their judgements of sensationalism differed substantially from those of the editors. Lai concluded that editors liked to believe that they understood their readers, and hence perceived their judgments as more similar, whereas students perceived themselves as more distant from the newspaper, and hence perceived their judgments to be less alike.

Grunig and Stamm (1973) distinguished between cognitions and evaluation in describing the orientations of those who were guided by social values, on the one hand, and economic determinism, on the other. They discovered that those who held liberal social values perceived that they communicated much more with people who shared their orientations, and the same was true for those who were guided by economic determinism. But although the social thinkers had clearer perceptions or cognitions of the actual state of housing, they did not evaluate possible solutions to the problem in the same way as did the poor. In contrast, the economic thinkers had a less clear idea about housing conditions, yet their orientation to solutions was more consistent with that of the urban poor. Neither group, however, was accurate in its perceptions of how the poor themselves evaluated the proposed solutions.

A 1973 study by Stamm, Bowes, and Bowes addressed the so-called "generation gap" between youths and adults. Differences in values between college youths and adults previously had been seen as a consequence of different degrees of maturation and different foci of interest. But in this case, although the adults misperceived the values of students, students accurately judged the perceptions of adults. Viewed together with the results of the Hong Kong study, we are encouraged to accept students' judgments about the nature of adult public opinion with greater confidence.

FROM EVALUATION TO COGNITION

As we have shown, many co-orientation studies have been concerned with perceived agreement or disagreement and with evaluative judgments. Only the Grunig and Stamm (1973) study attended explicitly to cognitive effects, that is, simply "knowing" what the other person thought. Whereas the evaluative component asks if people agree or disagree, or like or dislike, the cognitive dimension asks simply if people are *aware* of the foci of the opinions of others. Because even the simplest problem is multifaceted, mutual awareness may center on one of the several cognitive aspects of problems as we have defined them.

Several scholars have identified cognitive elements similar to those that we have proposed, although they have not introduced them as elements in a system. For example, our colleague Kepplinger and Noelle-Neumann (1979) reported opinions about the consequences of problems and their possible solutions. A study of television coverage of the oil crisis of the 1970s by Theberge (1982) observed that television coverage emphasized causes and solutions.

Interestingly, many more opinions about the oil crisis were directed to the causes of the crisis than to solutions to it. This appears to be a rare case in public opinion. The oil crisis might have affected people so intimately that they, and the media, were more ready to blame people and institutions (for causing the problem) than they were able to propose solutions. This finding addresses the question we asked earlier about what kinds of problems lend themselves most to the formation of opinions about the consequences, causes, or solutions. This question forces us to think about such problems as AIDS, drug and child abuse, and abortion.

In summary, there has been ample precedent for our cognitive approach, and it may be viewed as complementary to attitudinal or evaluative approaches. Added to our previous question—What are you thinking about?—would be the question "What do you think about it?"

THE STUDENT DATA

We derived our data from reponses to four questions:

1. What students perceived to be the focus of attention of public opinion (As we suggested, the cognitive parameters included the consequences, causes, or solutions to problems.)
2. The cognitive parameters they themselves had focused on
3. What they mentioned to someone else
4. What they perceived that someone else had discussed with them

Actual statements made by students illustrate how we determined their foci of attention and their perceptions of the foci of others.

An American fourth-year student from the University of Washington saw a dual focus of attention of public opinion with respect to the problem of inflation. First, he saw its consequences. Inflation was a "two-headed monster." Shifting from consequences to solutions he observed that it would take a great deal (of effort and sacrifice) to correct it.

He was most concerned about solutions to the problem. His own opinion was that the problem must be solved immediately to avert a depression. That was the opinion that he expressed to fellow students. But he did not perceive himself as co-oriented to those students. They did not understand the consequences of inflation, he said, and they wished to blame President Reagan (Ronnie) for it; that is, they demonstrated an orientation to causes rather than to solutions.

A German woman philosophy student from Mainz saw dependence on the United States as the most important problem. She perceived that public opinion was critical of the consequences of that dependence. She, herself, believed Germany should evolve into a neutral state. There should be a real democracy and not just the appearance of it. So she was at the stage of suggesting solutions to the problem. She told a friend that addressed the possible consequences of the problem (of dependence). She perceived that her friend also was afraid of war and power politics, that is, consequences, and perceived co-orientation with her with respect to this aspect of the problem.

Quite clearly, the focus of attention of this German student was primarily on the consequences and solutions to the problem of German dependence, but she perceived herself as more co-oriented to consequences than to solutions. She was "ahead" of her colleague on that aspect of the problem.

A Japanese student perceived that public opinion was attentive to the prospect of possible revisions to the Constitution that would permit an increase in defense spending, that is, a disposition toward solutions to constitutional problems. But he did not feel that the public was aware of the consequences of that solution or the causes of the problem. He wished to maintain the protections contained in the Constitution; that was his solution to the pressures for rearming. However, he did not discuss this opinion with anyone because he feared that his view was unpopular. Hence the cognitive foci were on solutions, but he feared public disagreement concerning policies.

This student said he listened to the opinions of his peers about solutions in a university class, but he did not comment. Again, there was a common cognitive focus on solutions, and once more he did not perceive others as sharing his views. Quite interestingly, this student made no references to the causes or consequences of problems. It is possible that the debate over the Constitution was at a stage that transcended discussions of these aspects of the problem.

A Chinese second-year history student from Hong Kong University was concerned with problems of population and thought there was public opinion of two kinds—both for and against severe restrictions on illegal immigration. Thus he saw a focus of public attention on proposed solutions, a sharing of his personal concern. He asserted that the government should return all illegal immigrants to China once they were discovered. This was a serious problem, he said, alluding to consequences that threatened the very existence of Hong Kong.

Relating to co-orientation, he told his friends (as a solution) that the government should act on this problem. A conversation with his friends, he remembered, revealed their tendency to oppose the action, although representing a similar orientation to solutions. Another student pointed to the political uncertainties that faced Hong Kong (consequences of the transfer of sovereignty in 1997) and perceived that public opinion also was concerned about the same consequences—a perception of co-orientation at that cognitive level.

As we review these individual statements we may discern that students tended to focus on two or sometimes all three aspects of a problem, which tended most often to be consequences and solutions to problems rather than causes. This is not surprising, of course, for it is more difficult to delve into the causes of problems than to assess their effects or propose solutions.

TOWARD A COMPARATIVE VIEW

Because students as individuals are essentially similar across cultures, we expected similarities to emerge when we compared them as groups. But students are also products of different cultures and face different situations, so we also expected to observe some differences.

As shown in Figure 7.1 and Table 7.1, students were most similar in their tendencies to address consequences and solutions to problems rather than their causes. This was not surprising, for adducing the causes of problems requires special expenditures of energy and time. Obviously students encountered problems in managing these personal resources.

The pattern of orientation for American students was more like that of Japanese and Hong Kong than German students. There was a much greater degree of emphasis given to each orientation, however. American students were much more oriented to solutions than to causes or consequences, this bent being consistent with a culturally induced faith in the probability and the efficacy of solutions. But like the other student groups,

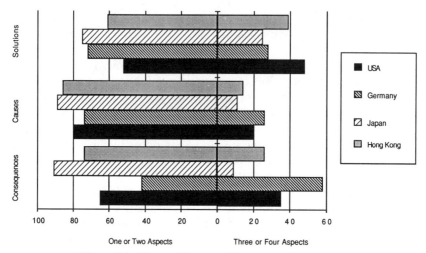

Figure 7.1. Extent of Focus on Three Aspects of Problem

they were oriented less to the causes of problems than to the consequences or solutions. However, they inquired into causes more than did the Japanese or Chinese students, again possibly because of cultural values that assure access to problems even while they are being managed by professionals or governments.

One might think that being a participant in a social movement and/or observing at first hand the consequences of a social problem would bring attention to the causes of problems, but this did not turn out entirely to be the case. German students were most activist and participatory and, consistent with our hypothesis, most observed consequences of problems from that vantage point. However, German students inquired into the causes of

TABLE 7.1. EXTENT OF FOCUS ON THREE ASPECTS OF PROBLEMS

Number of Aspects Mentioned (%)	Germany (n = 367) (78%)	United States (n = 515) (81%)	Japan (n = 395) (59%)	Hong Kong (n = 291) (42%)	
Consequences					
One or two	42	65	91	74	
Three or four	58	35	9	26	(128)
Causes					
One or two	74	80	89	86	
Three or four	26	20	11	14	(71)
Solutions					
One or two	72	52	75	61	
Three or four	28	48	25	39	(140)

problems only slightly more than did other students. It is possible that they were dealing with problems for which causes were well understood, or their problems might have been at an early stage of emergence, too early to assess causes. Yet the similarities across the groups argue against that kind of reasoning. The most likely explanation is that German students, as activists, were more involved in consequences than either in causes or solutions.

Japanese students were least likely to address the causes and the consequences of problems. This tendency is due, in part, to the fact that they reported fewer orientations to all aspects of problems. The Japanese students were more oriented to solutions than either causes or consequences.

It is interesting that Hong Kong students devoted more of their attention to solutions to problems than to their consequences. A reason may be found in their constant awareness of problems and their desire to solve them. Chinese students find themselves in the midst of problems of transportation, housing, population, and employment. All these situations are local in nature; even the most casual visitor to Hong Kong may see evidence of problems of housing and transportation being addressed.

Overall, American students (81 percent) expressed the most opinions, followed by the German (78 percent), the Japanese (only 52 percent), and the Hong Kong students (only 42 percent). Thus American and German students were more similar than Japanese and Hong Kong students, who were substantially different from the Americans and Germans but roughly equivalent to one another.

TOWARD A STEP THEORY

One of the advantages of our cognitive focus is that the three aspects of consequences, causes, and solutions suggested steps in a process.

In combining the percentages of the "three or four" references across Figure 7.1 as consequences (128 total), solutions (140), and causes (71), we observed that students referred most often to solutions to problems, then consequences, and finally causes. We would surmise on the basis of these data that soon after the emergence of a problem people will demand solutions to it; an alternative explanation is that we caught more students at the solution stage of their problems.

If the first surmise is true, logic proposes that a problem first emerges in an awareness of its effects or consequences, which leads at some point to a consideration of solutions. Dealing with the causes of a problem, when considered, intervenes at some point between consequences and solutions. The cause of a problem is, however, the step that the fewest persons address. To translate steps into a process, we must think of them as following on one another in a meaningful and systematic way. Carter (1965) suggested that identifying foci of attention, although simple at first glance, carried implications for observing process.

THE COMMERCIAL POLLS

One of the tests of our cognitive approach was to determine if it had generalizable qualities. Thus we examined all relevant public opinion polls in the archives of the Roper Center during the oil crisis. Did these polls focus on the consequences, causes, and solutions to problems? If so, would our findings on the dominance of solutions, consequences, and causes be validated? The review of the polls showed that, generally speaking, more polls asked the respondents about solutions than about the causes or consequences.

For example ABC News, Louis Harris and Associates, and NBC-AP each asked if respondents favored or opposed oil price deregulation if it would lead eventually to lower prices; they asked also if the respondents favored or opposed a windfall profits tax on oil companies, and if these revenues should be used to create new mass transportation? Each of these questions addressed proposed solutions to problems related to the oil crisis. The CBS-New York Times polls also asked about possible outcomes or solutions: Would the companies seek to produce more oil? Should alternate sources of energy be used, such as nuclear power, coal, and shale rock, given the risks and potentials?

Some questions also addressed causes of the oil crisis. Harris asked if rising oil prices were a cause of inflation. CBS News and the *New York Times* asked who caused the problem; for example, how much should government regulations be blamed for causing the crisis? How much of the blame should be placed on Middle East oil producers, on domestic oil companies, on the president, on consumers, or simply on a true shortage of oil? Yankelovich, Skelly, and White pollsters asked if the oil crisis was caused by a desire on the part of oil-producing countries to punish the United States for its policies.

The Harris, CBS-*New York Times*, and NBC-AP polls all asked individuals to describe the nature and consequences of the crisis; that is, was there a problem, and if so, what was it? For example, was the crisis a real crisis or fabricated for some other purpose such as price gouging? Roper asked about scarcities that would be produced by the shortage of oil and the inconveniences that these shortages would bring about. And Roper asked, as well, about possible ways to control oil prices, given the shortages, and things people could do to maintain the availability of and to conserve oil-based products (solutions).

In review, the three cognitive elements were present. Poll questions were focused on the consequences, causes, or solutions to problems. But more extensive analysis must be carried out to see if any logic is implicit in these steps.

- Is there a polling logic that explains when a pollster is most likely to ask questions about the consequences, causes, or solutions?
- Is there a public opinion logic of the same nature?
- Is there a media logic that rationalizes a set of relationships?

The answers to these questions await research on a multitude of publics, events, and social problems and issues.

COGNITIVE CO-ORIENTATION

Figure 7.2 and Table 7.2 show the extent to which the students perceived that they were co-oriented cognitively to their peers and/or to public

		Perceptions of Co-orientations			
	Orientations to Cognitive Aspects:	With Publics		Interpersonally	
		.r	Sig.	.r	Sig.
USA (N=678)	Causes	-.04	.15	.12	.001
	Consequences	.12	.001	.22	.001
	Solutions	.21	.001	.26	.001
Germany (N=493)	Causes	-.01	.46	.14	.01
	Consequences	.34	.001	.48	.001
	Solutions	.15	.001	-.07	.10
Japan (N=667)	Causes	.35	.001	.31	.001
	Consequences	.10	.01	.31	.001
	Solutions	.54	.001	.50	.001
Hong Kong (N=639)	Causes	.03	.29	.03	.25
	Consequences	.14	.001	.32	.001
	Solutions	.39	.001	.39	.001

Figure 7.2. Orientation to Cognitive Aspects of Problems and Perceptions of Co-orientation.

TABLE 7.2. ORIENTATIONS TO COGNITIVE ASPECTS OF PROBLEMS AND PERCEP-
TIONS OF CO-ORIENTATION

| Orientations to Cognitive Aspects | Perceptions of Co-Orientations | | | |
| | with Publics | | Interpersonally | |
	.r	Sig.	.r	Sig.
1. United States				
Causes	−.04	.15	.12	.001
Consequences	.12	.001	.22	.001
Solutions	.21	.001	.26	.001
2. Germany (*n* = 493)				
Causes	−.01	.46	.14	.01
Consequences	.34	.001	.48	.001
Solutions	.15	.001	−.07	.10
3. Japan (*n* = 667)				
Causes	.35	.001	.31	.001
Consequences	.10	.01	.31	.001
Solutions	.54	.001	.50	.001
4. Hong Kong (*n* = 639)				
Causes	.03	.29	.03	.25
Consequences	.14	.001	.32	.001
Solutions	.39	.001	.39	.001

opinion to aspects of social problems—to consequences, solutions, or
causes. Were the perceptions of co-orientation greater for peers or for the
public? Were perceptions similar or different in the four cultures?

Our measures of cognitive co-orientation were determined by comput-
ing Pearson correlation coefficients for the correspondence of answers to
the four questions (own opinion, perceived public opinion, opinion expressed to peer, and peer expression in response). The correlation computed for the first two questions showed the degree of correspondence
between the individual's opinions and perceptions of public opinion. The
correlation of the second two questions represented perceived peer communication, that is, correspondence between what the individual perceived
that he or she discussed and what he or she perceived the other person said
in response.

In terms of the Stamm, Bowes, and Bowes (1971) findings reported
earlier, it was not surprising to observe the degree to which the students
perceived co-orientation between themselves and the public. But the extent of it was somewhat startling. Significance reached the .001 level in 17
of 24 of the paired comparisons, and in another two instances it achieved
the .01 level. Thus the students perceived in most cases that they and
others were talking about much the same thing, whether with respect to

each other or to members of the general public. There were only five paired comparisons in which this was not the case, all of them related to the causes of problems. As we have pointed out, causes are not as easily recognized or understood as are consequences or possible solutions.

We assumed also that students would be similar in some respects across cultures in their perceptions of public opinion and peer groups. The similarities would come about because of their equivalence in status in each society. But differences would also be apparent, attributable to culture and to the uniqueness of situations.

The greatest likelihood of perceived co-orientation across the four groups involved the consequences of problems. As we have noted previously, these are the easiest aspects of a problem to observe. The perceptions of causes or even solutions to problems should be more subject to values and conditions in a culture. Thus substantially greater co-orientation was perceived across the four student groups with respect to consequences (and solutions) than to causes of problems. Surprisingly, students perceived greater co-orientation in most cases to the general public than to peers. In the eyes of students, the university setting did not seal them off from the greater community.

Except for Hong Kong students, the overall patterns of perceived co-orientation were very similar across the four groups. American students were not unlike the German, Japanese, and even the Hong Kong students in most respects.

Cultural and situational factors distinguished the groups in only two important respects: Japan was the only country in which a substantial number of students felt that they shared perceptions with the public about the causes of problems. There were no other positive correlations of this kind. One possible basis was situational; the students identified as the most important problems those that were of common interest to them and to the society and not uniquely attributable to their own interests. These would include such problems as trade, defense buildups that challenged the Constitution, and the adoption of consumerism values, problems that were of common concern. A second reason was cultural—the close sense of affiliation within the family as well as the workplace.

Hong Kong students, in contrast, did not co-orient to each other or to the public with respect to causes of problems. The reason may be found in the nature of the situation in Hong Kong. The students there concentrated on a greater number of problems than did any of the other students; this result implied a greater range of steps, as well, and thus less probability of co-orientation. There is an implication that cultural groups that focus on fewer steps do so by consensus and are essentially collective in their orientation to social life.

A SECOND ANALYSIS

It should be remembered that the aspects of problems about which the students were communicating had their location in the problematic situations they had defined. In effect, they were talking about the consequences, causes, and solutions to those problems. Looking directly at the problematics—about which students had discussed consequences, causes, and solutions—might some of them, more than others, produce perceptions of co-orientation?

Since we had not asked directly about co-orientation to problematic situations, we cannot answer that question directly. But we might approximate that result by looking at the most important problem that the students discussed and relating to it the extent of co-orientations to aspects of that problem, that is, to the causes, consequences, and solutions.

We followed a simple procedure. We isolated each problematic situation, such as "need for value," "loss of value," and so on. We then tallied each instance of co-orientation to the causes, consequences, and/or solutions to that problem. The results are presented in Table 7.3 as the total number of instances of co-orientation with respect to each problematic situation. These were calculated for perceptions of publics as well as peers.

The results are proportions of 100 percent in each case. Thus, for example, in the case of the United States—where the problematic situation was need for value—54 percent reported co-orientation with both the public and peers either to the causes, consequences, or solutions to the most important problem. By including all three conditions we inflated the values, somewhat, but this should not greatly disturb the comparisons. Based on this example, Figure 7.3 and Table 7.3 show the extent of perceived co-orientation to general public opinion and to peers with respect to problematic situations that describe need for value.

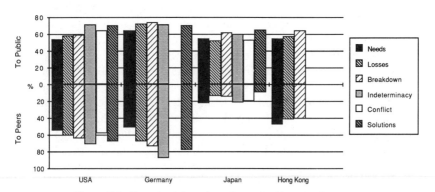

Figure 7.3. Perceived Co-orientation to Problematic Situations

TABLE 7.3. PERCEIVED CO-ORIENTATION TO PROBLEMATIC SITUATIONS (IN PER-CENTAGES)

Problem Situations	United States		Germany		Japan		Hong Kong	
	Perceived Co-Orientation to							
	Public	*Peers*	*Public*	*Peers*	*Public*	*Peers*	*Public*	*Peers*
	(1)	(2)	(1)	(2)	(1)	(2)	(1)	(2)
Need	54	54	64	51	55	23	55	48
Loss	58	61	72	68	52	14	57	42
Breakdown	59	64	74	74	62	15	64	41
Indeterminacy	71	71	71	88	60	22	++	++
Solution	64	58	++	++	53	20	++	++
Conflict	70	68	70	78	65	10	++	++

++ Insufficient N.

First, the general level of perceived co-orientation is high. In the cases of each problematic situation American students perceived that they were as much oriented to the opinions of the general public as to those of their peers. This finding might be due to two factors: (1) students' perceptions shared with the public's a high degree of salience with respect to the problems, and (2) students' and the public's perceptions depended on the media.

German students produced slightly higher scores for co-orientation than the other three groups. It was possible that the participatory politics of German students caused them to project their concerns on the society and perceive that they were sharing foci of attention with its members.

Japanese students perceived co-orientation more dramatically with publics than with peers. Cultural factors hint at a basis for this finding. For one thing, it would be improper at the interpersonal level for Japanese students to introduce into a conversation any problematic or conflictual situations. At the same time, the sense of awareness that exists in Japanese society would explain the students' marked tendency more to identify their concerns with those of the general public.

It thus would be easier to project one's beliefs on an anonymous public than to validate one's perception of another person, particularly if the matter were controversial.

Hong Kong students perceived themselves to be more in touch with the public than with one another, but not nearly to the extent as in Japan or for the same reasons. Perceived co-orientation in the Chinese case might be due to the kinds of problems that were mentioned, most of them occurring in the intimate and crowded physical environment that was shared equally by students and by adults.

SUMMARY

We employed a comparative perspective to analyze the extent to which students demonstrated similarities and differences in perceiving a common focus of attention with respect to cognitive aspects of problems. This perspective applied not only to perceptions of public opinion but to peer communication as well.

We approached the concept of co-orientation as a cognitive rather than an evaluative dimension. The cognitive elements incorporate the consequences of a problem, its causes, and possible solutions. These dimensions contribute to a sense of structure and process. Each element of structure—consequences, causes, and solutions—could be seen to represent steps in a process of opinion formation. First the individual forms opinions about the consequences of a problem, and then the solutions, and some individuals inquire into causes.

As a related step, we compared perceptions of co-orientation in relation to each kind of problematic situation and described our expectations for similarities and differences in behavior across cultures and with respect to perceptions of publics and peers. We demonstrated the relevance of both structural similarities across cultures and unique differences in cultures and situations.

This approach to public opinion is an extension of our efforts to substitute cognitive and process-oriented concepts for topical and evaluative approaches to news, as described in Chapter 4.

CHAPTER 8

The Intercultural Dimensions of Interpersonal Communication

Decades ago Katz and Lazarsfeld (1955) "rediscovered" interpersonal communication as a powerful source of influence in the 1940 American presidential campaign. But despite the provocation of those findings, there was little opportunity at that time to test the applicability of the concept to other political cultures.

Scholars recently have begun to examine the nature of informing and influence in other cultures. In a recent comparison of the levels of comprehension of radio news by American and British audiences, Robinson and Levy (1986) discovered the two kinds of audiences were similar: As the number of conversations about the news increased, considerably higher comprehension occurred. Information did not sink in or become "deep processed" by many individuals until it had been related to the norms and attitudes of peers and colleagues in that culture. The researchers added, "Indeed, one might even conclude that until news is put to such communicative use, it is of minimal societal consequence" (p. 234).

Another study in Britain by Gunter (1984) showed that talking about the news had at least as powerful an effect on comprehension as using the media; thus interpersonal communication clarified messages and tapped a consensus of shared meanings.

These and other studies have been valuable because they have fortified our knowledge about the relationships between media use and interpersonal communication in multicultural settings. They have another cultural utility, as well, for they help us to distinguish between the often-merged concepts of *information* and *influence*. This is a valuable conceptual clarification because it permits the comparative researcher an opportunity to observe the relationships of information and influence in a variety of cultures. As we will see, some cultures rely greatly on personal networks to diffuse influence as well as information.

One of the most culturally intriguing questions that this chapter pursues is the reason(s) for the dramatic differences in dependency on interpersonal communication for *information* between the Japanese students and others in the comparison groups. Why did the Japanese students express so little dependency on interpersonal communication as a source of information?

Did they get sufficient information from the mass media and thus did not require interpersonal communication for information? This answer does not seem plausible. Japanese students used mass media only slightly more than other students, although they used more varieties of media than the other groups. Even that fact, however, would not rationalize the lack of use of so intimate a source as interpersonal communication.

Did they have fewer interpersonal contacts? Our data in Chapter 7 on perceptions of public opinion and communication did not support that conclusion. Japanese students, as much as other students, reported discussions with their peers and perceptions of similarities with them on the focus of their attention.

Did they actually gain and/or exchange as much information as other groups but assess it in different terms, that is, as culturally defined "information" that from the Western perspective would be viewed as "influence"?

We have one piece of evidence that seems to argue the cultural case for more actual equivalence. Figure 8.1 describes the relationship between the use of interpersonal communication and personal observation to identify problems and the use of mass media and qualitative media. Although

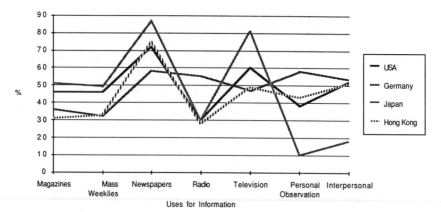

Figure 8.1. Comparative Uses of Mass Media and Interpersonal Communication for Information.

fewer Japanese students cited interpersonal communication and personal observation as primary sources of information, those who did so also reported more use of mass media and qualitative media. The difference is substantial for qualitative media and less significant for mass media when compared to U.S. and German students.

What these data point to are generally similar connections between nonmedia and media use among Japanese, U.S., and German students. The stronger connection in the case of the Japanese argues for the connectedness of one to the other and argues against nonuse of interpersonal communication and personal observation for information.

To attack these questions from another perspective we have incorporated an analysis of intercultural communication without media interaction, hoping to extract from the intercultural communication literature some suggestions about how media-interpersonal communication dependencies might function in Japan as well as in other cultures.

A culture may or may not utilize mass media for both information and influence. Japanese students expressed a culture in which mass media are used primarily for information and interpersonal communication is used primarily to diffuse culture.

This use contrasts with the Western concept of influence, which describes the larger social context in which information is contained. Culture, in the Western sense, thus spells influence. It would predict that American and German students, notably, would utilize interpersonal communication and observation as extensions of media for both information and influence. These are normative cultural manifestations for each of those societies. Mindful of these kinds of nuances of cultural meaning, Nakanishi (1986), among others, recommended that studies be carried out in single countries before comparative analyses to prevent confounding of meaning.

THE MASS MEDIA CONNECTION

In considering the mass media connection, that is, the relationships between media use and interpersonal communication, we asked a number of questions:

1. To what extent did each of the student cultures report similar or different dependencies on mass media and nonmedia (interpersonal communication and observation) for information and/or influence?
2. How much similarity of behavior existed among the student cultures, and how much of it was attributable to the equivalence of students' roles?
3. What elements of culture and/or specific situations produced differences in communications behavior?

Figure 8.1 and Table 8.1 compare the uses of mass media and interpersonal communication for information. In examining our data we found that our expectations for observing similarities across the student groups generally were supported. These similarities seemed to be explained by the equivalent roles of students and their place in the broader culture. However, differences in culture also contributed to some striking differences.

Examples of similarities included the following:

1. When preferences were rank-ordered, newspapers were the first source of information for students in each of the four cultures.
2. Television was the next most cited source of information.
3. Other than Japan, the three groups used nonmedia sources to the same extent, including both personal observation and interpersonal communication. As we have pointed out, these were remarkably different for Japan.
4. These behaviors held not only across mass media but for qualitative media as well.

The differences were explained by cultural and situational factors:

1. Fewer German students watched television, explained in part by a cultural tendency to depend on radio and a situationally defined aversion to the more controlled and less satisfying content of television news.
2. More Japanese students watched television, attributable in part to culturally defined attractions to television as a visual and active medium coupled with a lesser use of radio.
3. Fewer German and Hong Kong students read magazines, perceiving them as elite media. But this tendency was common to a lesser ex-

TABLE 8.1. COMPARATIVE USES OF MASS MEDIA AND INTERPERSONAL COMMUNICATION FOR INFORMATION

	United States	Germany	Japan	Hong Kong
Mass media				
Magazines	46	36	51	31
Mass weeklies	46	32	49	33
Newspapers	72	58	87	75
Radio	30	55	30	28
Television	60	47	81	49
Non-mass media				
Personal				
observation	38	58	10	43
Interpersonal	52	53	18	51

NOTE: Qualitative media included prestige media and opinion publications.

tent across all four groups, contributing further to the idea that in certain respects students in all cultures will demonstrate similarities in media uses.

4. The mass weeklies were seen by German and Hong Kong students as less adequate than newspapers. However, Japanese accorded their mass weeklies the unique role of entertainment as well as information. American students alone had access to such "class mass weeklies" as *Time* and *Newsweek*.

5. A situational factor that seemingly suggested equivalence between the Japanese and Hong Kong students was the similar degree to which problems such as housing, population, and pollution could be observed first-hand in those crowded Asian countries. Given this equivalence, we could expect that references to personal observation as a major source of information would be similar.

This did not turn out to be the case, however. Japanese students, in contrast to Hong Kong students, did not elevate these directly observable problems to the level of most important problems. Rather, they turned to other, more personally manageable (i.e., private) problems as their foci of attention. As Japanese students defined the situation, it was a governmental, bureaucratic, and media role to deal with "public" problems, even if they, themselves, witnessed them. Except under unusual conditions, public problems were not to be treated as private problems. Thus Japanese students were in consonance with what the media defined as "public" and "private" saliences of problems. In contrast, other students deemed most important the problems they, themselves, observed.

Given the greater use by the Japanese students of mass media—television, newspapers, magazines, and mass weeklies (not, however, radio)—for information, we might also have assumed that Japanese students had a greater appetite for information from interpersonal sources as well.

As we have pointed out, however, our data show that many fewer Japanese students described interpersonal communication as a source of information. Fewer Japanese students said they discussed their opinions with their peers, and fewer reported that they perceived the existence of public opinion—despite the fact that as many Japanese students reported that they themselves held opinions.

CULTURAL ASPECTS OF COMMUNICATION

Answers to findings of the kind we have just described must be sought in analyses of cultures. We are fortunate to have accessible to us a number of studies that have compared the influence of cultures on the communication behaviors of Japanese and American students. These extend along a number of cultural and situational dimensions. Unfortunately, we do not have the same wealth of studies to compare German or Chinese students. But because our other German and Chinese data are so similar to that of the American students who have been studied in relation to the Japanese, we may make some guarded inferences in relation to those groups. In fact, Hall (1977) classified both Japanese and Chinese cultures as "high context," and Nakanishi (1986) concluded that the findings of Wolfson and Pearce (1983), who studied Chinese interpersonal communication, also permitted insight into Japanese patterns.

As discussed in Chapter 1, intercultural communication studies depend for their uniqueness of approach and productivity on their ability to relate culture to communication. Nakanishi, among others, described Japanese society as being homogeneous in terms of race, language, and basic value orientations. In Kunihiro's (1976) terms, members of Japanese society share a great many aspects of daily life and consciousness. This view echoes Hall's (1977) description of Japan as a high-context communication society, in which most of the information is either in the physical context or internalized in the person, and little is in the coded, explicit, transmitted part of the message.

Nakanishi (1986) emphasized that messages exchanged among Japanese may not be easily understood by those who do not share the same contextual information since the Japanese language often seems to be vague and indirect to those who do not understand what is being communicated. A Japanese person communicates by effective use of language and viewing the communication in a holistic context rather than striving for complete clarity and openness. Nonverbal feedback and situational cues permit individuals to move from the general to the specific and from the opaque to the transparent. Adaptability is important, and being more specific or vague than the situation warrants is a sign of insensitivity (*yabo*).

Just as we have distinguished information from influence, in the Japanese tradition it is important to discern the relationship aspects of the communication from its context (*sasshi*). Mushakoji (1976) observed that in Japan it was considered a strength to be able to catch on quickly so that one could adjust to the position of the other before it was completely stated.

Several of the Japanese-American communication studies were carried out through collaboration of American-trained Japanese scholars and American scholars. Understandably, the researchers were directed to those traditions of interpersonal communication studies that were considered to be important both to Japan and to America. We are able to place trust in these studies because they were carefully cross-translated for both Japanese and American nuances, and both cultures were reflected equally.

The foci for study included communication apprehension, self-monitoring, uncertainty reduction, high- and low-context cultures, and language. Nakanishi studied self-disclosure, another high-priority concept in intercultural communication, completely in the Japanese context. As we summarize these studies, we describe their implications for our own data analysis.

Communication Apprehension

This research tradition in interpersonal and intercultural communication examines the importance of communication apprehension. McCroskey, Gudykunst, and Nishida (1985) described the concept as a fear or apprehension of engaging in the act of communicating without respect to the content of the communication or the language—one's own or the other's—that is employed. The scholars compared Japanese students who were speaking in Japanese and English.

The results demonstrated that Japanese students were just as apprehensive whether they were speaking their native language or another language. This was an unusual behavior because students in other cultures invariably were less apprehensive when speaking their own languages. The researchers concluded that Japanese cultural norms did not encourage talkativeness but rather valued reticence. The Japanese student would lose fear or apprehension only when it was clear that it was appropriate to speak.

If we accept the premise that Japanese culture requires a major preliminary step in communication, that of determining the appropriateness of the situation, we may see that the first step taken by any Japanese would be to obtain or give information about the definition of the situation rather than to give or to get information about the subject at hand. Thus, communication apprehension may be seen as a fear of taking an inappropriate step. It is less surprising, therefore, that the Japanese students were least likely to report interpersonal communication as a major source of information.

Social Distance

Wiseman, Hammer, and Nishida (1987) asked American and Japanese students to assess the status of the other to determine the amount of perceived social distance. The Japanese students actually knew more about the American students than the Americans knew about the Japanese. Yet the Japanese perceived more social distance between them and, as a consequence, were less willing to express an opinion.

In contrast, U.S. students perceived a greater social distance between themselves and Japanese students, and they were more willing to risk expressing an opinion. For Japanese students, shyness and reticence were more appropriate behaviors than expressing opinions. Given these characteristics, they would perceive greater social distance. Underlining these differences, American students culturally also perceived less social distance and thus were even more encouraged to express their opinions, as is reflected in our data.

Social Status

In a related context, Johnson and Johnson (1975) concluded that Japanese students were more sensitive than American students to the social statuses of other persons and, as a consequence, were less assertive in their behavior. Japanese students also were more vague (incorporated in the language itself), more indirect, more sensitive to verbal cues, and treated silence as attentively as words.

Students were asked in a number of situations to answer such questions as "I would" or "I would not tell" a person an opinion or ask for one on public issues. The Japanese students were less likely to engage in these direct inquiries. Obviously, they preferred an approach that was less explicit and direct, emphasizing interdependence and harmony.

In a parallel study that produced similar findings Nisugi (1974) contrasted Japanese cultural traits revealed in communication—such as delicacy, politeness, vagueness, gentleness, abstractness, warmth, and sensitivity—to the more mechanical English-language characteristics of rhythmic syntax, specificity, objectivity, practicality, and systematic and concise approaches. One might surmise that the English and German sytaxes and styles lent themselves more to exchanging information about opinions, as seems reflected in our data.

Language Relevance

Hall (1976) posited a framework of high- and low-context cultures. The Japanese language was identified as offering the greatest cultural context among other high-context Asian languages, whereas English and German, the other languages represented in our comparative analysis, were identified as low-context languages. As Hall explained,

> A high context language...is one in which most of the information is either in the physical context or internalized in the person, while very little is in the coded, explicit part of the message. A low context message is just the opposite; the mass of information is vested in the explicit code. (p. 79)

This is another way of describing the outcomes we already have observed, that is, that the more highly contextualized Japanese language took precedence over culturally manifest information exchange. The interpersonal context carried the advantage of a heavy quotient of prior understandings. Its informational content was vested in the social situation. Thus Japanese themselves would not describe their activity as an overt form of information exchange despite the fact that a great deal of information was incorporated.

As H. Nishida (1985) described the Japanese context, the language itself displays the ability of parties to express respect and positive regard for one another. This expression cannot be accomplished if one does not understand the language and culture:

> In high context cultures the focus in initial interaction is not upon predicting individual behavior in general but whether the other person will follow the norms and conventions appropriate in the context. This information does not come from the content of the verbal message but rather from knowledge of the other's background and the relationships between the people involved. (Gudykunst et al., 1986, p. 569)

Self-Monitoring

A member of a high-context culture would tend, therefore, to direct a great deal of effort and energies to what Snyder (1974) described as "self-monitoring." Out of concern for social appropriateness, the individual becomes highly sensitive to self-presentation and expression by others. These observations then guide his or her own behavior.

It is important to note that T. Nishida (1977) pointed out that although the self-monitoring concept had not been tested in Japan, it contained elements of applicability. Okabe (1983) indicated that in a culture of *sasshi* or *omoiyari*, both words meaning "considerateness," to communicate well means to understand and perceive the inexplicit, even to the point of deciphering the faintest of nonverbal nuances. One implication for our data is that the reports by Japanese students on interpersonal communication of information were minimized because the transfer of information was too subtle to be picked up by the question.

Conditions of Ambiguity

Gudykunst and Nishida (1984) placed both American and Japanese students in conditions of uncertainty and found that they used different coping strategies. The Japanese students were much more reluctant to engage in self-disclosure or to ask questions directly of one another. Rather, they attempted to reduce their uncertainty by themselves. Here, again, the demand by the culture for greater personal control and autonomy would make it more difficult for the Japanese student to ask for or give information except under very appropriate conditions.

It is difficult to summarize the import of all these concepts, but we might say briefly that Japanese interpersonal communication is both relational and informational. Interactions are heavily contextual and take information into account more implicitly than explicitly. Knowledge does not emanate only from the explicit content of the message but also from the context of the exchange. We must, therefore, conclude that the tendency for Japanese to minimize interpersonal communication as a source of information is explained by cultural definitions of information. What for Westerners might be seen as influence would be perceived by Japanese as information, but not so called.

The need for conceptual equivalence as a guide to deriving valid comparisons is illustrated by the studies of intercultural interaction that we have cited. There seems little doubt that the observations that were made in the experiments reflected the actual behavior of the American and Japanese participants. Yet there remains a nagging question of situational equivalence in the experimental setting. The cultural question that needs to be asked is whether Japanese students viewed the experiment as a "private" setting or a "public" one. In each case, they might have behaved differently.

In discussing value systems and communication in Japan, Midooka (1985) outlined a number of traditional values and beliefs that still influence Japanese behavior despite the impact of new values and beliefs. They represent, in these terms, a latent structure which may be reawakened within the individual and have the power to influence behavior in a situation.

Midooka lists some of these as avoidance of conflict as a way of maintaining a peaceful existence, an emphasis upon a modest self (Proverb; A talented hawk hides his claws), and a corresponding belief that quality will be recognized. Further, the Japanese is not encouraged to think of himself or herself as an individual but as a contextual unit that includes both self and others—a relationship. Thus communication behavior varies greatly with the nature of the interaction.

The experimental situation calls into focus the Japanese concept of the "circle of Nakama." Two possible circles exist—an intimate one of family, relatives, friends, and colleagues, and the social and familiar bonds that tie them together. This is an environment that is easily accepted; it incorporates laws of cause and effect, or *En*, one's fate. These ties between *Nakama* which are bounded by *En* are not easily broken. The Japanese may communicate easily within this group. They may also be assertive with someone of equivalent or lower status in the group.

Status and role are thus important within the group. Japanese communication patterns are affected by age, position, tenure, wisdom, sex, and family status. Thus experimental communication situations involving Japanese and American students must take these and other factors that express *Nakama* into account.

Outside the relatively friendly atmosphere of *Nakama* other patterns assert themselves—expression is more controlled and deferential. This invokes *Keigo*, the polite, honorific mode. The Japanese who recognizes the most subtle differences between the two kinds of situations and can adapt to them readily is considered to have a good personality, and that quality determines employability in an organization. Presumably, the random assignment of Japanese to experimental groups would address this difficulty.

Other communication patterns that express cultural values also may assert themselves in situations. One of them is a generalized tendency to represent oneself as shy, to be relatively silent, to maintain a certain caution through ambiguity rather than definiteness, and to smile as a sign of a desire for harmony. In that way the person expresses modesty as well.

Substantial ambiguity arises between the Japanese necessity to shield real intentions, *honne*, and official conduct, *tatemae*. To avoid revealing his own opinions the Japanese will speak in terms of general principles which do not bring harm to anyone. This is another aspect of *tatemae*.

An evident problem with *tatemae* is that the generalities that are produced are not likely to bring about action. In recognition of that possible problem a great deal of preparation of the setting must be carried out. This is described as *ne-mawashi*, a preliminary process where problems are worked out in intimate informal settings so that the formal meeting may proceed without controversy and come to a predetermined conclusion. Again, the experimental situation must take possible conflictual elements into account.

THE AMERICAN EXPERIENCE

Posed against the intuitive, almost existential approach to information and communication that we have just discussed, American culture prescribes a contrastingly explicit orientation. Philosopher Robert Hutchins, former president of the University of Chicago, once described American experience as rooted in the "civilization of dialogue." The spirit of Western civilization was the spirit of inquiry: Its dominant element was the *logos*; nothing was to remain undiscussed. Everyone was to speak his or her mind, and no position was to be left unexamined. The exchange of ideas between and among people was held to be the path to the realization of the potential of the race (Peterson, 1973).

Peterson (1973) noted that whereas Americans sought dialogue, Japanese did not; even if the form were dialogue, the content was monologue. No matter how much a Japanese negotiated, no agreement was made on the basis of a thorough statement from both sides as to the bases for the differences, an approach idealized by Westerners.

Western institutions and social processes have expressed their confidence in the value of the spoken language: representative government, the jury system, the lecture system, tutorials, debating, and so on. Dialectics have set up Western constructions of logical propositions; movement back and forth among the propositions encourages feedback and interaction.

In reaching an understanding or decision, Westerners present large numbers of potentially relevant facts and ideas, and participants move to the next level of understanding through repetition of the back-and-forth movements. It is a method that takes time and effort and, of necessity, involves not so much a language of decision as a language of process. In contrast, Isamu (1972) has described oriental languages as more "practical" in approach, skipping process and going on to a conclusion.

In describing problems of dialogue between Japanese and Europeans, Abe (1972) was amazed to observe how scattered and disjointed Japanese conversation appeared to be from the Western perspective. There appeared to be no apparent logical coherence between speakers; yet they came to agreeable conclusions. The reason was that verbal expression, however itself fragmentary and unsystematic, nonetheless carried emotional, communal values.

While in Japan it would be common to ask, "What do you think of this?" and the answer might be "I like it"; in Western cultures the individual would offer a reason for *why* he or she "likes it." And when other persons enter into a situation, Westerners move onto a rational plane and employ logical thinking to persuade; but Japanese, even if certain they are correct and no less logical, make no direct attempts to persuade.

Japanese have been taught to respect the feelings of others and surmise thoughts rather than question people directly, whereas the Western pattern is quite to the contrary. Similarly, although confrontation is permitted to develop in American encounters, its occasion in the Japanese context is considered to be offensive and disagreeable, as to a sense of beauty.

Japanese try to keep interpersonal relations harmonious through nondialectic means. The result is that Western dialectic and the linguistic tools necessary for debate are not honored, much less given the impetus to bloom.

Forms of unspoken communication such as *haragei* (the art of subtle communication) and *me wa kuchi hodo n i mono o ii* (the eyes say as much as the mouth), are in constant use, and they work to support the esthetic ideal.

One might think of Americans and Japanese, therefore, as having "attitudes" toward language. Whereas Japanese use language to ensure the process of assimilation of one to the other (described by Peterson as a process in which the effort is made to make the strange seem familiar), Americans use language to define differences as well as similarities in points of view. The English language, unlike Japanese, does not carry the implication that both parties to a communication already are part of one organic whole. Rather, in English one's identity is constantly subject to redefinition.

English as a language also distinguishes between the self and the other, whereas Japanese—despite much ethnic diversity—shares a great deal of the other's consciousness. Explanations through language often are unnecessary. An intuitive, nonverbal communication of the sort that develops among family members living under the same roof also diffuses throughout the society.

These Western modes and motivations for communication are reflected both in the nature of American communication research and in its foci of attention. American scholars have studied very explicitly the processes of information exchange and influence. Much to the point in our comparisons, the Western studies of the diffusion of information reflect the highly explicit nature of information giving and receiving and its uniquely cultural characteristics as process. Acculturation also explains the social purposes that researchers in the West have pursued, such as efforts by one person to influence another. In these terms one must be struck by the dichotomy in Western thought in the perceptions of information and influence.

RESEARCH OPERATIONS AS EXEMPLARS

American communication research illustrates the acculturation processes that we have described. Gantz and Trenholm (1979) reviewed several studies that examined psychological and social needs expressed by the sharing of information. The importance of their work is not to be minimized. One study (Fink, Serota, Woelfel, & Noell, 1975) found that passing along information helped to reduce anxieties that an individual felt about an event; the same psychological principle was applied to the need to cope with situations that were discrepant with the expectations held by the individual (Gantz & Miller, 1974) because the existence of the discrepancies provoked people to talk about them. Many individuals who passed along information were motivated by altruism and a desire to relate to others (O'Keefe & Kissel, 1971). Thus communication in Western thought appears to be a means to attain a relationship, whereas communication in Japanese culture serves to express a relationship.

One is led by evidence of this kind to characterize American communication culture as flowing from a more open system and a more heterogeneous and therefore "discrepancy-prone" society, where information is deemed essential by individuals to address those discrepancies. As we have suggested, whereas Japanese motivations are tied to the perceptions of group consciousness, American motivations express the needs of the individual or the perceived needs of others—their interest in or need for knowledge and a desire to get acquainted, to note reactions to information, and to modify attitudes. Self-indulgent motivations include self-interest; acquiring information; asserting one's knowledge, dominance, or position; seeking clarification; acquiring status or approval; assessing the other; and simply passing time.

These motivations for communication have been reduced to four factors: (1) the desire for information, (2) the desire to establish social status, (3) the need for expression, and (4) the desire to explore possibilities for social contact. It is culturally important that only one of these motivations assumes common consciousness, such as sharing feelings or determining the commonality of interests, as so characterizes Japanese culture.

Troldahl and Van Dam (1971) inquired into the extent of face-to-face communication of the news and the environments in which it was most likely to occur. They discovered that in the large industrial and financial center of Detroit, about 30 percent of respondents said that in the preceding two weeks they had offered their opinions to someone, and 20 percent recalled that someone had volunteered an opinion to them. When we compare this "volunteering" behavior to the subtleties observed in Japan, we are struck by the differences in style.

Troldahl (1971) found that those who perceived themselves more as givers of information than askers did not in all situations markedly display more knowledge or use of media. This finding gave rise to the hypothesis that the demand for exchange in the American context is explained more by personality than by social rules or intellectual propositions. But it should be noted that culture permits this variation without any sanctions. Troldahl found supporting evidence for this hypothesis: Persons who were most gregarious in personality did not wait to be asked for their opinions, more often initiating communication and more often giving than asking for information. In the Japanese context any expressions of personality would be viewed in very negative terms, for these might work against harmony in the group.

BASES FOR GENERALIZATIONS

These marked differences in behaviors between Japanese and Western styles of communication raise questions concerning the conditions under which behaviors might be more generalizable. Perhaps the most evident "leveling" process occurs under conditions of crisis or indebterminacy. Such situational factors might demand of the individual a degree of information diffusion that transcends the constraints of culture.

We need to carry on comparative analysis of communication during critical events—natural disasters, for example, in which information exchange by interpersonal means would be essential. Similarly, where social institutions broke down in their functioning there would be a need for alternative channels of information and communication. By examining communication in the situational context we may come closer to a basis for comparison.

There is ample precedence for comparative studies of this kind on the diffusion of information about important events. Hanneman and Greenberg (1973) predicted the likelihood of exchanging information about important events in the news, and Haroldsen and Harvey (1979) described conditions under which diffusion of information most likely would take place. They suggested that the more extraordinary or "shocking" the event, the more likely that people would exchange information and opinions about it.

A Diffusion Test Case

This was the case when a group of researchers was organized in 12 countries in Europe, Asia, and America to observe the diffusion of news about the assassination of Sweden's Prime Minister Olof Palme (Rosengren 1987). The researchers took into account differences in media structures, cultures, political place in the international system, and other factors. United States, West German, and Japanese scholars observed diffusion processes among politicians, journalists, and the public as three distinctive groups. Actually, comparatively little information was passed along interpersonally; most was through mass media. The United States and Japan were characterized as "television" countries, whereas Germany was a "radio" country.

THE GERMAN EXPERIENCE

Very few studies have been conducted in West Germany on aspects of interpersonal communication. Conditions under which media are most relevant to interpersonal communication in Germany have not been spelled out adequately enough to propose a theory or to encourage a comparative approach to the question. Kepplinger, who carried out the West German phase of the Olof Palme diffusion study, observed this gap in the social science literature in West Germany and concluded that it came about more as a matter of academic priority than cultural disinterest.

Kepplinger and Martin (1986) did undertake, however, a unique effort to observe how often and under what conditions the content of the mass media was a stimulant to interpersonal communication. The approach taken was to observe the extent to which students actually referred to the mass media in the discussion of social problems. We may remember that German students expressed a stronger sense of identification with the media than did the other three groups. We might expect them to refer to the media, therefore, in discussions about participatory politics.

Although Kepplinger and his colleague did not test that explicit hypothesis, they adopted a research technique that could answer the question. The procedure they adopted was to introduce an observer into the everyday activities of the students at places where groups of students tended to gather. These included apartments, campus settings, and coffee shops and cafeterias. The observers simply made a note of any references that were made to the mass media. They did not write down what was said, only that the media had been mentioned. Nonetheless, a number of observations could be made.

First, mass media tended to be mentioned more in small groups than in large ones. Overall, 71 percent of the students referred at some point to the media. But a reference to the media did not necessarily produce a reply in that genre. Only a fourth of the replies to "media mentions" themselves mentioned the media.

Second, mentions of the media were affected by the intensity of a discussion. Did media enter the discussion more often in the heat of argument or at a less impassioned point in the discussion? Apparently there was no connection between the intensity of discussions and references to media. Thus media did not seem to be introduced as arbiters of difficult situations.

Third, the observers classified participants as active or passive. Here there were dramatic implications for media use. When individuals played passive roles in the conversation, only 8 percent mentioned media; but when individuals tended to dominate the discussion, some 87 percent mentioned the media.

This finding varied dramatically by media:

- Those who mentioned newspapers did so equally if they were passive participants or dominated the discussion.
- Those who mentioned radio tended to mention it only slightly more if they dominated the discussion, but in any case, radio refer-

ences tended to occur in noncontroversial and more frivolous areas of the discussion.

- Those who mentioned television tended to do it most often if they dominated the discussion.
- Qualitative sources were used more to attack the positions of others than to defend one's own position.

Although we lack comparable data, we would speculate that this use of communication by German students in interpersonal communication would contrast dramatically with the discussions of the other student cultures.

THE CHINESE EXPERIENCE

There also is little to summarize with respect to the Chinese experience. Yasunari (1969) pointed out that the Chinese, in contrast to the Japanese, have been characterized in cultural terms as given to excessive and even exhaustive expression and endless argument. He contrasted this social behavior with artistic values, in which Chinese value empty space in their brush paintings.

Norinaga (1763) similarly labeled the Chinese approach as "pompous verbosity," together with a proclivity to debate constantly the rights or wrongs of various positions and to try to define the principles behind every policy or action. He referred to Chou Enlai's flashing eyes portrayed in film and photographs as being prepared to devastate an opponent in biting argument. The "sayings" of Confucius, and recently Mao, were legendary, testifying to the Chinese love of discourse—which may be compared with the Western *logos*.

We can only hope that more empirical work into the interpersonal communication of the Chinese will be stimulated and extended to intercultural dimensions.

SUMMARY

There has been renewed research interest in the concepts of information and influence that encourages an interest in multicultural studies of interpersonal communication. American and Japanese cultures were juxtaposed in terms of the extent of their dependence on information as contrasted with influence. Cultural parameters were held responsible for seeming differences in the uses of interpersonal communication for information.

Ultimately, it was suggested that comparative analysis might well be directed toward traditions of diffusion of information with respect to important events as affording a basis for comparability. The impact of "shocking" events may bend communication rules or even break them.

Data were presented that addressed the relationships between interpersonal communication (information and influence) and use of nonmedia and media (mass and qualitative) sources. Both similarities and differences were observed, the former attributed to structural factors of equivalence and the differences being explained by cultures and situations.

An extensive literature was developed that compared Japanese and American cultural influences on communication. Examples also were provided from the German and the Chinese experiences. We generalized that communication was closely aligned to culture and to language.

To gain insight into the Japanese concept of information, it is helpful to look at policy studies on information flow in Japanese society.

Takasaki and Ozawa (1983) were responsible for the most sweeping of those studies. It is important to point out that they represented the research interests of two powerful institutions, the Research Institute for Telecommunications (Takasaki) and the Nippon Telegraph and Telephone Public Corporation (Ozawa). They also inspired investigation by the late Ithiel DeSola Pool that information flow could be measured for all media—as well as nonmedia—and then compared directly. Ultimately, they created a method for translating all media and nonmedia output into the unit of "the word."

This unit of analysis produced an "integrated indicator" that permitted volume of information flow to be compared across all sources of information. The researchers assessed and compared the number of word units transmitted by television, movies, letters, newspapers, and magazines. Volume of information transmitted by telegraph, telephones, television, books, and newspapers then could be compared directly with the number of word units diffused by other media as well as nonmedia. The formula for calculating word units was many years in the making.

As a matter of social policy, the researchers sought to determine the ratio of word production from all sources to word consumption by audiences. Three critical questions were posed:

1. What was the ratio of word production to word consumption?
2. Was there overproduction or underproduction of "words"?
3. What was the cost per word unit of each information source?

Cultural insight into the significance of the information volume approach is permitted by reflecting on the reasons for framing these questions and the omission of others. To illustrate, no questions were asked either about the transmission of information by interpersonal means or about the acquisition of information by personal observation. One implication of this priority is that formal media, not interpersonal communication or observation, were the most important means for communicating information in society.

The collection of data by Takasaki and Ozawa was begun in 1977, and data points were plotted every five years. Based these data, the researchers concluded that total information supply was increasing more rapidly than the gross national product. This gain was attributed to the proliferation of telecommunications and broadcasting media during that 25-year period. But the researchers also observed that information consumption increased at a much slower pace than supply. They concluded that the ability to process information was humanly limited. Social policy required, therefore, the innovation of a variety of information sources and the improvement of access to them. Additional insight into the Japanese view of communication is gained by the recommendation by the researchers that steps to be taken to improve the information flow ratio (of production to consumption) should be regarded as "*social* policy rather than *communication* policy" (p. 26).

CHAPTER 9

Agenda Setting in the Multicultural Context

The challenge to agenda setting in the multicultural context is to be comparative. Not every political system is equivalent to the American model; not every political culture encourages the media to set their own public agendas. Politicians and bureaucrats often reserve for themselves the power to set agendas, utilizing media and other institutions as each situation requires.

Agenda-setting processes in every society depend on the interactions of government, institutions, and the media; in each case similar functions are served. But some political cultures permit more initiative on the part of media than do others—and at different stages of the process. Thus the American conception of a single step in agenda setting from media to the public tends to understate the process. If we are to engage in comparisons, we must work toward a model of agenda setting that will specify not only the media but other actors as well. That model will suggest a number of steps, a variety of approaches, and a range of effects.

In terms of approach, the American mass communication model has defined agenda setting as a "cumulative" process; that is, as the amount of attention given to a story by the media increases over time, more agenda-setting effects are produced. This approach has been accepted multiculturally. More recently, however, our German colleagues have suggested that in addition to the purely cumulative impact of the reporting of events, special effects are produced by sudden and intermittent surges in emphases—what they propose as an "impulse model."

The agenda-building approach follows the cumulative model but looks at the added impact, over time, of other actors playing a role. Typical examples involve media collaboration with interest groups, government, or soical institutions. Cook and colleagues (1983) described a television investigation, which when aired, produced agenda-setting effects not only for the public but also for policymakers. These policymakers had wroked hand-in-glove with the television reporters and praised each other's efforts. People who recognized this alliance concluded that the problem must be taken seriously; that is, the cumulative weight of media emphasis and the promise of government actions demanded attention.

Cook and colleagues (1983) observed,

> Most agenda-setting studies stop at the point of examining the impact of the mass media on the public. This is presumably because the researchers assume that the normative wheels of democracy then begin to roll and the public pressures elected officials who, being responsive, consequently set to work to change policies and programs. But is this linear progression in fact what happens once the public agenda has changed? (p. 18)

Agenda building lends itself to comparative analysis because all governments *build* agendas to bring about desired actions rather than looking only to the media to see if an agenda has been set:

> Agenda-building...is a problem particularly appropriate for comparative analysis. It occurs in every political system, from the smallest to the largest, from the simplest to the most complex, while at the same time there are important variations in its form and structure. (p. 27)

More recently Rogers and Deering (1988) proposed an agenda-building model which differentiated among media agendas, public agendas, and policy agendas. Referring to the pioneering work of Lazarsfeld and Merton (1948), they noted that agenda setting was an outcome of the experience and interpersonal communication engaged in by elites. They suggested that agenda setting be studied as structural dependencies between government and media—much of it in a spirit of cooperation.

To Rogers and Deering (1988), to resolve cultural biases in agenda-setting studies it was necessary to conduct them in a wider range of nations and to view them comparatively. Until 1988 only 12 countries had initiated studies of this kind, most of them Western, democratic countries as well as Japan. Only a few had been carried out in Third World or socialist nations:

> The parochial history of agenda-setting research deprives us of learning to what extent the media agenda, the public agenda, and policy agenda in

other societies differ from, or resemble, those found in the United States. Future research in other countries, preferably in a comparative design, could contribute toward our understanding of how the mass media, via public opinion, influence society as well as interaction between policymakers and the media. (p. 584)

AN AGENDA FOR AGENDA SETTING

The concept of agenda setting as advanced by McCombs and Shaw (1972), as McCombs himself has noted, produced agenda setting in its own right; it told researchers what to do research about without telling them exactly what to do. Although described earlier as an alternative to a "maximal effects" approach, McCombs (1981) placed agenda-setting research in the mainstream of mass communication research:

> The metaphor of agenda-setting, which has recently been of such interest to mass communication researchers, is a succinct statement about the social impact of the mass media. It captures the idea so long cherished by social scientists that the mass media have a significant impact on our *focus of attention and what we think about.* (p. 121; our emphasis)

McCombs acknowledged Chaffee's (1980) observation that as hypothesis regarding effects, agenda setting had limited success, but as a general functional requirement of society, the concept of agenda setting was indispensable. The idea was not to look for media influence and directional effects but to view agenda setting as of assistance to individuals in organizing their thoughts and activities so that they could function adequately in society.

McCombs (1981) also stressed the concept of message elements or content but was nonspecific about their behavioral properties. In discussions with the authors he welcomed the idea that message elements might be defined cognitively, at the same time creating a basis for multicultural comparisons. Whereas social institutions and processes might be quite different from one society to another, cognitive processes of individuals are largely equivalent and thus comparable. McCombs saw agenda setting in its problematic aspects—social problems emerging along paths defined by Blumer (1971) (see Chapter 3) and individuals engaged in problem solving as a way of satisfying their "need for orientation" to social life.

McCombs (1988) more recently summarized the evolution of agenda-setting research in ways that incorporate Chaffee's observations. McCombs indentified a four-step process of studies of agenda setting that incorporated, first, the testing of the basic hypothesis itself, then the specification of contingent conditions, followed by the expansion and broadening of the agenda of research objects, and finally a widening of the focus to incorporate those actors and agencies which contributed to what we later will describe as a "multistage" "agenda-building" hypothesis. The key developments in each of these stages included:

1. The testing of the basic hypothesis was advanced by experimental studies by Iyengar and Kinder (1985) that demonstrated agenda-setting effects of television across a number of public issues. Although the experiments distorted some conditions, McCombs conceded, they did isolate the particular effect of establishing the salience of an event.

2. The specification of contingent conditions led to the exploitation of the familiar concept of "need for orientation." So a function of agenda setting was to permit the audience to locate themselves in relation to an event or issue, for instance, to map their surroundings. The productivity of the theory was enhanced by its demonstrated linkage to existing research traditions.

3. Expanding the agenda was accomplished by looking for agenda-setting effects with respect to a variety of objects and their attributes. Thus stereotyping and image building became conceptualized as agendas of attributes and status-conferral as an agenda of persons.

4. The widening of the focus of agenda setting adds up to what we have begun already to describe as a multistep, agenda-building theory. Thus various actors, such as public relations practitioners, gatekeeping operatives, elite newspapers setting agendas for other newspapers, the news reporting and writing process, and so on all contribute to the steps that are taken that set agendas for a number of participants in the process of mass communication.

McCombs' Foreword to this volume acknowledges our efforts to achieve a "conceptual elaboration" of the agenda-setting dependent variable into three distinct effects rather than into only one.

1. *Thinking about:* A media report does not influence the respondent to give attention to something that is given salience in the message, that is, to think about it. Very possibly, the audiences will give higher salience to thinking about something else if, of course, they think at all. In that sense, as we illustrate in Figure 9.1, audiences, themselves, decide what, exactly, to think about;

2. *What to think about:* This is the classic preoccupation of agenda-setting research; in this case the audience acts upon the basis of the salience that the media have given to the object. They think about it in some of its permutations.

3. *Exactly what to think:* In this case the audience not only acts on the basis of the degree of salience accorded to the message by the media but learns, and utilizes, elements of the message.

McCombs sees the specification of three kinds of effects as permitting

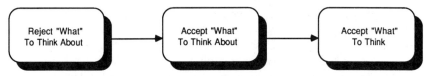

Figure 9.1. Expanding the Cognitive Basis of Agenda Setting

fuller analysis of message elements that contribute to effect. Previously, content has been approached as "categorical," that is, topical categories such as politics, social issues, personae, and events. Later in this chapter we will propose ways in which the three effects of our dependent variable might be specified.

In cataloguing a list of problems they associated with the agenda-setting approach, Gladys and Kurt Lang (1981) were early to point to the need to specify exactly what was meant by "thinking about." After all, they suggested, the idea of "thinking about" was the thrust of the theory. Could "thinking about" imply merely an awareness of the importance of a problem?

The Langs concluded that this was not the case—that simple awareness could not be the meaning of the dependent variable that was intended by the agenda setters. Many people become aware of the importance of many problems, but that doesn't mean that they think about all of them. Thus agenda setting that produced "thinking about" meant that a process was at work—cognitive processes, as we have defined them.

The Langs felt their way into two kinds of problematic situations that we have described. At one level there were personal concerns about events or policies that became transformed into problems. These represented the needs and deprivations felt by publics.

At the second level there were those problems that in their definition as problems evoked controversy or conflict—aspects of those problems became "at issue." We may derive from this thinking the proposition that, generically, there were two kinds of cognitive dynamics that produced "thinking about": problems and issues. All problems, as they observed, did not become "at issue."

> A personal concern can...be identified as one of the most important problems facing the country [or] as an [issue] object of considerable public controversy. (p. 451)

But the dynamics of the entire agenda setting process involved not only the thinking of audiences but the actions and thinking of those who were responsible for the events—political actors, social critics, interest groups, and journalists—our multistage, multieffects model.

Our own agenda in this chapter is to evaluate elements of agenda setting that are most important for comparative analysis, such as cognitive processes, taking into account implications for culture. We must restrict ourselves to a limited, cognitive perspective, acknowledging that on a variable-by-variable basis the potential for comparative analysis is virtually endless, given the number of studies and the contingent conditions. McCombs (1981), himself, described a legion of studies, and Winter (1981) summarized them as rooted in an array of "stimulus" and "audience" attributes.

Our concerns with culture and meaning lead us to a more complex agenda-setting model than was proposed originally, one that includes not only multiple actors and multiple channels but multiple effects as well. The multiple effects center on the concept of "thinking about." Little of the research into agenda setting has addressed message elements conceptually. Thus it has left unanswered McCombs' questions about the message elements that represent the focus of attention in agenda-setting studies— "what to think about." Does agenda setting invariably cause the individual to focus on "what to think about" or may it be as much the case that media saliences motivate audiences "only to think," without actually directing them to a topic?

If we can assume that the media produce message elements that are interpreted in various ways by audiences, it becomes clearer that the media are not likely to succeed as much in proposing what should be thought about as in saying, in effect, that there is food for thought. In these terms we must conceive of agenda setting as producing *multiple effects* rather than the usually cited single effect of "thinking about." Most agenda-setting data, if reanalyzed, might suggest the minimal focusing effect that we have suggested; that is, that media most often cause audiences to think without being able to place on their agenda exactly *what to think about.* To explain: One may be motivated to think without convergence on what to think about; similarly, one might be motivated to think about without being instructed exactly what to think about. Variable cognitive effects must be isolated and operationalized so that they can be more easily observed.

Our purpose is to utilize the cognitive concept of the problematic situation as an indicator of thinking; the particular problematic situation, as a meaning state, identifies what it is that the person is thinking about. For example, if an individual constructs a problematic situation as loss of value, that represents the meaning that the individual has attached to it. The act of problematizing would be an agenda-setting effect of "only thinking," which might accept or reject the media agenda for "thinking about." Figure 9.1 pictures three possible agenda-setting effects: only thinking, what to think about, and what to think. We present evidence from our content analyses and survey data to establish that problematizing occurs in this way and is present in the multicultural context.

FROM A ONE-STEP TO A MULTISTEP PROCESS

The idea that agenda setting should be observed as a one-step process involving media and audiences, minimizing the roles of other actors who are parties to the process, might be viewed as an early preconception of American communication research. The assumptions built into the one-step process supposed an American and Western democratic press system that enjoyed considerable autonomy in its efforts to set public agendas. This approach persisted despite the recognition that sources set agendas for journalists and journalists functioned reciprocally for sources as part of an intricate pattern of mutual dependencies and interactions.

Because he is a political scientist and not a communication scholar, Cohen (1963) may be assumed to have advanced the "what to think about" thesis in the context of political management, not communication. The larger point, made by other political scientists, is that politicians, interest groups, and other actors are partners with the media in any agenda-setting process. In this scenario the process usually begins with ideas and actions advanced by government officials, bureaucracies, interest groups, experts, and social critics. These actors vary in their relative importance from event to event, problem to problem, and issue to issue. One would expect that to be the case in any political culture.

To be comparative, therefore, the agenda-setting model would incorporate many actors and steps in the process, leading to the interaction between the media and their audiences. Further, if we added our three cognitive orientations—"only thinking," "what to think about" and "what, exactly, to think"—the agenda-setting model would account for multieffects as well as multisteps. As McCombs (1981) proposed, this addition would fit agenda-setting research into a total mass-communication paradigm. Refer to Figure 9.1 for our construction of the three kinds of cognitive effect.

The multistep model that we have proposed—incorporating policymakers, media, and publics—only hints at the number and variety of actors who play roles in the agenda-setting process. A historian looking at the complex interactions between policymakers, press, and publics during the emergence of Israel as a nation-state, described it as a study in "dance steps," with changing partners and varied routines. Agenda setting must be studied in its situational context. Evensen (1988) concluded:

> [the agenda-setting process]. . . is not a unidirectional but a multidirectional process, with the "dancefloor" a site of struggle among competing

partners...influence does not flow in one direction...nor are power relations fixed. (p. 2)

Which partner is leading on the dancefloor in any event is subject to change...the press played an important part in highlighting policies from which the public could choose. In the end, policy helped to shape events of which [the press] was a part. (p. 27)

The late John Dewey, the disciplined teacher and pragmatist, might better have written the script for the agenda-setting hypothesis and, obviously, well prior to the more recent innovators who have been credited with the idea. His distinction between simple awareness and reflectivity described in *How We Think* (1909), read today, agrees with our view that agenda-setting should be articulated at a number of stages of thinking rather than only at the level of equivalence of salience of media content and audience response.

Dewey would have seen simple awareness as the least demanding of the conditions of "thinking about" or reflectivity that he proposed. We would assume that agenda-setting researchers had more in mind than "simple awareness" as the most important agenda-setting effect. Had this been the case, agenda-setting effects would have been limited merely to pointing to the existence of a problem of some kind, rather than inducing audiences actually "to reflect" upon it. As Dewey put it with some piquancy, this would suggest only "a penny for your thoughts" (p. 2) because they would not be worth any more than that amount.

Other steps in thinking suggested by Dewey, which we also propose, made greater demands upon the individual and, in terms of agenda-setting processees, represent a standard of thought that the media would be expected to stimulate as a function of agenda setting. To Dewey, any significant agenda-setting effects would call upon the media to produce conditions of "reflectivity"—stressed in Japan as a cultural parameter—in their audiences in which they would, as an example, judge the probability of the significance of a problem to which the media have accorded "salience." Having done this, audiences then would decide how much reflectivity and reasoning they would bring to bear upon the problem.

It is important to note, also, that Dewey saw that the end product of reflectivity was conviction and belief. Having judged that an event or condition deserved one's attention and thought, the individual would be bound to think it through to a conclusion that would lead to belief and action. Hence, as we will propose, it might be more pragmatic to view agenda setting as being articulated by steps in a process, from simple awareness to reflectivity and thence to belief and action. The media thus would play a role not only in stimulating thought but would contribute, through the information that the media provided, to the steps by which audiences came to terms with *what* to think.

THE JAPANESE CONTEXT

The Japanese context offers a unique example of a multistep, multieffects model. For one thing, the Japanese journalist operates more within a structured and formal social and political context than do journalists in the comparison countries. The public also operates according to the rules. Individuals in Japan are less likely to intervene directly in the political process and are more likely to be represented by interest groups. These groups relay their needs to the bureaucracies in the ministries, all of which are functioning core parts of government. Beyond this, political factions and parties represent constituents. The organization of Japanese society suggests, in fact, that we might expect the strongest kind of agenda-setting effects where they occur, that is, not merely "only think" but "what to think about" and "what to think."

We may illustrate this process by an agency such as NTT, the national telecommunications system, which represents not only domestic and foreign telephonic and other wireless agencies but also MPT, the Ministry for Posts and Telegraph. These smaller ministries and their bureaucracies, as parts of the government, are amenable to interest group representation. Unions, which represent workers, utilize networks to communicate their needs and, on occasion, demands.

Business and industry look to the Ministry of International Trade and Industry (MITI) for representation. Farmers look to the Ministry of Agriculture. The bureaucracies of these government agencies do not take passive roles; they relay claims between and among the various layers of agriculture, govenment, business, industry, trade, and consumer groups. It is only when these institutions fail to operate, which has occurred in rare cases, that interest groups take their complaints directly to the government, usually to local government.

ACCESS AND INTERACTION

Political parties and factions take conditions of access and interaction into account and maintain communication with the bureaucracies and the ministries as a way of becoming sensitive to their needs. The relationships among the media, the government, and its bureaucracies are equally close. Audiences' perceptions of the value of the media in setting agendas are heightened by their awareness that the media "are in the know."

This has not always been the case. After World War II and up to the 1970s, the Japanese press was viewed as contentious. The press during this period was too ideological, too aggressive, and too crude as judged by a normative model of expectations for behavior. But degrees of conservatism have set in, although some newspapers have retained their independence. *Asahi Shimbun*, a prestigious Japanese national newspaper, has been known for being anti-American, anti-South Korean, pro-Chinese, pro-North Korean, and pro-nonaligned nations.

In a number of closely interrelated empirical studies Feldman (1985, 1986a, 1986b, 1987) pointed to the extent to which members of the Japanese Diet read newspapers and utilized contacts with journalists to obtain information about pertinent issues. This, he points out, is a complex but constantly ongoing process and carries implications for our multistep agenda-setting model:

> Politicians differ in their assessment of...sources...[of information]... depending on to which camp their party belongs. The ruling L.D.P. members have a high regard for...newsmen. Members of the opposition parties see their own colleagues as prime sources of information....The fact that many pressure groups and various business circles are constantly in contact with political parties and politicians suggests, of course, that there will be variations...depending upon the political climate in a certain time. (1987, p. 379)

One finding by Feldman (1985) was that politicians used different media at different times, but that they constantly used media. He also observed (1986a) a correlation between the extent to which Diet members met with local newspapers and their tenure in the Diet. This pointed to a close affiliation between the practice of politics and the process of mass communication. At the same time, however, Feldman (1986b) pointed out that Diet members also maintained a high degree of contact with national newspapers, more often with *Asahi*, the most prestigious, but extending to other "big nationals" as well. Feldman (1987) noted the degree of importance that politicians attributed to contacts with the press.

As discussed earlier concerning a U.S. study, when it is apparent that specific media or journalists are accenting government policies or programs, the audiences may infer that what is being portrayed in the media must, at the least, be thought about. In such cases the agenda-setting effects are likely to go far beyond simply thinking to what to think about and even *what, exactly, to think*.

These actors and structures, and relations between them, were visualized as a pluralistic model by Kabashima and Broadbent (1986). It points in the case of Japan to:

1. Strong influences by agriculture and the media on both the bureaucracy and the cabinet of the ruling Liberal Democratic Party, coupled with the strong influence of business on the cabinet but *not* on the bureaucracy

2. Only moderate influence by labor on the bureaucracy, but strong influence by labor on the media and opposition parties
3. A strong influence by citizens' movements, excluding women's movements, on the media, but only moderate influence by the citizens' and women's movements on opposition parties

Thus a multistep, interactive agenda-setting model would identify the actors, the direction, and the strength of their relations. One would then identify contingencies such as the nature of events (and other stimuli) and audiences. One would also predict agenda-setting effects from a chain of interactions rather than from the journalist or the media.

The role of the media is central to any model. One must assess the strength of the relations among the media, business, the cabinet, the bureaucracy, labor, and citizens' movements. All relations imply interaction, not simply one-way dependencies. The power of the media to set agendas, or to "build them," is ruled by the accessibility of journalists to the dominant actors. Because most Japanese journalists perceive themselves to be nonideological and, where partisan, split between left and right, there is enhanced potential for access and interaction.

A reflective Japanese scholar has offered an intriguing formulation of the relationship of tri-polar forces of government, press, and public opinion that carry implications for agenda setting. The question is the extent to which these forces converge in their efforts and opinions. If government and press converge, as we may see in the example of publics' perceptions of collaboration between the government and television, then agendas for publics would incorporate not only what to think *about* but probably what *to think*, as well. Akita Tsujimura (1976) sees tri-polar relationships between government, press, and public opinion as forces that control not only agenda setting but social action. Where all forces converge there is the greatest likelihood of social action as well as mutual agenda setting.

Tsujimura says, however, it is a relatively rare event in Japanese public life for government, press, and public opinion to be in unanimity, either in favor of a policy or opposed to one. An example of unanimity was the belief that the Soviet Union should return to Japan the northern islands that the Soviet Union acquired after the settlement of World War II.

A more usual condition is that two forces are aligned on one side and the third force disagrees with the position that is taken. One example was the situation in which the Japanese government and the press were in agreement on a proposal for restoring diplomatic relations with the Soviet Union. In this case the press was seen as taking the initiative, winning the acquiescence of the government, but failing to persuade publics to adopt the idea. In cases of this kind the press successfully played an agenda-setting function for government and publics, encouraging both of them to think about the recognition problem.

Tsujimura contends that more often the government and publics share concerns that are not joined in by the press. In the cases of the San Francisco Peace Treaty and the rearmament/reinforcement of the Self-Defense Forces, the press criticized the government. But public opinion polls indicated that the public supported the government. In this case the press did not set the public agenda but, rather, offered an alternative agenda that was ignored. The press failed to establish in either the government mind or the public view an alternative to be thought about seriously.

That same kind of gap may develop when there is agreement by the public and the press and the government attempts to sidestep their agenda. Tsujimura sees the Lockheed and Tanaka corruption scandals as instances of the press not merely suggesting to publics what to think *about* but precisely *what to think*. The press acted as the watchdog of government and succeeded in establishing the public agenda.

Tsujimura also sees it as possible for one of the tri-polar actors to suggest agendas that the two other parties will ignore. This was exemplified when the government revised the U.S. security treaty in 1960. In this case the press thwarted efforts by government to set a public agenda. The press similarly saw itself isolated when it supported a National Railways strike that inconvenienced publics and antagonized the government. Neither the government nor publics wished at this time to think about the rights of workers. When publics reject both government and press alternatives, there is no agenda. That may be the most common condition.

Tsujimura's formulation was not intended to address agenda setting but actions and attitudes in relation to social problems; yet it carries exciting implications for the reformulation of agenda setting as a multiactor and multiattitudinal as well as a more complex cognitive process.

Ito (1988) also cautions against the concept of national consensus-building as a conscious effort on the part of any actors other than government leaders in power. In Japan, consensus is most often sought within partisan political or social groups, as in the political caucus or in the political faction. The journalist who has access to a group or faction in many cases will observe and report within that context and contribute to consensus-building within that group. But the journalist, per se, is not working toward *national* consensus.

Ito points out that the Japanese tendency toward "consensus" much more often applies to intimate groups than to public efforts that are directed to national consensus, for that often is difficult to achieve. In the political context, Japan's active parties run the spectrum from conservative to Communist, including even a Buddhist party. Journalists do not consider it their role to create consensus among the parties, and certainly it is not their job. Yet it is easier to create public consensus in Japan than in the United States or even Germany, not only because of greater cultural and ethnic homogeniety but geographical factors such as its island character, limited size, and extensive means of transportation and communication.

PENETRATION AS A STIMULUS CONDITION

The Japanese press system might be thought of as an unique stimulus condition. They boasts a unique, almost complete capacity to reach audiences. Tamura (1987) noted that a few daily newspapers such as *Yomiuri*, (9 million), *Asahi* (7.7 million), and *Mainichi* (4.1 million) together with two other national newspapers account for a daily circulation of almost 25 million. Feldman (1987a) and others cited more dramatic figures obtained from *Nihon Shimbun Nenkan*, the Japanese newspaper association yearbook for 1985. They estimated a total circulation of 67 million of which the "Big Five" account for 38.5 million, or 57 percent of all circulation. Whichever the figure, this degree of penetration far exceeds that of daily newspapers in any of the comparison countries. In addition, Japan supports seven news-transmitting television networks, more than the five in the United States, four in Great Britain, and two in Germany.

Japan also has the largest per capita newspaper circulation of the comparison countries, more than double that of the United States and a third higher than that of Germany. Japan lags behind the United States and Britain only in radio sets in use. Overall, a concentration of audiences, many in high-density urban settings (21 percent in cities of 900,000 or more), lends Japanese media ready access to a substantial proportion of the population.

One might consider cultural factors as well. Weaver (1983) believed that American media suffer a "temporal gap" in their efforts at agenda setting. The gap occurs when media accent problems at one time, and those problems only later become salient for the public. This process becomes inverted when problems are more salient to the public than to the media at a particular time. Weaver said that these gaps occur in the American context because of the varied nature of social units and their relative degree of integration in society.

In Japan the individual is expected to maintain a constant awareness of societal rules and demands. Thus temporal gaps in agenda setting, whatever the other considerations, are less likely to occur. Some observers assert that social organization in Japan is so unique, in fact, as to limit the bases for multicultural comparisons. This view suggests, at the least, that cultures, as expressed in their social organization, ought to be taken into account in comparative studies of agenda setting.

Weaver's (1983) findings point to the need for a more careful examination of political cultures. For example, Weaver points out that American political studies have found that the media set the agendas for issues in the early part of a compaign, whereas in the later stages the media set agendas for candidates' personalities. Approached comparatively, we might speculate that in political cultures such as Japan and Germany, where the major political actors and the lines of succession in political parties are well known, party images would be more important than candidates' images. Both would be emphasized at all stages, not only at a single stage of a campaign.

Media also demonstrate agenda-setting influences on one another. Patterson (1980), for example, found a reciprocal agenda-setting process in which television and newspapers set political agendas for each other as well as for their audiences. Noelle-Neumann and Mathes (1987) came to this same conclusion. They suggested that agenda setting be thought of in two terms: the "event as an event" and "an event as news." The media would be most effective in their efforts at agenda setting when they advanced values that were "consonant" with normative values in their definition of the situation, thus helping to establish an agenda for themselves as well as for the public.

FROM CUMULATIVE TO IMPULSE MODEL

Beyond the structural and cultural questions we have raised about the context for agenda setting, comparative questions must be asked concerning the conditions under which agenda setting is most likely to occur in any society. Our German colleagues observed that some media practices are more likely than others to produce agenda-setting effects. They suggested that we observe effects that have occurred not only because of the continuing emphasis the media have given to a problem—the so-called "cumulative" model—but also because of the extreme variability in the coverage of problems, the so-called "impulse" model.

Simply put, in the impulse model we may imagine news stories that are unusually timely and important in their implications and send an unexpected surge of power through the communication system. As a part of this surge, a sequence of stories may be published on an unanticipated schedule, each in its degree of importance multiplying rather than simply increasing the degree of importance of the first reports. Whereas in the cumulative model the agenda-setting researcher would look for a linear relationship between the emphasis placed on a story by the media and the number of people who believe that the story describes an important problem, in the impulse model the agenda-setting researcher would calculate the extent of change in emphasis by the media with the amount of change in attention by the audience.

German researchers (Kepplinger, Donsbach, Brosius, & Staab, 1986; Kepplinger, Gotto, Brosius, & Haak, 1988) measured change in the impulse model by looking at the differences in the number of television news stories about political issues over time and the differences in the number of people who thought the stories were important over that time period. They hypothesized that the more stories (cumulative model) and the more change in the number of stories (impulse model), the more awareness on the part of the public and the more acceptance of the nature of the problem. This acceptance of the nature of the problem would provide evidence that audiences had accepted what they should think about—which comes close to meeting the expectations American researchers have entertained for thinking about a problem. Mere awareness, however, appears to fall short of that expectation.

The actual results of the German studies favored the impulse rather than the cumulative model. The amount of change of emphasis predicted agenda-setting effects more than the cumulative model—steady but not spectacular increases over time. this finding applied to both awareness of problems and acceptance of the nature of problems. The German researchers also observed reverse agenda-setting effects:

1. Sometimes increased coverage brought about increased public awareness; then television increased its coverage somewhat. In this way the public, once sensitized, set an agenda for television.
2. There also was a reverse effect resulting from increased awareness by the public when television decreased its coverage once it had achieved agenda-setting effects.

The German authors perceived also that public opinion had a somewhat stronger agenda-setting effect on television news than vice versa. They suggested that their findings for television news be compared with newspaper effects and be considered comparatively, across cultures, as well. To this point they asked if television news, generically, produced agenda setting more related to an awareness of events then acceptance of the nature of problems or an understanding of them.

THE EQUIVALENCE OF MEANINGS

Whatever the nature of agenda setting—whether cumulative or impulse models—the equivalence of meanings must be assured if comparative analysis is to be carried out successfully. This need for clarification applies to the meaning of the very concept itself. As we learned from our discussion in Chapter 8 on interpersonal communication, multicultural analysis rests on a basis of common meanings. The initial terminology emerged, primarily, from the American research. As a critical example, the phrase *thinking about*—which is integral to the "minimal effects" condition of agenda setting—has been defined only loosely in American studies. European studies and our own comparative analysis have forced us to think in terms of the several agenda-setting effects we have suggested—only thinking, what to think about, and what to think. Up to now, the meaning of *thinking about* has rested on vaguely stated cultural parameters.

Thinking about also has implied an active audience to American researchers, but other cultural conceptions have required only that audiences recognize that the media and public have assigned a high degree of importance to a topic. A clearer conception of agenda setting—whether it means only awareness or acceptance of the nature of the problem, or if it means only salience and not actually "thinking about"—needs to be achieved. Otherwise, researchers will continue to find themselves working with a vaguely defined specification of effects.

There have also been demands for a greater clarity and bases for comparability of "message" and "audience" variables. Becker (1982) asked, "What, exactly, in the message was being thought 'about,' and who, exactly, was doing the thinking?" Becker argued that media assign meanings to messages by the "type of message display" they employ. If, in comparing media messages, as we did in Chapter 4, it became evident that one medium used different display factors than another, this factor would be weighted to permit comparative measures of the salience of a story.

We actually encountered this condition in our data: Japanese newspapers and television emphasized visual factors, in the first instance by the use of multiple headlines, graphs, and cartoons, and in television by a high quotient of entertainment and dramatic use of color and movement. German newspapers also used multiple headlines, in contrast to the lesser elements of display that characterized the American and Hong Kong newspapers. Edelstein and Hoyer (in press) observed the dramatic front-page display techniques used by *Aften Posten*, among other Norwegian newspapers, to highlight major stories that were to be found on inside pages.

THE MEANING OF MINIMAL EFFECTS

There is no greater need for clarity of definitions for comparative analysis than with regard to the concept of minimal effects. For instance, the pioneering work of McCombs and Shaw (1972) suggested that thinking about is a minimal effect of agenda-setting, whereas persuading an audience what to think is a maximal effect. This evaluation of minimal and maximal effects was derived from a model of presidential politics. Understandably, campaign managers attempt to persuade voters what to think and to vote accordingly. If one accepts these behavioral goals, persuading the public what to think would clearly be a maximal effect; persuading people only to think about voting would be, relatively speaking, a minimal effect.

Edelstein (1988) argued that getting people to think about something augured much more for communication than did persuading them exactly what to think. Thinking about implies an active audience, whereas being told what to think suggests a passive audience. Weaver (1984) earlier had taken exception to the minimal effects element of agenda setting on analagous grounds. He argued that the minimal effect of agenda-setting produces secondary effects that have great consequences for communication. For one, agenda setting "primes" audiences so that they become more sensitized to information. Both Edelstein and Weaver thus took the position that the term *thinking about* implied more extensive *communication* behavior than had been considered by the agenda-setting researchers. Weaver suggested that, in any case, whereas the media could propose, the audiences would decide.

The political context has affected thinking about agenda setting in other ways as well. It might become necessary, particularly in the comparative context, to identify agenda-setting rules for political as contrasted to social problems.

Political and Social Agendas

A number of practical as well as conceptual reasons should persuade us that agenda-setting effects should distinguish between political campaigns and more broadly defined social problems. The conditions that govern these two kinds of situations tend to be markedly different:

1. Political campaigns are founded in competition, whereas voting choices require behavior rather than opinions.
2. Campaigns also operate within prescribed time frames, giving them sharper boundaries and clearer focus than social problems, or even social issues.
3. Whereas cumulative knowledge is brought to bear on parties, candidates, issues, and elections, each social problem is different.
4. Interest groups or coalitions generally are topic bound, and less knowledge is transferred from one problem to another.

A comparison of agenda-setting effects in the political and social contexts can be seen in the Japanese data. Although societal norms of consensus in Japan tend to color the debate about social problems, political competitiveness is the norm. During election campaigns posters and pictures are tacked to telephone polls and buildings, loudspeakers attached to automobiles blare messages to passersby, and political parties and interest groups attempt to mobilize their constituencies to vote.

In the less well-defined environment of social problems, one typically encounters less public activity and debate. Much of what is occurring takes place in negotiations among government, interest groups, bureaucracies, media, and the perceived public. One is tempted, therefore, to hold different expectations for the agenda-setting capacity of the media during a political campaign than in the consideration of a social problem.

Testing the Proposition

Despite the logic of the situation, evidence from a number of Japanese studies has demonstrated only limited agenda-setting effects with respect to political campaigns—this despite the extensive penetration of Japanese media. Rather than independent media effects per se, agenda setting was tied more to variables, in the audience, such as the extent of political participation and knowledge about and interest in politics. This tie was strengthened by the influence of social networks such as family and peers. The evidence also suggested that agenda-setting effects could not be generalized as less true for social problems than for political issues and campaigns. Rather, the effects in each case depended on the nature of the problem.

Takeshita (1983) utilized a design that enabled him to correlate audience agendas with media agendas on political issues that had emerged in off-election periods. Agenda-setting effects were noted in fewer than half of the instances, and these were limited. Of some interest was the fact that newspapers were more effective than television, but the affected audiences for both media demonstrated the most interest in politics.

The communication outcomes were more provocative. With respect to newspapers, agenda setting was associated with only a modest degree of political discussion with family and peers. Where individuals engaged in a great deal of discussion, and where they least discussed politics, they expressed the least need for newspapers. Thus feeling oneself to be a member of an active social network precluded the need for newspapers to set agendas; and for those who lacked a sense of participation in a social network it was evident that the newspaper could not fill that gap. Curiously, people did not tie television news to interpersonal communication.

Kobayashi (1983) directly compared media agenda setting in political campaigns with performance on social problems. With respect to broadly defined social, economic, and political topics, the two leading dailies, *Yomiuri* and *Mainichi*, despite their circulations, demonstrated only limited agenda-setting effects. Newspapers with less circulation that were politically radical or appealed only to special interests also demonstrated little ability to set agendas.

Kobayashi found that only people of lesser occupational statueses were amenable to agenda setting, paralleling some American studies. Apparently people in those statuses operated in a less informative social milieu and thus were more susceptible to news. But there were no meaningful correlations of media and audience saliences by such demographic elements as age (only by low-occupation women), level of political knowledge, education, party identification, housing, or years of residence in the community. Media credibility in its narrower sense of accuracy did not produce a greater agenda-setting dependency.

Kobayashi again found that newspapers produced more effects than television, partly because only 12 percent of television news touched on politics. Other news was devoted to personalities and random events. Japanese television news seldom embraced commentary.

Takeuchi and Takeshita (1987) analyzed the content of four leading national dailies—*Yomiuri, Mainichi, Asahi,* and *Sankei.* Overall some weak effects were found among those audiences who were most exposed to the media, but these effects were rendered questionable by the fact that they applied only to those persons who were most interested in local politics and in the political campaign itself. A finding of this kind would, in the Japanese context, be considered as an argument for a multistep approach. It would be reasoned that consensual activities had the effect of muting media effects and that both media and audiences were demonstrating a similar degree of interest in consensual politics. In these terms, the strongest argument for agenda setting would be found at other steps in the process, for example, with regard to unseen actors.

CONTEXTS OTHER THAN POLITICAL

Takeshita (1984) also compared the agenda-setting effects of ten selected social, economic, and political (other than campaign) topics emphasized by *Yomiuri* and *Asahi* and the evening network news programs. He utilized a panel design to interview respondents at three different times. However, only one of eight topics generated strong agenda-setting effects. These occurred in the two newspapers at time 2 and time 3 for a value-added tax measure, a pivotal social issue in that Prime Minister Nakasone was thought to have lied to the nation about his intentions to levy a value-added or sales tax. Television produced effects between time 2 and time 3, explained by the fact that television had accorded substantial attention to this topic.

Takeuchi and Takeshita (1987) reported mixed effects from a number of studies. However, they introduced a methodological caveat. They concluded that some studies by Kobayashi (1983), Maeda (1978), and Horie (1982) did not demonstrate effects because they did not represent media content but the *audience's perceptions* of that content. Iwabuchi (1986) did, however, conduct a content analysis and, like Kobayashi, attributed only random effects to demographics such as age, sex, and education.

Takeshita (1988) actually compared the reports of respondents' agendas with perceptions of public agendas. Having anticipated that this was a less demanding test of agenda setting, we were not surprised that greater results were shown. Both newspaper and television users showed effects between times 1 and 2, and 2 and 3.

Takeshita at first had thought that agenda setting would be seen most clearly among those who were most attentive to the political campaign; that is, the more people are interested, the more responsive they are to newspaper content—or vice versa. But this did not prove to be the case. Rather, it was the less politically conscious groups that were more responsive to newspaper influence. Those who were most interested and who most used the media nonetheless appeared to be least affected by the media's agenda priorities.

Iwabuchi (1988) inverted agenda-setting effects as representing the influence of publics upon the media where there is a widely controversial issue and public attitudes have been expressed. The issue in question was the proposed, then withdrawn, value-added or sales tax. Iwabuchi concluded that the public anti-sales-tax movement and an awareness of the direction of the vote in local elections influenced media content and emphases in the subsequent national elections. Thus the mass media's ability to set an agenda was enabled by the existence of a climate of opinion.

EARLIER GERMAN STUDIES

In Germany, earlier studies were in the pattern of the Japanese studies— multistep and multieffects. The question explored was "What agenda-setting effects were engendered by what political actors?" Kepplinger (1985) compared men and women on their awareness of reasons for unemployment. The results showed that, the greater the coverage by German media, the less discrepancy occurred between either increasing or decreasing awareness. One could see intimations of an impulse model in these findings. A second German study (Mathes, 1987) showed a remarkably high correlation between the German audience's responses to the "most important problem" and newspaper and television coverage of that problem. At issue was the dismissal of a distinguished German army general for alleged homosexuality, one of the most controversial disputes in recent memory. This was a story that carried great impact, one that again would imply an impulse model at work. As might be expected, agenda-setting effects were concentrated in the first ten weeks, when the issue had a shock effect on a previously unaware public. Again, these data are subject to interpretation by an impulse rather than a cumulative model.

Kepplinger and Roth (1979) credited the German mass media with more than agenda setting in the creation of the oil crisis by eroding consumer confidence in oil supplies at a time when imports of crude oil actually had increased. Weighed against actual oil imports and levels, no real crisis of oil supply existed in Germany, yet in early September 60 percent of media reports described the supply situation as bad or worsening. More than telling the public only what to think about, the media provided a frame of reference for what was thought. All the more curiously, media references dropped precipitously at the time a real crisis might have occurred. Hence there was a supply reality and a media reality, with the public more responsive to the latter.

STAGES OF EFFECTS

Some German studies found that the agenda-setting effects of media in critical economic and social situations may operate by stages. At the first stage the media create broad awareness, what it thought of as a minimal agenda-setting effect. But it swiftly encourages thought and even behavior by individuals and the society. The media may, in that way, contribute to a significant increment of social change. Illustrating this thesis is a study by Kepplinger and Hachenberg (1985), which described media legitimization of deviant social behavior by students resisting the draft, leading ultimately to changes in the laws that defined the limits of behavior. At each stage of this social/legal change, mass media coverage increased proportionately.

Newspapers and magazines produced more than 900 articles on conscientious objecting. The *Frankfurter Rundschau*, one of the newspapers in our German sample, alone published 26 percent of these articles. The motives and goals of the objectors were presented in a predominantly positive or neutral light; they were justified in 40 percent of all references, treated neutrally in 43 percent, and criticized in only 17 percent. The point of view taken by the newspapers was predicted by political ideologies. The *Frankfurter Rundschau* was ideologically sympathetic to and least critical of student objectors. Kepplinger and colleagues point to two critical areas for discussion:

1. The media are responsible for the creation and functioning of a critical mass of public opinion. Chain reactions may then occur within the social structure involving a public who has not been exposed directly to the media. These people respond to the reactions of others to media content.
2. The recognition of social change by a larger public occurs in response not to media but to personal observations of changes in social behavior and social norms. That is why social change may be perceived as sudden and dramatic. Overlooked in this perception are the intervening steps, in which interest groups, bureaucracies, social critics, and media have played their roles.

The German studies also cast light on the agenda-setting effects reported in Japan of the Nakasone incident, in which the Prime Minister had reversed a tax policy that he had stood on for reelection. At the point of actual implemantation of the policy—which had been discussed widely in the press—the public reacted strongly. Thus agenda setting occurred as a result of a critical event (impulse model) that impinged on an undercurrent of sentiment (cumulative) that was antecedent to action. Once the action was reported, the society responded. That behavior extended beyond simply thinking, or even thinking about, to what was thought.

SOME HONG KONG STUDIES

Our Hong Kong studies addressed less dramatic events and circumstancs and contributed much less to theory. One study found a stark contrast of structural forces in media penetration to those in Japan. In contrast to the remarkable degree of diffusion of Japanese daily newspapers and television, in Hong Kong both newspaper and television diffusion were politically and culturally fragmented. The two English-language newspapers, the *South China Morning Post* and the *Hong Kong Standard*, come closest to being able to define "official" issues or problems defined by the British governors, but they fall far short of the capacities of Japanese media.

A myriad of Chinese-language newspapers, some with far greater circulation than the English-language newspapers, nonetheless lack the power to set agendas. In reference to the observation made by Cook and colleagues (1983) that audiences are aware of media potential, Hong Kong Chinese know that English-language newspapers usually are more "in the know" than the Chinese newspapers; this same effect holds for television in which two English-language stations are more representative of official views, whereas the two Chinese-language stations, one Mandarin and the other Cantonese, splinter the Chinese audiences.

A study by Yee (1987) acknowledged the inability of media to set agendas directly for audiences. The study assumed that only interest groups could affect policies and that the media would appeal to those groups. In our model, these would be key actors in a multistep agenda-setting process. Yee asked members of interest groups to rate the importance, to themselves personally, of four subissues relating to nuclear energy problems: Chernobyl, World Environment Day, a petition-signing event, and an official ceremony in Beijing celebrating the opening of a nuclear energy plant. Interest group members were asked to assess when they had begun to work toward the definition and resolution of the issues. Assessments of their initiatives were compared with timetables of content of the two newspapers—one a leftist paper, the other rightist—and a third (control) publication, a magazine. Yee confirmed that the media reacted to interest groups more than establishing agendas for them.

EXPLORING THE COGNITIVE REALM

As we approached our own data we took the view that in the absence of a clearly defined concept of thinking about, we needed to adopt a cognitive approach that would permit us to observe behavior. We utilized one of our cognitive variables—the problematic situation—as reflective of a thinking process. The problematic situation also offered the promise of a comparable unit of description, for all students in the four cultures reported that they thought about problems by problematizing them.

It will be remembered that in Chapter 4 we utilized the problematic situation to specify the dynamics of news. In this analysis we learned that both the media and students addressed the same kinds of problematics. We also utilized the problematic situation in Chapter 6, where we identified it as a motivational state. This category filled a gap between need and activity in the conceptualization of actual uses of television and newspapers for solving problems. The problematic situation would also function as the cognitive link to thinking about, which is at the core of agenda-setting effects.

We may take some recent examples of media content that contain problematic situations. Let us imagine that we are readers and we are experiencing agenda-setting effects that cause us to think about the news. The data is May 13, 1988, and we are in Seattle, looking at the afternoon daily, the *Seattle Times*:

- *Headline:* Boeing Looks Like Winner in $4 Billion-Plus Jet Order
- *Problematic:* Winning the contract was a positive outcome of an earlier condition of uncertainty. This characterization was portrayed by the headline and probably thought about by many Seattle readers in similar terms. If so, two kinds of agenda-setting multiple effects model occurred—what to think *and* what to think about.
- *Headline:* Seattleite Charged with Smoking on Plane
- *Problematic:* This is a violation of the law. Because it is a Seattle person, it also represents a sense of loss to the community. That problematic situation of loss of value is what many Seattle readers thought about, and they may, as well, have believed the report. Hence two agenda-setting effects seemed likely, both what to think about and what to think.
- *Headline:* Juror Said, "I Didn't Know About Auburn Cyanide Deaths"
- *Problematic:* The newspaper headline portrayed a state of uncertainty expressed by the juror. Some readers thought about this allegation of a state of uncertainty but may or may not have believed the statement. Thus agenda setting for them occurred to the extent that they were persuaded what to think about but not what to think.
- *Headline:* Negotiators Settle Snags on Missile Pact
- *Problematic:* The headline reports a step toward a solution in the negotiations for a missile pact. This representation of a problematic situation is likely to be accepted, in principle, by many readers. In this case they are likely to learn what to think as well as what to think about.

These represent only a few of the many problematic situations that are implicit in headlines (and stories) in one day's newspaper. The data for the four groups of students reflect approximately six months of newspaper coverage. We match up the weight of that content with the interests of students, expressed by their formulation of problematic situations. Our two kinds of data identify possible links between what the newspapers represented as problematic situations in their stories and what the students cognized as situations in their own minds.

Our essential questions, therefore, were the extent to which media content—arrayed topically and also with respect to problematic situations—could be reconciled with the emphases given to it by students in the four cultures. Because of our interest in cultures we formulated the hypothesis that we would observe the least divergence in the most closely knit cultures, which we identified as Japan and Germany. We saw Chinese culture in Hong Kong as being disrupted by colonical control.

TESTING THE CULTURAL HYPOTHESIS

Figure 9.2 and Table 9.1 compare news defined in topical terms with survey data for newspapers and student groups. We substracted the scores for newspaper coverage (NC) from survey data of students (SD) for each topic. We then summed the differences (TD) and divided by the number of topics. This process yielded a mean difference (MD) score. The cultural hypothesis suggested that German and Japanese students, the most cohesive groups, would reflect greater convergence between students and media than the other groups.

With a mean difference score of 5.4, Japanese students lent support to the cultural hypothesis by demonstrating the least divergence between

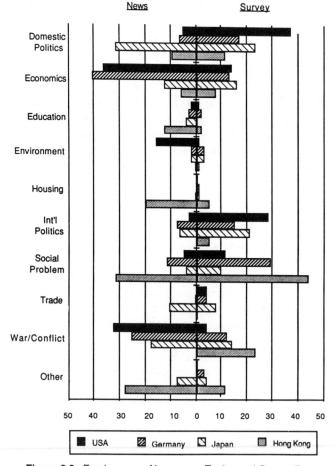

Figure 9.2. Emphases on Newspaper Topics and Survey Data

TABLE 9.1. EMPHASES ON NEWSPAPER TOPICS AND SURVEY DATA

Topics	Germany		United States		Japan		Hong Kong	
	NC	SD	NC	SD	NC	SD	NC	SD
Domestic politics	37	5	17	7	23	32	11	10
Economics	14	37	13	41	16	13	8	6
Education	1	2	2	3	—	4	2	13
Environment	1	16	3	2	3	2	1	1
Housing	—	—	1	—	1	1	5	20
International politics	28	3	15	8	21	7	5	—
Social problems	11	5	29	12	10	4	44	32
Trade	4	—	4	1	8	11	—	—
War/conflict	4	33	12	26	14	18	23	—
Other			3		4	8	11	28
Totals	101	101	99	100	100	100	99	100
Total	136		82		54		80	
MD	13.6		8.2		5.4		8.0	

NC = topically categorized news content.
SD = survey data from students.
TD = total differences.
MD = mean differences.
NOTE: Because of low frequencies several categories were collapsed. Energy (4 percent) and technology (3 percent) were combined with economic news; population (3 percent), institutions, (1 percent), and psychological (3 percent) were combined with social problems.

newspaper topics and their own responses. Thus the agenda of the Japanese students came closer to the agenda of the newspapers than was true for the other students.

We were surprised to observe that the German students demonstrated the greatest mean differences between newspapers and their own definition of the situation. We saw that result as revealing a gap between the concerns of youths and those of the larger culture, reflected by media content. But this difference did not exclude the symbiosis German students had demonstrated with the newspapers along ideological lines. Also, although most German students shared a great many of the concerns of the *Frankfurter Rundschau*, the more liberal newspaper in our sample, they were less likely to be as responsive to the agenda of the *Mainzer Zeitung*, a respected but more moderate newspaper. Moreover, although the German students might disagree with the topical emphasis of newspapers—for they were highly participant regarding a limited number of issues—they might be cohesive concerning the ideological context of those concerns. Finally, the greatest discrepancies occurred, first, with domestic politics and international relations—in which the students felt they were able to play little part—and second, with economic problems and issues of war and conflict. Here students felt themselves to be most involved, not only in terms of economic self-interest but ideologically as well. Therefore, we should expect to observe greater convergence between German students and the press along meaning dimensions. We look for evidence of this finding in Figure 9.2.

The fit between newspapers' and students' agendas in the United States and Hong Kong was consistent with our expectations. The American variance was somewhat similar to that of the German students— primarily in discrepancies between media attention to domestic politics, international relations, and social problem and students' attentiveness to economic issues and war and conflict.

Hong Kong proved to be a special case, however. There was a degree of consensus between students and the media concerning the salience given to social problems (such as crime and divorce). But there was divergence with respect to some social problems; students demonstrated much more concern about housing and education than did the media; and although the media were attentive to war and conflict, students found these concerns outside of their competence. This focus reflected the global interests of the British crown colony but not the interests of politically unfranchised students.

We also rank-ordered the data to gain another perspective, but only a minimal variation in the picture emerged. We therefore are not presenting the tabled data.

THE MEANING HYPOTHESES

Figure 9.3 and Table 9.2 represent our effort to contrast the media and student agendas that reflected "thinking about" as a behavior, utilizing the concept of problematic situations. As we had done for topical headings, we asked about the fit of emphases by audiences and media. To illustrate: If the media and audiences stressed losses of value to the same extent, consonance would be achieved. If the media stressed losses of value but survey data did not reflect this emphasis, there would be a lack of consonance. We again subtracted the scores for newspaper coverage (NC) from survey data (SD) for each problematic situation. We then summed the difference (TD) and divided by the number of problematic situations. This process yielded a mean difference (MD) score.

Figure 9.3 reveals few associations between students' perceptions of problematic situations and portrayal of problematic situations in newspapers. We might conclude, therefore, that students were more attuned to topics in the abstract than to the problematics in which they were couched by newspapers. This is an important finding to be able to demonstrate empirically. It means that it is easier to demonstrate topical agenda setting than meaning agenda setting. It then follows that although many news

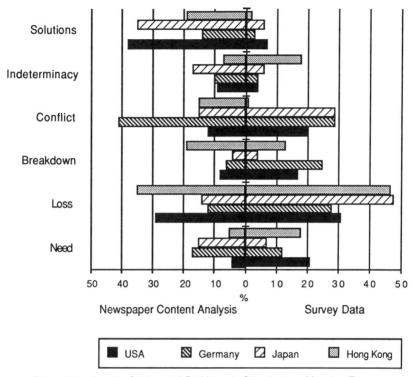

Figure 9.3. Agenda Setting and Problematic Situations as Meaning Terms

TABLE 9.2. AGENDA SETTING AND PROBLEMATIC SITUATIONS AS MEANING TERMS

Problematic Situations	United States		Germany		Japan		Hong Kong	
	SD	NC	SD	NC	SD	NC	SD	NC
Need	21	4	12	17	7	15	18	5
Loss	31	29	28	12	48	14	47	35
Breakdown	17	8	25	6	4	4	13	19
Conflict	20	12	29	41	29	15	1	15
Indeterminacy	4	9	4	10	6	17	18	7
Solutions	7	38	3	14	6	35	2	19
Totals	100	100	101	100	100	100	99	100
	TD = 72		TD = 71		TD = 98		TD = 73	
	MD = 12		MD = 12		MD = 15.5		MD = 12	

SD = survey data.
NC = newspapers content analysis.
TD = total differences.
MD = mean differences.

stories cause their readers to think, they might not be defining what to think about.

By and large the mean differences (MD) were similar across the four student groups. The largest difference along meaning dimensions occurred with Japanese students. Japanese newspapers tended much less than did students to emphasize problematic situations involving loss of value, and they were much more likely than students to point to solutions to social problems. As we have noted previously, many Japanese students in our sample described losses of value associated with their personal concerns about the educational system, breakdown of morals, and the loss of family ties and traditional values.

In each culture the media were far more attentive to solutions to problems than were the students. This finding raised a larger question: Is it possible that the media generically are more oriented to solutions than are the readers?

In the context of solutions, German students and newspapers were least consonant, possibly because of the active role played by students in calling attention to particular problems; the media appeared to reflect the orientations of institutions attempting to cope with those problems—even during a national election, when the media publicized candidates' glib assertions that there were more problems than solutions. Thus the real gap between media perceptions of attempts to solve social problems and public perceptions may be even greater than is reflected in the student data.

Each of the four student groups expressed more of a sense of loss of value than was portrayed by newspapers. The greatest discrepancy was observed in Japan. This finding is a telling reversal: whereas Japanese students demonstrated the greatest consonance topically with newspapers, they were most divergent in the meanings that they assigned to those topics.

A similar phenomenon occurred with the American students. Although there was a modest association of newspaper emphasis and survey data on topics, there were substantial discrepancies between newspapers and students in the meanings that were represented by those topics. As indicated earlier, American students felt personal and social deprivations that were not reflected in newspaper content.

Both American and Japanese students perceived more social conflict in their environment than was reflected in newspapers, whereas German and Chinese students perceived less. In the U.S. case this finding largely represented differences in the emphasis accorded by the media to activist causes. In the Japanese case the discrepancy implied a sense on the part of students that their concerns with problems such as social conflict were not shared by the media—despite the fact of national elections going on in Japan at that time. In Germany, in contrast, the greater competition generated by the elections contributed to higher scores for social conflict in the media. In Hong Kong, students did not identify with the kinds of international conflict portrayed in the media. These largely reflected concerns of the colonial British government.

There were some areas of consonance, however. Both students and media gave the least attention to conditions of indeterminacy. American and German students related similarly to the treatment by their media of breakdowns in social institutions. Here, again, students saw more failures in institutions than did the media. Nor did students feel that effective steps had been taken to cope with those problems.

Elections accounted for the fact that Japanese newspapers reflected more indeterminacy than was experienced by students. Newspapers weighed the probabilities of the various races, whereas students appeared to be somewhat aloof to the course of political events, the races representing foregone conclusions. In contrast, students in Hong Kong expressed more concern about political uncertainties—related to the shift of political sovereignty from Britain to China in 1997—than were portrayed by newspapers.

BARRIERS TO AGENDA SETTING: PERSONAL DIMENSIONS

It is almost obligatory at this point to observe that there are many more barriers to agenda setting than factors operating to facilitate such effects. One of the most obvious barriers to a dominant media role, of course, is the life experience of the individual, in which most of a 24-hour cycle is taken up with the everyday processes of living—work, home, family, sleep, recreation, entertainment, and other time-consuming activities. Our questions, however, have gone beyond private to public lives.

Here too, however, the individual appears to be more active in his or her own milieu than are the mass media. For example, agenda-setting studies of the mass media have revealed that personal observation of events and interpersonal communication are actual barriers to agenda setting by the media. Atwater, Salwen, and Anderson (1985) observed that certain members of the publics—those who discuss problems a great deal, rather than those who discuss problems very little—were more aware of agendas set forth by the media. Yet they established their own agendas, and these took priority over those of the media. Apparently, discussing matters with others helps to set one's own agenda. In contrast, those who used the media but had less contact with other people depended more on the media agendas. The same authors Atwater, Salwen, and Anderson, (1984) tested the effectiveness of interpersonal communication in contributing to agenda-setting effects by the media in their coverage of an environmental issue. They discovered that the more people discussed environmental issues, the less likely the media were to influence the priorities they set for those issues.

Other researchers observed similar phenomena. Zucker (1978) and Hong and Shemer (1976) found that interpersonal contacts were more instrumental in setting agendas than were the media. Erbring, Goldenberg, and Miller (1980), reporting similar results, characterized this phenomenon as dramatizing the difference between the impact of "front page news and real world cues."

Two student studies are relevant, both of which were conducted during political campaigns. Mullins (1977) found that discussion actually enhanced the effectiveness of the media in setting personal agendas; in the political context it did not substitute for it. But Weaver, Auh, Stehle, and Wilhoit (1975) found that interpersonal discussion during a senatorial campaign decreased media effects.

We may only speculate that many of the meanings that the students attached to problems represented their own personal definition of the situation rather than an assessment of a social condition. Certainly Chapter 8 demonstrated the extent to which students engaged in personal observation and interpersonal communication. These data testified to the fullness of their personal agendas. We might conclude in relation to this evidence that the social environment always is public, but meanings are private.

SUMMARY

We specified a number of conditions of agenda-setting research that required conceptual clarification if multicultural studies were to be carried out effectively. These included specification of *meaning*, especially the phrase *thinking about*, the *minimal effects* hypothesis, and the concept of *problematic situations* as meaning objects. Our comparison of topical and meaning categories led us to observe that topics, because they incorporate a variety of meanings, provide a better, although conceptually looser, fit between media content and audience's responses.

Because of the pluralistic nature of societies, a multieffects agenda-setting approach was suggested that would take into account the concept of agenda building. The roles of social institutions suggest that agenda setting is more than a one-step process between media and audiences; rather, it is one of several steps in a chain of influence. We described models that incorporated impulse as well as cumulative effects, which suggested that agenda setting proceeded in stages that were accompanied by multiple effects.

We cited a number of Japanese, German, and Hong Kong studies that tested the multistep, multieffect approach to agenda-setting and other media effects. The Japanese studies showed few agenda-setting effects, either in the case of social problems or with respect to the political process. In contrast, the German studies argued strongly for an impulse model and a multistage process to explain substantial media effects. Hong Kong studies reflected the dominance of a government-dominated media system.

We suggested another potentially significant area of inquiry: Whereas media and audiences seemingly achieve more consonance in addressing topics in the news, meanings that are assigned to those topics appear to diverge dramatically. This finding reminds us of our earlier suggestion that when agenda-setting researchers test the proposition that media advise audiences what to think about, they must be explicit about meaning referents. "Topics" are not equivalent to "meanings." Thus we must conclude that people do not think about topics but about the meanings that are implicit in those topics.

The observations of the German scholar Habermas (1962) appear to be relevant to our multistep model. He theorized that the strain of institutions within a society—political parties, bureaucracies, education, business, and media—worked toward a relative degree of autonomy for each institution rather than an interdependence of resources and actions. That fact might help to explain the inability of the media consistently to set agendas for the public.

Finally, researchers should look to personal observation and interpersonal communication for agenda-setting effects. In some cases, these will minimize and outweigh the impact of the media alone.

CHAPTER 10

Transcending the Debate: A Constructivist Approach to Methodology

One of the dichotomies posed in communications research is that of the open versus the closed-ended question. Schuman (1986) concluded that although the closed-ended approach was more efficient, the open-ended approach was more sensitive, particularly in less defined situations. He recommended that both approaches, or modifications of them, be used in the same study, but he conceded that in practice this was seldom done.

One of our purposes in this chapter is not so much to "revisit" the debate as to "redefine" it. Our methodology may be said to have been open-ended in form, yet it was, at the same time, closed-ended in order and structure. Although the students responded to questions in their own words, thus reflecting open-endedness, the questions were ordered and structured to limit, in closed-ended effect, the responses.

Beyond transcending the debate over open versus closed-endedness, another purpose in this chapter is to test more broadly the relevance of our concepts. We have done so by constructing closed-ended scale items for each concept. These items may be utilized by research colleagues and applied to a variety of substantive problems.

However, our first approach is better considered as *constructivist* rather than either open- or closed-ended. Thus termed by Swanson (1981), the constructivist approach has developed methods that have maximized the participation of respondents in the data-gathering process and, as a consequence, have enhanced the exchange of information and *communication*. Methodological decisions have become information and communication decisions. As researchers reach points of decision about methodology, they consider the potential for enhancing or limiting the exchange of information and communication.

Opinion research during the Vietnam War was a case in which closed-ended items and even approaches to constructivism failed in part. There was a dawning realization that because all the early polls on Vietnam used the same methodological approaches and asked similar closed-ended questions, all yielded similar results. The closed-ended questions constrained respondents by the specification of both a limited number of alternatives (not always the most relevant ones) and values that were associated with them. Those results pictured the public as supporting the war; the president thus was able to point to the polls as a way of defending his policies.

A Stanford University research team finally challenged not merely the findings of these studies but also the methodologies they employed (Verba et al., 1967). The team shifted to a more constructivist format, one that offered respondents a greater range of alternatives and a larger number of values for judging them. The respondents were permitted to select among the alternatives and the values that were presented to them. However, they could not themselves volunteer alternatives or supply their own values.

Nonetheless, the methodology assured a more constructivist approach. By engaging in selection, respondents became more active participants in the opinion-reporting process. To this extent they were able to construct their own pictures of reality. But the methodology nonetheless limited the number of alternatives and the values that could be attached to them; as a consequence, individuals who were faced with justifying their choices of alternatives were forced to utilize values that were not their own, and to this extent they constructed false pictures of reality. Constructivism had been taken to a point, but possibly not far enough.

Edelstein (1973) concurred with the objectives of the research strategy that Verba and colleagues (1967) had adopted and sought to extend the approach to its maximal potential. It required the additional step of allowing respondents to supply both their own alternatives and their own values. Edelstein pointed out that this approach took into account two types of errors that often occurred when the researcher undertook the construction:

- *Type 1: solution-errors:* This occurred when the respondent was asked to "agree" or "disagree" with or to "support" or "reject" alternatives with which s/he previously was unfamiliar and which s/he had not evaluated previously.
- *Type 2: evaluation-errors:* The respondent might be familiar with the solution that had been proposed, and might have a rationale for accepting or rejecting it, but that rationale was not contained in the pollster's statement. Hence the respondent "evaluated" alternatives on the basis of unfamiliar criteria. (p. 87)

Both Type 1 and Type 2 errors produced problems of construction and thus failed to stimulate meaningful communication. In Thurstone and Chave's (1929) long-stated terms, respondents were forced to relate to someone else's definition of the situation. Decades later Cantril (1965), recognizing the nature of research challenges that were being posed by the emergence of new populations and technologies, called for research that would assess newly emerging problems in meaningful contexts.

To accomplish this goal in realistic terms, he said, individual respondents should be permitted to describe their own psychological environments as free as possible of any point of view brought to the situation by outside observers. Cantril explained that in the cross-cultural context people had to be understood in their own terms:

> Clearly, an accurate appraisal of an individual's reality can never be obtained if he is forced to make choices of selections between categories, alternatives, symbols or situations as these are posed in the usual type of questionnaire.

Cantril (1965) nonetheless acknowledged the methodological dilemma of open versus closed-ended items, adding, "Yet, without some...preconceived classification, how can a final research instrument be obtained that allows for quantitative comparison?" (pp. 21–22). Those considerations led to the invention of what Cantril described as a "self-anchoring scale" in which the respondent would place himself or herself in relation to others. Thus the respondent would be helping to "construct" the measurement.

Respondents also were permitted to set the agenda in terms of their own perceptions, goals, and values. These could be wishes or hopes, frustrations or deprivations. The respondent placed himself or herself on that ladder both "now" and in the future. The place on the scale would be relative in each culture; hence although absolute values might be different, relative values in each culture would be preserved and individuals could be compared cross-culturally concerning how they saw themselves in relation to others within and across cultures.

More recently we have seen a recognition of the importance of permitting respondents to utilize their own frame of reference, growingly referred to as "schema" and "frames of reference." McLeod and colleagues (1987) observed that a growing body of research makes a compelling case for the schematic approach. Lau and Sears (1986) suggested the use of open-ended survey questions for this purpose, and Lau (1986) argued that individuals were consistent over time in their construction of schema. This stability of individual structuring carries implications for both conceptualization and methodology.

STRUCTURAL PARAMETERS

In our search for cross-cultural comparability, we have stressed the utility of the concept of structural equivalence. We have used the term *structure* to describe social institutions that represent the functioning of societies. But structure also may be viewed in terms of its meaning for the individual, as has been suggested for cognitive structures. These structures describe the ways in which the individual constructs situations and processes information to deal with those situations. Cognitive structures permit multicultural comparison at the point at which individuals think and communicate.

Mitchell (1980) took a structural approach to cognitions that is of special relevance to our concerns. He established that important problems have many aspects or foci of attention; these made up the structure of cognitions about a problem and governed the ways in which problems were typified by the individual. Mitchell pointed out that the nuclear energy debate involved at least six foci of attention: transporting and disposal of nuclear waste, reprocessing, emission, proliferation, access to information and loss of prolitical control, and even meltdowns, as was threatened at Three-Mile Island and occurred at Chernobyl.

Two major ideas were central to Mitchell's (1980) observations. One was that so-called problems or issues are multidimensional rather than unidimensional. There was no single nuclear energy problem nor any single substantive problem of any kind. All had numerous aspects to which the public gave its attention. The second idea was that the constituency of the public differs dramatically for each aspect of a problem. Different publics are more or less interested in and capable of addressing each aspect of a problem or subissue.

Mitchell's (1980) approach was thus analagous to the schema approach and to our attention to aspects of problems that were the foci of public opinion, that is, the consequences, the causes, and the solutions to problems. As respondents consider different aspects of problems, gaps in the foci of communication could occur. Polling questions addressed to social problems might demand that respondents deal with aspects of a problem with which they are unfamiliar.

Aspects of problems also taxed the analytical capabilities of respondents. In the Vietnam study, respondents who said that they "could not decide" how the war should be brought to an end gave a variety of reasons for that response. "It was too difficult to decide"; "it was not up to them to decide"; they had "too much information," "not enough information," and/or the "wrong information." They said that "if they decided they would have to defend their decisions"; that they didn't have "confidence" in their decisions; and that people, in any case, didn't listen to them. These personal inadequacies represent structural as well as substantive problems of communication in data collection.

There have been other efforts to take constructivist approaches to data gathering. To enhance the communication potential of questions on voting choices, Stamm (1985) required respondents to "imagine" situations and to deal with more "processual" concepts of a candidate's image. Each respondent was asked to interpret the relevance of candidates' images and think beyond candidate-attribute relations to other qualifying conditions. What was meaningful about an image was not simply its attributes but the connections and/or associations that were made. Reeves, Chaffee, and Tims (1982) urged a study of processing mechanisms as a way of understanding what was being communicated. Carter (1978) made a distinction between learning about candidates and issues and constructing or "imagining" them.

Bogart (1972) also conceptualized research requirements in communication terms. He characterized polling methodologies simply as mechanisms by which the public became sensitized to itself and by which journalists and political leaders appraised the public's sense of things. Thus the quality of the mechanisms determined the effectiveness of public communication. Both the form and the substance of questions became important in this process.

THE COMPARATIVE CONTEXT

A constructivist approach may also enhance the potential for comparability across cultures because the questions may be more value free. In permitting students to describe what they themselves considered to be the most important problems, students could be compared to one another in value-free terms. The basis for comparability was found not in the *substance* of the problem but in its *importance*. Substantively, each problem might be different, but it was comparable because it was of equal salience or importance to each student, and in these terms conceptually equivalent.

To permit each student in our study the maximum freedom to describe his or her own most important problem, the questionnaire was, in form, open-ended—but open-ended in the narrow sense, that is, not in the approach. The procedure of being taken through a series of steps required the students to state the logic of their situation, and a structure thus was defined.

Although closed-ended in structure, the open-endedness of form required that responses be coded. This was a demanding process, but steps were taken to ensure its success. All coding was carried out by carefully trained graduate students in each country under the direction of a faculty and graduate-student supervisor. Preliminary tests of reliability were conducted until 90 percent reliability was achieved. At that point the coders proceeded on a "referral" basis: All questions were referred to a coding supervisor.

We faced a dilemma that all comparative researchers face at many decision points: choosing among methods for their appropriateness for the task at hand, their relative efficiency, and the resources at the command of the research team. Noelle-Neumann and Kepplinger (1981) pointed out,

> When international research groups are co-operating, two different attitudes can be observed with regard to the questionnaire. One group advocates an unstructured questionnaire (as far as possible), employing open-ended questions, a minimum of specified, pre-coded responses, so as to obtain the respondents' natural reactions and to obviate the danger of response alternatives artificially creating opinions.
>
> The other group holds the view that an unstructured interview is only suitable for exploration in the preliminary phases of a survey, and they believe that a measuring method, designed to offer the possibility of repetition, comparison, and checking, has to work with structured questionnaires, as otherwise the principles of measuring and statistical analysis cannot be observed or applied. (pp. 116–18)

To resolve this problem in their study, Kepplinger and Noelle-Neumann (1981) used both approaches, interviewing one sample with an open-ended questionnaire and the other with a closed-ended instrument, utilizing the resources of the Allensbach Institute of Public Opinion. We carried out the same exercise but on an ad hoc basis.

DECISION POINTS IN THE COMPARATIVE PROCESS

Earlier comparative studies (Edelstein, 1973, 1974) helped us to anticipate some of the decision points we would encounter in implementing our approach. These problems were challenging when we first encountered them for we were attempting to compare individuals in settings where the cultures were diverse and the political structures were dramatically different. There were great economic and political disparities, and the character and richness of media systems were highly diverse.

We found bases for comparability, however, in the common context of individuals living in urban settings, of meanings that individuals assigned to our concepts, and of the ways in which individuals addressed and coped with the personal and social problems that they described.

Many problems of comparability nonetheless were challenging.

Disparities in the Extent and Diversity of Media Systems

In comparing Seattle to the two Yugoslav cities of Belgrade and Ljubljana, we observed that there were far fewer broadcasting channels in the latter (television and radio). Our conceptual remedy was to test the proposition that although the number of channels might vary greatly across cultures, the comparative question was the *availability* of channels of each kind; that is, were radio, television, newspapers, opinion magazines, and so on equally accessible as sources? If so, there was equivalence in those terms.

Availability of Content

A similar question of comparability arose about the availability of categories of media content, that is, news versus entertainment, and their quality. Again, although the amount of content in various categories within each channel varied across cultures, the conceptual question was the actual availability of each kind of content; was it or was it not available?

Problem Equivalence in Societal Terms

Problems were deemed to be equivalent at the individual level if each problem were equally salient to individuals, whatever the nominal designations. However, an important and related question arose: Were the most important problems in one culture more important than the most important problems in another culture? To test this question empirically, we compared the frequency distributions of the most important problems in the four cultures. A similar pattern of distributions implied similar degrees of importance. We found that this condition existed, so we could make the necessary comparisons.

A Situational Approach

As McLeod and colleagues (1987) suggested, we took a situational rather than a cross-situational approach. We reasoned that it was easier for the respondent to report on communication or media use in an important situation of his or her own definition than across situations that had been defined by an investigator.

Conceptual Equivalence

We gained conceptual equivalence by the cross-cultural relevance of our cognitive variables—the problematic situation and aspects of public opinion. These cognitive variables enabled us to compare students on the common meanings assigned to problems, no matter their topical identification.

Cultural Equivalence

A question of comparability was presented because of the inclusion of both Eastern and Western cultures. Were concepts such as the "problem" and "problematic situation" similarly understood and applicable in Japan and Germany, in Hong Kong and the United States? Through the translation and discussion processes with colleagues and students, we observed that the concepts were, indeed, comparable in their meanings across cultures.

THE VALIDATION OF CONCEPTS

Social scientists must rely on validated concepts and standardized procedures to advance knowledge in a field. Data gathered by standardized procedures permit much easier replication and comparability. We therefore took steps to translate our constructivist approach into scale items that were replicable for each of our major concepts. Within this approach we retained two basic controls on data collection.

1. We would discuss only those problems that were most salient to students.
2. We would deal with this behavior in a bounded situation rather than across situations.

Our pretest data were obtained from an intact group of adults who were waiting to be impaneled for Superior Court duty as jurors in King County, Washington. They had been randomly selected from voter registration lists. King County bounds Seattle and its adjacent rural areas.

The selection processes of those subjects assured a degree of representativeness but fell short of randomness because many nonregistered citizens and those persons who were excused from duty were not accessible. The nonregistered group tended to be of the lowest level of education and income and the other groups were of the highest education and income, so canceling-out factors were at work.

There were, however, compensating advantages to our strategy. Data collection was minimal in cost, and accessibility to the respondents was assured. Each morning the jurors were gathered in a large room to wait until they were summoned for duty—which meant that they had time on their hands. Our data-gatherers were described as members of the faculty and graduate students in the School of Communications. More important, perhaps, subjects were told by court house officials that the school, out of its research funds, had purchased amenities for the personal use of the jurors; in this way a 90 percent rate of cooperation was achieved.

Three pretests were conducted, each comprising from 85 to 147 inter views. The items were derived from statements made by the students. A set of four Likert statements, utilizing a five-point scale, was constructed for each major concept:

1. Perceptions of problematic situations
2. Orientations to causes, consequences, and solutions to problems
3. Uses of sources of information
4. Evaluation of those utilities

As in the open-ended surveys, each respondent was asked to describe the three most important problems facing the country and then to specify the problem that was most important to him or her personally. We computed Pearson product moment correlations between individual scales and each scale item against the correlation of the other three items. The second procedure told us the extent to which each item correlated with a cluster of items as well as with individual items.

We set minimum acceptable correlation coefficients of .24. Although the lower limits explained a limited amount of variance, they produced reliability coefficients at greater than the .001 level. Many of our scales demonstrated higher coefficients, as high as .62, explaining more than 36 percent of the variance. We rejected a number of items that were correlated at .001 levels of significance because they did not meet our minimum requirements for explaining variance.

FIRST CONCEPT: THE PROBLEMATIC SITUATION

One of our major concepts was that of the problematic situation; it addressed the meanings that individuals attached to the problems that faced the country and what they themselves believed to be the most important problems.

The six scales for problematic situations emerged as follows:

Loss of Value

Four items were designed to tap what students had reported in surveys as wastes of money, time, energy, and resources. (Correlations are shown after each item.)

All four items were retained from the loss of value scale:

1. It (the problem) is so costly.
   (wasteful, .28; energy, .38; resources, .33)
2. It has wasted so much time.
   (costly, .28; energy, .54; resources, .37)

3. . . . taken up so much energy.
   (costly, .38; wasted, .54; resources, .60)
4. . . . used so many resources.
   (costly, .33; wasted, .37; energy, .60).

As shown, all items correlated at a minimum of .28, and one correlated at .60.

Need for Value

Needs incorporated a number of dimensions, from simply wanting to hold on to what one has to having new needs, demands, wishes, and desires. We discovered that, empirically, "desire" was not associated with needs to the extent that our criterion for explaining variance had stipulated. Hence we dropped it from the scale.

Three of the four items were retained:

1. Try to hold on to what they [people] have.
   (needs, .45; demands, .41; desires, .18)
2. Meet only their most immediate needs.
   (holds, .45; demands, .33; desires, .21)
3. Make new demands.
   (hold, .41; needs, .33; desires, .35)

As can be seen, the dropped item, "indulge wishes or desires," correlated only .18 with one item ("hold onto what one has").

Indeterminacy

We observed that students had defined indeterminacy in terms of uncertainty, ambiguity, questioning, and inability to take action.

Again, three of the four items were retained, as follows:

1. It is difficult to know what to do.
   (what is happening? .37; do first? .51; how? .44)
2. . . . to know what to do first.
   (what is happening? .23; to do? .51; do first? .52)
3. . . . to know exactly how to do it.
   (what is happening? .18; what to do? .44; do first .52)

One item was dropped, "It is difficult to know what is happening," because it correlated only .23 with "what to do first" and only .18 with "how to do it."

Social Conflict

We had incorporated two paradigms of conflict in this scale, one *within* the individual, and the other *between* individuals, groups, or nations. We assumed conflict to be a generic and therefore organizing concept, but as our data indicated, this was not the case. The items relating to nations did not correlate highly with conflict in the individual or among friends or within groups. Therefore, the item relating to nations was dropped from that scale and another scale was created for nations, world organizations, terrorism, trade, and so on.

1. The problem is creating conflict within many individuals.
   (friends, .50; groups, .24; nations, .08)
2. ...among many friends.
   (individuals, .50; groups, .41; nations, .15)
3. ...among many groups.
   (individuals, .24; friends, .41; nations, .20)

The item describing conflict between nations correlated only .18 with individuals, .15 with friends, and .20 with groups.

System Breakdown

We incorporated four kinds of system breakdown or dysfunction: the fairness of the system to its users, the quickness with which the system responded to problems, its strength or endurance, and its efficiency in the use of resources.

We faced a dilemma here; two items failed to meet the minimum degree of correlation with the other three items. Each did, however, satisfy the criterion with respect to two items, although different in each case. We decided that we would retain these items but seek to improve them by examining their relationships to other concepts.

1. The system is not fair.
   (quickness, .29; strength, .24; efficiency, .27)
2. ...is too slow to react.
   (fairness, .29; strength, .47; efficiency, .14)
3. ...breaks down too easily.
   (fairness, .24; quickness, .47; efficiency, .26)
4. ...wastes resources;
   (fairness, .27; quickness, .14; strength, .26)

Solutions

We also designed a scale that incorporated approaches to problem solving. The lack of substantial correlations suggests that our respondents did not perceive them as discrete alternatives. We had postulated the continuum from changing objectives, to revision of priorities, to cancellation of old programs and experimenting with new programs. The correlations were positive, as we have suggested, but they failed to meet the level that we had established.

1. To solve this problem we should change our objectives.
   (revision, .54; cancellation, .14; experiment, .21)
2. ...revise our priorities.
   (Change, .54; cancel, .26; experiment, .20)
3. ...cancel existing programs.
   (Change, .14; revise, .26; experiment, .02)
4. ...experiment with new programs.
   (Change, .21; revise, .20; cancel, .02)

The least congruous of these items was experimentation; it did not correlate adequately with any other item; each of the other three items correlated adequately with any other item.

In summary, through our first three pretests we derived reliable Likert scales of three to four items for each of five problematic situations. We are developing new scales directed to perceptions of international conflict and alternative approaches to problem solving.

RETESTING CO-ORIENTATION

We devised four sets of scale items to measure co-orientation to cognitive aspects of problems. These were based on statements about one's own opinion, perceptions of public opinion, and expressing and hearing opinions from others.

Our data from these scales supported what we had obtained from our interviews with students, where we did not use scales:

1. As in the student data, there was more of a tendency for respondents to perceive that cognitive co-orientation was occurring than non-occurring. This finding applied both to perceptions of public opinion and opinion exchange with others.
2. Again as in the student samples, where there was not co-orientation, respondents portrayed themselves more than their partners as addressing more complex opinions, that is, describing the causes

and solutions to a problem rather than merely the nature of the problem or its consequences.

3. At the lowest level of complexity, that is, simply being aware of the nature of a problem rather than understanding its consequences, causes, or solutions, individuals were most likely to perceive public opinion about this aspect of the problem, were very likely to mention it to someone else, and perceived also that the other person had mentioned it to him or her.

(We had not coded "nature of the problem" in the student data.)

4. At the lowest level of abstraction, that is, consequences of the problem, the adult respondents, as had the students, perceived similarities in the orientations of others.

5. As we observed with students, substantial variation occurred with respect to the causes of problems, an orientation that makes greater demands on the individual. There were substantial discrepancies between a respondent's claim that he or she had focused on the causes of problems and perceptions of a similar orientation by the public. And respondents perceived themselves as telling about the causes of problems much more than hearing about them.

6. A similar phenomenon occurred with respect to perceptions of public opinion about solutions to problems. We constructed two sets of scale items for orientations to solutions. One set asked if *anything* could be done; the second, what *should* be done.

The phenomenon that we just observed repeated itself, in part. The respondent perceived that she or he "told more than heard" about the "need for something to be done." But respondents perceived a more balanced exchange with respect to "what, exactly, should be done." Apparently, once someone believes that *something* can be done, he or she is more ready to tell exactly *what* should be done.

(We did not distinguish between "demands for solutions" and "actual solutions" in the student data.)

In summary, our co-orientation scales reproduced, to a surprising extent, the data we had obtained from the students. The scales might therefore be used by communication researchers to examine cognitive coorientations to social and political situations.

INTERPERSONAL COMMUNICATION

Almost everyone in the adult sample reported interpersonal communication about the most important problem. We were interested in the nature and extent of the linkages that existed among friends, family, neighbors, and fellow workers. If someone talked to a friend, who else was he or she most likely to speak to?

Beginning with the size of correlations, a person who discussed a problem with his or her family was most likely also to discuss it with a friend, then with a neighbor, and then with a fellow worker. The differences were not great, however—family, .42; neighbor, .37; and fellow worker, .30. No other relationship exceeded .30. We drew the implication that the nature of a problem as well as the generic character of a relationship helped to predict the configuration of a communication network. Families shared kinship problems, whereas neighbors and fellow workers shared roles and interests such as class and politics.

THE PROBLEMATIC SITUATION

When a person defined a situation as problematic did he or she perceive it in multidimensional ways or in only one way? If problems were multidimensional, was there a tendency for certain problematics to cluster in given situations? Finally, were there special links between certain problematic situations and sources of information?

In answer to the first question, respondents in most cases incorporated more than one dimension. They tended, in fact, to incorporate several dimensions.

1. Persons who saw loss of value (or personal deprivation) in a situation also were likely to see needs for value, indeterminacy, and social conflict—these at the .001 level. They also saw institutional breakdowns and needs for solutions as a part of that situation, although significance approached only the .05 level. Thus a sense of personal deprivation was tied to almost all other problematics.
2. At the other extreme, an orientation to solutions to problems correlated highly only with the perception of institutional breakdowns (.001); we might derive from that finding a sense that solutions to broadly defined social problems are linked, inevitably, with the functioning of social institutions that, presumably, might be able to address those problems.
3. Needs for value correlated highly, as indicated, with a sense of deprivation and personal loss to the individual (.001). With this factor came a perception of the existence of social conflict (.01). Thus personal deprivation and need might be construed as likely to be associated with perceptions of social conflict and might possibly be triggered by those perceptions.

These findings carry implications for the assessment of public opinion:

1. There is never "only one thing wrong" and, therefore, only one basis for an opinion in a given situation. Rather, each situation incorporates a number of problematics, each of which depends on the other and/or is a consequence of or antecedent to the other.
2. Given that observation, it becomes more necessary to carry out longitudinal studies of the emergence of problems as problematics to determine the points at which other problematics intervene.
3. Further, it is a denial of the rich fabric of public opinion to assume that a few closed-ended questions may capture the richness of definition and detail that a respondent gives to a situation.
4. Finally, closed-ended items appear not so much to inform respondents as to redefine the problem. Thus closed-ended questions are obtrusive in structure as well as in content.

SOURCES OF INFORMATION

If problematic situations reflect cognitive dynamics, there should be relationships between problematic situations and the selection of sources of information. We explored these possibilities by looking at the relationships of the variables.

Loss of Value

Respondents reporting losses of value relied primarily on personal observation (.001) as a source of information; they also reported the use of qualitative media (.01). We inferred that losses of value or deprivation were more private than public, and that personal observation and qualitative media permitted more selectivity than other means. It was interesting to note the lack of correlation of loss of value and interpersonal communication. Apparently, some deprivations were too personal to communicate.

Need for Value

In contrast, those who reported needs for value tended to identify those needs with the public more than the private sphere. They were more likely to use mass media (.08) and somewhat less likely to use qualitative media (.07) than in conditions of loss of value. But as with loss of value, personal observation again was most relevant (.01).

We originally had hypothesized that those who expressed new needs as contrasted with familiar losses would require a greater number of sources of information to cope with that definition of the situation, and that expectation was confirmed (.01).

Indeterminacy

We hypothesized that pure indeterminacy was the most cognitively difficult situation in which an individual might find himself or herself. That inference was supported to some extent by the greater selectivity implied by the use of qualitative media (.04) as well as the general utility of mass media (.08).

Perceptions of Social Conflict

We were surprised by the lack of association of sources of information with perceptions of social conflict. The association held only with the mass media (.05). Thus qualitative media addressed solutions to problems more than the earlier stages of conflict. And social conflict was not observed at first hand or discussed in interpersonal terms.

Institutional Breakdowns

If institutional breakdowns were viewed as losses of value on a societal level, we might hypothesize that more communication would occur in that more critical condition. We found that use of mass media (.09) approached significance, but we gained somewhat more support for the hypothesis by the use of qualitative media (.05), interpersonal communication (.001), and special publications (.001).

Solution Orientations

The most demanding problematic situation was in the realm of demands for or steps toward solutions. There, as we had expected, an orientation to solutions was associated with use of qualitative media (.02), interpersonal communication (.04), use of special sources (.01), and personal observation (.04). Overall, we concluded that there were meaningful and systematic relationships between orientations to an array of problematic situations and uses of sources of information.

SUMMARY

We recast the question of open-ended versus closed-ended methods into a constructivist framework that enhanced the exchange of information and communication in the research setting. We reported on recent validation of open-ended questions as a means of permitting respondents to construct schemata or frames of reference that would allow them to demonstrate underlying consistency in their cognitive behavior over time. We described some of the comparative conditions that contributed to methodological decisions, and we then compared data that we had gathered by alternative research methods.

At the same time we reported on our development of validated, closed-ended scale items for each major concept. Our purpose was to make the concepts more accessible to other scholars.

We asked if these scales pointed to multidimensionality or singularity of meaning in a problematic situation. We concluded that the tendency was strongly toward multidimensionality. Thus problematic situations were complex rather than simple in their structures.

We asked if different problematic situations were associated with uses of different information sources. We tested several hypotheses, several of which brought support to the findings.

We are encouraged by these steps toward the development of validated and reliable measures. Schuman (1979) concluded that closed-ended items offered advantages *if* based on open-ended pretests. We appear to have approached that requirement.

CHAPTER 11

A Multicultural Review and Symposium

It is tempting and, of course, necessary to look back on a study that has required an enormous investment of time and resources by the authors, and then the readers.

Admittedly, it is more difficult to look ahead than to review what has been accomplished. But we take first things first and, subject to the limitations we have mentioned, review a number of our most important discoveries. We then think ahead to some of the challenges that face us.

We attempt this task in the form of a symposium, in which the authors speak to the reader and to each other from each of their perspectives. The American, German, and Japanese views are similar enough to be compared but different enough to be observed. These differences express themselves in the problems they address in their culturally determined point of view.

We set the stage for the symposium by outlining some of the major concepts that the authors agree have provided the thrust of the research and the bases for the comparisons. We have agreed that it is proper in this section to express at least a guarded enthusiasm about some of the steps we have taken toward accomplishing our goals. But we echo this joy not so much for what has been done as to express an optimism about the chances for attacking the many challenges that still need to be faced in comparative analysis. In these efforts we would welcome the participation of students and colleagues in our scholarly community, not only in our participating countries but in others as well. We see potential for using our concepts in historical and cultural analysis and we see applications as much to the developing countries as to postindustrial or "information societies," as we have come to think of them.

THE SYMPOSIUM PARTICIPANTS

Professors Edelstein, Ito, and Kepplinger agree that our study goes far to validate the promise of the comparative approach as we have used it. Certainly, we have demonstrated that its conceptual outlook distinguishes it from other approaches to the study of communication and culture. We believe the comparative approach has afforded us insights into each of the cultures that we might not have obtained with a different approach.

We recognize that the comparative approach, because of the differences in cultures, languages, and special conditions that it encompasses, demands creative conceptual and methodological approaches to achieve comparability. The reward for achieving the degree of success that we experienced was a bounty of generalizable knowledge about information and communication behaviors in the four cultures. It became apparent that youth culture was not merely a phenomenon that occurred within a culture but was likely to be present in all cultures, and was therefore generalizable on a global basis.

We acknowledge that practical as well as theoretical considerations had brought us to the study of youths. However, other practical considerations asserted themselves. It became desirable to bring to our student comparisons a number of related findings that had been found to be true for adults. These adult studies had been carried out at different times with different populations. One important step was to weigh one set of findings against the other—youth against adult—and we found that step to be productive and reassuring. The adult perspective also brought us face to face with a number of major traditions of communications research to which our concepts, without regard to findings, seemed to apply. In fact, we found that the concepts and data we had generated for youth cultures served as a window through which we could look at major traditions of research with fresh perspectives. We thus had moved by stages from a monograph describing youth cultures with a fresh set of concepts to a new look at a half dozen of the major traditions of research in mass communication. Although this aspect of the study was not originally intended, it became nonetheless a happy intellectual adventure.

Another major benefit of this approach, we agree, was the validation of our own data, made possible largely by our multicultural commitment of achieving conceptual equivalence. These comparisons did not cause us to lose any of the cultural nuances that would serve to explain differences in behavior. In fact, we were able to suggest that the field of mass communication should "go comparative." This suggestion caused us to expand models of communication and behavior to accommodate cultural variation. It was a highly worthwhile intellectual exercise.

The cultural variations were nonetheless important, and we could point to many of them:

Students in different cultures addressed different media for different reasons to understand social problems that they perceived were important to the society and with which they had identified personally.

Source credibility was of variable importance to the students, reflecting differences in the cultural context and variabilities in situations. These findings underlined the changing bases of evaluation of media sources of information multiculturally from a narrowly constructed definition of credibility to the ways in which media performed their roles and impinged on audiences. We need more research in Germany and Hong Kong, as well as in other countries, to validate these observations on a global scale.

We gained a universality—at one level—in approaching co-orientation, a vital area of communication research, as a cognitive rather than an evaluative process. This result enabled us to ask simply whether or not students in all cultures could perceive if the foci of their concerns were similar or different. Were they thinking or communicating about the same things or different things? And we observed a universality in their tendencies to focus on such cognitive orientations as the causes, consequences, and/or solutions to problems. But as we have suggested, we discovered cultural differences as well, and these have raised promising questions for research.

Why is it that in one culture, Japan, students perceived a more convergent focus of attention with general public opinion than with their peers? That is a most intriguing question, for that finding ran contrary to the findings in the other three countries. We have, in reporting those findings, risked less than definitive interpretations, so the question begs for further research. That research should not be confined to Japan, of course, but might be undertaken in comparative terms in all Asian countries.

We found it challenging as well to move beyond the theory of news proposed by Norwegian scholars Galtung and Ruge (1965)—which capitalized on topical and journalistically defined categories of news content—to a somewhat more complex theory suggested by Walter Lippmann's observation that news represented an "obtrusion" on the environment. Our theory had its genesis, therefore, in the properties of news, itself.

This focus of attention on news and not on its characterization or its social, economic, or political environment, was inspired by our cognitive variables, notably the problematic situation. It became apparent that what journalists intuitively characterize as news had its basis in conditions of discrepancy. These conditions of discrepancy have long been recognized intuitively as the essence of news not only by journalists but by audiences as well. It was the problematic situation that gave rise to readership and communication as behavioral responses. News as discrepancy provided insight into perceptions of news by cultures as well as by journalists and audiences.

We also agree that thinking multiculturally has encouraged a fresh approach to the concept of agenda setting. We transcended the American model of a one-step process from media to the public to a more complex relationship of source, journalist, and public and their reciprocal effects. The American approach reflected complex political and social norms. In one respect it was a pedagogical reaction to the concept of "powerful media" that reflected a transition in research orientations from "maximal" to "limited" effects of media. This changed vision reduced greatly the potential for building stronger effects into the agenda-setting model, although it promised that potential. The various proposals for a multistep agenda-setting and agenda-building process—incorporating key actors other than media, alone—promise to locate additional sources of media effects in the personal and institutional sources of information upon which reporters depend for information. We see additional excitement being built into an agenda-setting or agenda-building model by extension of the dependent variable—thinking about—to incorporate additional cognitive behaviors. We may distinguish among "only thinking," "thinking about," and "what to think about" as three—rather than only one—cognitive outcomes of agenda setting.

We also agree with other critics that the agenda-setting approach may have focused unnecessarily on behavioral effects other than communication effects. The question we have raised cross-culturally is whether more or less *communication* is brought about by an agenda-setting effect that encourages the audiences only to think, what to think about, or what to think. We would like to enquire, as well, if this effect varies by situation or events, by different media, and/or by cultures. We might also speculate that a multistep approach probably would promote interactive processes of communication among actors who represent institutions and other special interests in society. We may suggest that agenda-setting effects depend on the interactions of various actors, including those institutional sources that are most affected by the actions as well as by the appraisals of journalists who mediate them.

Our data support the conclusion that we must reexamine the *nonmedia* processes that in many situations substitute for the processes of mass communication. The student data also support the importance of making distinctions between the effects of *information* and those of *influence*. Our comparative perspectives, in which American, German, Japanese, and Hong Kong students used interpersonal communication and personal observation as substitutes for mass communication, pointed to the impact of cultures in defining the conditions under which media and nonmedia play their roles.

We experienced some satisfaction in being able to answer two questions about our proposed theory of problematic situations—the degree of productivity and its general relevance. In terms of productivity we were able to take several steps toward relevance.

First, we were able to model problematic situations as motivational states that helped to bridge gaps in the uses and gratifications approach. We feel that this suggestion might satisfy critics of uses and gratifications research who had pointed to a gap between needs (determined) and motivations (demonstrated).

Second, by the use of our cognitive variables we have been able to put another face on co-orientation effects. In addition to substituting cognitive effects for evaluative effects we have pointed to the implications of a cognitive model for identifying steps in the emergence of public opinion. This step model carries implications for events and cultures and encourages us to compare public opinion across a variety of cultures and different stages of development.

Finally, we saw our cognitive construction of problematic situations as leading to a theory of *news as discrepancy*. Here, again, there were numerous research challenges. How did journalists construct news as problematic situations as compared to perceptions by other actors—sources, social critics, and the public? We have learned enough about this subject to be encouraged that more might be learned about the different relationships and steps that lead to the formulation of news and thus the relationships between media and their audiences in different nations and cultures.

Having agreed on all these perspectives there still remain many aspects each of us should consider.

> EDELSTEIN: I guess it's my obligation to lead off, and I don't mind doing so. As we have considered each of the major traditions of research and reviewed the history of each variable in each of our societies, I have wondered, at times, how American concerns looked to each of our participants from other countries. The reason for this conjecture on my part, of course, is because so many of the variables had their genesis in American communication research and then were taken up by researchers in other countries, many of whom were trained in the United States.

> ITO: There are numerous examples from our perspective, and I can think of a number of them. For one, Japanese researchers believed that the uses and gratifications studies focused on people's interactions with mass media only because the American researcher's major concern was "what people do with media." It is important to emphasize, therefore, that our joint study dealt not only with mass media but also with such nonmedia channels as institutions, interpersonal communication, and even personal observation. The Japanese view is that these behaviors represent an essential part of the total information environment of the society. This permits us to ask how people interact with their information environment. We are so interested in this that we have developed a Japanese term to describe those situations— *joho kodo*, or "information behavior." Therefore, I am glad that light has been shed by our study on the viewpoint of the information behavior studies.

EDELSTEIN: I can agree with this but point out, as well, that we have been surprised to discover the many points of convergence. As an example, we seem to have a common basis for asking about the uses of information in your *joho kodo* approach. And when we have seen new developments in communication technologies we have seen corresponding change in what you describe as information environments—for example, the common approach to the concept of information societies.

ITO: I am impressed that these basic ideas were developed independently of Japanese information behavior studies and yet could be seen to have converged with our approach. Perhaps the most important similarity between the two approaches is a holistic view of how the individual interacts with those environments. In the larger sense, however, we would emphasize the importance of observing the flow of information through nonmass media channels as a way of assessing the effects of mass media. We all benefitted, of course, from the series of seminars that we held jointly with the School of Communications at the University of Washington and in Tokyo, in which Professor Kepplinger also participated. This contributed greatly to our ability to achieve a truly cooperative and collaborative effort.

EDELSTEIN: Professor Ito will recognize that this research is compatible with other Japanese interests. I am thinking particularly of those Japanese studies that centered on the information society that sought to standardize measures of information to permit the direct comparison of film, television, printed materials, and even voice. That was an innovative piece of work directed at achieving comparisons where none previously had been accomplished. To achieve an approximation of equivalence between different forms of information output was certainly mindful of the conceptual challenges that faced us as comparativists. We may think of our cognitive variables—which have information and information-processing elements in them—in similar terms. As a concept, the problematic situation accomplishes for us the same purposes as your unit of information accomplished for you, although applied to different problems. We created equivalent cognitive units of comparison without regard to topics, problems, or issues, just as your units of information cut across film, video, print, and voice.

KEPPLINGER: These conceptual tasks were challenging, so it is all the more important that we find applications for them. We have been able to apply the concepts across a number of important concerns. But we should use our concepts not only to gain perspective on concerns at one particular time but over time. In larger scope we need to place our concerns in historical perspective. We should do content analysis of media treatment of topics or issues and their meaning as problematic situations over time, say periods of five to 20 years. We should ask if media changed in the emphasis they placed on particular kinds of problematic situations over time, and why they did so. Would different kinds of events account for change, if it occurred, or might the media have learned to treat the same kinds of events differently? Was there societal change or media change?

We have too little longitudinal analysis of how media transform events into meaning terms. Coupled with this kind of analysis, of course, we should conduct large-scale surveys over the same periods of time. We might determine in this way if readers are getting closer to their media or drifting apart, and we might point to the kinds of events that contributed to any changes in convergence.

EDELSTEIN: You're suggesting a tight little paradigm there with four possible conditions occurring over time. In one case the events might be similar and media treatment of them might also be much the same; in the related and perhaps more interesting situation the events might be similar but the media treatment might be different. If we flip the coin and ask if the events are different, we might ask the same kinds of questions about treatment by the media. If events are different is media treatment the same, or is it different also? We might look to the changing structures of societies or changing practices of media for our answers to these questions. And as you have suggested, these patterns might vary by culture and by situations, for example, by patterns of social and economic development.

KEPPLINGER: At the risk of repeating myself, I want to emphasize how important it is to understand how media define topics in the news as problematic situations. We know they do not do this consciously but intuitively. We need to ask them, as well as ourselves, why they choose to emphasize one problematic situation over another. We also need to relate the media definitions to public definitions of the situation. As we point out in our discussion of agenda setting, it should not be viewed as the agenda setting of topics in the news but agenda setting of the problematics that are implicit in those topics. Topics in themselves are meaningless; they are merely categorical. I believe that when the media engage in the construction of topics as problematic situations they may have a great impact on the structure of public consciousness of the meaning of an event. Only longitudinal analysis, as I mentioned earlier, may address this question.

EDELSTEIN: What you are suggesting bears similarities to some of the earlier work of Wilbur Schramm (1959) in comparing media treatment of events such as the conflict over the control of the Suez Canal and the uprising in Hungary against the Communist government. He found differences in East and West in the amount of attention given to each of these critical events by First, Second, and Third World countries—but this was largely quantitative. I wonder how he might have reacted to our idea of viewing coverage in terms of the problematics that they reflected? He might have observed that the Soviet press saw Hungary as not merely an instance of social conflict but also as a potential loss of value, whereas the Western press portrayed conflict as a step toward a solution and saw Soviet repression as blocking those efforts by the "freedom fighters" at problem solving. As telling as it was, the sheer amount of space devoted to Suez and Hungary by East and West did not describe the meaning of the news that was conveyed by the construction of events as problematic situations.

KEPPLINGER: Although it might have been difficult to apply a problematics model to Suez and Hungary, as they happened, this does suggest that we inquire into the potential that exists for viewing the construction of problematic situations as elements in a step or stage model, for there appear to me to be elements of process implicit in the concept. Let us say that a person feels she or he has been deprived of something and suffers a sense of a loss of value; this might produce the motivation to express a need. This happens rather often as a commonsense observation. Other steps might then be possible. Perhaps the person takes a step toward a solution. In the process he or she experiences blocking by another person or by a bureaucracy. This might produce a sense of conflict as well, and produce confusion and uncertainty. The person then demands a solution after having first proposed one and been blocked in its application. All sorts of patterns could be developed.

We already have indications that individuals in societies can be more oriented to a state of loss or need. They may be overly pessimistic or optimistic in those regards. This triggers a lot of research potential. Is that society capable of taking steps toward solutions or does it become mired in bureaucratic blocking or uncertainties?

EDELSTEIN: We do have evidence of cultural tendencies as well as variations in our data. For example, we may think back to our discussion of the relationship of headlines to story content. The question we posed was whether or not headlines picked up the construction of the problematic situation that had been developed in the story. Most of the time this was the case, and we can attribute that to the constancy that is seen in many other ways in the editing of a newspaper. However, there were culturally defined differences. In terms of constancy, we characterized the American tendency as one of minimal variation between headlines and stories; both were highly objectified, presumably. The German pattern, in contrast, was great variation. We concluded that this was due largely to editors trying to force the public into making a voting choice. Thus while headlines demanded a clearer vision of the election, the reporter was observing the uncertainty that existed in readers' minds. The Japanese, like the Americans, portrayed a striking cultural bias. Whereas the American headlines and stories objectified events, the Japanese headlines sublimated story emphases on conflict and indeterminacy. And Hong Kong headlines reflected the tensions that existed between editors and reporters in the tense political atmosphere of that crown colony as it anticipated a shift of sovereign powers to China in 1997.

KEPPLINGER: These content analyses of the media are quite necessary, and I am glad that we undertook survey research to determine the fit of perceptions of problematic situations with respect to media and audiences. I am going to suggest as well that we should use surveys of problematic situations that are constructed by the public even if we don't always do media analysis. We need surveys at regular intervals to test the extent to which the distribution of problematic situations among the public changes over time.

It is important for us to know if the distribution of problematics is stable or shifting and how these perceptions are shaped by events and by cultures. For example, we may point in our study to the fact that both the Japanese and the Chinese students made more references to losses of value than did the American or German students. May we assume that these differences are attributable to their cultures or to the events that occurred within our research period? Is it possible that some cultures see problems more in terms of losses or deprivation than in terms of needs? If so, what accounts for this tendency? Was the fact of fewer references to problem solving on the part of German students part of a lasting German youth culture, or was this degree of pessimism due to a particular set of conditions? It is only if we ask these questions over time and across a number of kinds of situations that we will learn if we are dealing with cultures, that is, with national character, or with events.

EDELSTEIN: Speaking of the interactions of institutions and people reminds one very pointedly of the work of Ball-Rokeach and DeFleur (1976) and Ball-Rokeach (1985) and Gerbner and Gross (1976) to name a few who have reminded us of the success of media in rewarding their readers. I regret that we could not throw our net out wide enough to incorporate more fully their views as to the interdependency of media effects, as Professor Ito reminds us that we have taken complementary if not similar intellectual positions. Implicit in our discussions of media–audience mutuality of definition of the dynamics of news, the reciprocal effects of media and audiences on the agenda-setting process, as examples, is a Skinnerian postulate of reinforcement.

KEPPLINGER: Well, as I have said, I think as a social scientist one has the obligation to share one's thinking as well as one's data. Certainly, the thinking is there and it supports an active media hypothesis. It would be exciting to test those compatibilities of view more formally at some time. I am reminded of what Elizabeth Noelle-Neumann said of her theories of the climate of opinion and the spiral of silence: She was publishing them to be tested, not to be reified. I hope our courage also is rewarded by people testing our ideas, and those include the idea that the media actively advance problematic situations that they know will bring reader responses.

ITO: As Professor Edelstein knows, I have given thought to the research traditions that we represent. When Professor Edelstein first proposed his concept and methodology relating to the uses of communication, he contributed to that tradition. Our approach, along one dimension, falls into what I call an "events" perspective, where we capture people coping with problems of various kinds and communicating as a consequence of their interests.

But the media have an influence, too, and this is what you and Professor Kepplinger have discussed in relation to the work of sociologists such as Ball-Rokeach, DeFleur, Gerbner, and others who have defined active media. That is, if a person always uses certain media—as in our case, newspapers more than television—it is probable that s/he is influenced in a certain direction by the media contents. If many people choose a particular medium to know about a certain kind of problem, that medium has a strong influence upon the society as far as that problem is concerned. The various media influences, therefore, might depend upon the kinds of problematic situations that they define. I think the concept of media construction of a problematic situation, and audience responses to it, allows us to consider a question that previously has not been raised and could not previously have been answered.

We also should look behind some of this evidence for implicit effects. Again, a lot may depend on the problem. For example, although the Japanese and Chinese students both spoke of loss of value to the individual, the actual deprivations that they perceived could be attributed to social forces, such as the strain placed on the family and other traditional forms of social life by trends in economic development and vocational pluralism. Families have less time for each other, which leads to fragmentation of a social institution. So individual losses in the Asian context seem more readily transformed into family consciousness than in the Western cultures we examined. In future research we will want to explore these transformations as cultural forms. We tend to talk about structure and culture as phenomena that have a life of their own, yet we know that they are thoroughly intertwined. Yet as is so often true in life as well as in research, we need a way of talking about things. The reader should get out of our discussions that when the comparativist speaks of structures she or he usually is describing social institutions that express the functioning of the society as a cultural as well as an organizational entity. All societies create institutional structures such as government, business, education, social and health services, legal institutions, and so forth, for all societies have those functions to perform. But we must look at the cultural identities of institutions as well.

EDELSTEIN: I think comparativists have defined institutions as structures to create a kind of anthropomorphic being. Perhaps it is easier to compare societies at that very abstract level than to get down to cases. Certainly it helps to explain the number of comparative studies of media institutions, such as the press and broadcasting, which are viewed in their relationships to other institutions, such as government, education, and various bureaucracies.

Sociologists and critical researchers have tried to establish linkages among institutions, and we have referred briefly to the relationship of these perspectives to our own approach. Yet we did not make the "structural/cultural/communication" case as well as we might have. Professor Ito sees this more clearly with respect to the Japanese society. Perhaps it is because Japanese culture has specified a more synchronous relationship between institutions. The chain of influence and action is more clearly understood and communication can proceed more easily within those boundaries.

ITO: We have, of course, referred to this subject in other ways, but this is a good place to treat the matter in more detail. In Japan the concept of social structure is deeply ingrained in everyone. It is not something that has developed as a consequence of social change. Rather, with external change we have maintained internal stability. Our history has guided the ways in which social behavior and communication are to function. The linkage to communication is quite clear and equally profound. It centers on what sociologists recently have described as a "vertical" society, where social mobility occurs within an organization and cannot be achieved "horizontally" by jumping from one organization to another.

In feudal Japan, as in feudal Europe, social mobility was very limited both vertically and horizontally. But as a result of modernization and democratization in Japan, vertical mobility has become more possible than in some European societies. An able person may climb to the top of the organization or a group of organizations, whatever his or her birth might be. However, it is difficult to shift from one organization to another. In brief, there are many hierarchies within which mobility is high but between which mobility is low.

One consequence is that the Japanese system tends to suppress the development of social class in the classical sense because people's concerns are vertical and not horizontal. Executives are more loyal to their employees than to their stockholders or to executives of other organizations. In turn, Japanese workers are usually more loyal to their companies than to their peers in other organizations. Solidarity of workers across such automobile manufacturing groups as Toyota, Nissan, Mitsui, or Mitsubishi is almost nonexistent. Encouraging this development is the fact that salary levels are more equal within than across. More than 90 percent of Japanese believe they belong to the middle class. This is half again what is reported in most European countries.

This system keeps the society highly competitive. Losing to the competition is more fatal in Japan than in other societies because the members of one company cannot readily take their talents to the survivor in the competition. Even if they are hired, they will be forced virtually to start all over again, to make their way vertically in the new organization.

These elements of social structure affect communication very powerfully. In societies where horizontal mobility is high, as in the United States, people may be outspoken and straightforward, as our discussion in Chapter 9 of intercultural communication between American and Japanese students revealed. So if one does not like the boss or one's colleagues, one may quit and move to another organization, often at an increase in pay and status. In Japan movement of this kind is not possible; hence the people make efforts to avoid overt confrontation, emotional arguments, and needless debate.

This communication culture is transferred from parents to children, as we have seen. Japanese students do not talk as much about social issues with their peers because of the idea of the issue itself. An issue, as it is defined, invites confrontation. This is something that the Japanese student, as do Japanese adults, seek to avoid.

EDELSTEIN: What you are saying is increasingly seen as an unique aspect of Japanese culture, yet as you also point out, it might better be looked at as a point on a scale. Japanese do not always avoid, and Western cultures do not always confront. I am reminded of studies in both Norway and the United States of Scandinavian and American students who had been taught "consensual" skills by their parents along with an independence of thought. As a comparativist, I am of the mind that in groups that are as similar as our college students we might expect to see more universalities than differences in behavior where situations demanded it.

It is evident in our data that Japanese parents have transferred these values to their children. Our students did not discuss social issues extensively with their peers. While this does not mean that they did not form opinions or that they did not use many sources of information—including people, they tended not to discuss issues with those who were in their work setting as American and German students might do. It is interesting that the Chinese students behaved similarly to the Japanese more than did Americans or Germans.

KEPPLINGER: That is true not only of Japanese culture, as you have said, but of other Asian countries as well. We are also seeing evidence of this avoidance as expressions of political culture, and our construction of the problematic situation might lead us to ask about the perspectives of developing countries. Is it possible that some developing countries frame situations in such ways as to make them less able to take steps toward solutions simply because they refuse to construct those situations in terms of manageable problems or issues? In the same way, while understating the problems, they might tend to exaggerate steps toward solutions. We could determine if it were a cultural tendency if different developing countries, faced with similar events or conditions, problematized equivalent situations in different ways.

EDELSTEIN: We tried our approach in a doctoral dissertation by doing a content analysis of print media in a number of African countries. We did not have polling data, of course, to use as a basis of comparison, but we did construct models of social, economic, and political development that could be arrayed against one another. We found that some countries were more likely to claim steps toward solutions when the economic resources of those countries suggested that solutions were beyond their reach at that time. Thus steps toward solutions really were expressions of needs for solutions. We found it difficult to conclude, however, that this discrepancy was dysfunctional for the society. It might be an expression of culture. Certainly, the claims and the resources were at odds, and in objective terms that could be dysfunctional. We needed to know if African leaders and publics actually perceived reality in these ways or were simply playing out their roles on the cultural stage.

KEPPLINGER: A while ago we were talking about process. I think that our formulation of consequences, causes, and effects of problems and the co-orientation of students to those aspects suggest elements of process. First, of course, no matter how we construct public opinion questions, we are always asking about aspects of problems rather than problems in their entirety. No pollster can ask that many questions. So the offering to pollsters of this insight—that people form opinions about the consequences, causes, and solutions to problems, and talk about them—should meet with a warm reception.

However, I think the concept should be applied also to the journalist and to the media, for they are partners with pollsters in the public opinion process. We need to ask if, over time, media have become increasingly oriented to describing the causes of problems even when they are not competent to ascertain them. Our study of the oil crisis, as a case in point, pointed out how quickly the media called attention to the causes of the problems, and in neither case (the shortage crisis and the price crisis) were they correct in their analysis, nor did they bring the most competent experts to consider the questions.

A more recent case in Switzerland involved a mountain slide that killed many people and caused a great deal of damage. The media immediately cited the concerns that had been expressed by environmentalists to the effect that the continued logging of tress would cause a slide. However, another, earlier study had called attention to a geological fault that would bring about a slide. This report discounted any effects of tourism or logging but described the geological forces that caused the slide. Whether the media were right or wrong is of no particular moment. The question that must be asked is whether or not the nature of the media has changed over time so that there is more and more media concern about causes of events and problems. What are the societal and media forces that have coalesced to bring that change about? Is this as true of one country or culture as another? Would a longitudinal study identify other press tendencies—such as decreased attention paid to demands for solutions to problems in relation to proposals for solutions or actual steps toward solutions?

EDELSTEIN: We did bring some data to bear on those questions. First, we found that students were more likely to focus on the consequences of problems rather than on solutions or causes. On the face of it, that makes sense. And they perceived that their peers, and even public opinion, were at the same stage in their consideration of the problem. Culture, however, didn't seem to have much to do with it. So we might conclude that there is a universal tendency to look at how a problem has affected you and move from there to a consideration of what causes the problem and whether or not it is amenable to solution, and if so, how? But we must remember that not everyone goes beyond the effects of a problem to its causes and/or solutions. More comparative analysis on this question might be productive.

KEPPLINGER: As we seem to be doing now, comparative studies always seem to require a great deal of review and even second guessing. One puts in a lot of thought at the input stage, so later you have a good deal to think about, if your assumptions worked out, and so on. Also many decisions have to be made on the spot in a particular country, perhaps, when full opportunity for discussion among all the research teams is not feasible. We are fortunate to be able to express a degree of satisfaction with the concepts we adopted. The important aspect of that is the potential of our variables for other studies. The cognitive variables we have adopted make the researcher independent of the variety of topics and issues in a number of countries that ordinarily would plague the comparativist. Pollution doesn't mean the same in Germany as it does in the United States, and it certainly doesn't mean the same as it does in Japan. The problematic situation makes it possible for us to make direct comparisons; we don't have to compare topics or issues that are peculiar to one country. The comparative field needs variables of this kind that may easily be compared yet are sensitive to cultures.

ITO: Well, certainly transfers occur. Perhaps the term *information behavior*, which is a Japanese concept, will come to be adopted in the West just as was the information society concept. Similarly, although the problematics approach that is incorporated in this book was developed independently of Japanese research, I was happy to reveal at our conference at Keio University in 1983 that Japanese communication researchers had considered similar concepts.

We have also taken on overall perspective to the perceived effects of mass media and have tried to approach them in more manageable terms. We might look at mass media effects in just two ways: One set of theories assumes the homogeniety of content (and effects) of mass media, and the other theories assume heterogeniety. To illustrate, most theories that advance the concept of powerful media assume the homogeniety of media contents as well. These theories might be generally stated as Marxism and critical theory, events research, the spiral of silence, and agenda setting.

Many of these theorists, however, recognize that even if media content on a societal level may be heterogeneous or contradictory, the content to which each individual is exposed tends to become homogeneous because of many influences. These include accidental reasons such as mere accessibility or lack of time and effort to compare different contents. Other theories emphasize selective exposure and perception on the part of the receiver. According to these theories, people tend to be exposed to the media content that is congruent with their existing attitudes and avoid the media content that is incongruent with their attitudes. The uses and gratifications model emphasizes individual needs for media use. If an individual always uses the same media for the same purposes, even if the contents are not homogeneous in a strict sense, it is likely that he or she is affected at least by the characteristics of the content or latent values behind the content. The influence of violent TV programs or soap operas on the individuals who always watch them to satisfy certain needs is an example.

I see our study as assuming the heterogeneity of media content and, consequently, differences in effects, for theories of this kind must explain why individuals are influenced by mass media despite the fact that they are exposed to heterogeneous, which means often-contradictory, media content.

KEPPLINGER: Speaking to some of those points, the German empirical view, certainly, is essentially heterogeneous in its assumptions. But we accommodate the heterogeneous view of often-contradictory content by observing that any *responses* to media content depend on the presence of issues. No mass communication effects really can be observed directly unless there are issues to address. These issues produce not only contradictory but directly conflicting content.

German research shows that it is pretty irrelevant for the media to describe ongoing and stable patterns. These kinds of content make no demands on the individual or society. And as is articulated by the theory of news we have proposed, journalists seek to make demands on readers by posing problems—or as we have stated them—problematic situations. Our research is oriented toward problems and the ways in which media and people think about those problems. This focus deals with the essential aspects of mass communications and describes real mass communication effects. And it goes to the heart of Youichi Ito's (1987) formulation of the dichotomy homogeneous and heterogeneous approaches to effects.

EDELSTEIN: It would seem that the crux of the dichotomy between Professor Ito's homogeneous and heterogeneous approaches is that the critical theorists, particularly, would argue that similarities in behaviors are to be observed more often than differences and that the positivist empiricist merely focuses on the differences. Even those differences, the critical theorist will argue, are not important differences. They merely represent degrees of freedom, limited at that, and in most cases unimportant. Perhaps the comparativist takes a middle ground by taking into consideration the social and media structures that work toward homogeneity as well as attributing importance to differences that are produced by elements of culture.

ITO: A number of aspects of our study illustrate its predominantly heterogeneous orientation. The student respondents were asked which medium was most useful in knowing about the most important social problem. Furthermore, they were asked how useful that medium was. It becomes clear that if an individual is always exposed to a certain medium to know about a certain kind of problem—because it is most useful—it is probable that he or she is influenced in a certain direction by those media contents. As the uses approach suggests, there is a need, and the motivation to use the media is created by the awareness that the medium that is selected will satisfy the need.

Now let's take a case where a great many people choose the same medium to know about a certain kind of problem—one that treats certain problematic aspects of the situation, one may conclude that the medium that has been chosen exerts a strong influence with respect to that problem. So we should think of mass media effects as being more or less powerful in terms of certain kinds of problems and, of course, the problematics that are implied. Unfortunately, the introduction of the problem, and the problematic situation, has been absent from other heterogeneous approaches to media effects. If introduced, the problematic situation might help to clarify the thrust of other theories.

EDELSTEIN: Our data point to tendencies by newspapers to construct problematics in certain ways. Those were not always congruent with the ways that the students constructed them. But when that was the case we may assume that the media had a lot of influence and there was reciprocity with the audience as well.

ITO: We have abundant evidence of that in Japan. In our information behavior studies it was found that the information that people seek and the information they transmit outward tend to belong to the same category. During our anti-sales tax movement the people expressed an opinion and the media respondend. They then appeared to propose agendas that produced effects, not only in what to think about but also what to think. This had a powerful influence on the next national election. At the outset, the government had called their tax increase law *fukakachi-zei*, a "value-added tax." Recently, they changed the name to *uriage-zei* or "sales tax." We might borrow a term from Noelle-Neumann (1974) and call this a spiral of public opinion that developed through interaction between mass media and expressions of opinion. Examples of congruence of this kind need to be documented as they occur so that we can better understand the processes of public opinion formation.

It is important to note that our study found a great degree of congruence between perceptions of the focus of public opinion and students' own opinions, and there was congruence as well between the opinions of students and those persons with whom they talked. This finding means that people are not only passive receivers of information about their environment but also creators of it. The understanding of the two sides of people's information behavior, that is, reception and transmission of information, contributes to the understanding of the dynamics of public opinion.

EDELSTEIN: I hope each of you will comment on the data we observed for interpersonal communication and personal observation. The American and German students were particularly active with respect to interpersonal communication as most important sources of information, whereas the Japanese students referred to it much less. Yet Japanese students communicate, as they reported also, although they didn't set high value on the information content of it. The intriguing thing to me is that there is so little research about interpersonal communication both in Japan and in Germany. Only the Nishidas (whom we have mentioned) have established their careers as scholars in interpersonal communication, and most of that was done in collaboration with American colleagues.

KEPPLINGER: I'll answer first because my answer may be briefer. It's simply because our research institutes grew out of journalistic interests and activities. We don't think the study of interpersonal communication, and particularly intercultural communication, is unimportant, it's just that we have not devoted resources to those studies. We have studied interpersonal communication in relation to media behavior, as we reported in the study of the extent to which students actually referred to the media in their discussions of politics and in a comparative study of the diffusion of information about the assassination of Olof Palme, the Swedish prime minister. With us, it is a matter of neglect, and I don't know what can be done about it.

ITO: With us it's more a matter of culture. It is a well-known fact that Japanese people tend to avoid arguments or debates with other people. Osamu Nakano (1982) admits that in Japan the person who speaks his opinion first tends to dominate the situation because other people do not dare to challenge it, at least in that person's face. Therefore, Nakano argues that true "communication" in the Western sense does not exist in Japan. What exists in Japan is only a "chain of monologues." Because Japanese students do not talk about social issues with their peers does not mean that they do not form opinions. They are eager consumers of media and listen to other people. They just do not dare to discuss social issues with other people to the extent that German and American students do. It was interesting that Chinese students were more similar to Japanese in our data than to Americans and Germans. The Japanese communication culture may be an oriental or East Asian communication culture. A Japanese writer, Hotta (1957), once wrote that when one is "east of Burma" modest silence is a virtue, whereas "west of Burma" eloquence is a virtue.

EDELSTEIN: I hope we may look for more studies of interpersonal communication both in Japan and in Germany as well as in China, and I hope also that scholars such as the Nishidas will be able to extend their comparisons of Japanese students and American students to Japanese and Chinese and Japanese and Germans. In fact, studies of intercultural communication should be planned by scholars on more of a global basis than a merely accidental one if we are to gain a better understanding of the role of communication in and among all cultures.

ITO: Cultural differences are important, and we have demonstrated those differences at many points. But we should not misinterpret or overinterpret those differences. Even though there were dramatic differences with respect to the Japanese students in some categories of interpersonal communication, none of the actual behaviors could be said to be alien to the Japanese students. In our own data on the extent of use of mass communication and in the comparisons of Japanese and American students on styles of interpersonal communication it was always a case of more or less and never a case of absence or presence. So the data suggest a continuum of communication behavior along each dimension rather than an absolute scale. That is important to keep in mind, because it encourages us to ask about the situations in which more or less interpersonal communication, or a particular style of interpersonal communication, occurs.

We also must be cautious about our bases for evaluating the quality of communication; that is, we should be cautions about any tendency to characterize one kind of communication as good and another as bad. Fortunately, our cognitive approach has led us away from making value judgments of these kinds. But some value judgments might be read by others into our findings if we are not clear about it.

I can think of a number of examples. For instance, the comparisons of interpersonal communication styles of American and Japanese students that we cited pointed to the fact that Japanese students demonstrated more ambiguity, were less open and expressive, and so forth in academic studies of interpersonal communication. If the reader is not careful, it is possible to gain the impression that, qualitatively speaking, being more expressive is better than being less expressive. German students, as another illustration, incorporated more media perspectives into conversations about social problems. Is that better or worse than incorporating fewer media perspectives? I am happy that our comparative perspective suggests that particular behaviors are neither bad nor good; they are merely culturally normative. So we can see that the comparative approach transcends differences found in intercultural studies and teaches us to be cautious about the inferences that we draw from those observations. While it is understandable that normativeness may be invoked within cultures, it becomes dominance if it is introduced across cultures.

EDESTEIN: You are warning scholars about invoking normativeness in one culture upon another culture. It is difficult, of course, when intercultural communication occurs not to make culture-based observations. Certainly, we must strive consciously to achieve the necessary sensitivity. Only then will we be able to construct communication situations that intersect two or more cultures.

I'd like also to address your other point—the importance of the situational context. Clearly, there are two sides to that coin. One of them is the need to look at things situationally so that we do not leap to structurally or culturally based generalizations. We do, of course, expect to observe similarities in communication where social roles or statuses are similar. In fact, these social or "structural" forces sometimes assert themselves in the face of cultural influences or even the uniqueness of some situations. Yet the other side of this coin is that cultures may assert themselves more strongly than either social roles or situations. Thus it was not surprising that our students—similar as they were in role and status, and finding themselves in identical situations—nonetheless, at times, demonstrated interpersonal communication styles that were attributable to culture.

ITO: Yes. In fact, no one will disagree that Japanese cultural values inhibited those students in the situations into which they were placed. I find the comparative data to be interesting and valid, in the research context. It was good that Japanese scholars collaborated in that research. But I believe that if our Japanese colleagues had done the same research in Japan rather than in the United States, with the same collaborators, they would have discussed the findings in terms that more emphasized the Japanese experience. There is no real danger in experienced scholars misinterpreting the findings of studies of that kind, of course. But there is a broader danger in the tendency of publics to go beyond specific situations and the contexts in which certain findings emerge. As we all know, Japanese and other Asian cultures tend to be described in strokes that are too broad and that do not take culture and situations sufficiently into account.

EDELSTEIN: You have been very kind, Professor Ito, in telling me on occasion that I became "more Japanese" during my teaching at Keio University. I was quite pleased to hear that. But I know that we tend to impose Western criteria in some social situations. As an example, our journalists are very concerned about the idea of objectivity, thinking that it is a cultural concern rather than a product of the demands of daily journalism which your journalists, of course, also have learned to accept as products of the same environment.

ITO: Yes. These institutional demands, to which we respond similarly, should not, however, be transferred to the private realm. In that context we often hear that Japanese are less rational and more emotional than Westerners. But one should keep in mind that Japanese see similar phenomena from different viewpoints. While Westerners emphasize ideas of expressiveness, logicality, rationality, objectivity, and "persuasive communication," these tendencies are, indeed, suppressed in Japan under some circumstances. Yet Japanese can be expressive, logical, rational, objective, and even persuasive. The Japanese word *ri*, borrowed from the Chinese, means logical and rational. Without that rationality a social order cannot be maintained. Japanese must be logical, objective, realistic, and orderly when we make laws, write a book or academic article, and define rules. But while this style of communication is present in *public behavior*, we do not take these approaches in *interpersonal communication*. Behavior in the situation is controlled by cultural forms and values. Change the situation; you change the behavior.

EDELSTEIN: In the conferences held jointly by Keio University and the University of Washington—which we all remember fondly—I can recall a very touching paper by Professor Yoshiro Akutsu of International Christian University in which he distinguished between "information flow" and "sentiment flow." Your emphasis upon emotional qualities of communication brings back to mind the concept of "sentiment flow."

ITO: Well, without using that precise phrase, perhaps I can say simply that in interpersonal communication Japanese are basically emotional—as all human beings tend to be. While some cultures may believe that they are being logical, rational, and so on—and are engaged in "information flow"— they are employing rhetoric that justifies and rationalizes their emotional or evaluative orientations. If we Japanese insisted upon employing only an information-flow style we would not be able to reach consensus. In our interpersonal context form is essential. So if communication experiments convey to Japanese that they are expected to perform in the interpersonal mode then they will be unable to utilize an information-flow strategy; they will be forced by cultural norms to be ambiguous or roundabout in what they perceive as a situation approaching the intimacy of a group.

This is just my opinion, but I will take this a step further. Japanese do not necessarily trust persons who say they are rational and objective in the intimacy of interpersonal or group discussions. This becomes most obvious in conditions of interpersonal or group conflict. Westerners seem more to believe that, if they communicate rationally, logically and persuasively, conflict can be minimized and something approaching friendship will be established. To Japanese this seems to be rationalizing distrust. They believe resolution of the conflict is not likely to be achieved under these circumstances. If, in fact, some agreement were reached, it would be superficial and without understanding. Japanese therefore think that it is more practical to avoid discussions between individuals in conflict. Before "rational" discussions begin, emotional problems should be addressed.

EDELSTEIN: If you were to undertake some comparative analysis, and you were to use the Troldahl studies we described in Chapter 8, where would you start? Would you say that Americans and Japanese are too different to be compared or are you suggesting that we need to think through the bases for comparisons?

ITO: No. There are any number of bases for comparison. One comparison is suggested by our discussion of Western commitments to conflict-resolution by interpersonal communication and Japanese perspectives on the practicality of such efforts. We might say that Westerners are more optimistic than the Japanese about the power of interpersonal communication. As I have mentioned, the Japanese assume that even if people talk to each other they do not necessarily understand one another, so to keep harmony and good relations it is important to know what other people like and dislike. Given that knowledge, it is possible to avoid certain subjects.

So we might test the proposition that Japanese are more likely to use interpersonal communication to know more about the other while Americans communicate more to learn about the problem. It's possible that we might call the American approach "optimistic," while the Japanese approach would be more "pessimistic."

KEPPLINGER: The conceptualization of this research and the analysis that has flowed out of it really deserve more discussion, but I am afraid our discussion is concluding. Let me say, however, that the cognitive approach, and within that the problematic situation, has been extraordinarily productive. We have been able to construct a theory of "news as discrepancy," introduce the problematic situation as the "motivational state" in uses and gratifications research, and clarify the construct of "thinking" and "thinking about" to advance the cognitive dimensions of agenda-setting research. In the area of public opinion we structured opinions around cognitions of the *causes, consequences,* and *solutions* to problems. The productivity of the problematic situation is really quite extraordinary as a concept.

ITO: The concept of structure, as Professor McCombs pointed out, also was quite helpful to us in analysis. We used the concept of structure in a number of ways, of course. It described, first, the place of our students in the social structure. That had analytical value, for we could hypothesize that, given this equivalence in status, power, position, and so on, students would be likely to communicate similarly in similar situations. At the same time, we looked for differences in culture to explain variations in these behaviors. I think the readers would agree with us that we stated a reasonable set of expectations based upon "structural" considerations and that our expectations were confirmed very largely.

But in addition to social structures, such as our student groupings, we also used the term to describe social institutions such as the government, the bureaucracies, the family, the business order, and the media. I think the reader recognized that all these social institutions have a structural character. Their similarities, as well, contributed to our expectations that student communications in relation to those institutions would be similar unless, of course, cultural or situational factors intruded.

EDELSTEIN: I think you have also noted that students in each culture held different perceptions as to the viability or integrity of those institutions, including the press. Where students perceived any breakdown in their functioning, we saw different communication uses of the media. In Germany, particularly, we saw different communication loyalties—to the mass media rather than to qualitative media. German students, as political activists, found the mass media were most sympathetic to their actions, and they perceived that the mass media also had taken on a socially critical and responsible role.

ITO: This discussion is relevant to the Japanese situation as well. Somehow, Westerners perceive our institutions as homogenous, but the fact is that our system encourages a great deal of dissent and even conflict, as observable in our media. So it is important to keep in mind the variable nature of political, social, and media institutions and to be alert to patterns of social communication that occur as a consequence of different and often temporary institutional cooperation.

KEPPLINGER: We have come up with a stimulating array of concepts growing out of the problematic situation. But we haven't talked nearly enough about the importance of testing our theories on a broader basis among college youth—perhaps an Asianwide study. It would be wrong to stop now. How are Soviet and Chinese youth communicating in their new environments of *glasnost* and *perestroika* in the USSR and in the climate of modernization in China [in the newer economic zones in the coastal areas]? It is clear that college youth, as well as the more highly educated classes, are not sharing equally in the new economic order as compared to peasants and entrepeneurs. Coupled with a loss of ideology, this carries the threat of student disorder.

EDELSTEIN: As Professor Ito is even more aware, we need look to Korea, as well, where students have exerted such a powerful influence upon their government and where economic development and the Olympic Games have renewed national confidence. How are Korean youth viewing the steps that are being taken toward democratic communication?

There are few Asian countries where college youth are not central to their emergence as societies. In India economic development promises to create real opportunities for millions of college graduates. What values are being preserved and what modifications of outlook and communication are being created?

As I write this I am talking with a professor from the University of the Philippines. He points out that college youth and the educated classes formed the core of the 1986 people-power revolt that put Corazon Aquino in power. Many of the millions of demonstrators came out of the universities and from the educated elites, including among them many religious and business leaders. Here was evidence that the values of college youth were echoed in the larger society.

ITO: Japan has addressed the equilibrium between values of college youth and economic and social development as a whole. We have provided opportunities for college students, and this has produced a stable although still inventive society. Our culture reinforces values that promote orderly development among all sectors of the society.

We also see development in other Southeast Asian countries, although each culture determines its own path and its own equilibrium. If we are to generalize about the communication and values of college youth we need to plan a research strategy and program. We have concepts and research instruments, and we have a global outlook. I agree with Professor Kepplinger that our concepts and purposes have carried us to a new starting point. We need to decide: "What next?"

EDELSTEIN: Professor Ito will remember that we thought first about student behavior but wished to incorporate other publics, as well. Perhaps that is a next step—to compare students not only with one another but with other publics, as well. That is the only way in which we can truly demonstrate on a global basis the place of students in societies. So we should take new steps to advance our goals as comparativists—to achieve understandings of the common bases of communication among a diversity of nations and cultures. That would be our contribution to a more understandable global society.

EDELSTEIN: Thank you for these very personal perspectives. We'll now speak again with one voice as we look ahead.

LOOKING AHEAD

Our individual comments in many respects did look ahead but we might summarize a group view. We can say that our experience helped us to look ahead in a number of directions.

We became persuaded that substantially more attention must be paid to the values and communication of subcultures among world societies. Youth is an important subculture, but it represents only one identifiable social grouping. We may think ahead to a variety of other subcultures that should be defined and their behaviors explored and compared.

Although there were no substantial differences in outlook or behavior between men and women in our sample of university students, this equivalence should not be interpreted to extend to general populations. A more comprehensive comparison should be carried out that will allow us to theorize about the communicating roles of women as cultures become increasingly subject to pluralistic and other forces.

These comparisons should be projected in both time and space. By comparing the communication roles of women in a number of representative cultures, more reliable generalizations about the potential for communication development should be derived. A study of the emergence of women's communication roles should provide a highly reliable and generalizable index of social development.

Similar comparisons should be projected for the elderly, for ethnic and racial minorities, for other social classes, and for those who are governed by geography or climate. Comparative analysis will help us to validate a communications theory that brings us closer to general laws of behavior. We cannot gain a world view if we continue to base our inquiries on research in bounded cultures, each of which imposes its own constraints on behavior.

In the same sense, we must project on a worldwide basis the relevance of major concepts that address the functions and uses of mass communication. Which of our concepts are culture bound, and which are culture free? The comparative approach, by utilizing an analytical model of structure/culture/situation, enables us to test the multicultural efficacy of any number of concepts.

We need also to advance our methodological thinking to allow us to keep pace with theoretical perspectives. We cannot advance our thinking without advancing our methodological approaches. We will continue our efforts to construct validated scales that permit other social scientists to extend the relevance and the efficacy of cognitive concepts. Each must be observed systematically in a number of environments under a variety of conditions.

Because of the nature of our data and the requirement that we limit our efforts across time and space, we have not been able to extend our cognitive theories to other mainstream mass communications research. We look forward to any challenges of that kind that present themselves. Nor have we been able to extend the generality of our findings to a world youth culture. That limitation is built into the comparative approach—the availability of resources, time, and physical presence. Those many colleagues who have collaborated in this study nevertheless have demonstrated the enormous potential that exists for collaborative, comparative research and our ultimate attainment of a world view.

References

FOREWORD

Gilbert, S., Eyal, C., McCombs, M., & Nicholas, D. (1980). The state of the union address and the press agenda. *Journalism Quarterly*, 57:584–588.

McCombs, M. (1987). Effect of monopoly in Cleveland on diversity of newspaper content. *Journalism Quarterly*, 64:740–745.

———. (1988). Concentration, monopoly, and content. In R. Picard, et al. (Eds.), *Press concentration and monopoly*, Norwood, NJ: Ablex.

McCombs, M., Gilbert, S., & Eyal, C. (1982). The state of the union address and the press agenda: A replication. Paper presented to the International Communication Association: Boston, MA.

PREFACE

McCombs, M. E. (1981). The agenda-setting approach, In D. D. Nimmo & K. R. Sanders (Eds.), *Handbook of Political Communication*. Newbury Park, CA: Sage.

Smith, A. G. (1966). *Communication and culture: Readings in the codes of human interaction*. New York: Holt, Rinehart and Winston.

CHAPTER 1

Almond, G., & Verba, S. (1963). *The civic culture: Political attitudes and democracy in five nations*. Princeton, NJ: Princeton University Press.

Asante, M. K. (1980). Intercultural communication: An inquiry into research directions. in D. Nimmo (Ed.), *communication yearbook 4*. Beverly Hills, CA: Sage.

Asante, M. K., Newmark, E., & Blake, C. A. (1979). *Handbook of intercultural communication*. Beverly Hills, CA: Sage.

Babbili, A. S. (1987). *Surveying the landscape:* Recent trends and developments in international communication studies. Association for Education in Mass Communications and Journalism, San Antonio, TX.

Becker, S. L. (1976). Directions for intercultural communication research, in L. A. Samovar & R. E. Porter (Eds.), *Intercultural communication: A reader,* 2nd ed. Belmont, CA: Wadsworth.

Bendix, R. (1963). Concepts and generalizations in comparative sociological studies. *American Sociological Review*, 28:532–539.

Beniger, J. R., & Westney. D. E. (1981). Japanese and U.S. media graphics as a reflection of newspapers' social role. *Journal of Communication*, 31:14–27.

Benjamin, R. W. (1977). Strategy vs. methodology in comparative research. *Comparative Political Studies*, 9:475–484.

Bonnell, V. E. (1980). The uses of theory, concepts and comparison in historical sociology. *Comparative Studies in Society and History*, 22:156–173.

Boulding, K. B. (1959). National images and international systems. *Journal of Conflict Resolution*, 3:120–131.

Buchanan, W., & Cantril, H. (1953). *How nations see each other: A study in public opinion*. Urbana, Ill.: University of Illinois Press.

Cantril, H. (1965). *The pattern of human concerns*. New Brunswick, NJ: Rutgers University Press.

Carey, J. W. (1982). The mass media and critical theory: An American view. In M. Burgoon (Ed.), *Mass communication yearbook 2*. Beverly Hills, SA: Sage.

———. (1985). Overcoming resistance to cultural studies. In M. Gurevitch & M. R. Levy (Eds.), *Mass communication yearbook 5*. Beverly Hills, CA: Sage.

Carter, R. F. (1981). Measuring public opinion and assessing agenda setting. Presented to Mass Communication and Society Division, Association for Education in Journalism, Kent, Ohio.

Casmir, F. L., (1978). A multicultural perspective of human communication. In F. L. Casmir (Ed.), *Intercultural and international communication*. Washington, DC: University Press of America.

Chaffee, S., McLeod, J., & Atkin, C. (1971). Parental influence on adolescent media use. *American Behavioral Scientist*, 14:32–40.

Conrad, R. (1955). Social images in East and West Germany: A comparative study of matched newspapers in two social systems, *Social Forces*, 33:281–285.

Dajani, N. & J. Donohue (1973). Foreign news in the Arab press: A content analysis of six Arab dailies. *Gazette*, 14:155–170.

Dance, F. E. X. (1978). Human communication theory: A highly selective review and two commentaries. In B. D. Ruben (Ed.) *communication yearbook 2*. New, Brunsiwick, NJ: Transaction Books.

Daugherty, D., & Warden, M. (1979). Prestige press editorial treatment of the Mideast during 11 crisis years. *Journalism Quarterly* 56:776–782.

Deutsch, K. W. (1966). *Nationalism and social communication*. Cambridge, MA: MIT Press.

Donsbach, W. (1981). Legitimacy through competence rather than value judgments: The concept of jouralistic professionalism reconsidered. *Gazette*, 27:47–67.

Durkheim, É. (1938). *Les regles de la methode sociologique* (Paris: Alcan, 1895). G. E. B Catlin (Ed.), *The rules of sociological method* (translated by S. A. Solvay & J. H. Mueller). Chicago: University of Chicago Press.

Edelstein, A.S. (1962). Since Bennington: Evidence of change in student political behavior. *Public Opinion Quarterly*, 56:45–77.

———. (1974). *Communication and decision-making: A comparative study of the U.S. and Yugoslavia.* New York: Praeger.

———. (1982). *Comparative communication research.* Beverly Hills, CA: Sage Publications.

Edelstein, A. S., Bowes, J. E., & Harsel, S. M. (1982). *Information societies: Comparing the Japanese and American experiences.* Seattle: University of Washington Press.

Edelstein, A. S., & Hall, E. P. (1979). Sources of images of modern and traditional Japan: Situational and cognitive perspectives. *Studies of Broadcasting,* 15:5–30.

Ellingsworth, H. W. (1976). Personal communication to T. B. Saral. Cited in Consciousness theory of intercultural communication. Paper delivered to the International Communications Association, Portland, OR.

———. (1977). Conceptualizing intercultural communication. In B. Ruben (Ed.), *Mass communication yearbook 1.* New Brunswick, NJ: Transaction Books.

Fischer, H., & Merrill, J. (1976). *International and intercultural communication.* New York: Hastings House.

Fujiwara, N. (1969). Televiewing of Japanese people. *Studies of Broadcasting,* 7:55–104.

Galtung, J. (1971). A structural theory of imperialism. *Journal of Peace Research,* 8:81–118.

Galtung, J., & Ruge, M. H. (1965). The structure of foreign news. *Journal of Peace Research,* 2:64–91.

Gerbner, G., & Gross, L. (1976). Living with television: The violence profile. *Journal of Communication,* 26:173–199.

Gerbner, G. & Marvanyi, D. (1977). The many worlds of the world's press, *Journal of Communication,* 27:52–56.

Giffard, C. A. (1984). The inter-press Service: News from the third world. *Journal of Communication* 34:41–59.

———. (1985). The inter-press service: New information for a new order. *Journalism Quarterly,* 44:17–23.

———. (1987). The myth of new communications technologies as a quick fix for information imbalances. *Keio Communications Review,* Spring 1987.

Goodenough, W. H. (1970). *Description and comparison in cultural anthropology.* Chicago: Aldine.

Hachten, W. A. (1987). *The world news prism: Changing media,* clashing ideologies (2nd ed.). Ames: Iowa State University Press.

Hall, E. T. (1977). *Beyond culture.* New York: Doubleday.

Higson, J. M. (1968). Different emphases in the social scientist's conception of comparative method. *International Journal of Comparative Sociology*, 9:142–144.

Hirota, K. (1985). Computer communication and Japan's general public. *Computer Networks*, 10:1–5.

Holt, R. T., & Turner, J. E. (Eds.), (1970). *The methodology of comparative research*. New York: Free Press.

Howell, W.S. (1978). Theoretical directions for intercultural communication research. In M. K. Asante, E. Newmark, & C. A. Blake (Eds.). *Handbook of intercultural communication*. Beverly Hills, CA: Sage.

Hur, K. (1982). International mass communication research: A critical view of theory and methods. In M. Burgoon, (Ed.) *communication yearbook 6* (pp. 531–554). New Brunsurick, NJ: Transaction Books.

Ito, Y. (1978a). *Broadcasting in Japan*. London: Routledge & Kegan Paul.

Ito, Y. (1978b). Report at the final plenary session: Cross-cultural perspectives on the concept of an information society. In Edelstein, A. S., J. E. Bowes, and S. M. Harsel (Eds.), *Information societies: Comparing the Japanese and American experiences*. Seattle. WA.: University of Washington Press.

———. (1980). The johoka shakai approach to communication study in Japan. *Keio Commication Review*, 1:13–40.

———. (1981). The johoka shakai approach to the study of communication in Japan. In G. C. Wilhoit and H. DeBock (Eds.), *Mass Communication Review Yearbook #2*. Beverly Hills, CA.: Sage.

———. (1985). Implications of the telecommunications policy reform in Japan. *Keio Communication Review*, 6:7–17.

———. (1988). Conversations with the senior author, Seattle, WA. September.

Ito, Y., & Ogawa, K. Recent trends in johoka shakai and johoka policy studies. *Keio Communication Review*, 5:15–28.

Iwao, S., Pool, I. D., & Hagiwara, S. (1981). Japanese and U.S. media: Some cross-cultural insights into TV violence. *Journal of Communication*, 31:28–36.

Kayser, J. (1953). Report *One Week's News: Comparative Study of 17 Major Dailies for a Seven-Day Period*. Paris, France: UNESCO.

Kitahara, Y. (1984). Telecommunications for the advanced information society in Japan: Information network system (INS). *Journal of Telecommunication Networks*, Winter:338–343.

Kluckhohm, C. (1953). Universal categories of culture. In A. L. Kroeber, (Ed.) Anthropology today: An encyclopedic inventory. Chicago, Ill. University of Chicago Press.

Kocher, R. (1987). Bloodhounds or missionaries: Role definitions of German and British journalists. In M. Gurevitch and M. R. Levy (Eds.), *Mass Communication Review Yearbook No. 6*, Beverly Hills, CA: Sage.

Lasswell, H. D. (1968). The future of the comparative method. *Comparative Politics*, 1:3–18.

Lerner, D. (1958). *The passing of traditional society: Modernizing the Middle East*. New York: Free Press.

McCombs, M. E. (1981). The agenda-setting approach. In D. D. Nimmo & K. R. Sanders (Eds.), *Handbook of political communication*. Newbury Park, CA: Sage.

McLeod, J. M. & Rush, R. (1969a). Professionalization of Latin American and U.S. journalists. *Journalism Quarterly*, 46:583–590.

———. (1969b). Professionalization of Latin American and U.S. journalists, Part II. *Journalism Quarterly*, 46:784–789.

Maejima, M. (1973). The state and structure of information needs (Joho yokkyu no jittai to kozo). *Bunken Geppo*, 10:38.

Markham, J. W. (1961). Foreign news in the U.S. and South American Press. *Public Opinion Quarterly*, 25:249–262.

Marsh, R. M. (1967). *Comparative sociology: A codification of cross-societal analysis*. New York: Harcourt, Brace & World.

Martin, L. J. & Chaudhary, A. G. (1983). *Comparative Mass Media Systems*, New York: Longman, Inc.

Masuda, Y. (1979). Privacy in the future information society. *Computer Networks*, 3:164–170.

———. (1980). The information society as post-industrial society. Washington, DC: World Future Society.

Merrill, J. C., Bryan, C. R., & Alisky, M. (1970). *The foreign press: A survey of the world's journalism*. Baton Rouge: Louisiana State University Press.

Mowlana, H. (1970). A paradigm for comparative mass media analysis. In H. Fisher & J. C. Merrill (Eds.), *International and intercultural communication*. New York: Hastings House.

———. (1973). Trends in research on international communications in the United States." *Gazette*, 19:80–90.

———. (1986). *Global information and world communication: New frontiers in international relations*. White Plains, NY: Longman.

Nishida, H. (1987). Conversations with the senior author, Tokyo. May, June.

Nishida, H., & Nishida, T. (1981). Values and intercultural communication. In T. Nishida & W. B. Gudykundst (Eds.), *Readings in intercultural communication*. Tokyo: Geirinshobo.

Nishida, T., & Gudykunst, W. B. (Eds.), (1981). *Readings in intercultural communication*. Tokyo: Geirinshobo.

Nnaemeka, T. & Richstad, J. (1980). Structural relations and foreign news flow in the Pacific Region. *Gazette*, 26:235–257.

———. (1981). Internal controls and foreign news coverage: Pacific press systems. *Communication Research*, 8:97–135.

Nixon, R. B. (1960). Factors related to freedom in national press systems. *Journalism Quarterly*, 37:3–17.

———. (1965). Freedom in the world's press: A fresh appraisal with new data. *Journalism Quarterly*, 42:3–14.

Passin, H. (1963). Writer and journalist in the transitional society. In L. L. Pye (Ed.), *Communication and political development*. Princeton, NJ: Princeton University Press.

Pinch, E. T. (1978). A brief study of news patterns in 16 third world countries. Master of Arts thesis, Tufts University, Medford, MA.

Pisarek, W. (1981). Heroes of foreign news: A Polish perspective on newsmakers in socialist and nonsocialist countries. In G. C. Wilhoit and H. DeBock (Eds.), *Mass Communication Yearbook 2*. Beverly Hills, CA.: Sage.

Pool, I. D., Lasswell, H. D., & Lerner, D. (1952a). *The "Prestige Press": A comparative study of political symbols*. Cambridge, MA: MIT Press.

———. (1952b). *Symbols of democracy*. Stanford, CA: Stanford University Press.

Porter, R. E., & Samovar, L. A. (Eds.). (1973). Communicating interculturally. In *Intercultural communication: A reader* (2nd ed.) Belmont, CA.: Wadsworth.

Prosser, M. H. (1978). *The cultural dialogue: An introduction to intercultural communication*. Boston: Houghton-Mifflin.

Przeworski, A., & Teune, H. (1970). *The logic of comparative social inquiry*. New York: Wiley-Interscience.

Rachty, G. (1978). Foreign news in nine Arab countries. Master of Arts thesis, Tufts University, Medford, MA.

Radcliffe-Brown, A. R. (1952). *Structure and function in primitive society*. New York: Free Press.

Robinson, J. P. (1987). Letter to the senior author, May.

Rosengren, K. E. (1986). Media linkages between culture and other societal systems. In M. L. McLaughlin (Ed.), *Mass communication yearbook 9*. Beverly Hills, CA: Sage.

Samovar, L. A., Porter, R. E., & Jain, N. C. (1981). *Understanding intercultural communication*. Belmont, CA: Wadsworth.

Saral, T. B. (1979). Intercultural communication theory and research: An overview of challenges and opportunities. In D. Nimmo (Ed.), *Communications yearbook 3*. New Brunswick, NJ: Transaction Books. See (1977). Intercultural communication theory and research: An overview. In B. D. Ruben (Ed.) *communication yearbook 1*. New Brunswick, NJ: Transaction Books. (1975).

Schramm, W. (1959). *One Day in the World's Press: Fourteen Great Newspapers on a Day of Crisis*. Stanford, CA.: Stanford University Press.

Schramm, W., & Atwood, E. (1984). *Circulation of News in the Third World: A Study of Asia*, Hong Kong: CUHK Press.

Schramm, W., & Ruggels, W. L. (1967). How mass media systems grow. In D. Lerner and W. Schramm (Eds.). *Communication and change in the developing countries*. Honolulu: East West Center.

Scott, W. A. (1965). Psychological and social correlates of international images. In H. C. Kelman (Ed.), *International Behavior: A Social-Psychological Analysis*. New York: Holt, Rinehart and Winston.

Siebert, F. S., Peterson, T., & Schramm, W. (1956). *Four theories of the press*. Urbana: University of Illinois Press.

Skinner, B. F. (1972). *Beyond freedom and dignity*. New York: Knopf, 1972.

Sreberny-Mohammadi, A. et al. (1980). The world of the news: The news of the world. Report on Foreign Images, Paper presented at meeting of International Association of Mass Communications Research, Leicester, England.

Stevenson, R. L. (1988). *Communication, development and the third world: The global politics of information*. New York and London: Longman.

Stevenson, R. L., & Cole, R. (1980). Foreign news and the USICA debate over the New World Information Order. Parts 1 and 2, USICA Report 5–10–80. Washington, DC.

Stevenson, R. L. & Shaw, D. L. (1984). *Foreign news and the new world information order*. Ames: Iowa State University Press.

Stewart, E. C. (1972) *American cultural patterns: A cross-cultural perspective.* Society for Intercultural Education, Training and Research. La Grange Park, IL: Intercultural Communications Network.

———. (1974). Intercultural communication. In N. C. Jain and M. Schlow (Eds.), *Intercultural Communication: Proceeding of the Speech Communication Association Summer Conference.* New York: Speech Communication Association.

———. (1978). Intercultural communication. In F. Casmir (Ed.), *Intercultural and international communication.* Washington, DC: University Press of America.

Suchman, E. A. (1964). The comparative method in social research. *Rural Sociology,* 29:123–137.

Takasaki, N. (1978). The quest for quality of life for an information society. In (Eds.) A. S. Edelstein, J. E. Bowes, & S. M. Harsel. *Information societies: Comparing the Japanese and American experiecnes.* Seattle, WA.: University of Washington Press.

Tomasson, R. F. (1978). Introduction: Comparative sociology—The state of the art. *Comparative Studies in Sociology,* 1:1–11.

Tomita, T. (1978). Information and communication policies in an age oversupplied with information. In (Eds.) A. S. Edelstein, J. E. Bowes, & S. M. Harsel *Information Societies: Comparing the Japanese and American Experiences.* Seattle, WA.: University of Washington Press.

Triandis, H. C. (1972). Theoretical framework. In H. C. Triandis, (Ed.) *The analysis of subjective culture.* New York: Wiley Interscrence.

Wolfe, W. (1964). Images of the United States in the Latin American Press. *Journalism Quarterly* 41:79–86.

Yankelovich, D. (1972). *The changing values on campus.* New York: Pocket Books.

———. (1974). *The new morality: A profile of American youth in the 70's.* New York: McGraw-Hill.

CHAPTER 2

Akiyama, T., & Muramatsu, Y. (1985). Japanese value orientations (III): Changes over the decade 1973–1983. *Studies of Broadcasting,* 21:133–149.

Akuto, H. (1975). Changing political culture in Japan. In C. Hayashi (Ed.), *Changing values in modern Japan.* Tokyo: Nihonjin Kenkyukai.

———. (1978). The psychology and logic of party affiliation (*Seito shiji no shinri to ronri*). *Japan Echo,* 5:46–57.

Akuto, H., & Akiyama, T. (1971). Political process and public opinion. *Studies of Broadcasting,* 95–155.

———. (1973). Generation gap in contemporary Japan. *Studies of Broadcasting,* 9:191–216.

Akuto, H., & Kazama, D. (1975). Japanese value orientations: Persistence and change. *Studies of Broadcasting,* 11:21–38.

Atwood, R. (1984). Critical perspectives on the state of intercultural communication research. In B. Dervin & M. J. Voight (Eds.), *Progress in communication sciences.* NJ: Ablex.

Bloodworth, D. (1966). *The Chinese looking glass.* New York: Farrar, Straus and Giroux.

Brace, M. (1985). *Comparative youth cultures.* London: Routledge & Kegan Paul.

Budd, R. W. (1977). Perspectives on a discipline: Review and commentary. In B. D. Ruben (Ed.), *Mass communication yearbook 1.* New Brunswick, NJ: Transaction Books.

Casmir, F. L. (1978). A multicultural perspective of human communication. In F. L. Casmir (Ed.), *Intercultural and international communication.* Washington, DC: University Press of America.

Chaffee, S., McLeod, J., and Atkin, C. (1971). Parental influence on adolescent media use, *American Behavioral Scientist* 14:323–340, Jan–Feb.

Chen, J. (1987). The spontaneous student demonstration in China: 1919–1987. Masters thesis, University of Washington, Seattle.

Deutsch, K. W. (1968). *The analysis of international relations.* Englewood, NJ: Prentice-Hall.

Dodd, C. H. (1977). *Cross-Cultural Communication.* Dubuque, IA: Kendall-Hunt.

Durkheim, É. (1938). *The rules of sociological method.* Chicago: University of Chicago Press.

Edelstein, A. S. (1962). Since Bennington: Changes in students' political behavior. *Public Opinion Quarterly,* 26:564–577.

———. (1974). *Communication and decision-making: A comparative study of Yugoslavia and the United States.* New York: Praeger.

Edelstein, A. S., Bowes, J. E. & Harsel, S. M. (1982). *Information societies: Comparing the Japanese and American experiences.* Seattle, WA: University of Washington Press.

Equete Komission des 9 Deutschen Bundestages. (1983). *Jugenprotest im Demokratischen Staat II.* Bonn: Herausgegehen vom Deutschen Bundestag, Presse und Informationszentrum.

Gillespie, J. M., & Allport, G. W. (1955). *Youth's outlook on the future: A cross-national study.* Garden City, NY: Doubleday.

Guardo, C. J. (1982). Student generations and value change. *The Personnel & Guidance Journal,* 60:500–503.

Hall, E. T. (1977). *Beyond culture.* New York: Anchor Press-Doubleday. See also Hall E. T., Whyte, W. F. Intercultural communication. In C. T. Mortensen (Ed.), *Basic readings in communication theory.* New York: Harper & Row.

Han, Suyin (1972). Cited in Hoadly, J. S., Political participation of Hong Kong Chinese: Patterns and trends. *Asian Survey,* 13:604–616.

Harms, L. S. (1973). *International communication.* New York: Harper & Row. See also Harms, L. S. (1980). An emergent communication policy science: Context, rights, problems, and methods. *Communication,* 5:65–87.

Hoadley, J. S. (1967). Difference of opinion. *Far Eastern Economic Review,* 53: 249–251.

———. (1970). Hong Kong is the lifeboat: Notes on political culture and socialization. *Journal of Oriental Studies,* 8:206–218.

———. (1973). Political participation of Hong Kong Chinese: Patterns and Trends.

Asian Survey 13:604–616. See also Hoadley, J. S. (1970). Hong Kong is the lifeboat: Notes on political culture and socialization, *Journal of Oriental Studies*, 8:206–218.

Hoge, D. R. (1976). Changes in college students' value patterns in the 1950's, 1960's, and 1970's. *Sociology of Education*, 49:155–163.

Hoge, D. R., Luna, C. L., & Miller, D. K. (1981). Trends in college students' values between 1952 and 1979: A return of the Fifties? *Sociology of Education* 54:263–274. See also Hoge, D. R. (1976).

Holt, R. T., & Turner, J. E. (1970). *The methodology of comparative research*. New York: Free Press.

Howell, W. S. (1978). Theoretical directions for intercultural communication research. In M.K. Asante, E. Newmark, & C. A. Blake *Handbook of intercultural communication*. Beverly Hills, CA: Sage.

Hsieh, T. T., Shybut, J., & Lotsof, E. J. (1969). Internal vs. external control and ethnic group membership. *Journal of Consulting and Clinical Psychology*, 33: 122–124.

Hsu, F. L. K. (1955) *Americans and Chinese* (3rd. ed.). Honolulu: University of Hawaii Press.

Hughes, R. (1968). *Hong Kong—Borrowed place, borrowed time*. London: André Deutsch.

Ike, N. (1973). Economic growth and intergenerational change in Japan. *American Political Science Review*, 67:1194–1203.

Institut fur Demoskopie Allensbach. (1984). *Das Extreminsmus-Potentiale unter Jungen Leuten in der Bundesrepublik Deutschland* (2 vols.).

Jacob, P. E. (1957). *Changing values in college*. New York: Harper & Row.

Jugendwerk der Deutschen Shell. (1980a). *Die Einstellung der Jungen Generation zur Arbeitswelt und Wirtschaftsordnung, 1979*. Hamburg.

———. (1980b). *Jugend in Europa. Ihre Eingliederung in die Welt der Erwachsenen. Eine vergleichende Analyse der Bundersrepublik Deutschland, Frankreich und Gr. Britannien, 1977*. Hamburg.

Karl, W. (1970). Students and the youth movement in Germany: Attempt at a structural comparison. *Journal of Contemporary History* 1:113–127.

Kayne, J. B., & Houston, S. R. (1981). Values of American college students. *Journal of Experimental Education*, 49:199–206.

Kazama, D., & Akiyama, T. (1980). Japanese value orientations: Persistence and change (II). *Studies of Broadcasting*, 16:5–26.

Kepplinger, H. M. (1975). *Realkultur und Medienkultur, Literarische Karrieren in der Bundesrepublik*. Freiburg, Munchen: Alber.

———. (1978). Perception of social problems by local elites in West Germany and Lebanon," Paper, American Association for Public Opinion Research, Roanoke, VA.

———. (1981). Gesellschaftliche Bedingungen Kollektives gewalt. *Kolner Zeitschrift fur Soziologie und Sozialpsychologie*, 3:469–503. Darmstadt.

———. Conversation April, 1988. Mainz, West Germany.

Kim, Y. Y. (1979). Toward an interactive theory of communication acculturation. In D. Nimmo (Ed.), *Mass Communication Yearbook 3*. New Brunswick, NJ.: Transaction Books.

Kluckholm, C. (1951). Values and value orientations in the theory of action. In T. Parsons (Ed.), *Toward a general theory of action*. Cambridge, MA: Harvard University Press.

Kluckholm, F. R., & Strodtbeck, F. L., (1961). *Variations in value orientations*. Evanston, IL: Row, Peterson.

Kojima, K. (1977). Public opinion trends in Japan. *Public Opinion Quarterly*, 41: 206–216.

———. (1985). Changing Japanese value orientation: Its direction, process, and future. In *The structure of attitudes in contemporary Japan* (2nd ed.). Tokyo: NHK Broadcasting Culture Research Institute.

———. (1986) Youth and television in contemporary Japan—Analytical framework, background and characteristics. *Gazette*, 37:87–102.

Kojima, K. & Akiyama, T. (1985). Generation gap in contemporary Japan: Theme, method, results of analysis. *Studies of Broadcasting*, 9:191–216.

Kojima, K. & Kazama, D. (1975). Japanese value orientations: Persistence and change. *Studies of Broadcasting*, 11:21–38.

Krampen, G., & Wieburg, H. J. W. (1981). Three aspects of locus of control in German, American, and Japanese university students. *The Journal of Social Psychology*, 113:133–134.

Kroeber, A. L., & Kluckholm, C. (1952). Culture: A critical view of concepts and definitions. *Peabody Museum of American Archeology and Ethnology*, 47:1–223.

Lao, R. C. (1977). Levenson's IPC (Internal-External Control) scale: A comparison of Chinese and American students. *Journal of Cross-Cultural Psychology*, 9:113–124.

Lattmann, D. (1980). Stationen einer literarischen Republik. In D. Lattman (Ed.), *Kindlers Literaturgeschichte der Gegenwart, Autoren, Wereke, Themen, Tendenzen seit 1945*. Band: *Literatur der Bundesrepublik l*. Akutalisierte Ausgabe: Frankfurt: Fischer.

Levine, A. (1980). *When dreams and heroes died: A portrait of today's college student*. San Francisco, CA: Jossey-Bass, publishers.

Levitt, C. (1984). *Children of privilege: Student revolt in the sixties*. Toronto: University of Toronto Press.

Lichter, S. R. (1979). Young rebels. A psychological study of West German male radical students. *Comparative Politics*, 12:27–48.

Lipset, S. M. (Ed.) (1967). *Student politics*, New York: Basic Books, Inc.

Lipset, S. M., and Schaflander, G. M. (1971). *Passion and politics*, Boston: Little, Brown and Co.

McClosky, H. (1968). Political participation. In D. L. Sills (Ed.) *International encyclopedia of the social sciences, 12* New York: Macmillan.

Manabe, K. (1980). Patterns of political and social attitudes: A cross-national comparison. *Kwansei Gakuin University Annual Studies*, 20:87–102.

———. (1982). Japanese value orientations: Persistence and change. Paper delivered to Kwansei Gakuin University, Japan.

———. (1983). Political involvement and political information. *Kwansei Gakuin University Annual Studies*, 32:1–16.

———. (1984). Political involvement and political Information. *Kwansei Gakuin University Annual Studies*, 32:83–103.

Martin, L. J. (1976). The cultural communicator: The contradiction of intercultural communication. In H. D. Fisher & J. C. Merrill (Eds.), *International and intercultural communication*. New York: Hastings House.

Martin, L. J. & Chaudhary, A. G. (1983). *Comparative mass media systems*. New York: Longman.

Muramatsu, Y. (1975). Views of the Japanese youths toward television. *Studies of Broadcasting*, 11:39–62.

Naka, H. (1977). *Japanese youth in a changing society*. Tokyo: The International Society for Educational Information.

Nicasio, P. M., & Saral, T. B. (1978). The role of personality in intercultural communication. *Mass communication yearbook 2*. New Brunswick, NJ: Transaction Books.

Nishida, H., & Nishida, T. (1981). Values and interculturnal communication. In T. Nishida & W. B. Gudykundst (Eds.), *Readings in intercultural communication*. Tokyo: Geirinshobo.

Nishida, T., Gudykunst, W. B. (Eds.). (1981). *Readings in intercultural communication*. Tokyo: Geirinshobo.

Noelle-Neumann, E., & Kocher, R. (1987). *Die Verletzte Nation. Uber den Versuch der Deutschen, Ihren Charakter zu Andern*. Stuttgart: Deutsche Verlags-Anstalt.

Parsons, T. (1951). *Toward a general theory of action*. Cambridge, MA: Harvard University Press.

Payne, G. (1973). Comparative sociology: some problems of theory and method. *British Journal of Sociology*, 24:13–29.

Pazy, A., & Lomranz, J. (1980). Value conceptions of American and Israeli Youth. *The Journal of Social Psychology*, 111:181–187.

President's commission on campus unrest. (1970). *Campus unrest*. U.S. Government Printing Office: Washington, DC.

Prosser, M. H. (1978). *The cultural dialogue: An introduction to intercultural communication*. Boston: Houghton-Mifflin. See also Prosser M. H. (1976). Intercultural and international communication. In H. D. Fischer & J. C. Merrill (Eds.), *International and intercultural communication*. New York: Hastings House.

Raschke, J. (1988). *Soziate Bewegungen. Ein Historisch-Systematischer Grundig*. Auflage Frankfurt/New York.

Research Committee. (1961). *A study of Japanese national character*. Tokyo: Institute of Statistical Mathematics.

Rokeach, M. (1973). *The nature of human values*. New York: Free Press.

———. (1979). Value theory and communication research: Review and commentary. In D. Nimmo (Ed.), *Mass communication yearbook 3*. New Brunswick, NJ: Transaction books.

Rosengren, K. E. (1986). Media linkages between culture and other societal systems. In M.L. McLaughlin (Ed.), *Mass communication yearbook 9*. Beverly Hills, CA.

Roth, R., & Rucht, D. (1987). *Neue Soziale Bewegungen in der Budesrepublik Deutschland*, Studien zur Geschichte und Politik, Schriftenreihe, Band 252.

Saral, T. (1977). Intercultural communication: An overview. In B. Ruben (Ed.), *Mass communication yearbook 1*. New Brunswick, NJ: Transaction Books.

Shively, A. M., & Shively, S. (undated, approx. 1972). Value changes during a period of modernization—The case of Hong Kong. Paper delivered to the Social Science Research Center of Chinese University of Hong Kong.

Shively, S. (1972). Political orientations in Hong Kong. Paper delivered to the Social Science Research Center of Chinese University of Hong Kong.

Skinner, B. F. (1972). *Beyond freedom and dignity*. New York: Alfred A. Knopf.

Stewart, E. C. (1972). American cultural patterns: A cross-cultural perspective. Report to the Intercultural Communications Network, Society for Intercultural Education, Training and Research.

————. (1978). Outline of intercultural communication. In F. Casmir (Ed.), *Intercultural and international communication*. Washington, DC: University Press of America.

Swingewood, A. (1977). *The myth of mass culture*. Atlantic Highlands, NJ.: Humanities Press.

Townsend, J. (1967). *Political participation in Communist China*. Berkeley: University of California Press.

Tyler, V. L. (1978). Intercultural communication indicators: A "languetics" model. In B. Ruben (Ed.), *Mass communication yearbook 2*. New Brunswick, NJ: Transaction Books.

Urban Council. (1966a). Report of the Ad Hoc Committee on the future scope and operation of the Urban Council. Hong Kong. (August)

————. (1966b). Report of the Working Party on Local Administration. Hong Kong. (November)

Weber, M. (1904). *The Protestant ethic and the spirit of capitalism*. New York: Scribner's.

Wong, A. K. (1970–71) Political apathy and the political system in Hong Kong. *United College Journal*, 8:1–10.

Yamamoto, K. (Ed.). (1968). *The college student and his culture: An analysis*. New York: Houghton-Mifflin.

Yang, C. K. (1959). *The Chinese family in the Communist revolution*. Cambridge, MA: MIT Press.

Yankelovich, D. (1971). *Profile of a new generation*. Survey for CBS News. New York.

————. (1972). *The changing values on campus*. New York: Pocket Books.

————. (1974a). *The new morality: A profile of American youth in the 70's*. New York: McGraw-Hill.

————. (1974b). *Changing youth values in the 1970's*. New York: McGraw Hill.

Youth Bureau, Prime Minister's Office. (1974). *Japanese youth in a changing society*. Tokyo.

————. (1978). *The youth of the world and Japan: The findings of the Second World Youth Survey*. Tokyo.

CHAPTER 3

Atwood, L. E. (1984). Problem perception and mass media use in Hong Kong. Paper delivered to the International Communication Association, San Francisco. May 24–28.

Berlyne, D. E. (1965). *Structure and direction in thinking.* New York: John Wiley.

Blumer, H. (1971). Social problems as collective behavior. Social Problems, 18: 298–306. See also Ross, R., & Staines, G. L. (1972). The politics of analyzing social problems. *Social Problems,* 20:18–40; and Spector, M., & Kitsuse, J. I. (1974). Social problems: A reformulation. *Social Problems,* 21:145–158.

Buchanan, W., & Cantril, H. (1953). *How nations see each other: A study in public opinion.* Urbana: University of Illinois Press.

Bunge, M. (1967). *Scientific research 2.* Berlin: Springer-Verlas.

Cantril, H. (1965). *The pattern of human concerns.* New Brunswick, NJ: Rutgers University Press.

Carter, R. F. (1965). Communication and affective relations. *Journalism Quarterly,* 42:203–212.

Carter, R. F., Pyszka, R. H., & Guerrero, J. L. (1969). Dissonance and Exposure to aversive information. *Journalism Quarterly* 46:37–42.

Center for Study of Social Policy (1977).

Dewey, J. (1910). *How we think.* New York: Macmillan.

———. (1916). *Democracy and education.* New York: Macmillan.

———. (1927). *The public and its problems.* New York: Henry Holt and Company.

———. (1946). *Problems of men.* New York: Philosophical Library.

Donsbach, W. & Stevenson, R. L. (1984). *Challenges problems, and empirical evidence of the theory of the spiral of silence.* International Communication Association, San Francisco, May 24–28.

Edelstein, A. (1973). Decision-making and mass communication: A conceptual and methodological approach to public opinion. In P. Clarke & F. G. Kline (Eds.), *New models for mass communication research: Sage annual reviews of communication research, Vol. II.* Beverly Hills, CA.: Sage.

———. (1974). *Communication and decision-making: A comparative study of Yugoslavia and the United States.* New York: Praeger.

———. (1981a). Continuing the search for validity in public opinion about social problems and social decision-making. In H. Baier, H. M. Kepplinger, & K. Reumann (Eds.), *Offentliche Meinung und Sozialer Wandelr.* Darmstadt: Westdeutscher Verlag.

———. (1981b). A problem-oriented reconceptualization of public opinion. *The Journal of Communication Inquiry,* 6:97–117.

———. (1982). *Comparative communication research,* Beverly Hills, CA: Sage.

———. (1984). *New variables for the study of public opinion and communication about social problems.* Paper delivered to the International Communication Association, San Francisco.

———. (1985a). *Comparative public opinion: Working within a tradition.* Paper delivered to the International Communication Association, Honolulu.

———. (1985b). *Perceived congruency in the communicating of opinions about social problems: A comparative analysis.* Paper delivered to the American Association for Public Opinion Research, Great Gorge, NJ.

Festinger, L. (1957). *A theory of cognitive dissonance.* Evanston, Ill: Row, Peterson.

Funkhouser, G. R. (1973a). The issues of the sixties: An exploratory study in the dynamics of public opinion. *Public Opinion Quarterly,* 37:362–375.

———. (1973b). Trends in media coverage of the issues of the '60s. *Journalism Quarterly,* 50:533–538.

Gallup, G. (1976–77). Human needs and satisfactions: A global survey. *Public Opinion Quarterly*, 40:459–467.

Getzels, J. W. (1979). Problem-finding and research in educational administration. In G. L. Immogart & M. J. Boyd (Eds.), *Problem-finding in educational administration: Trends in research and theory*. Lexington, MA: Heath.

Harms, L. S. (1980). Communication policy problems as world problems. *Communicator*, pp. 10–14.

Jensen, J. V. (1975). Metaphorical constructs for the problem-solving process. *The Journal of Creative Behavior*, 9:113–124.

———. (1978). A heuristic for the analysis of the nature and extent of a problem. *The Journal of Creative Behavior*, 12:168–181.

Judge, A. J. N. (1975). World problems and human potential. *Futures*, June:209–220.

Kepplinger, H. M. (1978). Perception of social problems by local elites and workers in West Germany and Lebanon. Paper delivered at the American Association for Public Opinion Research, Roanoke, VA, June 1–4.

Manis, J. G. (1974). The concept of social problems: Vox populi and sociological analysis. *Social Problems*, 21:305–315.

Noelle-Neumann. E., & Kepplinger, H. M. (1981). Report on the study in the Federal Republic of Germany. In *Communication in the community: An international study on the role of the mass media in seven communities* (pp. 20–33). Paris: UNESCO.

Nordbeck, N. (1971). Problem: What is a problem? Comments on some definitions of the concepts "problem" and "problem situation." *International Associations*, 7:405–408.

Page, B. I., & Shapiro, R. Y. (1982). Changes in Americans' policy preferences, 1935–1979. *Public Opinion Quarterly*, 46:24–42.

Pavitt, C. (1982). A test of six models of co-orientation. The effect of task and disagreement level on judgments of uncertainty, utility, and desired communication behavior. In M. Burgoon (Ed.), *Communication yearbook 5*. New Brunswick, NJ: Transaction Books.

Pecci, A. (1968). World problems in the coming decades. *American Behavioral Scientist*, 2:20–24.

Smith, T. W. (1980). America's most important problem—A trend analysis, 1946–1976. *Public Opinion Quarterly*, 44:164–180.

Spector, M., and Kitsuse, J. I. (1974). Social problems: A reformulation. *Social Problems*, 21:145–158.

Takashina, S. (1984). The role of broadcasting in regional Japan—From the report on the local broadcasting research project. *Studies in Broadcasting*, 20:91–131.

Zygmunt, J. F. (1986). Collective behavior as a phase of societal life: Blumer's emergent views and their implications. In G. Lang and K. Lang (Eds.), *Research in Social Movements: Conflicts and Change*. Greenwich, CT: JAI Press Inc.

CHAPTER 4

Aggarwala, N. (1979). What is development news? *Journal of Communication*, 29:181–182.

Altheide, D. L. (1976). *Creating reality: How TV news distorts events.* Beverly Hills, CA.: Sage.

Altheide, W. L. Snow, R. P. (1979). *Media logic.* Beverly Hills, CA.: Sage.

American Society of Newspaper Editors (1982). *The Newspaper in readers' minds: An analysis of readers' content perceptions.* New York: Newspaper Advertising Bureau.

Atwood, E. (1970). How newsmen and readers perceive each other's story preferences. *Journalism Quarterly*, 47:296–302.

Badii, N., & Ward, W. J. (1980). The nature of news in four dimensions. *Journalism Quarterly* 57:243:248.

Bagdikian, B. H. (1971). *The information machines: Their impact on men and the mass media.* New York: Harper Colophon.

Bauer, R. (1964a). The communicator and the audience. In L. Dexter and D. M. White (Eds.), *People, society and mass communication.* New York: Free Press.

———. (1964b). The obstinate audience: The influence process from the point of view of social communication. *American Psychologist*, 19:319–328. See also: The communicator and the audience, In (Eds.) L. Dexter and D. M. White (1964b). *People, Society and Mass Communication*, New York: The Free Press of Glencoe.

Becker, L. B. (1979). Reporters and their professional and organizational commitment. *Journalism Quarterly* 56:753–783/770.

Bennett, W. L. (1983). *News: The Politics of Illusion.* New York: Longman.

Breed, W. (1955a). Newspaper "opinion leaders" and processes of standardization. *Journalism Quarterly* 32:277–284.

———. (1955b). Social control in the newsroom: A functional analysis. *Social Forces*, 33:326–335.

———. (1956). Analyzing news: Some questions for research. *Journalism Quarterly*, 33:467–477.

———. (1958). Mass communication and socio-cultural integration. *Social Forces*, 37:109–116.

Brown, R. M. (1979). The gatekeeper reassessed: A return to Lewin. *Journalism Quarterly*, 56:595–601.

De Fleur, M., & Rokeach, S. B. (1982). *Theories of mass communication.* New York: Longman.

Donsbach, W. (1981). Legitimacy through competence rather than value judgments: The concept of journalistic professionalism reconsidered. *Gazette*, 27: 47–67.

Edelstein, A. S. (1966). The role and status of the newspaperman. Ch. III in *Perspectives in mass communication.* Copenhagen: Einar Harck.

Edelstein, A. S., Bowes, J. E., & Harsel, S. (1978). *Information societies: Comparing the American and Japanese experiences.* Seattle: University of Washington Press.

Edelstein, A., & Hoyer, S. (forthcoming). Testing the problematic situation as a theory of news in the Norwegian context. Oslo: Institut for Journalism.

Elliott, P. (1972). *The making of a TV series: A case study in the production of culture.* London: Constable.

Ettema, J. S., & Whitney, D. C. (Eds.). (1982). *Individuals in mass media organizations: Creativity and constraint.* Beverly Hills, CA: Sage.

Findahl, O. & Hoijer, B. (1981). Studies of news from the perspective of human comprehension. In C Wilhoit and H. DeBock (Eds.), *Mass communication review yearbook 2*. Beverly Hills: Sage.

Galtung J., & Ruge, M. H. (1965). The structure of foreign news: The presentation of the Congo, Cuba and Cyprus crisis in four Norwegian newspapers. *Journal of International Peace Research*, 2:64–90.

Gans, H. J. (1979). *Deciding what's news: A study of CBS evening news, NBC nightly news, Newsweek and Time*, New York: Pantheon Books.

Gerbner, G. (1980a). Aging with television: Images of television drama, and conceptions of social reality. *Journal of Communication*, 30:137–148.

———. (1980b) The mainstreaming of America: Violence profile No. 11. *Journal of Communication*, 30:10–29.

———. (1984). Political functions of television viewing: A cultivation analysis. In G. Melischek, K. E. Rosengren, & J. G. Stapper (Eds.) *Cultural indicators: An international symposium*. Vienna: Akademie der Wissenschafter.

Gerbner, G., & Gross, L. (1976). Living with television: The violence profile. *Journal of Communication*, 26:173–199.

Gibbs, J. P. (1982). *Social control: Views from the social sciences*. Beverly Hills, CA: Sage.

Gieber, W. (1960a). How the "gatekeepers" view local civil liberties news. *Journalism Quarterly*, 37:199–205.

———. (1960b). Two communicators of the news: A study of the roles of sources and reporters. *Social Forces*, 37:76–83.

———. (1964). News is what newspapermen make it. In L. Dexter and D. M. White (Eds.), *People, society and mass communication*. NY: Free Press.

Gitlin, T. (1978). Media sociology: The dominant paradigm. *Theory and Society*, 6:205–253.

———. (1980). *The whole world is watching*, Berkeley: University of California Press.

Gollin, A. (1982). The newspaper in readers' minds: An analysis of readers' content perceptions. Report to the Newspaper Advertising Bureau, Inc., New York.

Gunter, B. (1983). Forgetting the news. In E. Wartella and D. C. Whitney (Eds.), *Mass communication yearbook 4*. Beverly Hills, CA: Sage.

Gunter, B., Clifford, B., & Berry, C. (1980). Release from proactive interference with television news items: Evidence for encoding within televised news. *Journal of Experimental Psychology: Human Learning and Memory*, 6:216–223.

Habermas, J. (1962). Regersdig Offentlighet. Oslo: Gyldendal.

Hall, S. (1983). The rediscovery of "ideology." Return of the repressed in media studies. In M. Gurevitch, et al., (Eds.), *Culture, society and the media*. New York: Methuen.

Halloran, J. D. Murdock, G. and Elliott, P. (1970). *Demonstrations and communication*. London: Penguin Books.

Jensen, K. B. (1986). Making sense of the news. Aarhus, Denmark: Aarhus University Press.

———. (1987). Answering the question: What is reception analysis? *The Nordicom Review*, 1:3–5.

Johnstone, J. (1976). Organizational constraints on newswork. *Journalism Quarterly*, 53:5–13.

Johnstone, J. W., Slawski, E. J., & Bowman, W. W. (1972). The professional values of American newsmen. *Public Opinion Quarterly*, 36:522–540.

———. (1974). *The news people: A sociological portrait of American journalists and their work*. Urbana: University of Illinois Press.

Kepplinger, H. M. (1982). Visual biases in television campaign coverage. *Communication Research* 9:432–446.

Kepplinger, H. M. & Roth, H. (1979). Creating a crisis: German mass media and oil supply in 1973/74. *Public Opinion Quarterly*, 43:285–296.

Kojima, K. (1986). Generational change and journalism: Methodology and tentative analysis. *Studies of broadcasting* 22:79–107.

Lang, K., and Lang. G. (1960). The unique perspective of television and its effect: A pilot study. In W. Schramm (Ed.), *Mass Communications*. 2nd ed. Urbana, Ill; University of Illinois Press. See also Lang, G. E., & Lang, K. (1984). *Politics and television reviewed*. Beverly Hills, CA: Sage.

Lasswell, H. (1948). The structure and function of communication in society. In L. Bryson (Ed.), *The communication of ideas*. New York: Institute for Religious and Social Studies.

Lippmann, W. (1922). *Public opinion*. New York: Macmillan.

Luttberg, N. R. (1983). Proximity does not assure newsworthiness. *Journalism Quarterly*, 60:731–732.

MacKuen, M. B., & Coombs, S. L. (1981). *More than news: Media power in public affairs*. Beverly Hills, CA.: Sage.

McLeod, J. M. & Rush, R. (1969a). Professionalization of Latin American and U.S. journalists. *Journalism Quarterly*, 46:583–590.

———. (1969b). Professionalization of Latin American and U.S. Journalists, Part II. *Journalism Quarterly*, 46:784–789.

McLeod, J. M., Kosicki, P. Z., & Allen, S. G. (1987). Presented to Association for Education in Journalism and Mass Communication, San Antonio, Texas. Audience perspectives on the news: Assessing their complexity and conceptual frames.

McQuail, D. (1983). *Mass communication theory: An introduction*. Beverly Hills, CA.: Sage.

Martin, L. J. & Chaudhary, A. G. (1983). *Comparative mass media systems*. New York: Longman.

Mencher, M. (1987). *News reporting and writing*, Dubuque, IA: W. C. Brown Publishers.

Meyer, P. (1988). Defining and measuring newspaper credibility. *Mass Media and Public Opinion*, Proceedings, International Association for Mass Communication Research, Barcelona, Spain.

Miller, A. H., Goldenberg, E. N. & Berbring, L. (1979). Type-set politics: Impact of newspapers on public confidence. *American Political Science Review*, 73: 67–84.

Molotch, H., & Lester, M. (1981). News as purposive behavior: On the strategic use of routine events. In S. Cohen and J. Young (Eds.), *The manufacture of news*. Beverly Hills, CA.: Sage.

Nimmo, D., & Combs, J. E. (1983). *Mediated political realities*. New York: Longman.

Nordenstreng, K. (1985). Bitter lessons. In M. Gurevitch and M. R. Levy (Eds.), *Mass communication yearbook 5*. Beverly Hills, CA: Sage.

Ogan, C. L., Fair, J. E., & Shah, H. (1984). A little good news: Development news in Third World newspapers. In R. N. Bostrom and B. H. Westley (Eds.), *Communication yearbook 8*. Beverly Hills, CA: Sage.

Ogan, C. L., & Swift, C. (1982). Is the news about development all good? Paper delivered to the AEJMC, Athens, OH.

Paletz, D. L., & Entman, R. M. (1981). *Media, power, politics*. New York: Free Press.

Passin, H. (1963). Writer and journalist in the transitional society. In (Ed.) L. L. Pye, *Communication and political development*. Princeton, NJ: Princeton University Press.

Patterson, T. E. (1980). *The mass media election: How Americans choose their president*. New York: Praeger.

Pik, T. S. (1984). The professional orientation of Hong Kong journalists in Chinese newspaper organizations. *Communication and Society*, pp. 53–56.

Pool, I. D., & Shulman, I. (1959). Newsmen's fantasies, audiences, and newswriting. *Public Opinion Quarterly*, 23:143–158.

Righter, R. (1978). *Whose news*? New York: Times Books.

Robinson, J. P., & Levy, M. R. (1986). *The main source: Learning from television news*. Beverly Hills, CA: Sage.

Rosengren, K. E. (1980). Mass media and social change: Some current approaches. In G. C. Willhoit & H. DeBock, (Eds.) *Mass communication yearbook 1*. Beverly Hills, CA: Sage.

Roshco, B. (1975). *Newsmaking*. Chicago,: University of Chicago Press.

Schlesinger, P. (1978). *Putting "reality" together. BBC news*. London: Constable.

Schoenbach, K. (1983). *Das unterschatze medium: Politiche wirkungen von presse und fernsehen in vergleich*, Munich: Spiess.

Schramm, W. (1949). The nature of news. *Journalism Quarterly*, 26:259–269.

Schramm, W., and Atwood, E. (1984). *Circulation of news in the third world: A study of Asia*, Hong Kong: The Chinese University Press.

Schudson, M. (1978). *Discovering the news: A social history of American newspapers*. New York: Basic Books.

Schulz, W. (1976). *Die konstruktion von realitaet in den nachrichtenmedien*. Freiburg, W. Germany: Karl Alber.

Shoemaker, P. J., Mayfield, E. K. (1987). Building a theory of news content. *Journalism Monographs*, 103:1–136.

Snow, R. P. (1983). *Creating media culture*. Beverly Hills, CA: Sage.

So, C. Y. K. (1982). Towards a logic of journalistic practice. *Academic Journal*, pp. 50–55.

Sreberny-Mohammadi, A. (1985). The world of the news study. In M. Gurevitch & M. R. Levy (Eds.), *Mass communication review yearbook 5*. Beverly Hills, CA: Sage.

Stevenson, R. L. (1985). Pseudo debate. In M. Gurevitch and M. R. Levy (Eds.), *Mass communication review yearbook 5*. Beverly Hills, CA: Sage.

Stevenson, R. L., & Greene M. T. (1980). A reconsideration of bias in the news. *Journalism Quarterly*, 57:115–121.

Swanson, G. E. (1956). Agitation through the press: A study of the personalities of publicists. *Public Opinion Quarterly*, 20:441–456.

Tuchman, G. (1973). Making news by doing work: Routinizing the unexpected. *American Journal of Sociology*. 79:110–131.

———. (1977). Objectivity as strategic ritual: An examination of newsmen's notions of objectivity. *American Journal of Sociology*, 77:660–679.

Tunstall, J. (1971). *Journalists at work*. London: Sage.

Vilanilam, J. V. (1979). Ownership versus development news content: An analysis of independent and conglomerate newspapers of India. In J. A. Lent & J. V. Vilanilam (Eds.), *The use of development news*. Singapore: Asian media and Information Center.

———. (1980) Ownership versus development news content: An analysis of independent and conglomerate newspapers of India. In J. A. Lent & J. V. Vilanilam (Eds.), *The use of developments news*. Singapore: Asian Media and Information Center.

Weaver, D. G, & Wilhoit, G. C. (1986). *The American journalist: A portrait of U.S. news people and their work*. Bloomington: Indiana University Press.

White, D. M. (1950). The "gatekeeper": A case study in the selection of news. *Journalism Quarterly*, 27:383–390.

Williams, F. (1982). *The communications revolution*. Beverly Hills, CA: Sage.

Woodall, W. G. (1986). Information-processing theory and television news. Ch. 6 in J. R. Robinson & M. Levy (Eds.). *The main source: Learning from television news*. Beverly Hills, CA: Sage.

CHAPTER 5

Atkin, C. (1973). Instrumental utilities and information seeking. In P. Clarke (Ed.), *New models for communication research*. Beverly Hills, CA: Sage.

Blumler, J. (1979). The role of theory in uses and gratifications studies. *Communication Research*, 6:9–36.

Blumler, J. G., & Katz, E. (Eds.). (1974). *The uses of mass communications: Current perspectives on gratifications research*. Sage Annual Reviews of Communication Research. Beverly Hills, CA: Sage. See also McLeod, J. & Becker, L. The uses and gratifications approach. In D. Nimmo & K. Sanders (Eds.), *Handbook of political communication*. Beverley Hills, CA: Sage.

Carter, R. F., Pyszka, R. H., & Guerrero, J. L. (1969). Dissonance and exposure to aversive information. *Journalism Quarterly*, 46:37–42.

Chaffee, S. H. (1973). Contingent orientations and the effects of political communication. Presented to Speech Communication Association, New York.

Dehm, U. (1984a). *Fernsehunterhaltung. Zeitvertreib, flucht oder zwang?* Mainz: Hase & Kohler, p. 170.

———. (1984b). Fernsehunterhaltung aus der sicht der zuschauer. In M. L. Keifer (Ed.), *Media Perspektiven*, pp. 630–643.

Edelstein, A. S. (1973). An alternative approach to the study of source effects in mass communication. *Studies of Broadcasting*, 9:5–29.

Elliott, P. (1974). Uses and gratifications research: A critique and a sociological alternative. In *The uses of mass communication*. London and Beverley Hills, CA: Sage.

Festinger, L. (1957). *A theory of cognitive dissonance*. Stanford, CA: Stanford University Press.

Gerbner, G., & Gross, L. (1976). Living with television: The violence profiles. *Journal of Communication*, 26:173–199.

Ha, L. (1986). Women's programs in women's eyes—A uses and gratifications study in an informational programme setting. *Communication and Society*, pp. 24–34. See also Ho, W. K. (1983). The experience of television news audience in Hong Kong. *Communication and Society*, 4:5–14.

Hayashi, C. S. (1982). Report on the "how-do-people-spend-their-time survey" in 1980. *Studies of Broadcasting*, 18:93–113.

Hayashi, C. S., Aoyama, H., Nisihira, S., & Suzuki, T. (1970). *Nipponzin No Kokuminsei (II)*.

Hayashi, C. S., Aoyama, H., Nisihira, S., Suzuki, T., & Sakamoto, Y. (1975). *Nipponzin No Kokuminsei III*.

Hayashi, C. S., Nishira, S, Suzuki, T., Mizuno, K., Suzuki, G., Sakamoto, Y., Murakami, M., & Aoyama, H. (1982). *Nipponzin no kokuminsei (4): A study of the Japanese national character*. Tokyo: The Institute for Statistical Mathematics: Idemitsushoten, Tokyo.

Institute of Statistical Analysis (1983). Report to the Hoso-Bunka Foundation. In C. Hayashi (Ed.), *Media uses and gratifications: A comparison of Japanese and American Judgements*. Tokyo. The institute has conducted a number of *kokuminsei* studies over the past decade.

Japanese Newspapers Publishers and Editors Association (1984). *The Japanese Press 1984*. Tokyo: Nihon Shinbun Kyokai.

Johnstone, J. W. C. (1974). Social integration and mass media use among adolescents: A case study. In J. G. Blumler and E. Katz (Eds.), *The uses of mass communications: Current perspectives and gratifications research*. Beverly Hills, CA: Sage.

Johnstone, J. W. C., Slawski, E. J., & Bowman W. M. (1974). *The American journalist: A sociological profile*. Urbana: The University of Illinois Press.

Katz, E., Blumler, J., & Gurevitch, M. (1974). Utilization of mass communication by the individual. In J. Blumler and E. Katz (Eds.), *The uses of mass communication: Current perspectives on gratification research*. Beverly Hills, CA: Sage.

Katz, E., Gurevitch, M., & Haas, H. (1973). On the use of the mass media for important things. *Studies of Broadcasting*, 9:31–65. See also (1973) *American Sociological Review*, 38:164–181.

Kepplinger, H. M. (1984). Development of communication in postwar Germany: Remarks on media use and social change. In *Bulletin of Institute for Communications Research* (Keio University), 23:1–29.

Kiefer, M. L. (1984). West Germany: Mass communication 1964 to 1980. (Working paper). Frankfurt: Media Perspektiven.

Kocher, R. (1987). Bloodhounds or missionaries: Role definitions of German and British journalists, In M. Gurevitch and M. R. Levy (Eds.), *Mass communication review yearbook 6*. Beverly Hills, CA: Sage.

Lang, K., & Lang, G. (1960). The unique perspective of television and its effect: A pilot study. In W. Schramm (Ed.), *Mass communications*. Urbana, ILL: University of Illinois Press. 2nd ed.

————. (1970). *Politics & Television*. Chicago: Quadrangle Books.

McGuire, W. J. (1974). Psychological motives and communication gratifications. In J. G. Blumler and E. Katz (Eds.) *The uses of mass communication*. Beverly Hills, CA: Sage.

McQuail, D. (1983). *Mass communication theory: An introduction*. Beverly Hills, CA: Sage.

————. (1985). With the benefit of hindsight: Reflections on uses and gratifications research. In M. Gurevitch and M. R. Levy (Eds.), *Mass communication Yearbook 5*. Beverly Hills, CA: Sage.

McQuail, D., Blumler, J. G., & Brown, J. (1972). The television audience: A revised perspective. In D. McQuail (Ed.), *Sociology of mass communications*. Harmondsworth, Eng.: Penguin.

McQuail, D., & Gurevitch, M. (1974). Explaining audience behavior: Three approaches considered. In J. G. Blumler and E. Katz (Eds.), *The uses of mass communications: Current perspectives on gratifications research*. Beverly Hills, CA: Sage.

Palmgreen, P. (1984). Uses and gratifications: A theoretical framework. In R. Bostrom (Ed.), *Communication yearbook 8*. Beverly Hills, CA: Sage.

Palmgreen, P., Wenner, L. A., & Rosengren, K. E. (1985). Uses and gratifications research: The last ten years. In P. Palmgreen, L. A. Wenner, & K. E. Rosengren (Eds.), *Media gratifications research: Current perspectives*. Beverly Hills, CA: Sage.

Rosengren, K. E. (1974). Uses and gratifications, a paradigm outlined. In E. Katz & J. G. Blumler (Eds.), *The uses of mass communication: Current perspectives on uses and gratifications*. Beverly Hills, CA: Sage.

Rosengren, K. E., & Windahl, S. (1972). Mass media consumption as a functional alternative. In D. McQuail (Ed.)., *Sociology of mass communications*. Harmondsworth, Eng. Penguin.

Rubin, A. M. & Rubin, R. B. (1981). Age context and television use. *Journal of Broadcasting*, 25:1–13.

————. (1982). Older persons TV viewing patterns and motivation. *Communication Research*, 9:283–313.

Schulz, W. (1976). *Die Konstruktion von Realitat in den Nachrichtermedien; Analyse der Aktuellen Berichterstattung*. Freiburg: Karl Alber.

————. (1982). News structure and people's awareness of political events. *Gazette*, 30:139–153.

Takeuchi, I. (1986). On the uses and gratifications studies. *Studies of Broadcasting*, 22:31–57.

Tang, M. (1986). TV news—Factors affecting gratifications dimensions from TV news. *Communication and Society*, 33–38.

Tokinoya, H. (1981a). Seigiteki komyunkeishen "rito to manzoku 1". (Uses and gratifications and political communication 1). *Sogo Jahnarizumyu Kenku (Journalism Studies)*, 95:13–25.

————. (1981b). Seigiteki komyunkeishen "rtio to manzoku 2." (uses and gratifications and political communication 2.) *Sogo Jahnarizyumku Kenku* (*Journalism Studies*), 96:90–97.

Tokinoya, H. (1986). Rojin shiehosha no doki-jusoku ni kansuru kenkyu. (A study of old viewers' motives from the viewpoint of uses and gratifications.) *Shankai Ronengaku*, 23:64.

Weaver, D. H. (1980). Audience need for orientation and media effects. *Communication Research*, 7:361–376.

Weaver, D. H., & Buddenbaum, J. M. (1981). Newspapers and television: A review of research on uses and effects. In C. Wilhoit & H. DeBock (Eds.), *Mass communication yearbook 1*. Beverly Hills, CA: Sage.

Weiss, H-J. (1978a). Kommunkiatonsbedurfnisse und medienfunktionen: Ein forschungsbericht uber die ermittlung subjektiver bedingungsfaktoren der mediennutzung. In (Eds.) K. Berg and M. L. Kiefer, *Massenkommunikation, eine langzeitstudie zur mediennutzung und medienbewertung*. Mainz: Von Hase & Kohler, pp. 345–391.

———. (1978b). Medium buch: Ein forschungsbericht uber kommunikations-bedurfnisse und einstellungen gegennuber medien. *Buch und lesen: Bertelsmann texte, Heft 7*. Gutersloh: Bertelsmann Verlag, pp. 91–119.

Wright, C. (1959). *Mass communication: A sociological perspective*. New York: Random House.

———. (1975). *Mass Communication: A Sociological Perspective*. New York: Random House. See also Functional analysis and mass communication revisited. In J. G. Blumler & E. Katz, (Eds.), *The uses of mass communication: Current perspectives on mass communication*. Beverly Hills, CA, and London: Sage.

CHAPTER 6

American Institute of Public Opinion. (1958). *The public appraises the newspaper 1958*. Princeton, NJ: Gallup Poll.

———. (1961). *The Public Appraises the Newspaper 1961*. Princeton, NJ: Gallup Poll.

American Society of Newspaper Editors (1982). *The Newspaper in readers' minds: An analysis of readers' content perceptions*. New York: Newspaper Advertising Bureau.

———. (1985). *Newspaper credibility: Building reader trust*. Minneapolis, MN.

Anast, P. (1961). Attitude toward the press as a function of interests. *Journalism Quarterly*, 38:376–380.

Andreoli, V., & Worchel, S. (1978). Effects of media, communicator, and message position on attitude change. *Public Opinion Quarterly*, 42:59–70.

Atwood, L. E. (1984). *Problem perception and mass media use in Hong Kong*. delivered to the International Communication Association, San Francisco.

Beniger, J., & Westney, D. E. (1981). Japanese and U.S. media graphics as a reflection of newspapers' social role. *Journal of Communication*. 31:14–27.

Breed, W. (1955). Social control in the news room *Social Forces* 33:465–477.

Burgoon, M., & Burgoon, J. K. (1979). Predictive models of satisfaction with a newspaper. In D. Nimmo (Ed.), *Communication yearbook 3*. New Brunswick, NJ: Transaction Books.

Burgoon, J. K., & Burgoon, M. (1980). Predictors of newspaper readership. *Journalism Quarterly* 44:130–133.

Burgoon, J. K., Burgoon, M. and Atkin, C. K. (1982). The world of the working journalist. Report. Newspaper Research Project, Michigan State University, East Lansing, MI.

Carlson, E. R. (1960). Psychological satisfaction and interest in news. *Journalism Quarterly*, 37:547–551.

Carter, R. F., & Greenberg, B. S. (1965). Newspapers or TV: Which do you believe? *Journalism Quarterly*, 42:29–34.

Chaiken, S., & Eagly, A. (1976). Communication modality as a determinant of message persuasiveness and message comprehensibility. *Journal of Personality and Social Psychology*, 34:605–614.

Chan, J. M., & Lee, C-C. (1986). Journalistic paradigm on civil protector: A case study in Hong Kong. Paper presented (1981) at East-West Communication Institute, Honolulu. Paper presented (1986) at meeting of the International Communication Association, Montreal, Canada.

Chang, L. K. H., & Lemert, J. (1968). The invisible newsmen and other factors in media competition. *Journalism Quarterly*, 45:436–444.

Edelstein, A. S. (1973) An alternative approach to the study of source effects in mass communication. *Studies of Broadcasting*, NHK, Tokyo.

———. (1974). *The uses of communication in decision-making: A comparison of Yugoslavia and the United States*. New York: Praeger.

Edelstein, A. S., & Tefft, D. (1973). Media credibility and respondent credulity with respect to Watergate. *Communication Research*, 1:426–439.

Gannett Center for Media Studies (1985). *The media and the people: Soundings from two communities* (Edited by C. Whitney). New York: Columbia University. See also: American Society of Newspaper Editors (1985). *Newspaper credibility: Building reader trust* (Conducted by MORI Research Inc.). Washington, DC; Los Angeles Times-Mirror (1985), *The people & the press* (Conducted by G. Gallup in collaboration with M. J. Robinson, George Washington University). Los Angeles; Los Angeles Times Poll, *The media poll,* (I.A. Lewis, director), Times Mirror: Los Angeles, CA.

Gaziano, C. (1988). How credible is the credibility crisis? *Journalism Quarterly*, 65:267–278.

Gaziano, C., & McGrath, K. M. (1986). Measuring the concept of credibility, *Journalism Quarterly*, 63:451–62.

———. (1987). Newspaper credibility and relationships of newspaper journalists to communities, *Journalism Quarterly*, 64:317–328, 345.

Gollin, A. E. (1986). *Readers rate their daily newspaper: Measuring images and performance*. New York: Newspaper Advertising Bureau, Inc.

Greenberg, B. S. (1966). Media use and believability: Some multiple correlates, *Journalism Quarterly*, 43–667.

Greenberg, B. S., & Roloff, M. E. (1974). Mass media credibility: Research results and critical issues. *News Research Bulletin*, News Research Center, American Newspaper Publishers Association, 6:35–44.

Gunter, B. (1983). Forgetting the news. In E. Wartella, D. C. Whitney, & S. Windahl (Eds.), *Mass communication review yearbook 4*. Beverly Hills, CA: Sage.

———. (1988). Attitude extremity and trust in media. *Journalism Quarterly*, 65:279–287.

Gunter, B. C., & Lasorsa, D. L. (1986). Issue importance and perceptions of a hostile media, *Journalism Quarterly*, 63:844–848.

Hovland, C., Janis, I. L. & Kelley, H. H. (1953). *Communication and Persuasion*. New Haven, CN: Yale University Press.

Ito, Y. (1987). Memorandum to author.

Izard, R. S. (1985). Public confidence in the news media. *Journalism Quarterly*, 62:247–255.

Jacobson, H. K. (1969). Mass media believeability: A study of receiver judgments. *Journalism Quarterly*, 46:20–28.

Japanese Newspapers Publishers and Editors Association. (1984). *The Japanese Press, 1984*. Tokyo: Nihon Shinbun Kyokai.

Johnson, S. D. (1984). International communication media appraisal: Tests in Germany. In R. N. Bostrom & B. H. Westley (Eds.), *Communication yearbook 8*. Beverly Hills, CA: Sage. See also Johnson, S. D. & Tims, A. R. (1981). Magazine evaluations and levels in readership: A cross-national comparison. *Journalism Quarterly*, 58:96–98.

Keating, J. (1972). Persuasive impact, attitudes and image: The effect of communication media and audience size on attitude toward a source and toward his position. Doctoral dissertation; Ohio State University, Columbus.

Kepplinger, H. M. (1984) Development of communication in postwar Germany: Remarks on media use and social change. In *The Bulletin of the Institute for Communication Research, #23*. Tokyo: Keio University.

Lee, R. S. H. (1978). Credibility of newspaper and TV news. *Journalism Quarterly*, 55:282–287.

Lemert, J. (1970). News media competition under conditions favorable to newspapers. *Journalism Quarterly*, 47:272–280.

Los Angeles Times Poll (1985). *Public and press: Two viewpoints*. Los Angeles, CA: Times Publishing Co.

Meier, N. R., & Thurber, J. (1968). Accuracy of judgments of deception when an interview is watched, heard, and read. *Personal Psychology*, 21:28–30.

Meyer, P. (1988). *Defining and Measuring Newspaper Credibility*. Paper presented at Barcelona, World Association for Public Opinion. July 24, pp. 40–60.

Meyer, T. J. (1974). Media credibility: The state of the research. *Public Telecommunications Review*, 2:48–52.

Miller, A. H., Goldenberg, E. N., & Erbring, L. (1979). Type-set politics: Impact of newspapers on public confidence. *American Political Science Review*, 73: 67–84.

Mulder, R. (1980). Media credibility: A uses-gratifications approach, *Journalism Quarterly*, 57:474–476.

Noelle-Neumann, E., & Piel, E. (Eds.). (1983). *Allensbacher Jarhbuch der demoskopie 1978–1983). Vol. 8.* New York: K. G. Sauer.

Office of Prime Minister (1981) Youth Affairs Administration, Report, Values of Youth. Tokyo, Japan.

Reagan, J., & Zenaty, J. (1979). Local news credibility: Newspapers vs. TV revisited. *Journalism Quarterly*, 56:168–172.

Richardson, B., Detweiler, J. S., and Bush, M. B. (1988). Linkages between journalists' community associations, attitudes and expression of viewpoints on selected issues. Paper presented to Association for Education in Journalism and Mass Communication, Portland, Ore. July.

Roberts, D. F., & Leifer, A. D. (1975). Actions speak louder than words—sometimes. *Human Communication Research*, 1:257–264.

Robinson, J. P., & Levy, M. R. (1986). *The main source: Learning from television news.* Beverly Hills, CA: Sage. See also. (1986). Interpersonal communication and news comprehension. *Public Opinion Quarterly*, 50:160–175.

Roper, B. W. (1985). *Public attitudes toward television and other media in a time of change.* New York: Television Information Office.

Saito, K. (1986). The rising credibility of newspapers: Results of the sixth comprehensive nationwide survey on the credibility of newspapers. *The Japanese press 1986.* Tokyo: Nihon Shinbun Kyokai.

Shaw, E. (1973). Media credibility: Taking the measure of a measure. *Journalism Quarterly*, 50:306–311.

Tan, A. S. (1981). *Mass communication theories and research.* Columbus, OH: Grid Publishing Co.

Washington Post Poll (1981). Radnor, PA: Chitron Research Services.

Westley, B. H., et al. Some correlates of media credibility. *Journalism Quarterly*, 41:320–330.

Woodall, W. G., Davis, D. K., & Sahin, H. (1983). From the boob tube to the black box: TV news comprehension from an information processing perspective. In E. Wartella, D. C. Whitney, & S. Windahl (Eds.), *Mass communication review yearbook 4.* Beverly Hills, CA: Sage.

Yu, D. B. (1981). *The role of newspapers in political communication: A case study in Hong Kong.* Hong Kong: Chinese University of Hong Kong.

CHAPTER 7

Allport, F. H. (1937) Toward a science of public opinion, *Public Opinion Quarterly*, 1:7–23.

Boorstin, D. (1973). *Democracy and its discontents.* New York: Vintage Press. See also (1971). *The image: A guide to pseudo events in America.* New York: Atheneum Books.

———. (1974). *Democracy and its discontents: Reflections on everyday America.* New York: Random House.

Bowes, J. E., & Stamm, K. R. (1975). Evaluating communication with public agencies. *Public Relations Review*, 1:23–37.

Breed, W., & Ktsanes, T. (1961). Pluralistic ignorance in the process of opinion formation. *Public Opinion Quarterly*, 25:382–392.

Carter, R. F. (1965). Communication and affective relations. *Journalism Quarterly*, 42:203–212.

Davison, W. P. (1983). The third-person effect in communication. *Public Opinion Quarterly*, 47:1–15. See also (1958). The public opinion process. *Public Opinion Quarterly*, 22:91–106.

Fields, J. M., & Schuman, H. (1976). Public beliefs about the beliefs of the public. *Public Opinion Quarterly*, 40:427–448.

Glock, C. Y. (1952). The comparative study of communication and opinion formation. *Public Opinion Quarterly*, 16:512–526.

Glynn, C. J. (1986a). *The communication of public opinion*. Paper delivered to the American Association for Public Opinion Research, Pennsylvania.

———. (1986b). *Perceptions of others' opinions as a component of public opinion*. Paper delivered to the American Association of Public Opinion Research, Pennsylvania.

Glynn, C. J. & McLeod, J. (1982). Public opinion du Jour: Its impact on communication and voting behavior. Paper delivered to the Association for Education in Journalism and Mass Communications, Athens, GA.

Grunig, J. E. (1983). Communication behaviors and attitudes of environmental publics: Two studies. *Journalism Monographs*.

Grunig, J. E., & Stamm, K. R. (1973). Communication and coorientation of collectivities. *American Behavioral Scientist*, 16:567–591.

———. (1979). Cognitive strategies and the resolution of environmental issues: A second study. *Journalism Quarterly*, 56:715–726.

Kepplinger, H. M. (1981). Gesellschaftliche bedingungen kollektiver gewalt. In *Kolner Zeitschrift fur Soziologie und Sozialpsychologie*, 33:468–503.

Kepplinger, H. M., & Noelle-Neumann, E. (1979). Report on the study in the Federal Republic of Germany. UNESCO.

Kim, H. S. (1986). Co-orientation and communication. In B. Dervin and M. Voight (Eds.), *Progress in communication science 7*. Norwood, NJ: Ablex.

Lai, Y. L. (1983). Opinion agreement and accuracy between editors and readers in evaluating local sensationalism. *Communication and Society*, 45–47.

Lemert, J. (1981). *Does mass communication change public opinion, after all?* Chicago: Nelson-Hall.

Lippmann, W. (1922) *Public opinion*. New York: Harcourt Brace.

McLeod, J. M., & Chaffee, S. H. (1973). Interpersonal approaches to communication research. *American Behavioral Scientist*, 16:469–99.

Noelle-Neumann, E. (1974). The spiral of silence: A theory of public opinion. *Journal of Communication*, 24:41–51.

———. (1977). Turbulences in the climate of opinion: Methodological applications of the spiral of silence theory. *Public Opinion Quarterly*, 41:143–158.

———. (1979). Public opinion and the classical tradition: A reevaluation. *Public Opinion Quarterly*, 43:143–157.

O'Gorman, H. J. (1975). Pluralistic ignorance and white estimates of white support for racial segregation. *Public Opinion Quarterly*, 39:313–30.

————. (1979). White and black perceptions of racial values. *Public Opinion Quarterly*, 43:48–59.

————. (1980). False consciousness of kind: Pluralistic ignorance among the aged. *Research in Aging* 2:105–128.

O'Gorman, H. J. & Garry, S. L. (1976). Pluralistic ignorance—A replication and extension. *Public Opinion Quarterly*, 40:449–458.

Salmon, C. T., & Kline, F. G. (1984). The spiral of silence ten years later: An examination and evaluation. Cited in W. Donsbach and R. L. Stevenson, Challenges, problems, and empirical evidence of the theory of the spiral of silence. Paper delivered to the Panel on The Spiral of Silence Theory, International Communication Association, San Francisco, May 24–28.

Stamm, K. H., Bowes, J. E., & Bowes, B. (1973). Generation gap a communication problem? A co-orientational analysis. *Journalism Quarterly*, 50:629–637.

Taylor. D. G. (1982). Pluralistic ignorance and the spiral of silence: A formal analysis. *Public Opinion Quarterly*, 46:311–335.

Theberge, L. J. (1982). *Coverage of the oil crises: How well was the public served? Vol. l. A qualitative analysis.* Washington, DC: Media Institute.

Tichenor, P. J., & Wackman, D. (1973). Mass media and community public opinion. *American Behavioral Scientist*, 16:593–606.

Weaver, D. H. (1980). Audience need for orientation and media effects. *Communication Research* 7:361–376.

CHAPTER 8

Abe, Y. (1972). *Dialogue with Western Europe*, pp. 222–223, (Seio to no taiwa), Tokyo: Kawade Shobo Shinsa.

Abe, Y. & Wiseman, R. (1983). A cross-cultural confirmation of the dimensions of intercultural effectiveness. *International Journal of Intercultural Relations*, 7:53–68.

Atwood, L. E., Sohn, A. B., & Sohn, H. (1978). Daily newspaper contributions to community discussion. *Journalism Quarterly*, 55:570–576. See also Atkin, C. (1972). Anticipated communication and mass media information seeking. *Public Opinion Quarterly*, 36:188–199. Edelstein, A., & Larsen, O. (1960). The weekly press contribution to a sense of urban community. *Journalism Quarterly*, 37: 489–498. Funkhouser, R., & McCombs, M. (1871). The rise and fall of news diffusion. *Public Opinion quarterly*, 35:107–113. Katz, E. (1960). Communication research and the image of society: The convergence of two traditions. *American Journal of Sociology*, 65:435–440.

Barnlund, D. C. (1975). The public self and the private self in Japan and the U.S. In J. C. Condon & M. Saito (Eds.), *Intercultural Encounters with Japan*. Tokyo: Simul Press.

Carter, R. F. (1965). Communication and affective relations. *Journalism Quarterly*, 42:203–212.

Chaffee, S. H. (1968). Sensitization in panel design: A coorientational experiment. *Journalism Quarterly*, 45:661–669.

————. (1973). Applying the Interpersonal perception model to the real world. *American Behavioral Scientist*, 16:465–468. See also Chaffee, S. H. (1982). Mass media and interpersonal channels: Competitive, convergent, or complementary? In C. Gumpert & R. Cathcart (Eds.), *Inter/Media: Interpersonal communication in a media world* (2nd ed.) New York: Oxford University Press.

Chaffee, S. H., et al. (1969). Experiments on cognitive discrepancies and communication. *Journalism Monographs*, 14.

Fink, E. L., Serota, L. K., Woelfel, J. D., and Noell, J. (1975). Communication, ideology, and political behavior: A multidimensional analysis. Paper presented to Political Communication Division, International Communication Association: Chicago, ILL.

Gantz, W., & Miller (1974). Exploring the motives to discuss political news: An experiment and a field study. Paper delivered to the International Communication Association, New Orleans.

Gantz, W. & Trenholm, S. (1979). Why people pass on news: Motivations for diffusion. *Journalism Quarterly*, 56:365–370. See also Deutschmann, P., Danielson, W. A. (1960). Diffusion of knowledge of the major news story. *Journalism Quarterly*, 37:345–355. Greenberg, B. S. (1964). Person to person communication in the diffusion of news event. *Journalism Quarterly*, 41:489–494. O'Keefe, T. M., & Kissel, B. C. (1971). Visual impact as an added dimension in the study of news diffusion. *Journalism Quarterly*, 42:298–303.

Gudykunst, W. B. (1983). Uncertainty reduction and predictability of behavior in high and low context cultures. *Communication Quarterly*, 31:49–55.

Gudykunst, W. B., & Nishida, T. (1984). Individual and cultural influences on uncertainty reduction. *Communication Monographs*, 51:23–36.

Gudykunst, W. B., Nishida, T. Koike, H., & Shiino, N. (1983). Japanese and American close friendship. In R. W. Bostrom & B. H. Westley (Eds.) *Communication yearbook 7*. Beverly Hills, CA: Sage.

————. (1986). The influence of language on uncertainty reduction: An exploratory study of Japanese-Japanese and Japanese-North American interactions. In M. McLaughlin (Ed.), *Communication yearbook 9*. Beverly Hills, CA: Sage.

Gudykunst, W. B., Yang, S. M., & Nishida T. (1985). A cross-cultural test of uncertainty reduction theory: Comparison of acquaintances, friends, and dating relationships in Japan, Korea, and the United States. *Human Communication Research*, 11:407–454.

Gunter, B. (1984). *News Awareness, a British survey*. London: Independent Authority Research Dept.

Hall, E. T. (1977). *Beyond Culture*. Garden City, NY: Doubleday.

Hanneman, G. J., & Greenberg, B. (1973). Relevance and diffusion of news of major and minor events. *Journalism Quarterly*, 50:433–437.

Haroldsen, E. O., & Harvey, K. (1979). The diffusion of "shocking" good news. *Journalism Quarterly*, 56:771–775.

Hwang, J., Chase, L., & Kelly, C. (1980). An intercultural examination of communication competence. *Communication IX*, pp. 70–79.

Isamu, K. (1972). *Language and the world* (Kotoba to sekai). Tokyo: Shinchosa.

Johnson, C. L. & Johnson, F. A. (1975). Interaction roles and ethnicity: The Japanese and Caucasians in Honolulu. *Social Forces*, 54:452–466.

Katz, E., & Lazarsfeld, P. (1955). *Personal influence*. New York: Free Press. See also Lazarsfeld, P. F., Berelson, B., & Gaudet, H. (1944). *The peoples' choice*. New York: Duell, Sloan and Pearce.

Kepplinger, H. M. (1985). Meinungsverteilung und Medienwirkung: Eine empirische Untersuchung zur Balance Theorie Fritz Heider's. In *Politik und Kummunikation*. Munchen: Oehlschlager (Ed.) U. Saxer.

Kepplinger, H. M., & Martin. V. (1986). *Functions of mass media in interpersonal communication*, 12:58–66.

Kim, Y. Y. (1979). Toward an interactive theory of communication acculturation. In D. Nimmo (Ed.), *Communication yearbook 3*. New Brunswick, NJ.: Transaction Books.

Kunihiro, M. (1976). The Japanese language and intercultural communication. In *The silent power: Japan's identity and world role*. Tokyo: Simul Press.

McCombs, M. E. (1981). The agenda-setting approach. In D. Nimmo & K. R. Sanders (Eds.), *Handbook of Political Communication*. Newbury Park, CA: Sage.

McCroskey, J. M., Gudykunst, W. B., & Nishida, T. (1985). Communication apprehension among Japanese students in native and second languages. *Communication Research Reports*, West Virginia University, 2:11–15.

McLeod, J. M., & Chaffee S. H. (1973). Interpersonal approaches to communications research. *American Behavioral Scientist*, 16:469–500.

Midooka, K. (1985). Value systems and communication patterns in Japan. Paper delivered to ICA. Honolulu.

Mushakoji, K. (1976). The cultural premises of Japanese diplomacy. In *The silent power: Japan's identity and world role*. Tokyo: Simul Press.

Nakane, C. (1974). The social system reflected in interpersonal communication. In J. Condon & M. Saito (Eds.). *Intercultural encounters with Japan*. Tokyo: Simul Press.

Nakanishi, M. (1986). Perceptions of self-disclosure in intitial interaction: A Japanese sample. *Human Communication Research*, 13:167–190.

Nishida, H. (1985). Japanese intercultural communication competence and cross-cultural adjustment. *International Journal of International Relations*, 9:247–269.

Nishida, T. (1977). An analysis of a cultural concept affecting Japanese interpersonal communication. *Communication*, 6:69–80.

Nisugi, M. (1974). Images of spoken Japanese and spoken English, In (Eds.) J. C. Condon, and M. Saito, *Intercultural encounters with Japan: Communication—contact and conflict*, Tokyo: The Simul Press.

Norinaga, M. (1763). *Shibun Yoryo, Bk. 2*, cited in H. Isheguro, (1985). Myths and false dichotomies. *Social Research*, 52:363–181.

Okabe, R. (1983). Cultural assumptions of East and West: Japan and the United States. In W. Gudykunst (Ed.), *Intercultural communication theory: Current perspectives*. Beverly Hills, CA: Sage.

Peterson, A. W. (1973). Psychological problems of Japanese students in facing English. *The New Current Report*, June:1–3.

Robinson, J. P., & Levy, M. (1986). *The main source: Learning from television news*. Beverly Hills, CA: Sage.

Rosengren, K. E. (Ed.). (1986). Special issue on news diffusion. *European Journal of Communication*, 2:135–142.

Rosengren, K. E. (1987). Introduction to A special issue on news diffusion. *European Journal of Communication* 2:135–142, 227–255.

Snyder, M. (1974). The self-monitoring of expressive behavior. *Journal of Personality and Social Psychology*, 30:526–537.

Takasaki, N. & Ozawa, T. (1983). Analysis of information flow in Japan. Information, economics and policy, 1:177–193.

Tichenor, P. J., & Wackman, D. B. (1973). Mass media and community public opinion. *American Behavioral Scientist*, 16:593–606.

Troldahl, V., & Van Dam, R. (1965). Face-to-face communication about major topics in the news. *Public Opinion Quarterly*, 29:626–634.

———. (1971). Face-to-face communication about major topics in the news. *Public Opinion Quarterly* 35:315.

Tsujimura, A. (1980). *Some characteristics of the Japanese way of communication.* Paper delivered to the East-West Communication Institute, Honolulu.

Wackman, D. B. (1973). Interpersonal communication and coorientation. *American Behavioral scientist*, 16:537–550.

Wiseman, R., & Abe, H. (1986). Cognitive complexity and intercultural effectiveness: Perceptions in American-Japanese dyads. In M. McLauglin (Ed.)., *Communication yearbook 9.* Beverly Hills, CA: Sage.

Wiseman, R. L., Hammer, M. R., & Nishida, H. (1987). Critical perspectives on the state of intercultural communication research. In B. Dervin & M. J. Voight (Eds.), *Progress in communication sciences.* Norwood, NJ: Ablex.

Wolfson, K., & Pearce, W. B. (1983). A cross-cultural comparison of the implications of self-disclosure in conversational logics. *Communication Quarterly*, 31:249–256.

Yasunari, K. (1969). *Japan, the beautiful, and myself* (U; tususukushii Nihon no watakushi). Tokyo: Kodansha.

CHAPTER 9

Atwater, T., Salwen, M. B., & Anderson, R. B. (1984). Influence of media and interpersonal agendas on personal agendas. Paper delivered to the AEJMC, Madison, WI.

———. (1985). Interpersonal discussion as a potential barrier to agenda-setting. *Newspaper research journal*; 6:37–43.

Becker, L. B. (1982). The mass media and citizen assessment of issue importance: A reflection on agenda-setting research. In D. C. Whitney, E. Wartella, & S. Windahl (Eds.), *Mass Communication Review Yearbook 3.* Beverly Hills, CA: Sage. See also Weaver, D. H., Graber, D. A., & McCombs, M. E. (1979). Agenda-setting influence on public agendas. In S. Kraus (Ed.), *The Great Debates: Carter vs. Ford 1976.* Bloomington: Indiana University Press.

Becker, L. B., & McLeod, J. (1976). Political consequences of agenda-setting. *Mass Communication Review*, 3:8–15.

Benton, M. & Frazier, P. J. (1976). The agenda-setting function of the mass media at three levels of "information holding." *Communication Research*, 3:261–273.

Blumer, H. (1971). Social problems as collective behavior. *Social Problems*, 18: 298–306.

Chaffee, S. (1980). Presidential debates—are they helpful to voters? In G. C. Wilhoit & H. de Bock (Eds.), *Mass communication review yearbook 1*. Beverly Hills, CA: Sage.

Cobb, R., Ross, J. K. & Ross, M. H. (198). Agenda-building as a comparative political process. *American Political Science Review*, 70:126–138.

Cohen, B. C. (1963). *The press and foreign policy*. Princeton, NJ: Princeton University Press.

Cook, F. L., Tyler, T. R., Gioetz, E. G., Gordon, M. T., Protess, D., Leff, D. R., & Molotch, M. L. (1983). Media and agenda-setting: Effects on the public, interest group leaders, policy makers, and policy. *Public Opinion Quarterly*, 47:16–35.

Dewey, J. (1909). *How we think*. Boston: D. C. Heath & Co.

Downs, A. (1972). Up and down with econology—The issue-attention cycle. *Public Interest*, 28:28–50.

Edelstein, A. (1988). Communication perspectives in public opinion: Traditions and innovations. In J. Andersons, (Ed.), *Mass Communication Yearbook 11*. Beverly Hills, CA: Sage.

Edelstein, A., & Hoyer, S. in press. Testing the functions of news in the Norwegian context.

Erbring, L., Goldenberg, E., & Miller, A. (1980). Front-page news and real-world cues: A new look at agenda-setting by the media. *American Journal of Political Science*, 24:16–49.

Evensen, B. J. (1988). Truman, Palestine and the press—A study in agenda-setting dance steps. Paper delivered to Association for Education in Journalism, Portland, July 2.

Feldman, O. (1985). Relations between the Diet and the Japanese press. *Journalism Quarterly*, 62:845–849.

———. (1986a). Meetings with the mass: Tendencies of Japanese politicians. *Political Communication and Persuasion*, 3:225–243.

———. (1986b). Japanese politicians' exposure to national and local dailies. *Journalism Quarterly*, 63:821–833.

———. (1987). Accessibility to news: Sources of information for Japanese politicians. *Government Information Quarterly*, 4:371–381.

Glass, D. P. (1985). Evaluating presidential candidates: Who focusses upon their personal attributes? *Public Opinion Quarterly*, 49:517–534.

Graber, D. (1972). Personal qualities in presidential images: The contributions of the press. *Midwest Journal of Political Science*, 16:46–76.

Habermas, J. (1962). *Borgerlig offentighet*. Oslo: Oslo University. See also J. Habermas. Toward a theory of communicative competence. In H. P. Dreitzel (Ed.), *Recent Sociology*.

Hirose, M. (1984). Seito to atsuryoku dantai (Pressure groups and political parties). *Jurisuto*, 35:54.

Hong, K., & Shemer, S. (1976). Influence of media and interpersonal agendas on personal agendas. Paper delivered to the AEJMC, Madison, WI.

Horie, H. (1982). Mass society and mass democracy. In H. Horie (Ed.) *Tohyo-kodo to Seiji-Ishiki*. Tokyo: Hokuku Shuppan.

Ito, Y. (1988). Conversation with senior author, Seattle, Sept. 1988.

Iwabuchi, Y. (1986). Mass media information and issue choice. In H. Horie & M. Ememura (Eds.), *Tohyo-kodo to Seiji-ishiki.* Tokyo: Keio-tsushin.

———. (1988). The influence of newspapers as seen in the sales tax issue. Presented to Japan Society for Studies in Journalism and Communication. Tokyo.

Iyengar, S., & Kinder, D. R. (1985). Psychological accounts of agenda-setting. In S. Kraus & R. M. Perloff (Eds.). *Mass media and political thought.* Newbury Park, CA: Sage.

Kabashima, I., & Broadbent, J. (1986). Referent pluralism: Mass media and politics in Japan. *Journal of Japanese Studies,* 12:329–361.

Kepplinger, H. M. (1975). *Realkultur und Medienkultur.* Freiburg: Alber-Verlag.

———. (1985). Massenmedien: Macht ohne verontwortung? In (Ed.) K. J. Wilbert, *Reden wir morgen in sprechblasen?* Koblenz: Handwerk-sammer.

Kepplinger, H. M., Donsbach, W., Brosius, H-B, & Staab, J. (1986). Media tenor and public opinion: A longitudinal study of media coverage and public opinion on Chancellor Kohl. Paper delivered to World Association for Public Opinion Research, May 14–18, St. Petersburg, Fla. See also, by the same authors, Medientenor und Bevolkerungsmeinung: Eine empirische studie zum image Helmut Kohls. *Kolner zeitschrift for soziologie und sozialpsychologie,* 38: 247–279.

———. (1987). Erwiderung auf die kritick von Helmut Thomse, *Kolner zeitschrift fur soziologie und sozialpsychologie,* 39:746–782.

Kepplinger, H. M., Gotto, K., Brosius H-B, & Haak, W. (1989). *Der einfluss des fernsehens auf die politsche meinungsbildung,* Freiburg i. Br.: Alber Verlag. p. 295.

Kepplinger, H. M. & Hachenberg, M. (1981). Gesellschafliche Bedingungen kollektiver Gewalt. *Kolner Zeitschrift fur Soziologie und Sozialpsychologie,* 33:468–503.

———. (1985). Media and conscientious objection in the Federal Republic of Germany. In D. Paletz (Ed.), *Political communication research: Approaches, studies, assessments.* Norwood, NJ: Ablex. See also *Die aktuelle Berichterstattung des Horfunks: Eine Inhal analyse der Abendnachrichten und politischen Magazine.* Freiburg: Alber-Verlag.

Kepplinger, H. M., & Martin, V. (1986) Functions of mass media in interpersonal communication. *Communication.* 12:58–66.

Kepplinger, H. M., &Roth H.(1979).Creating a crisis:German mass media and oil supply in 1973/74. *Public Opinion Quarterly,* 43:285–296. See also Kepplinger, H. M. (1983) German media and oil supply in 1978 and 1979. In N. Smith & L. Theberge (Eds.), *Energy coverage—Media panic—An international perspective.* New York: Longman.

Kim, Y. C. (1981). *Japanese journalists and their world.* Charlottesville: University of Virginia Press.

Kobayashi, Y. (1983). Information and mass media. In N. Tomita and N. Okazawa (Eds.), *Joho to democracy.* Tokyo: Gakuyo-shobo.

———. (1985). Soten sentaku ni okero masu mejia eikyo ni kansuru keiryo bunseki. In Y. Kobayashi (Ed.), *Keiryo seijigaku.* Tokyo: Seibundo.

Lambeth, E. (1978). Perceived influence of the press on energy policy-making. *Journalism Quarterly,* 55:11–18, 62.

Lang, K., and Lang. G. (1960). The unique perspective of television and its effect: A pilot study. In W. Schramm (Ed.), *Mass Communications*. 2nd ed. Urbana, IL: University of Illinois Press.

———. (1981). Watergate: An exploration of the agenda-building process. In G. C. Wilhoit & H. De Bock (Eds.), *Mass Communication Review Yearbook 2*. Beverly Hills, CA: Sage.

Lazarsfeld. P. F. & Merton, R. K. (1948). Mass communication, popular taste, and organized social action. In (Ed.) W. Schramm, *Mass Communication* 2nd. Ed. Urbana: University of Illinois Press.

McCombs, M. (1981). The agenda-setting approach. In D. D. Nimmo & K. R. Sanders (Eds.), *Handbook of political communication*, Newbury Park, CA: Sage.

———. (1988). Setting the agenda: The evolution of agenda-setting research. Paper. Sommatie X, Veldhoven: The Netherlands.

McCombs, M. E., & Shaw, D. L. (1972). The agenda-setting function of mass media. *Public Opinion Quarterly*, 36:176–187.

———. (1977). Agenda-setting and the political process. In D. L. Shaw and M. M. McCombs (Eds.). *The emergence of American political issues: The agenda-setting function of the press*. St. Paul, MN: West Publishing Co. See also McCombs, M. E. (1981). Setting the agenda for agenda-setting research: An assessment of the priority ideas and problems. *Mass Communication Review Yearbook* 2: (pp. 209–211).

MacKuen, M. B. (1981). Social communication and the mass policy agenda. In M. B. MacKuen & S. L. Coombs (Eds.), *More than news: Media power in public affairs*. Beverly Hills, CA: Sage.

McLeod, J. M., Becker, L. B., & Byrnes, J. E. (1974). Another look at the agenda-setting function of the press. *Communication Research*, 1:131–166.

Maeda, T. (1978). Subscription papers and political consciousness. *Hogaku Kenkyu*, 51:311–338.

Mathes, R. (1987). Mass media and political conflicts in the Federal Republic of Germany: A model and a case study. Paper delivered to the Institut fur Publizistik, Universitat Mainz, West Germany.

Mullins, L. E. (1977). Agenda-setting and the young voter. In D. L. Shaw & M. E. McCombs (Eds.), *The emergence of American political issues: The agenda-setting function of the press*. St. Paul, MN: West Publishing.

Nihon Shimbun Kyokai (Nenkan?) (1985). *The Japanese Press, 1985*, The Japan Newspaper Publishers and Editors Assn.

Noelle-Neuman, E., & Mathes, R. (1987). The "event as event" and the event as news: The significance of "consonance" for media effects research. *European Journal of Communication*, 2:391–413.

Patterson, T. E. (1980). *The mass media election: How Americans choose their president*. New York: Praeger.

Pempel, T. J. (1982). *Policy and politics in Japan: Creative conservatism*. Philadelphia: Temple University Press.

Reich, M. R. (1984). Mobilization for environmental policy in Italy and Japan. *Comparative Politics*, 16:379–402.

Rogers, E. M. & Dearing J. W. (1988). Agenda-setting research: Where has it been, where is it going? In (Ed.) J. A. Anderson. *Communication Yearbook #11*, Beverly Hills, CA.: Sage.

Schoenbach, K. (1982). Agenda-setting effects of print and television in West Germany. Paper delivered to the International Communications Association.

Siune, K., & Borre, O. (1975). Setting the agenda for a Danish election. *Journal of Communication*, 25:65–73.

Takeshita, T. (1981). The agenda-setting function of mass media: State of research and associated problems. *Japanese Journalism Review*, 30:203–218.

———. (1983). An empirical examination of media agenda-setting hypotheses. *The Bulletin of the Institute of Journalism and Communication Studies*, 31:101–143.

———. (1984). The perspective of agenda-setting research: Theory and verification in mass communications effects studies. *Studies of Broadcasting*, 34:81–116.

———. (1987). Issue reports and the agenda-setting hypothesis. Paper delivered to the Japan Society for Studies in Journalism and Mass Communication, Fukuoka University.

———. (1988). Issue reporting and the agenda-setting hypothesis (Souten hodo to gidai settei kasetsu). In (Eds.) Faculty, Institute for the Studies of Journalism and Mass Communication) *Senkyo Hodo to Tohyo Kodo*. Tokyo: University of Tokyo Press.

Takeuchi, I., & Takeshita, T. (1987). The agenda-setting effect of mass media in a local election: A Japanese experience. Paper delivered to the Conference on Media and Politics in Japan, Kona, Hawaii.

Tamura, M. (1987). The information environment around the Japanese people. *Studies of Broadcasting*, 23:7–26.

Tokinoya, H. (1982). Gidai settei riron ni yoru kokoku koka no kenku (A study of the effects of advertising and agenda-setting theory). *Yoshida Hideo Kinen Zaidan Josei Kenku Shu*, 10:75–87.

Tsujimura, A. (1976). Public opinion and political dynamics in Japan: The tri-polar relationships of government, press and public opinion. English translation. Shiseido: University of Tokyo.

Weaver, D. H., (1982). Media agenda-setting and media manipulation. In C. Whitney, E. Wartella, & S. Windahl (Eds.), *Mass communication review yearbook 3*. Beverly Hills, CA: Sage.

———. (1983). *Media agenda-setting and public opinion*. Keio University, Tokyo.

———. (1984). Media agenda-setting and public opinion: Is there a link? In R. N. Bostrom (Eds.), *Communication yearbook 8*, Newbury Bark, CA: Sage.

Weaver, D. H., Auh, T. S., Stehle, T. A., & Wilhoit, G. C. (1975). A path analysis of individual agenda-setting during the 1974 Indiana senatorial campaign. Paper delivered to the AEJMC, Ottawa, CN.

Winter, J. P. (1981). Contingent conditions on the agenda-setting process. In G. C. Wilhoit & H. de Bock (Eds.), *Mass communication review yearbook 2*. Newbury Park, CA: Sage.

Yee, A. K. C. (1987). A study of the agenda-setting function of the mass media: An analysis of the Daya Bay issue in Hong Kong. Paper delivered to the Department of Journalism and Communication, Chinese University of Hong Kong.

Zucker, H. G. (1978). The variable nature of news media influence. In B. D. Rubin (Ed.), *Communication yearbook 2*. New Brunswick, NJ: Transaction Books.

CHAPTER 10

Bogart, L. (1972). *Silent politics: Polls and the awareness of public opinion*. New York: Wiley-Interscience.

Cantril, H. (1965). *The pattern of human concerns*. New Brunswick, NJ.: Rutgers University Press.

Carter, R. (1978). A very peculiar horserace. In G. Bishop, R. Meadown, & M. Jackson-Beeck (Eds.), *The presidential debates: Media, electoral and policy perspectives*. New York: Praeger.

Edelstein, A. (1973). Decision-Making and mass communication: A conceptual and methodological approach to public opinion. In P. Clarke & G. D. Kline (Eds.), *Current perspectives in mass communication research*. Beverly Hills, CA: Sage.

———. (1974). *Communication and decision-making: A comparison of Yugoslavia and the United States*. New York: Praeger.

Lau, R. R. (1986). Political schemata, candidate evaluations and voting behavior. In R. R. Lau & D. O. Sears (Eds.), *Political cognition*. Hillsdale, NJ: Lawrence Erlbaum.

Lau, R. R., & Sear, D. O. (1986). *Political cognition*. Hillsdae, NJ: Lawrence Erlbaum.

McLeod, J. M., Kosicki, G. M., Pan, Z., & Allen, S. G. (1987). Perspectives on the news: Assessing their complexity and conceptual frames. Paper delivered to the AEJMC, San Antonio, TX.

Mitchell, R. C. (1980). Polling on nuclear power: A critique of the polls after Three Mile Island. In A. H. Cantril (Ed.), *Polling on the issues*. Cabin John, MD: Seven Locks Press.

Noelle-Neumann, E., & Kepplinger, H. M. (1981). Report on the study in the Federal Republic of Germany, in UNESCO, *An international study on the role of the mass media in seven communities*. Paris.

Reeves, B., Chaffee, S., & Tims, A. (1982). Social cognition and mass communication research. In (Eds.) *Social cognition and communication*. Beverly Hills, CA: Sage.

Schuman, H. (1979). The open and closed question. *American Sociological Review*. 44:692–712.

———. (1986). Ordinary questions, survey questions, and policy questions. *Public Opinion Quarterly*, 450:432–442.

Stamm, K. (1985). Effects of the Bush/Ferraro Debate on Candidate Characterization. Paper delivered to the Association for Education in Journalism, Gainesville, FL.

Swanson, D. L. (1981). A constructivist approach. In D. D. Nimmo & K. R. Sanders (Eds.), *Handbook of political communication*. Beverly Hills, CA: Sage.

Thurstone, L. L., & Chave, E. J. (1929). *The measurement of attitude*. Chicago: University of Chicago Press.

Verba, S., Brody, R. A. Parker, E. B., Nie, H. H., Polsby, N. W., Ekman, P., & Black, G. S. (1967). Public opinion and the war in Vietnam. *American Political Science Review*, 61:317–333. See also Verba, S., Brody, R. A., Parker, E. B., N. H., Polsby, N. W., Ekman, R., Black, A. S. Rossi, P. H., & Sheatsley, P. (undated). Public opinion and the war in Vietnam.

CHAPTER 11

Ball-Rokeach, S. J. (1985). The origins of individual media-system dependency: A sociological framework. *Communication Research*, 12:485–510.

Ball-Rokeach, S. J., & DeFleur, M. (1976). A dependency model of mass media effects. *Communication Research*, 3:3–21.

Galtung, J. & Ruge, M. H. (1965). The structure of foreign news, *Journal of Peace Research*, 2:64–91.

Hotta, Y. (1957). *What I thought in India* (Indo de kangaeta koto). Tokyo: Iwanami Shoten.

Ito, Y. (1987). Mass communication research in Japan: History and present state. In M. L. McLaughlin (Ed.), *communication yearbook 11*. Beverly Hills,: Sage.

Iwabuchi, Y. (1988). *Uriagezei hoan ni miru shimbun hodo no eikyo* (The influence of newspapers as seen in the sales tax issue). Paper delivered to the Japan Society for Studies in Journalism and Mass Communications, Tokyo.

Nakano, O. (1982). Nihongata soshi ni okeru komyunikeishon to ishi ketti (Communication and decision-making in Japanese organizations). In E. Hamaguchi & S. Kumon (Eds.), *Nihonteki shudansghugi (Japanese Groupism)*. Tokyo: Yuhikaku.

Noelle-Neumann, E. (1974). The spiral of silence: A theory of public opinion. *Journal of Communication* 24:43–51.

———. (1984). The spiral of silence: A reply. In (Eds.), K. R. Sanders, L. L. Kaid, & D. D. Nimmo, *Political communication yearbook*, Carbondale, Ill: Southern Illinois University Press.

Schramm, W. (1959). *One day in the world's press: Fourteen great newspapers on a day of crisis*. Stanford, CA: Stanford University Press.

Index